Understanding Belarus and How Western Foreign Policy Misses the Mark

Understanding Belarus and How Western Foreign Policy Misses the Mark

Grigory Ioffe

ROWMAN & LITTLEFIELD
Lanham • Boulder • New York • London

Published by Rowman & Littlefield
A wholly owned subsidiary of The Rowman & Littlefield Publishing Group, Inc.
4501 Forbes Boulevard, Suite 200, Lanham, Maryland 20706
www.rowman.com

16 Carlisle Street, London W1D 3BT, United Kingdom

British Library Cataloguing in Publication Information Available

The hardback edition of this book was previously cataloged by the Library of Congress
as follows:

Ioffe, G. V.
  Understanding Belarus and How Western Foreign Policy Misses the Mark /
Grigory Ioffe.
     p. cm.
  Includes bibliographical references and index.
  1. Belarus—Politics and government—1991- 2. Political culture—Belarus. 3.
Post-communism—Belarus. 4. Belarus—Social conditions—1991– I. Title.
  DK507.817165 2008
  947.808'6—dc22

                                                              2007033736

  ISBN 978-0-7425-5558-7 (cloth : alk. paper)
  ISBN 978-1-4422-4212-8 (pbk. : alk. paper)
  ISBN 978-1-4616-4650-1 (electronic)

♾™ The paper used in this publication meets the minimum requirements of American
National Standard for Information Sciences—Permanence of Paper for Printed Library
Materials, ANSI/NISO Z39.48-1992.

Printed in the United States of America

In memory of my grandparents,
Yevgeniya Lvovna Leichtman (born Menaker)
and Victor Grigoryevich Leichtman,
natives of Mozyr and Petrikov, Belarus.

Contents

List of Figures and Tables ix

Introduction xi

1 Questions of Language 1

2 A Search for Identity 37

3 Culture Wars, Soul-searching, and Belarusian Identity 77

4 Belarusian Economy 105

5 Belarusian Political Landscape 135

6 Alexander Lukashenka and His Detractors 167

7 Opinion Polls and Presidential Elections 193

Conclusion 231

Bibliography 243

Index 249

About the Author 261

List of Figures and Tables

FIGURES

I.1 Belarus and its neighbors   xxi

I.2 Regions of Belarus   xxi

2.1 Belarusians in Belarus   55

2.2 Poles in Belarus   55

2.3 Russians in Belarus   56

3.1 Yury Drakakhrust   84

3.2 Andrei Dynko   89

3.3 A civilizational fault line   99

6.1 Alexander Lukashenka visiting an elementary school in Petrikov   168

6.2 Alexander Feduta   180

7.1 Oleg Manayev   194

TABLES

1.1 Language of Everyday Communication of the Voters in the March 19, 2006, Presidential Elections ... 8

4.1 Percentage Distribution of the Answers to the Question "Where Is Life Better Now, in Belarus or in Russia?" ... 114

4.2 Price Differential between Crude Oil Sold by Russia to the European Union and to Belarus ... 117

4.3 Change in Belarus's Exports and Imports, 2004–2005 ... 118

5.1 Percentage of Urban Population ... 137

7.1 Distribution of Responses to the Question "What Problems Does Your Family Face?" ... 196

7.2 "What Are the Most Acute Problems That the Country and Its Citizens Face?" ... 198

7.3 Responses to the Question "Name Five Countries Which in Your Opinion Treat Belarus in the Friendliest Way and Five Countries That Treat Belarus in the Least Friendly Way" ... 201

7.4 Percentage Distribution of Response to the Question "To What Extent Do You Tolerate Representatives of the Following Groups?" ... 202

7.5 The Relationship between Comparative Assessments of Quality of Life and Geopolitical Preferences ... 205

7.6 Time Series of Responses to the Question "If Presidential Elections Were Tomorrow, Whom Would You Vote For?" ... 213

7.7 Time Series of Responses to the Question "If the Position of President of Belarus and Russia Were Instituted, Whom Would You Rather Vote for in the Corresponding Election?" ... 214

7.8 The Official Count versus IISEPS Polls in the 2006 Presidential Elections in Belarus ... 215

Introduction

After communists, most of all I hate anti-communists.

—Sergei Dovlatov[1]

When I came to America, the *Seinfeld Show* was in its first season, and it soon became my tutor in English comprehension. In one of the episodes of the fourth season, by which time I thought I was trained enough to grasp much of New York City humor, a movie called *Rochelle, Rochelle* was first brought up. "A young girl's strange erotic journey from Milan to Minsk" was that fictional movie's tagline, and its ending, "from Milan to Minsk," captivated me. Quite possibly, it merely was the consonance of two "Mi's," but I was inclined to read more into its spell on me. The tagline, I reasoned, implicitly singled me out against the backdrop of the general public. Many Americans had at least heard something about Milan but nothing about Minsk, whereas I had visited Minsk twenty-five times, and shouldn't I just share what I had learned with those willing to listen?

In a strikingly similar way, a short article in a 2004 issue of *The Economist* magazine effectively singled me out and may have even talked me, subliminally, into writing this book. The article begins with Stanislau Shushkevich, the first post-Soviet leader of Belarus, telling "a wry anecdote that encapsulates how his country of 10 [million] people . . . has been neglected by the West. 'I've always liked your country,' an American congressman once told him, 'especially since you got rid of that Ceausescu fellow.'"[2]

One would think, I said to myself, that low name recognition and a cliché-ridden image made an odd couple. Apparently this is not so in the area of foreign policy. Belarus, a country that most Americans would fail to identify on a map, has been portrayed as "a virtual 'black hole' in Europe" and "an anomaly in the region."[3] It has been called a "modern sultanate," and popular attitudes ensuring support for President Alexander Lukashenka were labeled "mass psychological marasmus."[4] More recent descriptions of Belarus call it "an authoritarian cesspool,"[5] "a bastard of Europe,"[6] "an outpost of tyranny,"[7] and, juiciest of all, "the last dictatorship of Europe."[8]

This admittedly weird marriage between low name recognition and a cliché-ridden image of one and the same country was, however, only one of the driving forces behind my book-writing effort. The war in Iraq was the second. Apparently this war cast a long shadow on every topic with international and/or political overtones. As the first rationale behind that war of choice, discovering weapons of mass destruction, proved unsustainable, the second line of defense of the war effort appeared to be regime change and spreading democracy. "There has been, however, such a chaos since the Iraqi dictator fell that it became common to hear Iraqis yearn for the order imposed by his strong-arm rule. Even some Americans share this sentiment. 'I feel like we should let Saddam out of jail and say, "Sorry, we didn't realize you were so brutal because you had to be,'" a member of a U.S. Special Operations unit told *Newsweek*" in 2004 after a hard day's fighting.[9]

Certainly Belarus is no Iraq: it has no oil, it is dangerously close to a major nuclear power, and the Belarus Democracy Act costs American taxpayers only $27.5 million a year, not more than $2 billion a week.[10] But there are similarities nonetheless. Crucial among them are some profound reasons why in much of the non-Western world, people desire order more than democracy. Drawing from my thirty-eight years of life experience in the Soviet Union, I would say that one of those reasons (just one) seems to be a legitimate fear of evil, destructive, and simply inconsiderate behavior on the part of fellow countrymen, behavior that only a strong arm can restrain. This behavior need not be as drastic as suicide bombing. Proclivity to use brute force, theft, and bribery to achieve one's goals; lack of due respect and consideration for the well-being and feelings of a stranger; earning wealth in a heavy-handed and objectionable way, then flaunting it amidst people of average means; toleration of large social distances; ethnic and religious animosity—someone ought to keep these and other instances of adverse social behavior and attitudes in check. Apparently, some societies are unable to accomplish this without compulsion. This inability could, among other things, explain why democracy cannot be exported, much less imposed, by an outside force. Simply put, one cannot build democracy other than on the homegrown foundation of civility and trust. I find it important to stress that my family and I decided to act on our long-entertained idea to leave the Soviet Union when it finally began to embrace democracy. When that change occurred, my sense of security was gone.

A geographer by training, I also could not but agree with one colleague's observation that the war in Iraq revealed an astonishing lack of general and regional geographic literacy on the part of American foreign policy makers.[11] Though this assertion applied to the major international conflict, a relatively calm situation may be even more treacherous. When a large-scale conflict erupts, relevant cultural and geographic knowledge does get eventually delivered, as the case of Iraq seems to show, albeit too little, too late. If, however, there is no attendant sense of urgency, the search for effective policy may be never ending. This is what seems to be the case with the decade-old U.S. and European Union (EU) policy aimed at unseating Belarus's president Alexander Lukashenka. Despite his lasting (since 1996) ostracism by the West, his presidency is no less stable today than at any other time since he was first elected president in 1994. In late 2006, the EU offered Lukashenka reconciliation in exchange for his merely retreating to where his regime's repressive stance toward the opposition and independent media was in 2000, that is, when a presidential candidate was not in jail and more independent media outlets existed.[12] However, by 2000, the anti-Lukashenka policies had been in place for quite some time. It is all too obvious, then, that Western policies with regard to Lukashenka's Belarus have been strikingly ineffective.

It could be, I thought, that these policies had been ill advised in the first place. On top of that, the policy makers' thinking about Belarus, just like their thinking about Iraq, is slotted into ideological templates of Western making, whereas Belarus, like Iraq, ought to be understood on its own terms, which means in the context of its location, history, and identity. Just stating, as George W. Bush did, that "Belarusians deserve better"[13] misses the point. Americans deserve better too! They deserve politicians whose certitudes are not as rock solid as W's on issues they poorly understand, politicians who get off their high horses and ask someone in the know to enlighten them first.

In all fairness, though, scholarship on Belarus is part of the problem, and knowing this was my third, and perhaps most powerful, writing incentive. Nicholas Vakar's 1956 book on Belarusian history[14] remains the most well-researched and revealing source on Belarus by far. Its analysis is so cogent that most events and processes unfolding in Belarus today (i.e., half a century later) appear to find more credible and compelling explanation in Vakar's volume than in many subsequent writings. And yet, the scenery has changed so much since 1956 that only those already knowledgeable about Belarus can fully appreciate Vakar's lead in Belarusian studies. Actually Michael Urban's 1989 book added some important insights into much more recent, postwar processes of ruling-elite formation in the Belorussian (that was the spelling then) Soviet Socialist Republic (BSSR). Among other things, Urban showed that contrary to expectations, Moscow had "no more than a marginal influence on the circulation of elites in the BSSR"[15] and that indigenous factors proved to be the decisive ones. Urban conducted a detailed analysis on the competition between the two elite groups: the Partisans (who emerged out of the wartime resistance to the German occupiers) and the so-called Minsk City Industrial Group.

Since Belarus acquired statehood, two categories of books about it have been released: multiauthor collections of articles and individual monographs. I reviewed two out of four collections[16] for *Europe-Asia Studies*,[17] and the third one[18] is referenced in my article.[19] The collections, though, are eclectic by definition. Besides, with the exception of one article, they do not contain material devoted to Belarusian identity, the issue of truly existential importance for Belarus. The mainstream message on Belarusian economy contained in all but one of the post-Soviet books on Belarus is that Belarusian economic growth is either a hoax or something that is about to expire due to systemic flaws in the Belarusian economic model. Considering that such predictions have been in circulation since 1996, whereas economic growth in Belarus has since then (1) accelerated and (2) been recognized as genuine by such citadels of neoliberalism as the World Bank and the International Monetary Fund (IMF), a less ideological and more open-minded approach to Belarusian economy is overdue. To be sure, a more nuanced economic analysis is contained in an article by Mario Nuti,[20] and Ronald Hill went so far as to acknowledge that "Lukashenka reflects popular values and aspirations,"[21] a rare admission for Westerners. Overall, the multiauthor volume edited by Stephen White, Elena Korosteleva, and John Lowenhardt[22] is the most balanced Western view of Belarus since it acquired statehood.

Due to the sheer specificity of the genre, however, it is not multiauthor collections but the book-length monographs on Belarus released after the breakup of the Soviet Union that my book is expressly designed to provide an alternative to. The earliest of these monographs was authored by Jan Zaprudnik,[23] a pen name of Sairhei Mikalayevich Vil'chitski,[24] who consistently narrates one of several available perspectives on Belarus's nation building. The book's central idea is that Belarusians are the descendants of the Grand Duchy of Lithuania and that Russian colonialism prevents them from rediscovering their true European selves. While this idea does have a niche of its own in the overall discourse about Belarusian identity, no more than 20 percent (at the very best!) of Belarusians living in the Republic of Belarus identify with that ideological niche. Presenting it as the only interpretation of what it means to be a Belarusian, as Zaprudnik does, reflects a narrow, biased, and somewhat self-centered — Belarus-is-me — view.

The second major thread of Zaprudnik's account on Belarus is primordialism, an argument which contends that nations are not "imagined communities"; rather, they are ancient, natural phenomena, and so, one has a nation as obviously as one has a measure of height. Because no nationalism is required to shape a nation, a Slavic-speaking individual with ancestral roots in what is now called Belarus is a Belarusian. But if any such individual embraces Polish or Russian identity, as has happened many times in history, he or she is not a true Russian or Pole, and attempts are justified to uncover their true Belarusian selves.

The third major thread of Zaprudnik's portrayal of Belarus is blanket negativism about what happened to the country after 1944, when he left the country for Germany.[25] In a 278-page book about Belarusian history, the immensity of what was built on the totally and completely devastated Belarusian land after the war receives 5 pages in the chapter titled "Destruction by War and Russification (1941–1985)." In those five pages, forcible collectivization, "military underground airfields and rocket bases in forested areas of Belarus"[26] are mentioned first. After devoting one paragraph to the actual scale of industrial construction, the downside of the Soviet efforts is given center stage: "environmental requirements and social needs were neglected"[27]; during the postwar construction in Minsk, historical landmarks were not spared (despite the fact that in Minsk, the number of brick-made structures surviving the war at all was in the single digits); the Belarusian economy became perfidiously intertwined with Russia's; "building gigantic tractor and automobile plants in [Minsk] was devoid of any common sense"[28]; and "Belarus was forced to send its cattle to meat plants in the neighboring Baltic countries."[29] Nevertheless, astonishingly, "by Soviet standards Belarus fared well."[30]

Obviously, given the scale of wartime devastation whereby more than one-quarter of the population perished, as well as the fact that Belarus was no powerhouse before that war, the country fared well by any thinkable standards. Because, indeed, so much in modern Belarus owes its existence to the Soviet war effort and postwar developments, Zaprudnik's overriding negativism toward these very developments effectively marginalizes his stance on his native Belarus. For anyone to draw any reasonable conclusion, one must first have real facts to work with.

Two books by David Marples are devoid of Zaprudnik's extreme biases. Marples goes as far as to concede that Russia may even be a source of benign influences on Belarus because "Russia is like a curate's egg, i.e., not everything about it is bad."[31] Marples' first book on Belarus[32] contains the best analysis of the effect of Chernobyl on Belarus ever presented in English to date. According to Marples, Belarus's reaction to the Chernobyl disaster has been irrational because Belarusians did not respond to the challenge it presented as a nation. This irrationality is attributed to the Russification of Belarus, the sole conduit of which, according to Marples, has been the economic development pattern adopted by the Soviets. Marples's second book paints a vivid picture of political developments in Belarus during the 1990s and calls its economic growth a hoax produced by intentional falsification of national statistics. In contrast to Zaprudnik, Marples recognizes contrasting attempts to flesh out the Belarusian idea, including an attempt to cast Belarus as a state linked historically and psychologically with Russia.

Marples's many observations are revealing and valuable, but the baggage of a cold war warrior weighs down on their interpretation. Thus, for example, there were precious few freedoms in the Soviet Union, which was bad, but the "'uncontrolled freedom' to withdraw from the study of the Belarusian language"[33] and replace it with Russian was wrong. Most Belarusians "appear to believe that life under the Soviet Union was preferable to present-day existence and maintain deep distrust for democratic principles and a market economy,"[34] and yet, the Belarusian Popular Front (ostensibly embracing those principles) "might be perceived as the conscience of Belarusians as a nation."[35] Obviously then, least of all, Belarusians can be trusted to recognize their own conscience: someone from a faraway country must tell them what their conscience is. Belarusians suffer from a "general lack of awareness of historical background,"[36] but "the continued propagation of the achievements of the Soviet people during the war, and the Belarusian partisans in particular,"[37] is wrong, as if the war were not history, or there were no continuity to history anyway.

Marples does not express his views on nation building; nor does he invoke any reputable theory of nationalism. Consequently, his de facto approach to nation building in Belarus is exceedingly idiographic and events driven, with an attitude toward those events firmly rooted in a disturbingly simple ideological matrix: almost anything that reveals Belarusians' leanings toward Russia is undesirable.

My perspective on Belarus is poles apart from that of Zaprudnik and quite unlike that of Marples. Not only do I discern a plurality of equally meaningful and competing ways to flesh out the idea of Belarusian distinctiveness as a nation, but also I find the touchstone of each idea's vitality to be its acceptance by the Belarusians themselves. Based on available data, I conclude that Belarus used to be a major Soviet success story, and its post-1995 economic success has been genuine as well. Finally, I take guidance from the premise that Lukashenka's rule ought to be viewed in the context in which it truly belongs, that is, in the context of Belarusian history and identity, not some abstract political form (dictatorship) deceitfully imposed on allegedly benighted people whom better positioned and informed outsiders seek to enlighten and liberate.

To some extent, my disagreement with Zaprudnik and Marples may be linked to our dissimilar backgrounds, for no one can extricate himself from his past. (Whether the difference in opinion can be attributed solely to background, I doubt.) Unless one is a devout Stalinist, there is no question that in the vastness and variety of Soviet practices, many deserve condemnation. As someone who first entertained the idea of leaving the Soviet Union in my early twenties, did so at thirty-eight, was stripped of Soviet citizenship, and was awarded refugee status in the United States, I would be one to attest to that. Yet on the other hand, my formative experiences in the Soviet Union owe much to its educational infrastructure, the great Russian literature, and sundry ideas and contacts that had little, if any, ideological undertone. Above all, I benefited from the Soviet contribution to the victory over Nazism. Without the organized June 1941 evacuation from Belarus just one day prior to the German occupation of the town of Mozyr, I would not have been born. Most of my mother's and grandparents' friends and relatives, all natives of Mozyr, who chose to stay put perished in the Holocaust, and many Belarusian Jews perished at the hands of local Nazi collaborators, including quite a few in Zaprudnik-Vil'chitski's hometown of Mir.[38]

Born in Moscow six years after the war, I can also attest that despite all ideological strictures, there was in the Soviet Union some room for pursuit of personal fulfillment and happiness. To be sure, I was only one and a half years old when Stalin died, but even under Stalin, hard as it is to believe, many people managed somehow to be happy. And this is hard to believe because Soviet Stalinism was a more inward-oriented beast compared with German Nazism: while Germans suffered in the final phase of the war, they had been designated, by the ideologues of National Socialism, as its major benefactors. In contrast, Soviet Stalinism victimized the Soviet people in the first place. In my mind, therefore, Stalinism was lesser of the two evils.

After the war, in which the worst of those evils was crushed, my grandparents returned to Mozyr, and I first visited them at the age of three. Thereafter, they moved to Minsk, and I began to make frequent visits there to spend time with the extended family, which also included my uncle and cousins. On every visit, I saw new buildings commissioned and new construction sites launched. Minsk developed fast, and at one point my grandparents had to relocate, as their detached single-family home with a stove fueled by peat briquettes was set to be demolished to allow the expansion of a major radio factory. Minsk was the fastest growing of all the large Soviet cities, and the pace of change it underwent, which I witnessed beginning in the early 1960s, was astounding. This makes me think that the formative experiences of modern Belarus are intertwined with those of my own. Because the scale of wartime devastation of Belarusian cities was so enormous, almost every structure existing in those cities today was built after the war, as was every industrial enterprise. So, most Belarusians rightly regard the war effort and postwar developments as the birthmarks of the Belarus that they know. Whether one likes or dislikes this view may matter; what matters more is that it is an unassailable fact.

Earlier, I noted that my background may not entirely explain my disagreements with Zaprudnik and Marples. What I meant is that a profound difference exists between the researcher's perspective and that of the political activist. The former poses substantive questions, whereas the latter does not. The political activist "knows" the answers in advance, and so, his or her task is to furnish information to uphold a certain standpoint and campaign vigorously on its behalf. There is nothing wrong with doing this, but I am in a different line of work. And I deeply regret that some fellow researchers effectively mix the genres. They are in effect saying that when it comes to the specific case of Belarus, there is nothing to question because Congressman Chris Smith from New Jersey and Senator Jesse Helms from North Carolina, the promoters of the Belarus Democracy Act, have already explained everything. To them, Belarus is the last dictatorship of Europe, period. In the absence of broad public interest in, or even reasonably high name recognition for, Belarus, the sway that this formula and the above-mentioned lawmakers have had on opinion and policy makers mirrors the overriding control of the Central Committee of the Communist Party on all sorts of issues in the former Soviet Union. This might sound insulting to the honorable lawmakers, but the parallel is irresistible: When I hear Senator John McCain[39] using words like "authoritarian cesspool" with regard to Belarus, I am instinctively reminded of ritual curses (like *zapadno-germanskii revanshizm*, or the West German thirst for revenge) that I was exposed to growing up in the Moscow of the 1950s and early 1960s. Apparently I am not alone. "Regrettably there are circles in America which . . . tend to perceive Belarus as a proxy for the yet unfinished old foe, Russia,"[40] a German political commentator observed on a Radio Liberty broadcast.

Not everything, though, looks gloomy. The aforementioned Belarus Democracy Act funds many activities. While I am proud of using none of that funding in my book-writing effort, there is no certainty that those fellow researchers who avail themselves of it are bent on pleasing the act's initiators, even though they are not all that hard to please. Possessed by an itch to "liberate" Belarusians (or whomever) from "tyranny," they do not give much thought to what is going on; nor do they wonder if those earmarked for "liberation" ever wished for it. The Soviet Union was also big on unsolicited liberation, and the Soviet researchers did not always satisfy their political leaders either. This happened when researchers called some well-worn "truths" into question, which is exactly what this book intends to do. In order to accomplish this task, I seek answers to the following questions and try my best to keep all sorts of preconceived notions at bay:

1. Why is Russian the de facto language of everyday communication for the majority of ethnic Belarusians?
2. Why has the Belarusian language been marginalized?
3. What kind of ethnic identity evolved (is evolving) in Belarus that makes most Belarusians insensitive to "their own" national symbols and attached instead to those embodying their kinship with neighboring countries?
4. What is the status of the Belarusian national movement when viewed through the prism of the most reputable theories of ethnic nationalism?
5. What factors and events have deterred the national consolidation of Belarus, and what, if any, is the relationship between it and current challenges to Belarusian statehood?
6. What is Belarus's standing on major economic and social indicators? What are the roots and implications of economic success in the post-1996 Belarus, a success confirmed by the World Bank and the IMF?
7. Why does Belarus maintain economic ties predominantly to Russia, and what are the advantages and disadvantages of this situation for Belarus?
8. Why did Belarus reject market economy and democracy, and what is the nature of the Belarusian political regime?
9. What is the makeup of the Belarusian political scene, and what are its formative factors?
10. What are the roots of the Lukashenka phenomenon?
11. Is the fact that people support the Lukashenka regime rooted entirely in their passivity and lack of understanding of their own good?
12. What are the mass attitudes of Belarusians to statehood, economy, foreign countries, and so forth?
13. Are national surveys that reveal those values reliable?
14. What amount of falsification were the presidential elections in Belarus subjected to?

I seek responses to these questions on the combined basis of (1) the spatial perspective inherent in my human geography profession and fitting the nature of Belarus's predicaments, one of which is lasting existence "in the shadow of Russian and Polish cultures"[41]; (2) durable personal observations (from no fewer than twenty-five visits, including six visits to Belarus since its acquisition of statehood); (3) knowledge of theories of nation building (with particular emphasis on the contributions of Anthony David Smith, Ernest Gellner, and Miroslav Hroch); (4) knowledge of local languages (Russian, Polish, and Belarusian); and (5) awareness of nation-building and political discourses within Belarus and careful monitoring of Belarusian media.

The book is based on several earlier academic articles of mine, including "Understanding Belarus,"[42] "Culture Wars, Soul-searching, and Belarusian Identity,"[43] and "Unfinished Nation-Building in Belarus and the 2006 Presidential Election,"[44] Several particulars pertaining to the book's subject and to transliterating proper names are in order. Belarus is a medium-sized European country with a land area of 207,600 square kilometers and a population of 9.7 million people (2006). Located in Eastern Europe, Belarus (figure I.1) borders Latvia, Lithuania, and Poland (all three being members of the EU and the North Atlantic Treaty Organization), as well as Russia and Ukraine. Belarus consists of six regions, called oblasts (figure I.2), whose capitals, with their corresponding 2006 population numbers in parentheses, are Brest (298,300), Grodno (314,800), Gomel (481,200), Minsk (1,728,000), Mogilev (365,100), and Vitebsk (342,400).[45] A regional center, Minsk is also the national capital of Belarus. From 1921 to 1939, when Belarus was split into eastern (Soviet) and western (Polish) parts, the Grodno and Brest regions in their entirety were under Polish administration as were the western part of Minsk Oblast and the northwestern part of Vitebsk Oblast.

Belarus has two official languages, Belarusian and Russian. In transliterating proper names for this book, I take guidance from the dominant language usage in the Republic of Belarus. Thus, geographic names are transliterated from the Russian. Besides the fact that this is how most Belarusians living in the Republic of Belarus refer to their cities and towns, the alternative (i.e., transliterating from Belarusian) would be fraught with a dilemma. As chapter 1 explains, there are two competing Belarusian orthographies: the so-called classic (Tarashkevitsa) and nonclassic (Narkomauka). Thus, the city I referred to as Grodno is Goradnia in Tarashkevitsa and Grodna in Narkomauka. In Tarashkevitsa, Brest and Minsk are Berastse and Mensk, respectively—forms that are rarely used in day-to-day communication. In contrast, there is one standard Russian form for each of those and all other toponyms. People's names are transliterated from Belarusian if they are referenced in Belarusian-language texts and from Russian if they are referenced in Russian-language sources. This creates a few discrepancies that the reader should be aware of. For example Akudovich's first name is rendered as Valyantsyn (Belarusian) and as Valentin (Russian). Yury Drakakhrust becomes Yury Drakokhrust when his Russian-language publication is referred to. One exception to the above rule concerns Lukashenka. Although in Russian-language texts this name ends with "o" instead of "a," Lukashenka has become the habitual spelling in English, and I have no intention of deviating from that routine.

Figure I.1.   Belarus and its neighbors.
ESRI Data and Maps 2006 (www.esri.com/data/). Produced by Ilya Zaslavsky

Figure I.2.   Regions of Belarus.
ESRI Data and Maps 2006 (www.esri.com/data/). Produced by Ilya Zaslavsky

This book would not have been possible without the help and encouragement of George Demko, my lasting American friend and mentor. While writing this book, I greatly benefited from the advice and consultation of Yury Drakakhrust, a political analyst and editor at Radio Liberty in Prague. I am grateful to Alexander Feduta for his own insight and for referring me to Yury Drakakhrust. Curt Woolhiser invited me to participate in the conference "The Arts, National Identity and Politics in Belarus" (Harvard University, October 14–16, 2005). Not only did that conference stimulate my work on this book, but it also enriched me with some first-hand observations and impressions that proved indispensable for that work. I am immensely grateful to Ilya Zaslavsky, who produced the maps and contributed to the book's cover. Polly Jones significantly improved my English. Andrei Dynko helped procure some pictures. Bernd Kuennecke, my department chair, provided me with teaching-release time so that I could devote much of the spring 2007 semester to writing this book. I am indebted to Roger Clarke, former editor of *Europe-Asia Studies*, who took an unusual decision to publish my three-part article about Belarus, out of which this book has evolved. I am grateful to David Marples, whose views on Belarus are far apart from mine but who provided me with indispensable food for thought about the idiosyncrasies of a certain way of thinking about Belarus (and not just Belarus). Discussions with David at several conferences did much to hone my debating skills. Victor Winston and Andrew Bond from the Bellwether Publishing Company did a great job of publishing one of my debates with David Marples.[46] Last but not least, I am grateful to Jan Zaprudnik for pointing out my mistakes in transliterating Belarusian words and for criticizing my articles. Zaprudnik's thorough disapproval of my perspective on Belarus assured me that I am on the right track. Despite this assurance, I still make mistakes, for which I alone bear responsibility.

NOTES

1. Sergei Dovlatov, *Sobraniye Prozy v Triokh Tomakh*, vol. 3 (St. Petersburg: Limbus Press, 1993), 293; see also http://lib.ru/DOWLATOW/dowlatow.txt.

2. "The Dark Heart of Europe," *The Economist*, October 21, 2004, at www.economist.com.

3. Margarita M. Balmaceda, "Myth and Reality in the Belarusian-Russian Relationship," *Problems of Post-Communism* 46, no. 3 (1999): 3.

4. Steven M. Eke and Taras Kuzio, "Sultanism in Eastern Europe: The Socio-Political Roots of Authoritarian Populism in Belarus," *Europe-Asia Studies* 52, no. 3 (2000): 536.

5. John McCain, U.S. senator, speech at The New Atlantic Initiative Conference, Washington, DC, November 14, 2002, at http://minsk.usembassy.gov/html/mccain .html.

6. Alicja Boryczko, "Belarus—A Lonely Island," *Democracy International*, May 13, 2004, at www.european.referendum.org/up/up125a.html.

7. "Rice Names 'Outposts of Tyranny,'" BBC News, January 19, 2005, at http://news.bbc.co.uk/1/hi/world/americas/4186241.stm.

8. "Bush Calls Belarus Europe's Last Dictatorship," *NewsMax.com Wires*, May 6, 2005, at www.newsmax.com/archives/articles/2005/5/5/214450.shtml.

9. Christopher Dickey, "Death of a Tyrant," *Newsweek*, January 8, 2007, 22.

10. Dickey, "Death of a Tyrant," 20.

11. Alexander Murphy, "Geographic Illiteracy Led Us to Be Hoodwinked into War," *Chicago Sun-Times*, March 18, 2006.

12. Yury Drakokhrust, "Tri strategii otnositelno Belarusi i belorusskii tertius gaudens" (paper presented at the conference "Belarus and Big Europe: Problems and Prospects," Minsk, Belarus, February 23–27, 2007).

13. George W. Bush, press conference, Riga, Latvia, May 7, 2005, quoted in "Washington Set to Work for Change in Belarus," *RFL/RL Reports* 7, no. 19 (May 17, 2005).

14. Nicholas Vakar, *Belorussia: The Making of a Nation* (Cambridge, MA: Harvard University Press, 1956).

15. Michael E. Urban, *An Algebra of the Soviet Power: Elite Circulation in the Belorussian Republic, 1966–1986* (New York: Cambridge University Press, 1989), 57.

16. Ann Lewis, ed., *The EU and Belarus: Between Moscow and Brussels* (London: Federal Trust for Education and Research, 2002); Elena A. Korosteleva, Colin W. Lawson, and Rosalind Marsh, eds., *Contemporary Belarus: Between Democracy and Dictatorship* (London and New York: Routledge/Curzon, 2003).

17. Grigory Ioffe, review of the books Ann Lewis, ed., *The EU and Belarus: Between Moscow and Brussels*, and Elena A. Korosteleva, Colin W. Lawson, and Rosalind Marsh, eds., *Contemporary Belarus: Between Democracy and Dictatorship*, *Europe-Asia Studies* 56, no. 2 (2004): 323–26.

18. Margarita M. Balmaceda, James Clem, and Lisbeth Tarlow, eds., *Independent Belarus: Domestic Determinants, Regional Dynamics, and Implications for the West* (Cambridge, MA: Harvard University Press, 2002).

19. Grigory Ioffe, "Understanding Belarus: Questions of Language," *Europe-Asia Studies* 55, no.7 (2003): 1009–47.

20. D. Mario Nuti, "The Belarus Economy: Suspended Animation between State and Markets," in *Post-Communist Belarus*, ed. Stephen White, Elena Korosteleva, and John Lowenhardt (Lanham, MD: Rowman & Littlefield, 2005), 97–122.

21. Ronald Hill, "Post-Soviet Belarus: In Search of Direction," in *Post-Communist Belarus*, ed. Stephen White, Elena Korosteleva, and John Lowenhardt (Lanham, MD: Rowman & Littlefield, 2005), 9.

22. Stephen White, Elena Korosteleva, and John Lowenhardt, eds., *Post-Communist Belarus* (Lanham, MD: Rowman & Littlefield, 2005).

23. Jan Zaprudnik, *Belarus at a Crossroads in History* (Boulder, CO: Westview Press, 1993).

24. "Doktaru Yanke Zaprudniku—75 gadou," *Nasha Slova* 519 (2001), at http://tbm.org.by/ns/no519/zaprud.html (accessed July 20, 2002).

25. "Doktaru Yanke Zaprudniku—75 gadou."

26. Zaprudnik, *Belarus at a Crossroads*, 113.

27. Zaprudnik, *Belarus at a Crossroads*, 115.

28. Zaprudnik, *Belarus at a Crossroads*.

29. Zaprudnik, *Belarus at a Crossroads*.

30. Zaprudnik, *Belarus at a Crossroads*, 116.

31. David Marples, *Belarus: A Denationalized Nation* (Amsterdam: Harwood, 1999), xiii.

32. David Marples, *Belarus from Soviet Rule to Nuclear Catastrophe* (New York: St. Martin's Press, 1996).

33. Marples, *Belarus from Soviet Rule to Nuclear Catastrophe*, 33.

34. Marples, *Belarus from Soviet Rule to Nuclear Catastrophe*, 134.

35. Marples, *Belarus from Soviet Rule to Nuclear Catastrophe*, 135.

36. Marples, *Belarus from Soviet Rule to Nuclear Catastrophe*.

37. Marples, *Belarus from Soviet Rule to Nuclear Catastrophe*.

38. A Russian-language novel by Liudmila Ulitskaya, *Daniel Shtain, perevodchik* (Moscow EKSMO, 2007) draws heavily on interviews of some Belarusian and Jewish survivors from the town of Mir and describes what happened there during the war in great detail.

39. John McCain became the U.S. Senate's point man on Belarus after the retirement of Jesse Helms.

40. Online interview with Alexander Rahr, Belarusian Service of Radio Liberty, *Forum*, January 10, 2007, at www.svaboda.org.

41. Nina B. Mečkovskaya, *Belorussky yazyk: Sotsiolinguisticheskie ocherki* (Munchen: Verlag Otto Sagner, 2003), 28.

42. Grigory Ioffe, "Understanding Belarus: Questions of Language"; "Understanding Belarus: Belarusian Identity" *Europe-Asia Studies* 55, no.8 (2003): 1241–72; and "Understanding Belarus: Economy and Political Landscape," *Europe-Asia Studies* 56, no. 1 (2004): 85–118.

43. Grigory Ioffe, " Culture Wars, Soul-searching, and Belarusian Identity," *East European Politics and Societies* 21, no. 2 (2007): 348–81.

44. Grigory Ioffe, "Unfinished Nation-Building in Belarus and the 2006 Presidential Election," *Eurasian Geography and Economics* 48, no. 1 (2007): 37–58.

45. Population numbers are referenced at www.by.all-biz.info/guide/population (Belarus: Information Resources).

46. David Marples, "Elections and Nation-Building in Belarus: A Comment on Ioffe," *Eurasian Geography and Economics* 48, no. 1 (2007): 59–67; Grigory Ioffe, "Nation-building in Belarus: A Rebuttal," *Eurasian Geography and Economics* 1 (2007): 68–72.

Questions of Language

To Belarusify Belarus is an uphill battle at the moment.

—Valyantsyn Akudovich[1]

Belarusian is a Slavic language distinct from Russian and Polish, which are its close relatives but are farther apart from each other than each of them is from Belarusian. The same applies to Ukrainian, which is also midway between Polish and Russian. Based on the statistical analysis of coincidental lexemes in the translations of identical texts, like the Bible and the United Nations Declaration of Human Rights, Ukrainian is qualified as the closest relative of Belarusian.[2] In contrast to Polish, however, Russian, Ukrainian, and Belarusian are classed as East Slavic languages. The linguistic differentiation in the East Slavic realm began to develop in the twelfth and thirteenth centuries, when this realm was divided between historical Lithuania and the Muscovy.[3] Within the East Slavic group, Belarusian is closer to Russian than to Ukrainian.[4] Belarusian was codified later than any other Slavic language with national status; this happened in 1918, when Branislau Taraškievič published the first textbook of Belarusian grammar.[5] Other prominent linguists, like Yevfimii Karski and Nikolay Yanchuk, had contributed to developing standard Belarusian so that it could replace many spoken dialects. From the mid-1800s, when the first publications in Belarusian dialects were released, and to the very end of the 1800s, the Latin alphabet was invariably used. From the late 1890s on, more and more Belarusian-language publications used a Cyrillic script, which prevailed in Belarusian publishing[6] after 1918 and was the only alphabet used in Soviet Belarus. Interestingly, the first edition of Taraškievič's *Grammar for [Secondary] Schools* was printed in Latin characters; however, just a few weeks later, the Cyrillic version appeared, and all subsequent six editions of the book, including the last one released in 1943 in German-occupied Minsk, were Cyrillic.[7]

The latest alteration of standard Belarusian was its state-sponsored reform in 1933 in Soviet (eastern) Belarus. This reform left Belarusian with two orthographies, the so-called Tarashkevitsa (canonized by Taraškievič) and Narkomauka. The former was used before the 1933 reform, but it continued to be used in western Belarus prior to 1939. It has been used by the Belarusian diaspora in the West, and after 1991, it has reappeared in many unofficial publications in post-Soviet Belarus. Narkomauka is the result of the 1933 reform and has been used in Soviet Belarus and in all state-sponsored Belarusian-language publications in post-Soviet Belarus as well. In fact, the difference between Tarashkevitsa and Narkomauka extends beyond orthography into lexicon and grammar.[8] Among the authors who wrote in Belarusian and gained international recognition are Janka Kupala (1882–1942), a poet and a playwright; Jakub Kolas (1882–1956), a poet; and Vasil Bykau (1924–2003), a prose writer.

Belarusian has been one of the official languages of Belarus since the Belarusian Soviet Socialist Republic (BSSR) was proclaimed (1919). From 1924 to 1939, Russian, Yiddish, and Polish were also given official status in the republic, but since 1939, Belarusian has shared its official status only with Russian. In 1990 (that is, shortly before Belarus became independent), Belarusian was proclaimed the only official language, while Russian was given the status of a language of interethnic communication. However, based on the national referendum of 1995, Russian was reintroduced as one of the two official languages of Belarus. This reintroduction gained support from 83.3 percent of the voters.

TRASIANKA AND THE RIDDLE
OF BELARUSIAN LANGUAGE USAGE

To the chagrin of all the "nationally conscious"[9] Belarusian intellectuals, the actual frequency of use of standard Belarusian in everyday communication is low. Moreover, it has never been used en masse in Belarusian cities.[10] Aleh Trusau, chairman of the Belarusian Language Society (Tavarystva Belaruskai Movy, or TBM[11]), pointed out that Belarusians did not "own" their cities for two hundred years[12]; ethnic Belarusians established their numerical majority in cities only in the 1950s.

Regarding modern language usage in Belarus, census estimates seem to be of limited, if any, value. In the 1959 census, 93.2 percent of all those who identified themselves as Belarusians living in Belarus reported Belarusian as their native language.[13] In 1970, 90.1 percent did so; in 1979, 83.5 percent; and in 1989, 80.2 percent.[14] Even with this high (but declining) level of recognition of Belarusian as the native language, ethnic Belarusians were described as having "the lowest level of native language loyalty among the fourteen non-Russian Union Republic nationalities, and also [as ranking] first in knowledge of Russian as a second language."[15] Formal expression of loyalty, however, has little to do with actual standard or literary usage. The use of Belarusian of literary norm can hardly be high if one takes into account that, for example, in the late 1980s, only 0.2 percent of secondary school students attended schools with Belarusian as the language of instruction in urban areas of the republic.[16] Not a single such school existed in Minsk Oblast or even in *rayony* (minor civil divisions) centers, with the exception of the town of Mosty, Grodno Oblast. In the countryside, Belarusian-language schooling was more widespread, but most of these de jure Belarusian schools effectively taught students in Russian. Posters, science and math tests, and most extracurricular communication between pupils and their teachers were in Russian as well.[17]

The 1999 census drew a peculiar distinction between one's native language and that most frequently spoken at home. More than 80 percent of ethnic Belarusians (65 percent of the entire population of Belarus) identified Belarusian as their native language. Yet, only 41.3 percent of all Belarusians indicated that they spoke Belarusian at home, and 58.6 percent said they spoke Russian.[18] Russian was mentioned as the language of at-home communication by 77 percent of ethnic Belarusian urbanites. Several researchers called this situation paradoxical as it reflects the contradiction between the symbolic (badge-of-ethnicity) and direct (communicative) functions of one and the same language.[19]

The figure 41 percent of ethnic Belarusians equates to 37 percent of the entire population, or roughly 3.7 million people.[20] This is still a lot—one cannot hide this many—yet meeting people who converse in standard Belarusian is problematical, as if they are hiding somewhere or perhaps resort to Belarusian only in intimate settings.

No observer who has command of the Russian language—better still, Russian and Polish, as I do—would consider the above statistics believable. While in Belarus I listened to standard Belarusian on Minsk radio and TV broadcasts, in the Janka Kupala Drama Theater, and in the headquarters of the TBM. The sole Belarusian TV channel in Minsk at the time I watched it the most (1970s and 1980s) could be labeled Belarusian only with some qualification. News reports were in Belarusian, while shows and movies were in Russian. From 2002 to 2005, the situation was roughly the same as in the 1980s.

The way interviews were (and still are) conducted in the Belarusian-language shows on Minsk TV impressed me the most. While an interviewer would speak Belarusian, most interviewees responded in Russian, no matter which social strata they represented. Moreover, while some urbanites responded in Belarusian, rural residents responded overwhelmingly in Russian.[21] This "bilingual" interviewing sounds awkward to an outsider, but locals are apparently used to it. In no other Soviet republic (and I visited thirteen out of fifteen) had I heard or seen anything like this. To be sure, under the Soviets, all republics conducted TV and radio broadcasts in Russian and in the native language of the titular nationality, but not at the same time, and rarely was the native speech flow in the native-language broadcasts interrupted by Russian.

A Belarusian researcher observes that out of eighteen theaters that existed in Belarus in 1994, four were Belarusian-language theaters. However, "all the work involved in production of a Belarusian-language play [was] most frequently conducted in Russian."[22] The Belarusian phonetics of most actors leaves much to be desired. A revealing remark to this effect singles out one actor from the others at admittedly best theater in Minsk, the Janka Kupala Drama Theater: "Kin-Kaminsky is one of [the] rare actors in the Kupala Theater who does not mix up case and gender agreement."[23]

During many trips inside Belarus in the 1970s and 1980s, I tried my best to locate people versed in the same standard language I heard from the speakers on the single local TV channel in Minsk. In other words, I set out to meet people that use Belarusian in everyday life, committed to this cause by sheer curiosity augmented by my interest in languages and a sensitive phonetic ear. With the perseverance of an investigative journalist, I toured the country trying to intercept a Belarusian-language conversation in public transportation, diners, railway stations, urban streets, rural food stores, cinema foyers, and private residences. I succeeded extremely rarely. Where conversational language was most remote from standard Russian, like in Grodno Oblast (especially its northern part abutting the Lithuanian border), the vernacular sounded close to standard, though accented, Polish, in which I was also fluent. However, in most instances, I was only exposed to either standard Russian, or *trasianka*.

Trasianka (literally, a mixture of hay and straw[24]) is a product of what Tatyana Mikulich calls *mounaya interferentsyia*[25] (linguistic superposition). *Trasianka* is an ever-present phenomenon in Belarus. It is analogous to a similar Russian-Ukrainian mix called *surzhik*. A blend of Russian and Belarusian, *trasianka* is described by nationally oriented intellectuals as a "disgusting creature of Soviet assimilation,"[26] a "perversion of the language system," or a "Creolized pseudo-language."[27] David Marples calls it "a patois of Russian and Belarusian."[28] Today, *trasianka* is more of a phonetic than lexical mix. In other words, it is ever-increasingly an accented Russian speech with just two dozen or fewer localisms unknown in standard Russian. Phonetic features that help distinguish Belarusians include enunciation of unstressed vowels, particularly "a" and "ya," and a lack of soft consonants, especially, but not only, "ch" and "shch." For example, when offered a cigarette, a *trasianka*-speaking person may say "Blagodaru, ya ne kuru" (Thank you, I do not smoke), while a person speaking standard Russian would say "Blagodaryu, ya ne kuryu," and a standard Belarusian speaker would have to say "dzyakui" instead of "blagodaryu." In rural areas, especially in the countryside of western Belarus, local lexical infusions into Russian are more numerous than in cities.

One has to point out, however, that castigating *trasianka* is only possible in a politically and/or emotionally charged discourse, where implicit or explicit assumptions as to what constitutes the best (the most dignified?) language of communication in Belarus are made up front. Without such assumptions (tacit or overt), disparaging comments (e.g., *trasianka* is an artificial lingo, *trasianka* is a product of forceful Russification) are just clichés. In Russia proper, colloquial communication in many instances is tinged with lexical and, especially, phonetic deviations from standard Russian that are by no means less discernible than those currently used in Belarus. For example, Nikita Khrushchev and Leonid Brezhnev spoke with a distinctive Ukrainian-tinged southern accent, as does Mikhail Gorbachev. From this perspective, mocking *trasianka* for not being sufficiently Russian is utterly snobbish. At the same time, vilifying it for being insufficiently Belarusian, given the low frequency of standard-Belarusian speakers, does not seem to make sense at all. One researcher suggests that "by heavily stigmatizing and ideologizing mixed speech, Belarusian language advocates are in effect rejecting potential transitional Belarusophones."[29] Another researcher observes that *trasianka* often becomes "a means of self-identification and group solidarity."[30]

Historically, the largest cities of Belarus were like Russian-speaking islands in the ocean of various Belarusian dialects. When rural migration to Minsk and regional capitals intensified, *trasianka* developed as a result of the adaptation of rural migrants to their new environments. By now, most big-city residents communicate in Russian of literary norm, whereas *trasianka* is particularly widespread in small towns (like Shklov, the hometown of Alexander Lukashenka) and in the countryside.

The actual spread of standard Belarusian in everyday life remains shrouded in mystery, and even Belarus-based researchers profess ignorance in this regard.[31] "The exact percentage of those speaking Belarusian is unknown to anybody," writes Nina Mečkovskaya, a leading Minsk-based expert on the issue.

"They refer to different numbers: 43% of Belarus's population; 16% of small-town dwellers; 1.5%–2% of residents of Minsk; 3.8% of residents of Minsk; etc."[32] The nationally conscious are apparently content with the 1999 census estimate and quote it every time they accuse the authorities of neglecting the language of 41% of Belarusians. For example, Trusau emphasizes that "no sociological survey in a totalitarian society can be believed,"[33] but he feels comfortable with the above-mentioned census estimate of the spread of Belarusian. Many Belarusians are reluctant to get involved in an open discussion of language usage. Even Lukashenka, who prides himself on speaking his mind no matter what the audience,[34] occasionally resorts to indirect phraseology when it comes to the topic of language.[35] For example, speaking to the Gomel provincial administration in November 2001, he said that in Belarus, "there is no problem of choice between Russian and Belarusian because the people have decided for themselves which language to use."[36]

An accurate, or at least realistically sound, statistic of the standard Belarusian language usage in everyday life may be available but probably is not, as even the nationally conscious are not in unanimous agreement as to what standard Belarusian is. For some, it is Tarashkevitsa, while for some others it is Narkomauka. For many years, there have been an inordinate number of inconsistencies on Belarusian-language posters, plaques, and road signs across Minsk and Belarus at large. In May 2002, on the major highway linking Minsk with Warsaw, I recorded road signs that announced a town's name as Staubtsy and Stoubtsy (in Russian this would be rendered as Stolbtsy). A street in Minsk was for a long time named vulitsa Krasnaya ("vulitsa" being an indication that the plaque was in fact in Belarusian, not Russian), whereas now it is vulitsa Chyrvonaya. The U.S. Embassy is called Ambasada Zluchanykh Shtatau Ameryki, whereas the next-door Embassy of Ukraine is called Pasol'stva Ukraiyny. One would think that the equivalents of such words as "embassy," frequently on display, would be among the most standardized words in all national languages, but it is definitely not so in Belarusian. One Belarusian journalist came up with a fascinating set of posters and public announcements that marry Russian and Belarusian and thus display illiteracy in both languages. The set includes such widespread distortions as *yuga-zakhad* (instead of *paudniovy zakhad*), *opiarnyi* (instead of *operny*) *teatr, poyezd* (instead of *tsiagnik*) *dalei ne idze, magazin* (in reference to a retail outlet) instead of *krama*, and so forth.[37] Some researchers point out, though, that in Belarusian, the literary norm itself is unusually loose. This is due not only to the coexistence of Tarashkevitsa and Narkomauka but also to the insignificant number of people committed to literary norm.[38] When, however, an object in question is hard to pin down, one cannot possibly ask for accurate estimates of its recorded frequency!

Predisposition to comparison and measurement is, however, indestructible. Thus, during my pilot survey of secondary school teachers in Minsk, Vitebsk, and Grodno, just three out of sixty-two respondents (less than 5 percent) pointed to Belarusian as the only language in which they communicate at home, thirty-seven pointed to Russian as the only home language, eleven said that they use Russian and Belarusian intermittently, and nine said that they use *trasianka*.

By and large, available surveys are much more in line with my field observations than census statistics. According to a 1989 survey, Belarusian was reported as spoken by 10 percent of the Belarusian population, including 1.5 percent of all urbanites.[39] A 1999 representative survey of 1,081 Belarusian adults selected randomly through the country and polled by a Belarusian research firm contracted by the U.S. Department of State showed similar results: as many as 12 percent of respondents spoke Belarusian at home and 7 percent at work.[40] "In Minsk, where four-fifths of the inhabitants are of Belarusian nationality, almost everyone usually speaks Russian at home (86%) and at work (90%)."[41] Timothy Colton refers to a 1999 national survey of 1,507 Belarusian adults, of whom only 4 percent indicated that they spoke only Belarusian at home.[42]

Multiple national surveys by the Independent Institute of Socio-Economic and Political Studies (IISEPS),[43] conducted from 1995 to 2004, revealed that those using only Belarusian in everyday communication are within the 2 to 7 percent range; those using only Russian are within the range of 37 to 47 percent; and the rest communicate either in both or in a mixed language. These results were criticized as biased: after all, limited use of Belarusian in the public domain may compel those dedicated to Belarusian to switch willy-nilly to Russian at work. This criticism prompted the pollsters to reformulate their question. In a 2004 national survey, they asked about the dominant language of communication at home only. The result: 13.7 percent pointed to Belarusian only, 73.7 percent pointed to Russian only, 6.8 percent said they use both Russian and Belarusian, and 4.7 percent use a language other than Russian or Belarusian. All the remaining responses (using Russian and one other language, Belarusian and one other language, and Belarusian, Russian, and one other language) accounted for only 0.5 percent.[44] The distribution of the voters in the March 19, 2006, presidential elections (discussed in chapter 7) assessed by the March 26–April 6, 2006, national survey of IISEPS (table 1.1) also reflects the modest role of Belarusian.

A national survey from October 2006, which revealed a somewhat higher (7.8 percent) share of Belarusian-only users, also cast light on factors conditioning the choice of language of everyday communication. About two-thirds (63.7 percent) said that "this is the language I have been using since childhood"; 23.5

Table 1.1.   Language of Everyday Communication of the Voters in the March 19, 2006, Presidential Elections

	Voted for Kozulin (%)	*Voted for Lukashenka (%)*	*Voted for Milinkevich (%)*
Belarusian	1.3	3.7	3.2
Russian	75.4	55.5	69.7
Belarusian and Russian	12.4	14.7	11.6
Trasianka	10.0	24.8	15.5

Source: National survey of March 26 to April 6, 2006 (random sample: 1,496 people > eighteen years of age interviewed face to face; sample error is within 3 percent); www.iiseps.org. Those stumped for an answer and those unwilling to give an answer are not included in the table; this explains why in two cases out of three, the column sums add up to less than 100 percent.

percent said that "this is the most widespread language where I live"; and only 13 percent adhered to what may be interpreted as value-laden motivation: "this is the language of my people and my homeland."[45] Among the Russian-only speakers (52 percent), almost three-quarters (72.9 percent) referred to that language as the one they have been using since childhood. A reprimand routinely leveled by conscious Belarusian speakers on their Russian-speaking compatriots is that they have betrayed their mother tongue (*matchynaya mova*). The above statistics show that, at least in the immediate sense of the word, this accusation does not hold water: for most Russian-speaking Belarusians, Russian is effectively their mother tongue.

"BADLY OUTNUMBERED, THOUGH VERY VOCAL"

A candid public discussion of the linguistic situation in Belarus is rare because the issue is now politicized to the extreme. A suggestive language argument is contained in Mikhas Puzinovsky's article entitled "Why Do Belarusian Parents Choose Russian Language of Instruction in [Secondary] Schools?" published in the TBM's newspaper. The article describes the case of Oshmiany, a town in the Belarusian-Lithuanian borderland that is actually closer to Vilnius than to Minsk. This is one region in Belarus where (according to my observations) everyday communication in the countryside is not so much between standard Russian and Belarusian (i.e., *trasianka*) as it is between standard Belarusian and Polish. This is the only region of Belarus where *rayon* newspapers are still released in Belarusian; other rural *rayon* newspapers in Belarus used to be published in Belarusian but are now bilingual. In the early 1990s, twelve first-grade elementary school classes were open in Oshmiany with the Belarusian language for instruction, while there were only two Russian-language first-grade classes. At the time, it seemed a "return" to Belarusian was close at hand.

About the same proportion between Belarusian and Russian classes was maintained for several years. At the time Puzinovsky's article was published (2001), the students who entered Belarusian-language classes were in grades five to eleven and were used by school district managers as a live confirmation of the freedom of choice between the two official languages of the country, a freedom that, according to Puzinovsky, does not actually exist. Puzinovsky states that all (!) those parents whose children entered Belarusian classes chose Russian for their younger children or demanded to switch to Russian for their older children. Puzinovsky explains this situation as follows: First, people have lost their belief in the prospects for national revival. Second, the leaders of the country set the wrong example when they communicate with their fellow countrymen in Russian. (In the early 1990s, this was not the case; Belarusian leaders Stanislau Shushkevich and Mechyslau Hryb used Belarusian and Russian intermittently.) Third, there are no vocational schools and colleges using the Belarusian language for instruction. Fourth, the very introduction of the two official languages, as a result of a popular 1995 referendum, is at fault. "Only the status of the sole official language attached to Belarusian in 1990 and corroborated by the 1994 Constitution could rescue and resurrect the language that had been kept down over centuries by Rzeczpospolita [i.e., Poland], tsarist Russia, and under the Soviets. The official bilingualism helps supplant our language from use."[46]

One may infer from the statement just quoted that freedom of choice is evil; only if there is a state mandate to cut back on this freedom can Belarusian win the tug of war. Note that Belarusian linguistic nationalists routinely label themselves democrats. According to Marples, "The opposition (usually called 'democratic') forces [are] badly outnumbered, though very vocal."[47] Here, the quotation marks framing "democratic" are on target. This is not to say that the entire collection of reasons for disloyalty to the Belarusian language does not warrant scrutiny; it does. However, the alternative reasoning has to be considered as well. According to it, the leaders of the country communicate in Russian precisely because this is what most Belarusians do. Further, if the introduction of the official bilingualism is construed as a sort of tacit coercion, then introducing one official language and opening plenty of Belarusian classes without asking parental consent, as was done in 1992 and 1993, is even more coercive to begin with. According to Ustina Marcus, "By 1994, more than 230 schools in Minsk were to be teaching in Belarusian, which was well above the percentage of students whose parents wanted them to attend such schools. Thus, parents often found that even if they opted for Russian schools, there were no places in them and their children had to go to the Belarusian schools. Such policies were perceived as forced Belarusification and heightened non-Belarusian speakers' fears."[48]

Among sixty-two secondary school teachers whom I surveyed in May 2002, only thirteen (21 percent) responded that they would like to send their own children to a school with instruction in the Belarusian language, while twenty-nine said that they would not. The September 2005 national survey by IISEPS revealed that while 12 percent of secondary school students attend Belarusian-only schools, 9.4 percent of the parents would send their children to such schools if the school choice entirely depended on them; 36.1 percent of the parents would prefer a school with Russian only, and 49.7 percent would prefer Russian and Belarusian.[49] The latter suggests that many welcome Belarusian as long as it is not the only language of instruction.

In light of these findings, the position candidly expressed in Puzinovsky's article about Oshmiany is reminiscent of that taken by a group of Belarusian authors who in 1987 wrote letters to Gorbachev asking him to influence Minsk authorities so they would issue new laws through which the Belarusian language would gain in stature. There is no doubt that the top-down, legislative initiative to protect one's language may be instrumental, and even effective, in achieving this goal. What strikes one, though, is the inherently Soviet belief in the supremacy and primacy of such a measure, which is viewed as all but a universal master key: you just fix the law, and the linguistic situation changes. The prior experience of successful changes of this nature, most eloquently summarized by Miroslav Hroch,[50] is inconsistent with this belief. It is the bottom-up initiatives, specifically, the patient, everyday work of the national movement, that blaze the trail.

As a sign of positive change, the TBM began to advertise its activities in a way that does not alienate the Russian-speaking majority. A leaflet placed in seventy-two subway cars in Minsk in September 2002 and devoted to a month-long campaign in favor of Belarusian read,

> To participate . . . there is no need to organize rallies. . . . Everybody can become an exemplary defender of one's native language among one's family, acquaintances, and friends. Just say a greeting in Belarusian, in the morning say *Dobry dzen'*! to a colleague or neighbor [and] . . . in the evening say *Dabranoch*! Read a good poem in Belarusian, write a postcard in Belarusian to your family, and when you fill out utility payment forms, do it in Belarusian. . . . When three people talk to each other in Belarusian, the fourth one will join them who is currently too shy to himself begin such a talk. Perhaps we will make it that talking in Belarusian will have become a matter of course. After all, nobody will do this for us. . . . You have something to take pride in because Frantsishek Skaryna conversed in the language of your grandfathers and he was as smart as anybody. Remember the best, be your own self, be the first.[51]

In March 2007, one local branch of the TBM persuaded the bosses of the public transportation agency in the city of Baranovichi to switch the recorded next-stop announcements on local buses from Russian to Belarusian.[52]

Such gentle but persistent dissemination of the nationalist message on language may eventually become successful.

FORCIBLE RUSSIFICATION AND *POMIARKOUNASTS*

How the current linguistic situation came about is explained in different ways. On the one hand, a small, but vociferous, group of activists is involved in an uphill battle to make Belarusian the language of mass communication. On the other hand, a silent majority of ethnic Belarusians is by no means unreceptive to the activists' views but does not seem willing to put their message into practice. Today, sixteen years after independence, Minsk seems to be as firmly a part of the Russian-language information space as under the Soviets, although it is not as Moscow-centered as it used to be. Much has changed after 2002. Now, there are three Belarusian TV channels instead of just one, whereas Moscow-based TV channels are being squeezed out slowly but steadily. The major government daily *Belarus Segodnia*, a Russian-language newspaper, also bearing the logo of *Sovetskaya Belorussiya* as a clear mark of succession, offers an information and propaganda product of decent quality: its design is quite modern, and its content is anything but primitive. In Minsk, one of the admittedly "fossil" street names, Prospekt Gazety *Izvestia* (Avenue of the Newspaper *Izvestia*), was changed in 2005; it is now Prospekt Gazety *Zviazda* (Avenue of the Newspaper *Zviazda*), the only national daily in Belarusian. Other fossil names, however, such as *Prospekt Gazety Pravda* (Avenue of the Newspaper *Pravda*), as well as streets named after Vladimir Lenin, Yakov Sverdlov, Felix Dzierzynski, Moiysei Uritsky, and the like, remain.

Haphazard attempts at introducing Belarusian overnight by decree, made in the early 1990s, are now decried as radical and insensitive. Vadim Glinnik, a Belarusian-speaking architect, confessed that in the late 1980s and early 1990s, he used to create artificial conflict situations by intentionally speaking Belarusian with people who disapproved of it either because they did not feel comfortable using the language or for any other reason. Now he calls his erstwhile behavior reckless and admits that he feels more affinity with a Russian-speaking Moscow intellectual than a Belarusian-speaking truck driver.[53] Irina Khalip, a journalist, refers to her similar behavior as linguistic Jacobinism.[54] However, both Khalip and Glinnik and other interviewees claim that due to Lukashenka, precious years have been lost for the cause of gradual transition to Belarusian.

Another popular viewpoint is that Belarusians no longer speak "their" language due to *pomiarkounasts*, which literally means "moderation and self-restraint," but its actual contextual reading also spans patience, resignation, tolerance, and susceptibility to outside influences. *Pomiarkounasts* is widely and persistently referred to in informal discussions about the language and identity of Belarusians. The following popular joke makes sense of this myth: A Russian takes a train. He enters a train car, walks to his seat, and sits on a nail sticking out of it. With indignation and disgust, he pulls the nail out of his body and throws it out the window. Now, a Ukrainian takes a train and also lands on the nail. He also pulls it out with disgust and pain but stops short of throwing it away because that would be imprudent as the nail may be put to use in the household. Now, it is time for a Belarusian to undergo the same ordeal. When a Belarusian realizes he is sitting on a nail, he hurts just like his counterparts, but he thinks, well, who knows, maybe this is what's meant to be. With this in mind, he continues to sit still.

During a 2002 competition in wit, the so-called KVN—literally, the Club of the Cheerful and Quick Witted, a college student team from Minsk—put the same meaning in a different nutshell. Referring to the famous peeing-boy statue emblematic of Brussels, they suggested that a statue equally representative of Minsk and Belarus in general should be a nonpeeing boy; a boy epitomizing Belarus is not peeing, he is enduring.

As an element of the Belarusian self-portrait, *pomiarkounasts* does not lend itself easily to rational analysis. However, Russification does. There is no doubt that Russification took place in the Soviet Union, although it hardly resembled the state-run conspiracy that it was often considered to be in Sovietology writings. In the Soviet Union, there were such powerful overt vehicles of Russification to fall back on that the need to also involve anything covert or hidden from the public eye seems questionable. One such overt tool of Russification was service in the Soviet army, which is primarily why command of the Russian language was always higher among non-Russian men than among women. Another reason to adopt Russian was to move up in the ranks, whether in a managerial position (like working for a large, federally controlled enterprise in a supervisory, let alone top-management, position) or to gain political position (executive power at the federal level or in a Communist Party cell). All these required proficiency in Russian. Migration of ethnic Russians was also a powerful engine of Russification.

In many Soviet republics, therefore, the mass spread of the Russian language was to be expected with the infusion of ethnic Russians and other Russian-language speakers from without. However, the scale of this infusion into Belarus was more on a par with the least Russified Baltic state, Lithuania, than with, say, Latvia or Estonia, let alone Kazakhstan. In 1989, Russians accounted for 13.2 percent of Belarus's population, Poles for 4.1 percent, and Belarusians for 77.8 percent. By 1999, the share of self-identified Belarusians had increased to 81.2 percent, and Russians and Poles declined to 11.4 and 3.9 percent,[55] respectively, with no recorded outflow of these ethnicities.

All Belarus watchers agree that there was never a Russian community in Belarus that would in any way detach and position itself against the cultural mainstream. There is none today, when in all the other post-Soviet states ethnic Russians have organized themselves into cultural associations and sometimes separate political parties. And yet, the Russian language became nearly the sole communication medium in Belarus. This convinced some students of Belarus that "the language conflict in contemporary Belarus is not . . . an ethnic conflict; instead, it is to a far greater extent an ideological conflict *within* the majority ethnic group."[56] Only Ukraine showed some semblance of similarity with Belarus with regard to the adoption of the Russian language. The parallel with Ukraine is natural as only in Ukraine and Belarus are the languages of the titular nationalities very close to Russian. Upon closer examination, however, one realizes how much more the Ukrainian language is embraced in Ukraine than Belarusian is in Belarus. Even in the most Russified eastern Ukraine (e.g., Donetsk, Kharkiv, and Lugansk oblasts), Ukrainian is the language of everyday communication in small towns and the countryside.

Indeed, nowhere outside Russia proper has the Russian language gained such supremacy as in Belarus. Moreover, there have not been many autonomous republics (the second tier of ethnic autonomy in the Soviet Union) in which Russian would be as dominant among the people of the titular nationality as in Belarus, despite the fact that in many of them the titular nationality is not in the majority. Admittedly, there were cases (such as the Udmurt and Mordva republics of Russia) but, indeed, very few.

According to Nikolai Zen'kovich, "The extent of adoption of the Russian language [in Belarus] has no match among all the peoples of the Soviet Union."[57] "What the Belarusians demonstrated had no precedent in the entire world: native population en masse solicited that the authorities excuse their children from studying their native language in secondary schools."[58]

So, had Belarus been subjected to a particularly "lethal" type of Russification that targeted each and every native speaker?

RUSSIFICATION VERSUS BELARUSIFICATION

It is believed that the forerunner of modern Belarusian was the official language of the Grand Duchy of Lithuania from the fourteenth to sixteenth centuries. However, according to Yevfimii (Yaukhim) Karski, the premier

Belarusian linguist, the language actually used by the grand duchy's upper strata and practiced in courts was significantly detached from the popular vernacular and contained many borrowings from other languages.[59] Moreover, from the end of the sixteenth century, that language, the so-called *prosta mova*, had yielded to Polish not only among the Catholics but also among the Orthodox and Uniate subjects of the grand duchy. By the beginning of the eighteenth century, *prosta mova* had been supplanted not only in public life but also as the language of private correspondence, diaries, and recorded comments and observations. These were now conducted in either Polish or Russian.[60]

Anyway, there was at least a 150-year hiatus (beginning in the late 1600s) in the literary tradition that is now being cast as inherently Belarusian. Marples writes that in Belarus, "the national past could only be reconstructed through what can best be described as 'historical leaps' over centuries of uncertain existence."[61] If anything, this apt formulation pertains to language in the first place.

The earliest literary works in Belarusian that appeared after that pause were created on the basis of ambient rural vernaculars, with no immediate connection to the fourteenth to sixteenth centuries' literary norm of the grand duchy. The first Belarusian writers were bilingual. They wrote in standard Polish and in the peasant vernacular of the Kresy, which to them was eastern Poland. These people were genuine populists who wanted to bridge the gap between themselves and their serfs, and for this reason they began to use the Belarusian vernacular of the peasantry in their literary works. The narrow circle of Belarusian early literary monuments includes two anonymous poems, *Eneida Navyvarot* (Eneida Turned Inside Out), written between 1816 and 1828 and first published in 1845, and *Taras na Parnase* (Taras on the Parnasse), written in the 1850s and first published in 1889; a comic opera, *Sialanka* (1846) by Wincent Dunin-Marcinkewicz (1807–1884); and the 1890s poems by Frantsyšek Boguševič (1840–1900).[62]

Soon after the third (1795) partition of Poland, St. Petersburg academic philologists classed the rural vernacular spoken in the newly acquired areas between Grodno, Minsk, and Vilna (Vilnius) as a Polish dialect.[63] Only after two successive Polish rebellions (1830 and 1863), in which some valiant protectors of the Belarusian peasantry participated, did it dawn upon Russian scholars that the vernacular was in fact a dialect of Russian, not Polish.[64] Evidently, political contingencies of the time exerted demands not much different from those of today. The "truth," however, was in the middle: the vernacular in fact formed a bridge between Russian and Polish; it was related and yet peripheral to both but retained distinctions of its own.

According to Mikhail Bulakhov, the biographer of Yevfimii Karski, Karski believed that "the Belarusian language had been refined in a more or less satisfactory way so it could be used for literary purposes only in the late 19th–early 20th centuries."[65] After the publication of the Belarusian grammar in 1918, it was six more years before attempts to propagate the standards of a new literary language were undertaken. This endeavor took place in eastern Belarus, after it became a Soviet republic.

It was hindered, however, by the fact that urban areas of Belarus had long been linguistically alien to their environs: Yiddish, Polish, and Russian were spoken in those cities and towns. According to the 1897 census, the percentage of ethnic Belarusians in all towns with populations in excess of two thousand residents was 16.1 percent, while in towns exceeding fifty thousand residents, it was only 7.3 percent.[66] At the time, Mogilev was the only sizable city in Belarus in which Belarusian was spoken by more than 20 percent of the population. In Vilna, which educated Belarusians considered the major center of Belarusian culture prior to Vilna's incorporation into Poland in 1921, only 4.2 percent spoke Belarusian in 1897. In Minsk, which became the Belarusian capital, only 9.0 percent did. In all these and other "Belarusian" cities, Yiddish was the most widespread language, in most cases followed by Russian and Polish. In Vilna, however, the order was different: Yiddish was spoken by 40 percent, Polish by 30.9 percent, and Russian by 20.0 percent.[67] On the basis of the 1897 census, Steven Guthier wrote about "the extreme weakness of Belorussians in the free professions and middle class. At the turn of the century, Belorussians lacked the educated and articulate personnel as well as the financial resources to sustain an effective national propaganda effort."[68] The development of a Belarusian literary norm was additionally hindered by having to use two different scripts in Belarusian-language publications, Latin for the Catholics and Cyrillic for the Orthodox.

The situation began to change when Belarusians obtained their own republic. According to Zen'kovich, Soviet Belarus experienced three Belarusification campaigns, that is, organized attempts to implant the Belarusian language into public life and mass media: in the 1920s, in the early 1950s, and from 1988 to 1994.[69] To be sure, Belarusian never ceased to be an officially recognized language of Belarus since 1918. Mass publishing in Belarusian began soon after the 1917 revolution, and, as was shown above, most ethnic Belarusians considered it to be their native language when filling out census forms. Those three campaigns were crusades to make Belarusian the de facto language of communication in Belarus. However, none of them made significant headway.

The first of the campaigns has been glorified in the annals of the Belarusian national movement as the golden age of Belarusian nationalism. Indeed, from 1921 to 1929, the entire Belarusian national elite gathered in Minsk. In large part having Catholic backgrounds, they were lured from western Belarus, which Poland possessed from 1921 to 1939. The enthusiasm for Belarusification was genuine among liberal arts professionals and local party leaders. Belarusian was declared the language of official gatherings and all sorts of official paperwork. However, the starting point of Belarusification was exceedingly low in all the major cities, and newcomers to these cities continued to be linguistically assimilated into the majority. With the removal of restrictions imposed on Jews in terms of settlement, occupation, and education, younger Jews abandoned Yiddish en masse and switched to Russian.[70] Thus, the Russian-language component of the urban population became overwhelming. At the same time, the popular image of Belarusian as a peasant vernacular lingered.

By 1926, due to accelerated migration from the countryside, the share of ethnic Belarusians in the urban population had grown to 39.3 percent. At the same time, Jews accounted for 40.1 percent and Russians for 15.6 percent. Yet, only 20 percent of the urbanites listed Belarusian as their native language in 1926, whereas in the countryside, 76.9 percent did.[71] Note that when only 20 percent of urbanites claim to be Belarusian speakers while 39 percent of them claim to be ethnic Belarusians, this is a clear indication that the linguistic assimilation of Belarusians in cities occurred rapidly, even during the heyday of the Belarusian national movement. Guthier stresses that "the decline of the Belorussian language reflects language switches among Belorussians, not a large influx of non-Belorussians."[72] He also indicates a "pattern of denationalization for Belorussians in districts contiguous to Russian ethnic areas,"[73] a clear sign of contagious diffusion.[74] In Vitebsk, only 4.7 percent of the population spoke Belarusian in 1926, and in Gomel only 0.6 percent did. At the same time, Minsk, a newly designated Belarusian national center, led with an impressive 22.9 percent.[75] In Minsk, all of the multilayered administration was required to use Belarusian, and the Communist Party itself led the Belarusification campaign. Although in 1913 no Belarusian-language newspapers existed in eastern Belarus, in 1928 there were thirty.[76]

Several phenomena deserve attention in conjunction with the first Belarusification campaign: resistance to Belarusification, the so-called divergent language planning, and the 1933 Belarusian language reform. Curt Woolhiser furnishes insights into what he calls "attitudinal barriers to the broader use of Belarusian"[77] and "the persistence of [a] negative attitude toward the language on the part of much of [the] urban population, including many linguistically assimilated ethnic Belarusian workers and Party officials."[78] In the 1925–1926 academic year, only 12 percent of all lecture hours were delivered in Belarusian at the Belarusian State University, and no lec-

tures at all were given in Belarusian at the medical school.[79] Failure to propagate Belarusian quickly enough led some scholars and activists, like Jazep
Ljosik, to find fault in the orthography and other features of the Belarusian
language itself.[80] In an effort to reduce similarity with Russian, Belarusian
language planners "engaged in a specific type of divergent planning."[81] Indeed, compared with the 1906–1914 language of the *Nasha Niva* (a Vilna-
based Belarusian newspaper and an icon of the Belarusian revival movement), the Belarusian of the 1920s had significantly moved away from
Russian. Mečkovskaya gives a long list of lexemes that were initially used in
the *Nasha Niva* but were later replaced in view of their close similarity to
their Russian counterparts. It is hardly a coincidence that the academician
Yevfimii Karski, whose contribution to Belarusian linguistics is second to
none, left Minsk for Petrograd in 1921 and expressed his indignation at the
"forcible Belarusification" of the offices and the practice of firing bureaucrats
"with high proficiency in Russian" who, however, failed to master Belarusian. "Belarusification," wrote Karski in his letter to *Pravda*, "should go naturally without pressuring and discriminating against people brought up in
Russian culture."[82] "Forcible Belorussification" is a term also used by
Nicholas Vakar[83] in reference to the developments of the 1920s.

Predictably, if Belarusification could be expected to face the toughest resistance anywhere, it was in the easternmost and southern parts of the republic. Not only did extremely few people in Gomel and Vitebsk name Belarusian as their native language, but rural villagers themselves spoke dialects that
were close to Russian and occasionally (in Gomel Province) Ukrainian. At the
same time, the standard Belarusian implanted into schooling and official life
had been based on the more Polonized western Belarusian dialects.

The 1933 reform then came as a natural backlash. Of course, it was a typical Soviet campaign; it resorted to heavy-handed ideological ammunition
and had a drumbeat irrelevant to the actual purpose of reform. In the decree
of the Belarusian Council of the People's Commissars of August 26, 1933, the
alleged Belarusian National Democrats (which had become a code phrase for
traitors as early as 1930) were accused of "intending to tear away the Belarusian literary language from the language of the Belarusian working masses
and of thus creating an artificial barrier between the Belarusian and Russian
languages."[84]

However, applying the "curate's egg" principle introduced into Belarusian
studies by Marples, not every Soviet campaign was ill advised or irrelevant
in its entirety. One has to look beyond the façade to uncover its true emphasis and goals. It is noteworthy that the language reform in question was conducted under the aegis of "weeding out Polonisms," which *Pravda* made clear
in its 1934 article devoted to Belarusian language reform.[85] When modern

Belarusian nationalists claim that the 1933 reform pursued the goal of making Belarusian closer to Russian, they are on target. However, they usually fall short of mentioning that the mainstream vernaculars of eastern Belarus themselves were naturally closer to Russian than the western Belarusian dialects that had once inspired Branislau Taraškiewič and a few other Vilna-based promoters of the Belarusian national cause. In the words of one researcher, the 1933 reform "discarded grammar options whose genesis had been the southwestern dialects which at the time were spoken beyond the borders of the BSSR, in Poland"[86] and "reoriented the dialectal basis of Belarusian literary norm to the southeastern dialectal zone genetically close to southern Russian dialects."[87] If only to some extent, therefore, the reform pursued the goal of making standard Belarusian more acceptable to the actual speakers. Note that at the time of reform, western Belarus belonged to a hostile foreign country. Of course, reforming a language that had been codified only recently and was still used by a small minority of urbanites did not boost respect for that language. For decades thereafter, a joke made the rounds in Minsk that *Praletaryi usekh stran zluchaitsesia!* gave way to *Praletaryi usekh stran ednaitsesia!*[88] because *zluchaitsesia* sounded too close to *sluchka* (coupling). In fact, it was a switch from a more Polonized version (close to the Polish *łączcię się*) to a more Russified one (close to the Russian *soyediniaites*).

In the meantime, in western Belarus the official stance of Polish authorities with regard to Belarusian was mixed, and it worsened since communist propaganda from across the border incited insurgence. Described in great detail by Vakar[89] and Ivan Lubachko,[90] the situation was grim, and the Belarusian national cause did not have good prospects under the exceedingly unitary and assimilatory policies of Polish administrations.

According to Yury Koriakov, proficiency in the native language was higher in western Belarus than in eastern Belarus. Whereas in the East, the Russification "was more from below, more spontaneous and did not cause inner protest, the policy of Polish authorities caused conscious resistance, which could express itself in desire to preserve the language."[91] Comparing Polish and Soviet attitudes toward Belarusian national aspirations in the 1930s, Vakar observes that whereas repressive Polish authorities mainly targeted the symbols of Belarusian cultural separateness, repressive Soviets targeted the people who promoted those symbols.[92] Indeed, beginning in 1929, the Minsk-based Belarusian cultural elite was dealt a severe blow when many found themselves behind bars, and many lost their lives for alleged bourgeois nationalism and espionage for Poland. The Belarusian intellectual elite had, for the most part, lived previously in Vilna under Polish rule, and so leveling this charge against them was handy for the bloodthirsty Cheka-NKVD. Vicious purges were undertaken at the time in all the other Soviet republics, not excluding Stalin's native Georgia. The Belarusian writer Uladzimer Arlou believes that these purges were especially devastating in Belarus and Ukraine. Out of approximately two thousand Soviet authors purged, as many as four hundred represented Belarus, a disproportionately high number.[93]

The intellectuals from every former Soviet republic invariably argue that their respective losses were the most devastating. As the scale of earthquake damage depends not only on the quake's force (as measured on Richter scale) but also on the construction design and material subjected to destruction, so Belarus's nascent nationalism suffered more damage than an old and seasoned nationalism would have. The Belarusian national movement therefore entered the war in much weakened shape. Yet, the Belarusification campaign did not cease. "Even after a purge began of the Belorussian nationalist elite in 1929, the Soviet authorities replaced the old leadership with younger Belorussians. Such trappings of cultural nationalism as Belorussian language in the schools, administration, and literature continued to receive official support."[94] Whereas in 1928 there were 30 Belarusian-language newspapers, in 1938, that is, after much of the national elite was purged, there were 149,[95] whereas Russian-language newspapers numbered 48, and "the output of books in Belarusian (including works in geology, physics, and other non-humanities topics) in the BSSR was seven times higher than in 1928."[96]

After the devastating war,[97] ethnic Belarusians quickly became the ethnic majority in all the cities of Belarus, initially because of the drastic reduction in the number of Jews and later also because of the greatly accelerated rural migration.

My own observations from the 1960s on have led me to believe that mass adoption of the Russian language by Belarus urbanites (and later by rural folks as well) continued unabated: rural migrants in cities preferred to send their children to Russian-language schools and adopted Russian themselves as their language of everyday communication. By the late 1960s, one-third of all secondary school students in Belarus, almost exclusively urbanites, did not take Belarusian even as a separate subject at the Russian-language schools they attended.[98] In the mid-to-late 1960s, the 1970s, and much of the 1980s, I visited Minsk every year, and it was practically impossible to encounter a conversation conducted in standard Belarusian in the streets of the Belarusian capital. By the late 1970s, even *trasianka* had all but vanished, and I could only listen to it at the Komarovsky farmer's market close to my grandparents' home. With reference to data from the Institute of Art, Ethnography and Folklore of the Belarusian Academy of Sciences, Koriakov reports that in the late 1980s and early 1990s, only 1.5 to 2 percent of Minsk residents steadily used Belarusian.[99] This brings us to Guthier's grim prediction: "If the pattern of assimilation continues, then the ultimate result will be a national elite without a constituency."[100]

However, long before this prediction was made, one more attempt to implant the Belarusian language was undertaken through the Communist Party apparatus. In 1953, Mikhail Zimianin, an ethnic Belarusian and an appointee of Lawrentii Beria, was supposed to replace a Russian, Nikolai Patolichev. A survey with a critical assessment of the linguistic situation in Belarus was prepared, and Zimianin was dispatched from Moscow. He delivered a Belarusian-language speech at the June 1953 Belarusian Central Committee meeting, something that had not been done since the early 1930s. Also, a detailed appraisal highly critical of local and Minsk-based party authorities' attitude to the Belarusian language was issued. However, the fall of Beria thwarted Zimianin's appointment, and he was called off to Moscow.[101] Under no subsequent Belarusian leader—Kirill Mazurov, Tikhon Kiseliov, Piotr Masherov, or Yefrem Sokolov—did Belarusian become the working language of the Belarusian authorities, although some modest attempts were undertaken, notably under Mazurov, who in January 1959 delivered a speech in Belarusian at a reception in honor of the fortieth anniversary of the founding of the BSSR. The 1958 school reform accorded parents the right to choose the language of their children's secondary school instruction and to refrain from learning the titular language of each union republic. In Belarus more frequently than anywhere else, urban families chose this option.

An additional, yet indirect, argument in favor of spontaneous Russification reported by Zen'kovich also shows that in the 1980s, all Belarusian-language publications were subsidized by the state and yet did not sell. The only exception to the rule was the magazine *Rabotnitsa i Selianka,* which used to sell one million copies because of its free-of-charge appendix devoted to home dressmaking. The following excerpt from Zen'kovich is revealing:

The remaining periodicals in Belarusian barely reached circulations of 40,000–50,000 copies and were primarily spread through the system of state-paid subscription, so they ended up in state libraries, rural "palaces of culture," offices of political education, and "red corners" of animal farms. Even such a newspaper as the *Zviazda*, an organ of the Communist Party of Belarus . . . printed barely 60,000–70,000 copies during its heyday. And this is despite the indefatigable control of the Central Committee over its spread! The Russian-language counterpart of the *Zviazda*, the newspaper *Sovetskaya Belorussiya,* also an organ of the Central Committee, had a circulation of 200,000 copies in the 1980s.

The principal magazine of the Belarusian writers' union, *Polymia*, published in Belarusian, had a circulation from 6,000–8,000 copies. However, its Russian-language counterpart, *Neman* [also an organ of the same union], sold 200,000 copies. . . . The situation in book publishing was even more paradoxical. Book-stores were unable to sell even a small number of copies of the highly talented novels by Vasil Bykov released in Belarusian. But no sooner had the same nov-els been translated into Russian than even 200,000 copies were instantaneously grabbed by avid buyers.

In order to fill the auditorium of the Janka Kupala Belarusian Drama Theater, whose plays are in Belarusian, the authorities recruited soldiers, cadets, and col-lege students [who were assigned to attend certain plays]. Even the names of reputable playwrights did not help. . . . The tickets for the same plays in Russian [staged in the Russian Drama Theater] were sold in full for every performance, and people stood in long lines to buy them.[102]

Contrary to some nationalists' pronouncements, the Soviet Belarusian au-thorities undertook an earnest effort to sustain the Belarusian language in the public domain. The effort has been far above and beyond the actual and spon-taneous demand for this language as the means of daily communication. Zen'kovich attributes this inadequate demand to the fact that Belarusian has been traditionally viewed as a peasant, rustic language. Exactly the same at-titude, however, once applied to Lithuanian, Czech, and Slovak,[103] to name just a few, and yet the respective national movements crossed this hurdle.

LANGUAGE PRESTIGE AND CHANGES OF THE 1990S

In 1988, Adam Maldis, doctor of philology, who in the 1990s became one of the spiritual leaders of the Belarusian opposition, offered a suggestive ac-count of the situation:

A lot has been written about our national nihilism. . . . Our national woes began as early as the second half of the 16th century (while prior to that everything had been more or less fine . . .) when in pursuit of privileges the feudal aristocracy betrayed the people and began to adopt the Polish language and Polish culture. By the end of the 17th century, the ancient Belarusian language, which had been the official language in the Grand Duchy of Lithuania, had been supplanted from the officialdom and confined to home usage. Later, when Belarusian lands were incorporated into tsarist Russia, the upper strata switched to Russian with equal ease and in pursuit of the same privileges. As a result, by the beginning of the 20th century, Belarusians had not evolved as a nation.[104]

Admittedly, the above account does not entirely undermine the Russifica-tion thesis; yet, it weakens it quite a bit. At the very least, Russification sheds the aura of compulsion and begins to look like an all-but-consensual act. After all, many ethnic groups of the Russian Empire effectively retained their respective languages despite the fact that similar prestige considerations applied to them.

> Until people resume speaking in Belarusian in their homes, in their families, until speaking the language becomes effortless and fluent, until then neither day care nor secondary school nor a university nor, eventually, the man-in-the-street will adopt the language. However, families will begin to talk Belarusian only when it is viewed as prestigious and necessary—for conversing at work or school or for making a speech at a Supreme Soviet's session or a Party conference.[105]

As Maldis's article suggests, everything hinges on prestige. Prestige once nudged people to renounce their language, and prestige may now nudge them to readopt it. In the meantime, the situation looks grim: "Urban schools lack teachers of Belarusian, while many of those who teach Belarusian in the countryside do not know the language well enough themselves and are not fluent in colloquial Belarusian."[106] Note that the previous statement is about the countryside, the depositary of folk culture in every old-world country.

> The Council of Ministers decided to promote the teaching of the Belarusian language. The minutes of this decision qualified the situation as unsatisfactory, and they set out to conduct very thoughtful changes. Yet even this very document was written and accepted in Russian. . . . While issuing appeals to rectify the language situation and to adopt bilingualism, we remain unilingual. This reminds me of a physician who is taking the trouble to persuade his patient to throw away cigarettes while at the same time inhaling and enjoying a tantalizing tobacco smoke.
>
> When, however, the Belarusian language is heard once in a while, as at writers' meetings, the audience all but hoots at every language mistake by the orator.[107]

The latter confession sounds awkward: it appears that the language has retreated to the recesses of memory to such an extent that even purists question each other's command of it. Maldis concludes that one ought to "muster one's own will and cross the psychological barrier. This is not going to be easy at first, and a certain discomfort may even emerge."[108] If, however, Belarusians do not overcome this discomfort, then in the twenty-first century they "will fall short of geniuses. These will emerge but will belong to different cultures, as it was with Mickiewicz and Moniuszko."[109]

In the late 1980s, fresh winds from Moscow stirred nationally conscious people in Belarus to action. As at other crucial junctures in the region's history, the stimulus for change came from outside. Moreover, Belarus's Communist Party leadership was one of the most resistant to democratic change in the entire Soviet Union. Ales Adamovich, a prominent Belarusian writer who in the 1980s relocated to Moscow, labeled his homeland the "Vendee of Perestroika." As Alexander Motyl wrote in his characteristically titled 1987 book *Will the Non-Russians Rebel?* "The Belorussian contribution to dissent has been virtually nonexistent."[110]

However, change emanating from Moscow was irresistible, and several local initiatives developed as a direct result of it. Thus, in 1990, the Law on Languages in the BSSR was adopted, in which Belarusian was declared the official language of the republic and Russian the language of interethnic communication. According to that law, the Republic of Belarus was to "ensure comprehensive development and utilization of Belarusian in all areas of public life"[111] Two observations are noteworthy in this regard. First, Belarus appeared to be the next to last non-Russian Soviet Republic to adopt the law in support of the titular language; only Turkmenistan did that later.[112] This delay reflects the situation whereby some activists from among liberal arts professionals were truly concerned about language, but most rank-and-file Belarusians could not care less. Incidentally, the *Sovetskaya Etnografia* journal had published a review of the readers' letters on ethnolinguistic issues sent to national (Moscow-based) newspapers from January 1987 to January 1988. There were twenty-four letters from Ukraine and only one from Belarus (whose population is only five times smaller).[113] Second, the newly adopted language law was a means to protect a language on the brink of extinction, much like the article on language was in the Code of Laws (*Statut*) adopted in 1588 in the Grand Duchy of Lithuania. At that time, though, *prosta mova* (which some call Old Belarusian), was being relentlessly supplanted by Polish.[114]

Yet, the late 1980s and early 1990s were a period of great expectations on the part of "nationally conscious" Belarusians. Thus, the TBM was registered in 1991 (it actually emerged in 1989) and began to publish the *Nasha Slova* weekly. Unlike today, the TBM was one of the most visible public institutions in Belarus. In 1991 another Belarusian-language newspaper acquired the name of *Nasha Niva*, a symbolic passing of the baton from the eponymous 1906–1915 Vilna-based newspaper, which played a central role in the Belarusian "revival," that is, the period when Belarusians acquired national aspirations. After its "reemergence," the *Nasha Niva* began to use Tarashkevitsa, in violation of the post-1933 canon abided by all Belarusian-language publications released in Belarus, except during the 1941–1944 Nazi occupation. Considering that the self-imposed task of the editors in the early 1990s was to detach Belarusian from Russian even more than during the 1921–1929 period, a switch to Tarashkevitsa is understandable. Considering, however, that, as mentioned above, the original *Nasha Niva* used many Russicisms not recognized in Tarashkevitsa, the switch is ironic, as well as somewhat risky as it may alienate less-educated language users.

The TBM and the Belarusian Popular Front (Belarusky Narodny Front, or BNF), a political party founded in 1989, kept the issue of the dismal situation of Belarusian in public focus. In the early 1990s, it was still rare but possible to come across Minsk intellectuals conversing in Belarusian in public. A drastic increase in the number of Belarusian language classes followed. The share of first-grade classes with Belarusian as the language of instruction skyrocketed from 20 percent in 1989 to 75 percent in 1994.[115] In Minsk and regional capitals where just recently there had been no Belarusian-language secondary schools at all and a huge share of schoolchildren did not even take Belarusian offered as a separate subject, hundreds of classes with Belarusian as the only language of instruction were open. This was arguably the most shortsighted step of the third Belarusification campaign. Thousands of parents began to petition local, regional, and national authorities to revert to Russian as the language of instruction. In Grodno, a group of parents sued local authorities who had transformed a Russian-language school into a Belarusian-language school. The court threw the suit out on the grounds that the ethnicity of the petitioners recorded in their internal passports was Belarusian.[116]

After Lukashenka's sound electoral victory in 1994, a 1995 referendum helped reintroduce Russian as another official language of Belarus. As already mentioned, the idea was backed by a staggering 83.3 percent of the voters. Yury Drakokhrust, an associate of Radio Liberty, stated that "in the 1995 Referendum, the question about the national status of Russian was a kind of a locomotive [the contextual meaning of this word is between a tiebreaker and a sure bet] that pulled through positive responses to all the other questions as well."[117] (Other questions addressed restoring the slightly modified flag and seal of the Soviet Belarus's, economic integration with Russia, and changes in the constitution that would allow the president to suspend the Parliament in case it were to violate the constitution.) Earlier, the same author had written that Lukashenka's election had been "an act of revenge of the social outcasts on nationalists," only to be reminded that those voting for Lukashenka were too numerous to be labeled outcasts.[118]

By no means, however, was the 1995 referendum a bolt from the blue. It was preceded by a multitude of public initiatives. For example, the short-lived Movement for Democratic Reform petitioned the government to reintroduce Russian as one of the official languages as early as March 1992.[119] In the spring of 1993, the same institution, together with a reputable publishing firm, prepared a draft law to this effect. In November 1994, the United Democratic Party of Belarus appealed to the government that the right of parents to freely choose the language of instruction for their children should be respected. "Inasmuch as the realization of the parents' rights to choose the language of instruction of their children often leads to choosing the language with social advantages attached to it," wrote a strong advocate of Belarusification, "so the 'weak' and less prestigious Belarusian language would under this approach inevitably *fall victim to the expansion of democracy in Belarus*"[120] [emphasis added]. From the left flank of Belarus's political spectrum represented by the communists, the demands to restore the official bilingualism have been issued repeatedly since 1990. Many times was the question of language debated in the Belarusian Supreme Soviet (parliament), whose majority, however, resisted the idea of a language referendum in 1992 and 1993.

The newly elected president, however, took heed of all those initiatives. One of his first speeches was at the Minsk Pedagogical University. In contrast to Stanislau Shushkevich and Mechyslau Hryb, the former official leaders of the country, Lukashenka delivered his speech in Russian. To the question from the audience of why he was not speaking Belarusian, Lukashenka responded with a rhetorical question: "Is there anybody here who does not understand me?" When, thereafter, Lukashenka mentioned the excesses of Belarusification and suggested that they should be reversed, the audience burst out in applause.[121] In his December 1, 1994, speech at the session of the Gomel City Soviet, Lukashenka made an offensive statement cited ever since by the opposition media. "People who speak Belarusian cannot do anything but speak Belarusian. One cannot express anything great in that language. Belarusian is a pitiful language. There are only two great languages in the world, Russian and English."[122] Never did Lukashenka reiterate this disparaging comment or come up with a similar one. In a personal interview of May 2002, Uladzimer Arlou, one of the best-known Belarusian-speaking intellectuals, conjectured that Lukashenka had probably long regretted his words. Whether or not this is true, the tone of Lukashenka's subsequent pronouncements on language has been decidedly different. While legitimizing the use of Russian in Belarus, Lukashenka steers clear from denigrating Belarusian. "I do not understand those who say that one should reject Russian and switch to Belarusian only," he said during his November 2005 trip to his native Mogilev Oblast. "Let us leave our Russian and our Belarusian. And we will be calmly perfecting our native language without torment and revolutions."[123] Or more emotionally: "This is our Russian language, we have put no less heart and soul into it than Russians and Ukrainians. All of us have been nurturing contemporary Russian. So when the question arose about bilingualism, this is no bilingualism at all. This is our Russian. And we have made it the second official language. The overwhelming majority respects, loves, and speaks it" (applause).[124]

Many Belarus watchers are on target when they express their indignation about the treatment of Belarusian by Belarus's officialdom. However, all that

Lukashenka did in his December 1994 Gomel speech was let the cat out of the bag. That cat, however, had long been there, and I would not back any conspiracy theory with regard to it. Unfortunately, the problem is deeper and has local roots. The popular vote of 1995 legitimized the actual linguistic situation. It is true, though, that the referendum marked the beginning of an officially sponsored reversal of the 1990–1994 increase in the use of Belarusian in the public domain. And it is equally true that "vigorous support of Belarusian began to be perceived *by society* as an opposition-minded activity" [emphasis added].[125]

In the 1999–2000 academic year, there were only twelve secondary schools (4.5 percent) in the city of Minsk that taught in Belarusian.[126] In the entire country, the number of elementary school freshmen who studied Belarusian (as a language course, not as the language of instruction in other courses) dropped from 75 percent in 1993 and 1994 to 28 percent in 1997 and 1998, and from 58 percent to 4.7 percent in the city of Minsk.[127]

Some nationally conscious Belarusians experimented with speaking Belarusian in public settings, notably, in the local militia (police) headquarters upon being apprehended for their participation in political rallies or for "politically neutral" violations. (Militiamen are in most cases fresh recruits from the countryside or first-generation urbanites, that is, people who may be expected to have been more exposed to Belarusian than most lifelong residents of Minsk.) Such experiments, largely unsuccessful, were then publicized to attract attention to the extinction of the Belarusian language. Typically, local police urged the detainees to speak "the normal language," that is, Russian. Arlou related such an episode. His friend and colleague, a Belarusian historian from Poland named Yauhen Miranovich, came to Minsk and addressed a local militiaman in Belarusian, asking for directions. A militiaman immediately called for help, and then both militiamen demanded that Miranovich show his internal passport. Realizing that he was a foreigner, both were disappointed: "Oh, you are a Pole," exclaimed one of them. "And we thought you were from the BNF."[128] The BNF is believed to be the most radical wing of the Belarusian opposition. The episode clearly shows that speaking Belarusian—in the capital of Belarus—is a political statement.

The nationally conscious capitalize on this knee-jerk reaction of the authorities to the Belarusian language: as long as a *beneefovets* (a member of the BNF) is a bad guy in the eyes of Lukashenka henchmen, he is a good guy for the opposition minded. As a result, speaking Belarusian has become chic among some Minsk intellectuals. Arlou put it this way: "I remember when I was a college student, speaking Belarusian was perceived as a hallmark of provincialism at best and of being an uneducated bumpkin at worst. However, with the passage of time, such a perception changed: today, speaking Belarusian is perceived as a hallmark of being educated, access to the elite, and, no doubt, in the current political situation, also as a stamp of belonging to the opposition."[129] Ironically, it is the Lukashenka-led policy that deserves credit for such a change.

The likelihood that this new trend will affect the linguistic situation requires additional research, but my feeling is that it has not generated many converts outside the Minsk-based liberal arts elite. Also hindering the cause of Belarusification is the ongoing debate between the proponents of undoing the language reform of 1933 and its defenders.[130] Nina Mečkovskaya likens the Narkomauka versus Tarashkevitsa debate to the "romantic anachronism" of tenaciously holding on to both Latin and Cyrillic scripts in the beginning of the twentieth century, which is what Belarusian national activists used to do. "If, however, a movement for Belarusian becomes one of the aspects of practical policy," writes Mečkovskaya, "it is perilous for it to stay romantic. When romanticism trips onto real life, it either backs down (which is what most frequently happens in Belarus) or enters into a more or less acute conflict with life and in such a way becomes a factor of social destabilization."[131]

The most important change that has taken place, however, and one that the nationally conscious must be given credit for, is vastly enhanced public awareness of the linguistic situation. The nationally conscious have succeeded in instilling a feeling of guilt in the minds of intellectuals and encouraging their sense of personal responsibility for changing this situation. Instilling a feeling of guilt, however, is an ambiguous outcome at best. It creates a psychological predicament of a crossroads type, out of which there are normally two ways, not just one. The first way would be indeed to "muster one's will and cross a psychological barrier," as Maldis urged in 1988. The alternative way of easing the sense of guilt is to "kill the messenger." In Belarus, there seem to be many people for whom the psychological discomfort of switching to Belarusian is too high a price to pay for disposing of their alleged moral guilt. These people feel just as angry as the linguistic nationalists themselves. For many, switching to the language they simply do not know well is not worth a try. Their deep-seated misgiving is that sending their children to a Belarusian-language school would render them functionally illiterate in both Russian and Belarusian. This misgiving would be easy to dispel if the two languages were not as close to each other as Russian and Belarusian are. Certainly, mastering English in no way inhibits one's command of Russian and vice versa. However, when it comes to languages whose entire grammatical structures and a large part of their vocabularies are very much alike, confusion becomes a real problem.

Yet another aspect of the problem is that many of those silently protesting a switch to Belarusian consider themselves to be part of a broader information space and do not want to narrow it down for their offspring either. This information space is aggressive; it employs Russian and asserts itself not only through conventional media but also (and to an ever-increasing extent) through the Internet. For example, all the Moscow-based newspapers have their free-access sites, so one no longer needs to be a conventional subscriber. Belarusian is almost never used in software business and development, and there is no Belarusian thesaurus of computer-related terms.[132] On June 1, 2006, all Microsoft business in Belarus was transferred to the domain of the company's Russian branch. The news article containing information about this is titled "Microsoft Adjoined Belarus to Russia."[133] By and large, a not-so-successful showing of Belarusian nationalist causes in the polls[134] may attest to the fact that "killing the messenger" continues to be a popular reaction.

Yet some trends of the opposite nature make themselves felt as well. According to Trusau, the TBM has 10,500 members and works hard to spread the language. In Trusau's view, 90 percent of Belarus's entire population understands the language, and should the country's leaders use it publicly, the people would follow suit.

Glinnik said that whereas in the late 1980s he knew personally each and every resident of Minsk who spoke Belarusian in his or her everyday setting, today they number in the dozens of thousands.[135] Arlou, a native of Polatsak (better known as Polotsk), has two sons born in 1977 and 1982. Arlou's family had long switched to Belarusian, and his first son was exposed to it from his early childhood. When he was about six years old, he asked his father why his family and their closest friends spoke a language different from that spoken everywhere else in their town. However, when the boy was eleven he once gladly announced upon coming home from school, "Daddy, I have just run into some people talking in Belarusian, and they are not our friends!" Arlou was unable to give his first son education in Belarusian, but his younger son attended only Belarusian-language classes from the very beginning, a clear sign of progress. Arlou professes no quick solution to the problem, even if Belarusian speakers come to power. However, he believes that a kind of a beachhead is already there, with many intelligent people doing their work quietly and shaping up the "archipelago Belarus," a phrase attributed to a philosopher Valyantsyn Akudovich. According to Arlou, the national existence of an independent Belarus will sooner or later generate the need for the Belarusian language.[136]

Khalip, an ardent defender of the Belarusian national cause, who said that she would love for her yet-to-be-born children to be Belarusian speakers, told me that, whereas in the past salespeople in urban food stores would either frown if you addressed them in Belarusian or respond in Russian, now they are more likely to switch to Belarusian themselves.[137] Andrei Khadanovich, a

Belarusian poet, told me that in the liberal arts community, it is no longer a must to speak just Belarusian; switching from one language to another has become acceptable.[138] This climate of tolerance bodes well for the number of "converts" to Belarusian.

Whether cautious optimism is warranted remains to be seen. It follows from the annals of successful national movements that an impressive grassroots following ought to predate legislative initiatives. A mistake of the Belarusian-language promoters has been trying to reverse this order. Because the abrupt, forceful, and top-down introduction of Belarusian from 1992 to 1994 "elicited a strong feeling of protest,"[139] the backlash of 1995, which occurred under Lukashenka when Russian was reintroduced as another official language, was hardly avoidable. Ironically, this reaction would have been even more imminent had a genuinely democratic regime (that is, that responds to people's needs) been in place in Minsk.

CONCLUSION

Belarus remains part of the Russian-language information space, and the overwhelming majority of its people use Russian as their preferred language of everyday communication. What is more, for the majority of Russian speakers, this preference has to do with the dominant language of their families, so in effect Russian is their mother tongue. Estimates of Belarusian usage were grossly inflated by the Soviet-era censuses; the 1999 Belarusian census continued this tradition, albeit in a more moderate form. Surveyed secondary school teachers, a critical contingent as far as language is concerned, spoke Russian in their homes, and few felt any moral obligation to promote Belarusian. The exact frequency of standard Belarusian usage in everyday life is hard to assess, but it is most probably in the single digits percentagewise.

The issue of language is currently politicized, with most educated Belarusian speakers positioning themselves as "democrats." This self-image is unwarranted in cases where these self-proclaimed democrats oppose freedom of choice (e.g., the choice of language of instruction). Assertions that the current linguistic situation is due to the Lukashenka regime and that its more profound cause is forcible Russification are unwarranted.

Lukashenka is an easy target to blame, but doing so is irresponsible. While Lukashenka is an autocrat, a genuinely democratic leader would have been obliged to respond to the linguistic preferences of his fellow countrymen, just as Lukashenka did when in 1995 he reintroduced Russian as one of the official languages of Belarus.

Blaming Russification is a trickier issue. Russification did indeed take place all over the Soviet Union. However, because it has succeeded nowhere as much as in Belarus, local peculiarities must be considered foremost.

Belarusian is a Slavic language closely related to Russian and Polish. For centuries, it existed only in dialect form within a transitional space between the domains of these languages, with western dialects being close to Polish and eastern ones being close to Russian. In the beginning of the twentieth century, Belarusian of literary norm was exposed to stiff competition from two older and "aggressive" language environments, Polish and Russian, which had long dominated the urban areas of Belarus. That Russian and Polish linguistic expansionisms were at times state sponsored is beyond doubt. Yet, elements of spontaneity in language change in Belarus have been equally apparent.

Moreover, it appears that Belarusification (a mass switch to Belarusian) was also promoted by the state but did not yield significant results. Unlike in other countries long under linguistically alien influences, no critical mass of Belarusian speakers emerged that would sway the rest of the public. Blaming the "overwhelming odds," that is, the resistance of Russian speakers, may make sense. However, overcoming alien influences wherever they took place (e.g., in the Czech Republic, Lithuania, and Norway) has always been an uphill battle. That the crucial breakthrough never occurred in Belarus suggests that locals have not perceived Russian (in much of Belarus) and Polish (in the extreme west of the Belarusian "ethnographic territory") as "alien." So, the process of switching to these languages in the course of urban socialization has been effortless, smooth, and by and large spontaneous and voluntary. Pinning hopes on top-down, administrative means of Belarusification has not helped the cause of linguistic Belarusification either.

Some cautious optimism with regard to the possibility of eventually breaking this pattern of linguistic assimilation derives from the slowly, but surely, growing number of educated Belarusian speakers and from the very prospects of Belarusian independence. Should the latter be sustained, the demand for Belarusian may at some point achieve the requisite critical mass. However, this is not preordained, and hard, everyday work of the national movement is required, as is a tactful and careful way in which to conduct it.

NOTES

1. Valyantsyn Akudovich, "Zbelarusizavats Belarus pakul shto ne atrymayetsa," *Dom Litaratora*, a talk show of the Belarusian Service of Radio Liberty, February 23, 2007, at www.svaboda.org.

2. Nina B. Mečkovskaya, *Belorusskii yazyk: Sotsiolingvisticheskie ocherki* (Munchen: Verlag Otto Sagner, 2003), 79.

3. Yury Koriakov, *Yazykovaya situatsiya v Belorussii i tipologiya yazykovykh situatsii* (PhD diss., Moscow State University, 2003), 86.

4. Mečkovskaya, *Belorusskii yazyk*, 79.

5. Branislau Taraškievič, *Belaruskaia hramatyka*, 6th ed. (Mensk: Vydavetstva Shkolnykh Padruchnikau i Litaratury dlia Moladzi u Mensku, 1943).

6. "As for the scale of publishing in Belarusian, throughout the entire nineteenth century, 75 books were released in different local dialects; however, from 1901 to 1916, 245 books were released in Belarusian" (quoted in Koriakov, *Yazykovaya Situatsiya*, 29).

7. Mečkovskaya, *Belorusskii yazyk*, 61.

8. Mečkovskaya, *Belorusskii yazyk*, 131.

9. This is a calque from *svyadomyya*, a code word literally meaning "aware of."

10. The forerunner of modern Belarusian was used in the Grand Duchy of Lithuania until the end of the sixteenth century.

11. The Tavarystva Belaruskai Movy bears the name of Frantsyshak Skaryna.

12. Personal interview with Aleh Trusau, May 23, 2002.

13. Steven L. Guthier, "The Belorussians: National Identification and Assimilation, 1897–1970," *Soviet Studies* 29, no. 2 (1977): 274.

14. Tatyana M. Mikulich, *Mova i etnichnaya samasviadomasts* (Minsk: Navuka i Technika, 1996), 147–48.

15. Ralph S. Clem, "Belorussians," in *The Nationalities Question in the Soviet Union*, ed. Graham Smith (London: Longman, 1990), 115.

16. Mikulich, *Mova i etnichnaya samasviadomasts*, 150.

17. Koriakov, *Yazykovaya situatsiya*, 59; Mečkovskaya, *Belorusskii yazyk*, 31.

18. *Natsional'nyi sostav naseleniya Respubliki Belarus i rasprostranionnost' yazykov* (Minsk: Ministerstvo Statistiki i Analiza, 2001), 214–15.

19. Mečkovskaya, *Belorusskii yazyk*, 33; Koriakov, *Yazykovaya Situatsiya*, 43; Anthony N. Brown, "Language and Identity in Belarus," *Language Policy* 4, no. 13 (2006).

20. *Naseleniye Respubliki Belarus* (Minsk: Ministerstvo Statistiki i Analiza, 2000), 13.

21. For example, on May 26, 2002, on Minsk's Channel 1, I watched an interview with Leontii Biadulia, chairman of a famous collective farm in Grodno Oblast. Biadulia, a rural resident from western Belarus, replied exclusively in Russian to the questions posed in Belarusian. This bilingual TV interviewing and the fact that rural villagers respond in Russian are noted by Mečkovskaya, *Belorusskii yazyk*, 41.

22. L. A. Melnikova, "Dvuyazychiye v sfere kultury, iskusstva," in *Tipologiya dvuyazychiiya i mnogoyazychiiya v Belarusi* (Minsk: Navuka I Tekhnika, 1999), 160.

23. Mečkovskaya, *Belorusskii yazyk*, 32.

24. Some researchers make a special point that this mixture is of lower quality than pure hay. See Genadz Tsykhun, "Krealizavany produkt: Trasianka yak ab'yekt lingvistychnaga dasledavannia," *Arche* 6 (2000), 7, at http://arche.home.by/6-2000 /cychu600.html.

25. Mikulich, *Mova i etnichnaya samasviadomasts*, 41.

26. Personal interview with Aleh Trusau, May 23, 2002.

27. Alexandra Goujon, "Language, Nationalism, and Populism in Belarus," *Nationalities Papers* 27, no. 4 (1999): 668.

28. David Marples, *Belarus from Soviet Rule to Nuclear Catastrophe* (New York: St. Martin's Press, 1996), 31.

29. Curt Woolhiser, "Language Ideology and Language Conflict in Post-Soviet Belarus," in *Language, Ethnicity and the State*, vol. 2, ed. Camille O'Reilly (London/New York: Palgrave, 2001), 91–122.

30. Genadz Tsykhun, "Krealizavany pradukt: Trasianka yak ab'yekt lingvistychnaga dasledavannia," *Arche* 6 (2000), 7, at http://arche.home.by/6-2000/cychu600 .html.

31. See, for example, Andrei Yekadumau, "'Kul'tyrnyya realiya belaruska-rasiiskai integratsii," in *Belaruska-rasiiskaya integratsiya* (Mensk: Entsyklapedyks, 2002), 219.

32. Mečkovskaya, *Belorusskii yazyk*, 87.

33. Personal interview with Aleh Trusau, May 23, 2002.

34. The official website of the president of Belarus is www.president.gov.by/rus/ president/profile.shtml.

35. To be sure, on several occasions, Lukashenka went on record with disparaging comments with regard to Belarusian and was later lampooned by the opposition media.

36. "Kuropatskie sideniya," *Belaruski Rynok* 45 (2000): 25.

37. Dmitry Drygailo, "Doroga na 'Yuga-Zakhad,'" *Belorusskaya Delovaya Gazeta*, December 14, 2000, 12.

38. A. I. Padluzhny, "Prablemy variantnastsi belaruskai litaraturnai movy," *Belaruskaya mova u drugoi palove XX stagoddzia* (Minsk: BGU, 1998), 28–32.

39. L. V. Tereshkovich, "Obshchestvennye dvizheniya v sovremennoi Belorussii: Kratkii Kommentarii k Dokumentam," in *Grazhdanskie dvizheniya v Belorussii: dokumenty i materialy, 1989–1991* (Moscow: TSIMO, 1991), 20.

40. R. B. Dobson, *Belarusians Gravitate toward Russia: A Pull of Russian Language, Media Remains Strong* (Washington, DC: Office of Research, Department of State, October 11, 2000), 2–3.

41. Dobson, *Belarusians Gravitate*.

42. Timothy Colton, "Belarusian Public Opinion and Union with Russia," in *Independent Belarus: Domestic Determinants, Regional Dynamics, and Implications for the West*, ed. Margarita M. Balmaceda, James Clem, and Lisbeth Tarlow (Cambridge, MA: Harvard University Press, 2002), 30.

43. IISEPS is an opposition-minded Minsk-based think tank and polling firm headed by Dr. Oleg Manayev, a sociologist with an international reputation. IISEPS was subjected to harassment by the Belarusian KGB in December 2004. On December 27, 2004, the U.S. ambassador visited IISEPS as a sign of support for the beleaguered Belarusian nongovernmental organizations. On April 15, 2005, the Supreme Court of Belarus ruled to close down the institute. It is currently active as a nonprofit organization registered in neighboring Lithuania. Manayev has been repeatedly

warned by the General Prosecutor's Office that the continuation of polling in Belarus by an institution not registered in Belarus is a criminal offence. Manayev's response so far has been that the polling is conducted by a group of private citizens.

44. Yury Drakokhrust, "Dovediot li yazyk do Kieva?" January 26, 2005, at www.iiseps.by/press13.html.

45. IISEPS's national survey of October 2006, at www.iiseps.org.

46. Mikhas' Puzinowsky, "Chamu batski-belarusy u shkolakh vybirayuts' ruskuyu movu?" *Nasha Slova* 520 (2001), at http://tbm.org.by/ns/no520-523/20-21/vibar.html.

47. David Marples, *Belarus: A Denationalized Nation* (Amsterdam: Harwood, 1999), 60.

48. Ustina Marcus, "The Bilingualism Question in Belarus and Ukraine," *Transition*, November 29, 1996, 18. Quite a few identical opinions are related in Koriakov, *Yazykovaya situatsiya*, 46.

49. National survey of September 2005, at www.iiseps.org.

50. Miroslav Hroch, *Social Preconditions of National Revival in Europe: A Comparative Analysis of Patriotic Groups among the Smaller European Nations*, 2nd ed. (New York: Columbia University Press, 2000).

51. "TBM predlagayet grazhdanam govorit' po-belorusski," August 27, 2002, at www.bdg.by/newnews/news.

52. "Belaruskaya mova guchych u baranavitskikh autobusakh," Belarusian Service of Radio Liberty, March 20, 2007.

53. Personal interview with Vadim Glinnik, May 21, 2002.

54. Personal interview with Irina Khalip, May 27, 2002.

55. Calculated on the basis of *Natsional'nyi sostav naseleniya Respubliki Belarus i rasprostranionnost' Yazykov* (Minsk: Ministerstvo Statistiki i Analiza, 2001), 16.

56. Curt Woolhiser, "Language Ideology and Language Conflict in Post-Soviet Belarus."

57. Nikolai Zen'kovich, *Tainy ukhodiashchego veka* (Moscow: Olma Press, 2000), 327.

58. Zen'kovich, *Tainy ukhodiashchego veka*, 330.

59. Mikhail Bulakhov, *Evfimii Fiodorovich Karskii, 1861–1931* (Minsk: BGU, 1981), 181.

60. Mečkovskaya, *Belorusskii yazyk*, 23–25.

61. Marples, *Belarus*, 4.

62. Mečkovskaya, *Belorusskii yazyk*, 25.

63. Nicholas Vakar, *Belorussia: The Making of a Nation* (Cambridge, MA: Harvard University Press, 1956), 69.

64. Vakar, *Belorussia*, 73.

65. Bulakhov, *Evfimii Fiodorovich Karskii*, 195.

66. Steven L. Guthier, "The Belorussians: National Identification and Assimilation, 1897–1939," *Soviet Studies* 29, no. 1 (1977): 43.

67. Guthier, "The Belorussians: National Identification, 1897–1939," 45.

68. Guthier, "The Belorussians: National Identification, 1897–1939."

69. Zen'kovich, *Tainy ukhodiashchego veka*, 287–333.

70. My great-grandparents, who were born and lived in Belarus all their lives with the exception of 1941 to 1944 and died in the late 1950s, spoke Yiddish with each other. Their children, including my grandparents, spoke Russian with each other but still had some limited proficiency in Yiddish. All three children of my grandparents, my mother included, who were growing up in the 1930s, late 1940s, and 1950s in a medium-sized town in southern Belarus, know only few words in Yiddish and have been entirely immersed in the Russian of literary norm. This situation is representative of the overwhelming majority of the Belarusian Jews.

71. Guthier, "The Belorussians: National Identification, 1897–1970," 54–55.

72. Guthier, "The Belorussians: National Identification, 1897–1970," 55.

73. Guthier, "The Belorussians: National Identification, 1897–1970," 57.

74. "A form of spatial diffusion . . . occurring where spread is in a centrifugal manner outward from a source region. . . . It is well demonstrated by the spread of contagious diseases and the diffusion of those other phenomena that rely on touch or direct contact for their transmission. The process is strongly influenced by distance." John Small and Michael Witherick, *A Modern Dictionary of Geography*, 3rd. ed. (London: Arnold, 1995), 50. Contagious diffusion is often contrasted with hierarchal diffusion.

75. Guthier, "The Belorussians: National Identification, 1897–1970," 53.

76. Vakar, *Belorussia*, 59.

77. Curt Woolhiser, "Metalinguistic Discourse, Ideology, and 'Language Construction' in the BSSR, 1920–1939," the English original of an article published in French as "Discours sur la langue, idéologie et 'édification linguistique' dans la RSS de Biélorussie, 1920–1939." In *Le discours sur la langue en URSS à l'époque Stalinienne*, edited by Patrick Sériot, 299–337. Cahiers de l'ILSL no. 14 (Lausanne: University of Lausanne, 2003).

78. Woolhiser, "Metalinguistic Discourse."

79. Mečkovskaya, *Belorusskii yazyk*, 69.

80. Woolhiser, "Metalinguistic Discourse."

81. Woolhiser, "Metalinguistic Discourse."

82. Liudmila Rublevskaya and Vital Skalaban, "Okolonauchnyi spor," *Belarus Segodnia*, January 20, 2006.

83. Rublevskaya and Skalaban, "Okolonauchnyi spor," 139–40. Vakar carefully documents widespread and occasionally violent resistance to Belarusification, particularly in Gomel Province, whose communist leader was removed for conniving that resistance.

84. In the decree of the Belarusian Council of the People's Commissars of August 26, 1933, the alleged Belarusian National Democrats were accused of "intending to tear away the Belarusian literary language from the language of the Belarusian working masses and of thus creating an artificial barrier between the Belarusian and Russian languages." Ivan S. Lubachko, *Belorussia under the Soviet Rule, 1917–1957* (Lexington: University Press of Kentucky, 1972), 115.

85. Vakar, *Belorussia*, 153.

86. O. Skopnenko, "Movna situatsiya v Bilorusi i problemi norm biloruskoi literaturnoi movi," *Proceedings of the International Conference Derzhavnost ukrainskoi movi i movnii djsvit svitu* (Kyiv), 2000, at http://dzvinkaxxv.narod.ru/bud-skopn.htm.

87. Skopnenko, "Movna situatsiya."

88. These are the Belarusian versions of "Proletarians of all countries, unite!"—a motto from the *Communist Manifesto* by Karl Marx and Friedrich Engels. This motto adorned the front page of every Soviet newspaper.

89. Vakar, *Belorussia*, 119–36.

90. Lubachko, *Belorussia*, 127–38.

91. Koriakov, *Yazykovaya situatsiya*, 36.

92. Vakar, *Belorussia*.

93. Personal interview with Uladzimer Arlou, May 24, 2002.

94. Vakar, *Belorussia*, 59.

95. Vakar, *Belorussia*.

96. Woolhiser, "Metalinguistic Discourse."

97. Belarus did not regain its 1939 population (8.9 million people in current borders) until 1969. "Owing to the effects of the war, Belorussia lost a greater percentage of its population than any other region of the USSR; between 1939 and 1951, the population of Belorussia declined by 12.7%" (Clem, "Belorussians," 113)

98. Koriakov, *Yazykovaya situatsiya*, 40.

99. Koriakov, *Yazykovaya situatsiya*, 69.

100. Guthier, "The Belorussians: National Identification, 1897–1970," 283.

101. Zen'kovich, *Tainy ukhodiashchego veka*, 300–309.

102. Zen'kovich, *Tainy ukhodiashchego veka*, 191–92.

103. This is abundantly documented in Miroslav Hroch, *Social Preconditions of National Revival in Europe: A Comparative Analysis of Patriotic Groups among the Smaller European Nations*, 2nd ed. (New York: Columbia University Press, 2000).

104. Adam Maldis, "Davaite, nakonets, zagovorim," *Kommunist Belorussii* 3 (1989): 74–75.

105. Maldis, "Davaite, nakonets, zagovorim."

106. Maldis, "Davaite, nakonets, zagovorim," 76.

107. Maldis, "Davaite, nakonets, zagovorim."

108. Maldis, "Davaite, nakonets, zagovorim."

109. Maldis, "Davaite, nakonets, zagovorim," 73.

110. Alexander J. Motyl, *Will the Non-Russians Rebel?* (Ithaca, NY: Cornell University Press, 1987), 152.

111. Quoted in Koriakov, *Yazykovaya situatsiya*, 45.

112. Mečkovskaya, *Belorusskii yazyk*, 35.

113. Mečkovskaya, *Belorusskii yazyk*.

114. A. I. Zhurausky, *Gistoryya belaruskai litaraturnai movy*, vol. 1 (Minsk: Navuka i Tekhnika, 1967), 350–51.

115. M. A. Avlasevich, "Natsionalno-yazykovye problemy v Respublike Belarus," in *Materialy mezhdunarodnogo nauchnogo seminara, posvaschionnogo pamati o. v. ozarovskogo* (February 27–28, 1996) (Mogilev: Mogiliovsky Universitet, 1996), 6.

116. Mečkovskaya, *Belorusskii yazyk*, 36.

117. Retsidiv (interviews with experts), *Belorusskay A delovaya Gazeta*, February 18, 2003, at http://bdg.press.net.by/2003.

118. Mečkovskaya, *Belorusskii yazyk*, 127.

119. Siargei Zaprudsky, "Mounaya palitika u Belarusi u 1990-ya gady," *Arche* 1 (2002), at http://arche.home.by/2002-1/zapr102.html.

120. Zaprudsky, "Mounaya palitika u Belarusi u 1990-ya gady."

121. Mečkovskaya, *Belorusskii yazyk*, 127.

122. Mečkovskaya, *Belorusskii yazyk*.

123. Soobshcheniya pressluzhby prezidenta, November 14–18, 2005, at www.president.gov.

124. Alyaksandr Lukashenka, "Gosudarstvo dlia naroda" (speech at the Third All-Belarusian People's Convention, *Belarus Segodnia*, Friday, March 3, 2006), at www.sb.by/article.php?articleID=50217.

125. Mečkovskaya, *Belorusskii yazyk*, iv.

126. Yekadumau, "'Kul'tyrnyya realiya belaruska-rasiiskai integratsii," 217.

127. *Nasha Slova*, September 29, 1999.

128. "Tsi patrebna belarusam belaruskaya mova?" *Nasha Slova* 523 (2001).

129. "Tsi patrebna belarusam belaruskaya mova?"

130. Alexandra Goujon, "Language, Nationalism, and Populism in Belarus," *Nationalities Papers* 27, no. 4 (1999): 669.

131. Mečkovskaya, *Belorusskii Yazyk*, 45.

132. Kseniya Avimova, "Computer 'pa-belarusku' zagovorit neskoro," *Belorusskaya Delovaya Gazeta*, August 11, 2005.

133. "Microsoft prisoyedinil Belarus k Rosii," *Belorusskiye Novosti*, May 24, 2006, at www.naviny.by/ru/content/rubriki/2-ya_gruppa/kompyuter/24-05-06-01.

134. The above-quoted 1999 survey showed that only 11 percent of respondents believe that learning and studying in the Belarusian language are "very important." Together with "fairly important," the respondents total 32 percent. At the same time, learning and studying in Belarusian are not important for 62 percent of the respondents (Dobson, *Belarusians Gravitate*, 4).

135. Personal interview with Vadim Glinnik, May 22, 2002.

136. Personal interview with Uladzimir Arlou, May 23, 2002.

137. Personal interview with Irina Khalip, May 27, 2002.

138. Personal interview with Andrei Khadanovich, Warsaw, November 2006.

139. Vladimir Berezin, "Dlya kogo veshchayet Radyyo Svaboda?" *Nashe Mneniye*, May 14, 2005, at www.nmnby.org. In the words of Alexander Feduta, "I do not have a problem with Belarusian. The problem lies elsewhere. As every self-respecting person I cannot stand it when something is forced down my throat and I am reproached on account of inadequate patriotism" (Alexander Feduta, "Otvety na voprosy," *Nashe Mneniye*, May 19, 2005, at www.nmnby.org).

2

A Search for Identity

When the state means action, and the nation means a project, the identity of the nation-state is bound to be a lively battleground.

—Yann Breault[1]

In today's Belarus, an outright war of mythologies is under way, a clash of symbols and heroes. The national pantheon is split up and pervaded by inner conflict.

—Maxim Zhbankov[2]

When asked whether the oblivion of the Belarusian language will lead to the erosion of Belarusian identity, 23.3 percent of the school teachers covered in my May 2002 pilot survey[3] said yes, 15 percent chose the rather-yes-than-no option, 30 percent subscribed to rather-no-than-yes, 20 percent said no, and 11.7 percent had no opinion. In such a way, only one-fifth of the respondents firmly believed in the survival of Belarusian identity under current conditions. Overall, however, I felt that the situation required further insight.

Upon asking my Minsk correspondents orally and by e-mail whether maintaining Belarusian identity while speaking Russian is possible, I encountered two reactions:

1. Entertaining this possibility would only make sense if the native language were dead; however, it is not.
2. If Belarusians spoke Russian, what would be the difference between them and Russians?

The first reaction has been de facto analyzed in chapter 1: the language is not certifiably dead, but it is not a living language in the full sense of the word, especially in urban areas of Belarus. The second reaction is a rhetorical question; the difference is indeed small, and so the attainment of separate identity hinges on whether the goal of becoming truly different from Russians can become truly mobilizing. Valer Bulgakau, editor of the major Belarusian-language periodical *Arche*, recently mentioned that "whatever one publishes in a journal format—fiction, art, or language study—one cannot count on selling more than 1,000–1,500 copies. Belarusian culture has not yet mustered a bigger audience."[4] However, because the language problem in Belarus has little, if anything, to do with interethnic antagonisms—rather, it is a problem within Belarusian ethnicity[5]—ways of becoming truly different from the Russians are not readily apparent. According to Miroslav Hroch, "Linguistic assimilation [does] not always strike a decisive blow against the further development of a nationality: one need only cite the examples of Ireland and Norway."[6] In the case of Ireland, the historical religious difference from England played an important role.

RELIGION AND IDENTITY

Indeed, according to Anthony Smith, "Organized religion supplies much of the personnel and communication channels for the diffusion of ethnic myths and symbols. The priests and scribes not only communicate and record and transmit these legends and beliefs, but they also serve as the chief guardians and conduits of the symbolism which can link feudal or imperial elites to the peasant masses."[7]

However, one of the most acutely perceived vulnerabilities of the Belarusian identity probably lies in the area of organized religion. For Belarusian nationalism to assert itself vis-à-vis two older and aggressive nationalisms, Russian and Polish, it had to change the historic pattern of ethnic mobilization that had long dominated the area. In this pattern, Belarus was viewed as the Polish-Russian borderland, in which the Orthodox associated themselves with the Russians, and Catholics with the Poles, and after the collapse of the Uniate (Greek Catholic) Church, there was indeed little or no room for Belarusians per se.

Most residents of Belarus, by some accounts about 70 percent,[8] belonged to the Uniate Church from 1569 to 1839. Some scholars believe that its collapse, more than anything else, undermined the Belarusians' sense of being different from neighboring ethnic groups.[9] Indeed, the Uniates (who abided by Orthodox rites but recognized the supremacy of the pope) essentially represented a transitional, halfway creed between Roman Catholicism and Russian Orthodoxy. One may say that it was just as transitional as local vernaculars were between Polish and Russian. Two transitional features (language and creed) superimposed might have led to something qualitatively new, as it has in western Ukraine where the Uniate Church survived. However, blaming Belarusians' blurred identity on the Uniate's demise would invoke the chicken-and-egg conundrum if only because the Uniates' supreme clerics shifted to the Orthodoxy voluntarily,[10] and most Belarusians followed in their footsteps. Also, even at the time when most ancestors of today's Belarusians were Uniates, many in the upper classes were Roman Catholics.[11] It is therefore not a foregone conclusion that the Uniate Church might have succeeded in consolidating the ancestors of today's Belarusians.

It is tempting to assume, though, that in today's Belarus the issue of the religious underpinnings of identity is no longer important. First, there is confessional peace in Belarus wherein the Orthodox ostensibly have no problems with their Catholic neighbors. In Novogrudek, for example, a major *kosciól* (Polish for "church"), with its many Polish-language posters and prayer books,[12] is just one hundred meters away from a major Orthodox *tserkov'* (Russian for "church") where they preach in Russian, and there does not seem to be any major tension between the two at all. Second, despite the religious revival of the 1990s, "the influence of religion on social life is minimal."[13] Third, Protestant denominations, not traditional Orthodox or Catholic churches, are growing most quickly in today's Belarus.

All of this being said, however, the traditional religious divide appears to linger. People may not attend services, but most are keenly aware of their religious backgrounds, imprinted in many cases in their first names: Stanislaw or Jadwiga, for instance, are identified somehow as Catholic, while Ivan and Nadezhda are identified as Orthodox. Moreover, the Orthodox and Catholic churches retain their functions as the collective ambassadors of Russia and Poland. Thus, there is no self-styled or autocephalous Belarusian Orthodox Church.[14] Instead, there is a Belarusian branch of the Russian Orthodox Church. As for the Catholics, about half of all Catholic priests are citizens of Poland.[15] It is symptomatic that Alexander Lukashenka speaks of himself as an "Orthodox atheist" (an atheist with an Orthodox background), has made friends with Filaret,[16] the Orthodox supreme leader of Belarus, and is rumored to be suspicious of Catholics. Those of Catholic background, on the other hand, refer to Filaret as the biggest imposter and wheeler-dealer,[17] and Stanislau Shushkevich, whose background is Catholic, said that in his childhood he associated the Orthodox clerics with heavy drinking, while Catholics priests and monks appeared to him as decent, spiritual, and clean.[18]

LOCATION, ETHNONYM, AND IDENTITY

According to Nina Mečkovskaya, "The principal problem of Belarusian history has been the problem of cultural and political survival . . . 'in the shadow' of Russia and Poland. It is an unfavorable geopolitical fate to be the object of Russian and Polish assimilation and of two powerful and mutually antagonistic expansions."[19] Some Belarusian scholars even express their irritation over the fact that "all archetypes of Belarusian nationalist thinking are fixated on spatiality, more specifically on some space between somebody else's preset niches."[20]

In his famous book *The Ethnic Origins of Nations*, Smith wrote that "geopolitical location [may be] more important for ethnic survival than autonomy, provided that we underline the symbolic and sociological aspects of location."[21] In what follows, I pay attention to both aspects as they typify Belarusians. One thing, however, is clear from the outset: for a critical mass of people with Belarusian identity to squeeze in between Russians and Poles has been, and continues to be, entirely within the realm of possibility. This possibility cannot be discarded on the sole basis that Russian and Polish nationalisms are older and more aggressive and the respective heartlands are not far apart. In Europe and around the world, younger nationalisms succeeded despite overwhelming odds, and the distances between separate national cores in parts of Western Europe are often smaller than those between Moscow, Minsk, and Warsaw. In other words, there is plenty of "room" for Belarusians, provided of course that Belarusian nationalism succeeds in its crucial survival test: effectively rallying locals around various markers of Belarusian identity. This, however, has not been a smooth process by far.

Perhaps the most phenomenal feature of Belarusians has been a long-lasting absence of a common name that would be perceived as the token of their collective identity. Vladimir Picheta, one of the prime authorities on Belarusian history, wrote that the term *Weisse Rusen* (White Russia) was first used by German authors in the fourteenth century. During the reign of Ivan the Third (1462–1505), the official language of the Russian court appropriated this term. In 1654, "White Russia" was included in the official title of the Russian monarch (as the tsar of Great, Small, and White Russia).[22] However, the term in question was long used as a toponym, not a marker of ethnic identity.[23] Only by the end of the nineteenth century did some "pioneers" begin to use it in that capacity.[24] The meaning of the term is not quite clear. There are two most believable interpretations. According to one, White Rus' meant a part of Rus', which had no obligation to pay tribute to the Tatars in the twelfth century, as opposed to Black Rus', which did pay tribute to the Tatars.[25] According to the second interpretation by Oleg Trubachev, a Russian linguist who, incidentally, did extensive research on Belarusian, there were the following divisions of Rus' at large: Malaya Rus', the ancestral Russian land from which the expansion started; Velikaya Rus', land being colonized (land under expansion, for which Malaya Rus' was the "point of departure"); and White Rus', part of the ancient color-orientation pattern, according to which "white" means "west."[26] One can see that in neither interpretation was "Belarus" an ethnic homeland, at least originally. Other known interpretations of the term[27] do not change this conclusion. It would be safe to say that the words "Belarus" and "Belarusian" were embraced by most indigenous people of the Russian-Polish borderland only in the wake of the formation of the Belarusian Soviet Socialist Republic (BSSR). Among other things, this effectively means that the Soviet period was the longest time span of the Belarusians' nationally conscious existence. Under the BSSR, Belarusian became one of the official languages. Also, "Belarus" and "Belarusian" became part of the republic's national emblem and anthem, and the words circulated widely in regional print media and state documents, including, above all, internal passports initially issued for the urbanites and residents of border regions. These personal IDs included the mention of Belarus not only as one's place of residence but also as a person's *natsional'nost'*, or ethnicity. Prior to that essentially top-down imposition of the toponym "Belarus" and ethnonym "Belarusian," most regional residents of Slavic background introduced themselves as *tuteishiya*, which in the Polish language means "locals."[28] In regard to western Belarus, which from 1921 to 1939 was part of Poland, Curt Woolhiser mentions that as a self-designation, the term "Belarusian" first became common in rural communities in the Bialystok and Grodno regions only during the interwar period.[29]

This lasting anonymity is truly exceptional because a common name is the most basic indicator of belonging to a group. When Uladzimer Arlou and Gennadz Saganovich write that princedoms existing in what is now Belarus and the Smolensk province of Russia "formed an ethnically and linguistically homogenous region"[30] as early as the eleventh and twelfth centuries, they may be on target. But even seven to eight centuries down the road, a common verbal denominator of this homogeneity, one that would transcend localism, was missing, and that is puzzling. Even the many large-scale military campaigns that affected the region apparently failed to foment a truly collective sense of insecurity that would be conducive to shared identity. Some, like Mikola Yermalovich, believe that the original name of what is now called "Belarus" was Litva (Lithuania), which was subsequently usurped by a neighboring ethnic group, albeit by mistake.[31] Segrei Markov, a Russian political scientist, writes in this regard, "If one is having a tea together with members of the Belarusian opposition, they would put bluntly what they still hesitate to formulate publicly. 'Belarus,' they would say, 'is a colonial fabrication of Moscow. We are a separate people, ancient and different from Russians. We are successors of the Grand Duchy of Lithuania."[32] According to Vitaut Kipel, most people of the region used to identify themselves as *Litsviny*, or residents of Lithuania.[33] This may not be quite accurate: according to Mikhas Bich, as recently as the mid-nineteenth century, "Belarusian" as an ethnic name was widespread but limited to the easternmost part of modern Belarus; *Litsviny*, on the other hand, was a typical ethnonym for western and central Belarus, while in Polesie (southern Belarus), the term *Paliashchuk* was used.[34] All in all, the absence of a single ethnonym for the Slavic population of the region, prior to the commencement of the Soviet period, is undeniable.

SOCIAL STRUCTURE AND IDENTITY

The social composition of Belarusians may have inhibited the manifestations of their separate and unique ethnonational identity. Currently, 67 percent of Belarus's population lives in cities, but urbanization was grossly delayed, and as recently as 1926, the share of urbanites among ethnic Belarusians (8 percent) yielded to that of other ethnicities within the republic, notably, Jews, Poles, and Russians. A middle-class intelligentsia that "would invite masses into history"[35] was late in coming. As a result, in the beginning of the twentieth century, residents of Belarus had the least discernible sense of separate ethnic identity, and Belarusian nationalists did not seem to have much following among the predominantly peasant Belarusian masses. Most importantly, no sense of shared identity between the social classes had been forged in Belarus before the communist revolution in the Russian Empire. The upper and even middle (merchant and craftsman) strata pledged allegiance almost exclusively to the Russian, Polish, and Jewish causes.

However, to present social structure as the root cause of the blurred identity of Belarusians would probably be shortsighted. Miroslav Hroch studied in depth the nationalist movements of Europe's so-called nondominant ethnic groups, such as Czechs, Lithuanians, and Norwegians. He defines a nondominant ethnic group as that distinguished by the following "three deficiencies: it lacked 'its own' nobility or ruling classes, it possessed no state, and its literary tradition in its own language was incomplete or interrupted."[36] Belarusians fit this definition impeccably. Among Belarusians, as in other nondominant ethnic groups, the majority of the national movement's most active participants were of rural origin. In Lithuania, this share, according to Hroch's estimate, was as high as 90 percent.[37] One of the principal tasks of the national movement was then to ensure that separate identity would not fall prey to the vertical and horizontal mobility in which rural villagers become involved, so that, say, a Czech would not stop identifying with people of his stock when promoted in the ranks and/or when moving to an urban area. This outcome, however, could never be taken for granted in Belarus, and so it is not by chance that as recently as the 1970s, Jan Zaprudnik averred that urbanization in Belarus spelled loss of national character.[38]

BIRTH OF IDENTITY

In Belarus, awareness of ethnic distinctiveness began to develop among Catholic intellectuals in the mid-1800s. In a narrowly defined linguistic sense, it was an awakening, as the contemporary Belarusian vernacular was now construed as deriving from the Ruski language of the Grand Duchy of Lithuania (GDL). Ethnic awareness was an entirely new sensibility because those writing in western Russian in the grand duchy had not defined themselves in opposition to Russia; in fact, it was affinity to Russia that was important, while weakened contacts and growing Polonization had ultimately undermined the Russianness of the GDL. The idea of a separate Belarusian identity grew out of the folkloristic research of some Vilna University professors and students, notably Jan Barszczewski (1790–1851) and Jan Czeczot (1796–1847), whose language of everyday communication was Polish. Czeczot, for example, published in Wilno (Vilna) six collections of folk songs, most translated into Polish but some retaining the original vernacular and rendered in Latin characters.[39] Later, Wincent Dunin-Marcinkiewicz (1809–1884) and some others contributed to the sense of Belarusian self-awareness. Linking their folklore research with literary and official documents of the GDL (1253–1569), they concluded that they had inherited a cultural-historical legacy with all the trappings of a tradition distinctive from that of the Poles. As they uncovered the historical past of the Lithuanian and Belarusian peoples and became aware of the cultural rebirth of other "small nations," such as Czechs, Serbs, Croats, Bulgars, and Slovenes, these Catholic intellectuals became convinced that the formula *gente Rutheni, natione Poloni* (a Pole of Russian descent) did not quite fit their ethnic domain.[40] The poet Frantsyšek Boguševič (1840–1900) subsequently refined this idea, in 1891 telling his fellow countrymen that they were Belarusians and that their land's name was Belarus.[41]

The emergence of a Belarusian national idea (a step forward compared with the awareness of ethnic distinction) matured in the *Nasha Niva* literary circle, which from 1909 to 1915 published the eponymous newspaper in

Vilna. This circle also comprised mostly Catholics, a minority among Belarusian speakers. The preponderance of Catholics among the Belarusians, who were conscious of their belonging to a distinct ethnicity, is underscored by many authors, notably by Alexander Tsvikevich.[42] From 1909 to 1912, the *Nasha Niva* was published in two parallel versions: Lacinka (using the Latin alphabet) and Grazhdanka (using the Cyrillic alphabet). This practice inhibited the development of the Belarusian literary standard.[43] Among the Belarusian speakers, Catholics who preferred Lacinka were five times less numerous than the Orthodox, who did not just prefer Grazhdanka but were for the most part ignorant of the Latin script. However, the percentage of the *Nasha Niva*'s readers among the Catholics was 2.5 times higher than that among the Orthodox. This parallel publishing in two scripts was an early indication of the less formal and more profound cultural divide that would complicate the national consolidation of Belarusians for decades to come. It is also important to keep in mind that although Lacinka was popularly perceived as a symbol of high culture and of belonging to Europe, the Russian government was hostile to the idea of introducing the "Polish alphabet" to the peasant masses. Faced with this controversial situation and also strapped for cash, the editors of the *Nasha Niva* in 1912 switched to publishing entirely in Cyrillic.[44]

The city of Vilna, where the *Nasha Niva* was edited and published, played a significant role as the meeting place of nationally conscious Belarusians, and so from the perspective of Belarusian nationalism, Vilna was its most significant center. The first ever Belarusian-language elementary school was opened in that city in 1915.[45] The subsequent loss of Vilna, first to Poland and then to the newly emerging Lithuanian state as a result of the 1921 Riga Treaty and the 1939 border rearrangements, was hurtful for the Belarusian national cause. Early Belarusian writers called Vilna the "Belarusian Zion"[46] (Zmitrok Biadulia) and Krivitskaya Mecca (Uladzimir Zhylka).[47] According to Bich, "If Wilno University had endured for one or two decades longer, it would have become more Belarusian than Polish: dominant Belarusian elements in its environs would have won the tug of war with Polish influences, whose sources were on the ethnographic space of Poland per se."[48] This prediction is impossible to verify. However, to any impartial observer in the early 1900s, it would not seem likely that the Vilna metropolis would ever become the core area for the Belarusian national cause. In all fairness, though, it would seem equally unlikely at the time that Vilna would ever become Vilnius, the major center of Lithuanian culture and officialdom. Poles and Jews dominated the city,[49] its cultural landscape, and the iconography (architecture, billboards, public signs, attire, etc.) of the place. Polishness was promoted by the Catholic Church and the character of the local university, one of the principal centers of Polish nationalism. While Jews could not possibly raise any national claims on the city, it was in Vilna that Ben Yehuda (born as Eliezer Perelman in a shtetl of Luzhki, currently in Vitebsk Oblast of Belarus) set out to revive Hebrew. Later, his son, Ben-Zion, who became known by his pen name, Itamar Ben-Avi, became the first person in modern times to speak Hebrew as his native language because it was the only language spoken in Ben Yehuda's family. Vilna thus meant many things to many people.

Today's Vilnius is no longer a major center of Belarusian nationalism, although its most active leaders have long enjoyed the sympathy and support of Lithuanian authorities. Thus, in 1988, the first congress of the Belarusian Popular Front (BNF) convened in Vilnius. There are also some Belarusian-language publishers and one Belarusian-language monthly. About sixty thousand people in Lithuania are believed to be ethnic Belarusians based on records of Belarusian ethnicity in their Soviet internal passports. Yet, aside from Belarus itself, the only contiguous area where nationally conscious Belarusians can be found en masse is northeastern Poland.

IDENTITY FRUSTRATIONS: PENDULUM EFFECT

Situated between Poland and Russia both geographically and linguistically, the promoters of the Belarusian national idea identified themselves in opposition to either one or the other of Belarus's expansionist neighbors. Today, for obvious reasons, the bogeyman to disassociate oneself from is Russia, but historically Russia and Poland were used in that capacity intermittently, as springboards of sorts. In fact, Poland was to play this role first because the Belarusian national idea developed amidst Polish-speaking intellectuals who began to define themselves in opposition to that country. In their opposition, however, they stood a chance of falling into the embraces of Russia. Similarly, rebounding from Russia at a different point, Belarusian nationalist thinkers were to be on the lookout lest they become too Polish: a peculiar pendulum effect.

The pendulum analogy is irresistible; it is ensconced in the spontaneous imagery of the language used to describe the early stages of Belarusian nationalism. Thus, according to Zakhar Shybeko, the outcome of the 1839 conversion of the Uniates to the Orthodox Church means that Belarusians were "pulled away as it were from the Catholic Poles but drawn dangerously close to the Orthodox Russians."[50] Mečkovskaya writes that in Belarus, in the late 1800s to early 1900s, "anything that was elevated above the illiterate peasant existence, be that church, school, or officialdom, automatically became either 'Russian'(and Orthodox) or 'Polish' (and Catholic)."[51] Against this backdrop, to maintain Belarusian distinctiveness in writing, the editors of the *Nasha Niva* practiced the so-called divergent language planning, aiming at diminishing both the Russianness of Grazhdanka and the Polishness of Lacinka.[52] Interestingly, Woolhiser shows that currently, the Belarusian-language publications in Bialystok, Poland, contain a lot of Russicisms, whereas in the Grodno region, on the Belarusian side of the border, publications in Belarusian use many Polonisms.

In his important 1929 book, Alyaksandr Tsvikevich showed that long before any distinctive "Belarusian idea" emerged, educated Belarusians used to be assimilated either into Russian or Polish culture.[53] The ideological blueprint of Russification was the so-called West-Rusism, a theory that emphasized Belarusian peculiarity but only within the confines of the Russian cultural universe. The most prominent author and promoter of this theory was Mikhail Koyalovich (1828–1891). Born in Kuznica Bialystocka, in the Belarusian-speaking area's extreme West, wherein the Orthodox were a minority, Koyalovich was imbued with the idea of the high mission of Russian Orthodoxy. Born ten years later in Mostovliany, to the east of Kuznica (!), Konstanty (Kastus) Kalinowski (1838–1864) was imbued with the idea of the high mission of Polish Catholicism for the enlightenment and liberation of the local, and mostly Orthodox, peasantry. In a primordialist sense, that is, assuming that nation comes first and nationalism later, both Koyalovich and Kalinowski were Belarusians. But they were committed to dragging the "Belarusian pendulum" in opposite directions: for Koyalovich, the Belarusians' natural home was Russia; for Kalinoswki, it was Poland. Similar alter egos can be found in the next generation of Belarusians. Thus, Bronislaw Taraśkewicz (Taraškevič or Tarashkevich), the author of the first Belarusian grammar, was apparently raised in Polish culture. In the Vitebsk Drama Theater's production of Sakrat Yanovich's play *Arrest*, Tarashkevich talks about himself as a man of Polish culture and clarifies that this is different from actually being a Pole.[54] Tarashkevich's contemporary, Yevfimii Karski, the premier Belarusian linguist of all time and an ethnic Belarusian, was decidedly a man of Russian culture. As the rector of Warsaw University from 1905 to 1915, he was one of the most ardent Russifiers of Poland, not just Belarus. Tsvikevich shows that in 1917 Karski was in favor of introducing Russian-only secondary school instruction in Belarus; only if locals insisted would he concede to freshman-year instruction in Belarusian.[55] Several prominent people with Belarusian roots became known to the rest of the world as Poles, which prompted Ivan Solonevich, yet another Belarusian, to write, "Tyskiewicz's, Mickewicz's, and Sienkiewicz's are about as much Belarusian as I am, but they sold out [to the Poles], so the people were left without the upper stratum."[56]

According to Tsvikevich, the self-styled Belarusian national idea, which claimed that Belarusians were neither Russians nor Poles, had emerged only when both Poles and Russians happened to weaken their assimilatory efforts in their common borderland because of being preoccupied with what was going on in their respective national cores.[57] This, however, did not make the search for a distinctive Belarusian identity any easier. When Boguševič published his *Belarusian Pipe*,[58] considered to be a cultural treasure by the Western-leaning Belarusian nationalists, Karski, who was about to begin his own three-volume masterpiece, *Belarusy*,[59] devoted to the Belarusian language, referred to Boguševič's work as a "proclamation in Latin spirit with the precise aim to cause an upheaval in the Russian family."[60] By all accounts, therefore, the difficulties of finding a separate and unwavering niche in what was once called "an economically and culturally dead zone between Russia and Poland"[61] have been immense, which may in part explain the tenuous and fragile nature of Belarusian nationalism. Apparently even the cultural icons of Belarusianness had a hard time nurturing attachment to the Belarusian idea in their offspring. Thus, Boguševič's son was described as a "zoological Polish chauvinist" who even denied passing on the archive of his late father to interested Belarusian activists.[62] Vasyl Bykau, the major Belarusian author of our time, ruefully admitted that he had failed to raise his two sons "in a nationally conscious way, and so they grew in an essentially cosmopolitan urban environment."[63] Indeed, Bykau's son, Sergei, notes that until his father's last day, they communicated in Russian.[64]

The precarious nature of Belarus's geopolitical niche comes with some other complications, including the above-mentioned denominational pattern of ethnic mobilization. This means that in what used to be the Polish-Russian borderland, Catholics tended to identify with the Poles, whereas the Orthodox identified with the Russians, effectively leaving no room for Belarusians. Indeed, as mentioned above, in most Catholic churches of Belarus, Polish is routinely used. And, likewise, in the Orthodox churches, the language is Russian. This explains why in the annals of the Belarusian national movement, from its very inception to today, one comes across the same refrain: it is wrong to determine nationality by religion, and most self-proclaimed Poles in Belarus are actually Belarusians. A list of relevant quotations follows:

Fiodor Turuk (1921): "In Belorussia, Catholics from ancient times (*izdrevle*) identified with Poles, while Orthodox with Russian."[65]

Fiodor Turuk (1921): "The surviving Belorussian nobilities usually assign themselves to the Poles because of their Polish and Catholic upbringing."[66]

Alyaksandr Tsvikevich (1929): "Rallying for the Orthodox schools for Belarusians, the *West Russian Herald* had one more objective: it consciously confused religion with nationality, deliberately equating the Orthodoxy with Russianness. Just as there was no Russia outside the Orthodoxy, likewise a Belarusian Catholic simply did not exist. In that sense, West-Rusism was totally identical to Polonism, which also assigned nationality according to religion."[67]

Mikola Shkialionek (early 1940s): "It appeared that both competitors, Russia and Poland, were ready to divide Belarus according to a religious principle: the Orthodox Belarusians are Russians and the Catholic Belarusians are Poles."[68]

Tatyana Mikulich (1996): "The old principle of assigning nationality according to one's religion has survived to these days. In quite a few cases, in Belarus, people call themselves Poles, who do not have anything in common with the Polish nationality except religion."[69]

Wojtek Kość (1999): "Since the words 'Orthodox' and 'Belarusan'[70] are synonymous in the minds of Bialystok authorities, both groups are discriminated against equally. However, those two words are not synonymous."[71]

L. V. Tereshkovich (1991): "Denominational problems are extremely painful for the Belarusian national movement. In Belarus, Catholicism bears a distinctly colonial imprint, whereas the attitude of the Orthodoxy to the national movement is chilly, although the Orthodoxy has absorbed some regional features. . . . The overwhelming majority of Catholic priests are ethnic Poles who consider all Belarusian Catholics to be Poles. The Polonization conducted by the priests is also reinforced by widespread Polonophile views among youths."[72]

Jan Zaprudnik (1993): "The Uniate clergy . . . spoke better Polish and Latin than the language of their flock. Concepts of religion and nationality were inseparably welded: Orthodoxy was Russian, Catholicism was Polish, and Uniatism was plebeian, associated with eastern rites but Western ecclesiastical allegiance."[73]

Jan Zaprudnik (1993): "Strivings for Belarusian separateness were seriously hampered by the general identification of Catholicism with Polishness and Orthodoxy with Russianness—a psychological heritage of the age-old Russo-Polish competition in the Belarusian lands."[74]

Jan Zaprudnik (1993): "[In Belarus] identification of Orthodoxy with Russianness and Catholicism with Polishness is deeply seated in the popular mind. In fact, Belarusian renewal is an uphill struggle precisely because it has to deal with the heavy burden of past centuries—a burden not easily discarded."[75]

Jan Zaprudnik (1993): "The Polish minority in Lithuania consists fundamentally of indigenous inhabitants who consider themselves Poles exclusively because of their Catholic religion (the everyday language of these "Poles" is a dialect of Belarusian)."[76]

Jan Zaprudnik (1993): "Old clichés inherited from history are being reanimated now in the atmosphere of free expression: whereas eastern Orthodoxy is identified by many, either subconsciously or overtly, as the 'Russian faith,' Catholicism is presented as the Polish faith. Officially, Moscow and Warsaw are both content with this twist of mind and have been using it for their own expansionist purposes."[77]

Zaprudnik's exceptional tenacity in fighting the denominational pattern of ethnic mobilization may be self-defeating. First, if one fights an alleged myth this persistently, one actually lends it additional legitimacy. Second, and most importantly, objecting to the denominational pattern on the grounds that it is rooted in the popular mind-set is illogical. Ethnic allegiances and/or shared identity can exist only in popular mentality, which is their sole possible agent or substratum. There could hardly be a DNA or other objective scientific test that tells Belarusians from Russians or Poles. Criticizing popular mentality may make sense when it propagates "truths" rejected by science, such as that the earth is flat or that automobile tires can save one from lightning. But if people identify themselves in a certain way over and over again for a period of two hundred years, then telling them that they got it wrong after all constitutes a bizarre message at best. While physical anthropology (e.g., facial types) and language may in exceptional cases cast doubt on self-proclaimed ethnic identity, this is highly unlikely in a racially homogenous region with gentle language gradients, overlapping cultural influences, and unstable national borders. After all, the people in question do not claim to be Mongols, Arabs, or American Indians. They do not even claim to be French or German. The people in question are Slavs who live in what has been for centuries the Russian-Polish borderland and who just cling to one of its flanks. Having lived all their lives in between Russian and Polish national cores, all they want is to be identified with one of the two. Apparently the third alternative (i.e., espousing Belarusianness) has not swayed some of them. It seems the positive message of the Belarusian national movement (that is, a message defining who "we" are rather than who "we" are not) has not struck a cord with a sizable number of Belarusian speakers.

When Andrzej Sadowski, a researcher from Bialystok, Poland, studied the communities on both sides of the Belarus-Poland border, his survey included one question that was considered entirely normal on the Polish side but raised many eyebrows on the Belarusian side: what nationality do you belong to in your deepest conviction? People east of the border were surprised (whereas those west of it remained unruffled) because Soviet-style internal passports contained a clear-cut record of nationality. Unavailable in Poland, but available and required in Belarus, these IDs helped instill and fix the notion of one's belonging to a certain ethnic group—in fact, so much so that there appeared to be no need to doubt it, which is why the words "in your deepest conviction" seemed grossly redundant to many on the Belarusian side of the border. Sadowski aptly dubbed this phenomenon "passport ethnic awareness."[78]

HOW MANY BELARUSIANS? BELARUSIANS IN POLAND

According to the 1999 census, there were 8.159 million Belarusians living in Belarus.[79] According to the 1989 Soviet census, 2.127 million Belarusians lived in other Soviet republics,[80] for the most part in Russia, Ukraine, and Lithuania. But it is impossible to verify how many of these people are Belarusians "in their deepest conviction" (as per Sadowski). In contrast, the data available for the northeastern part of Poland (formerly Bialystok Voivodship, but currently part of Podlaskie Voivodship) allow one to attribute ethnicity to self-identification, the realm where ethnicity rightfully belongs, particularly in blurred cases in which people face more than one option.

The number of Belarusians in Poland has been debated since the reinstatement of Poland's statehood in 1919 and up to this day. The last Polish census that recorded nationality (narodowość) took place in 1921. In 1931, only a question on native language was included. Nicholas Vakar showed that in the census of 1921, all the natives of Roman Catholic faith were registered as Polish, and the total number of Belorussians was thus reduced from 3,700,000 to 1,041,760 under the assumption that "being Roman Catholic in faith, they would be completely assimilated within ten years or so."[81] The veracity of this assumption could not be tested at the time, and in 1939, Poland was partitioned for the fourth time in its history, with Bialystok and its environs accruing to Soviet Belarus. After the war, Bialystok and its environs were returned to renascent Poland, and a certain number of Belarusians remained west of the border, in Poland.

In later years, the Polonization process accelerated, but the postwar Polish censuses did not include entries on either nationality (ethnicity) or native language. According to Sadowski's survey of the mid-1990s, no Catholics of northeastern Poland identified themselves as Belarusians.[82] On the other hand, there were 286,000 people of Orthodox faith in what used to be Bialystok Voivodship of Poland. These people accounted for 40 percent of that voivodship's entire population. Of these, 53 percent identified as Poles and 28.2 percent as Belarusians.[83] Based on these data, one can estimate the number of self-identified Belarusians in Poland at 80,600.

Looking forward to its accession to the European Union (EU), Poland reintroduced the ethnicity (narodowość) entry in its census form. The EU requires accountability with regard to each member nation's treatment of its minorities; no accountability can be enforced without counting those minorities in the first place. As a result, the 2002 Polish census revealed that there were just 48,700 Belarusians in Poland, a much lower number than previously thought. Note that the 2002 census was the first to require people to explicitly identify their ethnicity since 1921. Out of Poland's 48,700 self-identified Belarusians,

46,400 lived in Podlaskie Voivodship.[84] Although the number is significantly lower than was estimated in earlier years, Belarusians have the broadest territorial base of all Poland's minorities. Ethnic Germans, for example, are three times as numerous as Belarusians, but in no single *gmina* do they account for more than 50 percent of the population. Belarusians, however, make up more than one-half of the population in four *gminy*. In Poland, *gmina* is a civil subdivision of the lowest level. Somewhat analogous to rural Soviet administrations in the republic of Belarus, it encompasses several rural villages. The higher-level civil division is *powiat*, somewhat analogous to Belarusian *rayon*. In Hajnówka Powiat, which abuts the border with Belarus, about 40 percent are self-identified Belarusians. Thus, Belarusians are the only minority in Poland that can claim local autonomy in view of their contiguous and pronounced territorial base. Whether or not this will be pursued depends to some extent on the local community leaders.

These leaders acknowledge the fast-paced assimilation of their coethnics. According to Miranovich, for example, many Belarusians "renounce their legacy in order to advance their career and to increase their sense of security."[85] According to Jan Maksimyuk, circulation of the *Niva*, the major Belarusian-language newspaper in Poland, dropped from ten thousand in the late 1960s to less than one thousand now.[86] Apparently, the homogenization pressure in today's Poland is quite real but falls short of interpersonal confrontations. The distribution of self-identified Belarusians among communities with varying percentage share of the Orthodox gives some insight into this sort of pressure. Krzystof Goss uncovered a regularity: the higher the percentage of the Orthodox, the more willingness there is to identify as Belarusian, and vice versa. In fact, only in the overwhelmingly Orthodox communities do people overwhelmingly identify as Belarusians. But when Catholics account for just 15 to 25 percent of the community's population, the rest being Orthodox, then the percentage of self-identified Belarusians within the rest of the population drops to about 50 percent. And when the Orthodox are a minority themselves, precious few among them identify as Belarusians. For example, among the Orthodox residents of Bialystok, only 15 percent say they are Belarusians.

Polonization has been progressing along several channels, with language and religion being the most important. Mixed Orthodox-Catholic marriages usually take place in the *kosciól*, not the *cerkiew*, and kids born to those mixed families are usually baptized as Catholics.[87] When in 1976 I first visited Bialystok and stayed with an Orthodox family, the two teenage girls in that family emphasized that they spoke correct Polish, unlike their older relatives in Hajnówka. Statements like these from youths bear evidence of strong homogenizing pressures. According to the Russian 1897 census, 83.3

percent of Sokolski Powiat identified as Belarusian speakers, and it was the most Belarusian *powiat* within the current borders of Poland. In 2002, just 1 percent of the Sokolski Powiat population identified as Belarusian.

SPATIAL DISTRIBUTION OF ETHNIC GROUPS

A transborder area comprising Grodno Oblast, Belarus, and Podlaskie Voivodship, Poland, is a transitional region both linguistically and culturally, which is particularly characteristic of the areas abutting the current Polish-Belarusian border. These include about a dozen westernmost *rayony* of Grodno Oblast (notably Grodno, Lida, Wolkowysk, Voronovo, and Shchuchin) and a similar number of *gminy* in the easternmost part of former Bialystok Voivodship (notably the environs of Hajnówka, Bielsk, Siemiatycze, and Sokólka).[88]

Now, the major aspect of transborder symmetry is that there are people identifying themselves as Poles to the east of the state border and as Belarusians to the west of the border. Also, most Poles in Belarus and the overwhelming majority of Belarusians in Poland alike are rural villagers.[89]

Yet, symmetry is limited in scope, and there are important asymmetrical features that also engage attention. First, the 1999 Belarus census recorded 396,000 Poles,[90] whereas there are no more than 46,400 self-identified Belarusians in the transborder regions of Poland. Available observations show that the latter figure is significantly short of the actual number of Belarusian speakers in Polish Podlasie (or Podlaskie Voivodship). In contrast to that, on the Belarusian side of the border, the actual number of those using Polish in an everyday setting is significantly less than the number of self-proclaimed Poles.[91] In other words, here identity is stronger than its linguistic basis.

On the Belarusian side of the border, most secondary schools are Russian-language schools. Polish schools were terminated in 1948. Local Poles have long appealed to the authorities to restore Polish-language schools, and some were reopened in the late 1980s. Currently, Polish is taught as a subject in twenty-eight schools in Grodno Oblast. Also, in the late 1990s, two secondary schools with Polish as the only language of instruction were opened: one in Grodno (560 seats) and one in Wolkowysk (198 seats).[92] Interestingly, not all the students who attend these schools are Poles according to their internal passports. On the Polish side, no exclusively Belarusian schools exist as no local demand for such schools has been recorded in annual surveys of parents. So, all the schools here are Polish-language schools, but in some, Belarusian is taught as a separate subject. Sadowski surveyed two lyceums located in Hajnówka and Bielsk, linguistically the most Belarusian places in the area, and determined that 39 percent of students in one lyceum and 50 percent in the other identify as Poles, while only 23 percent in each lyceum identify as Belarusians.[93]

These findings illustrate how spatial continuity is giving way to abrupt transborder changes under the homogenizing influence of statewide tendencies. Indeed, according to Sadowski, 43.6 percent of self-identified Belarusians in Poland use Polish in contacts with colleagues and friends, and 24.8 percent use Polish in contacts with family. On the other hand, in the border regions of Grodno Oblast, 54.2 percent of Poles and 57.2 percent of Belarusians use Russian in contacts with friends and colleagues; in contacts with family, 40.6 percent of Poles and 44.4 percent of Belarusians use Russian.[94]

It appears that Belarusian national agitation is kept alive exclusively by the Orthodox in Poland, whereas in Belarus people with Catholic backgrounds have been in the forefront of the anti-Russian strand of Belarusian nationalism. The April 2002 declaration of the BNF and Christian Conservative Party takes the Orthodox Church on directly: "Active Russification of the Belarusian population is conducted by the Orthodox Church, which has traditionally acted in Belarus as an anti-national force."[95]

The explanation for this particular asymmetry is twofold. First, the religious affiliation or background of the Orthodox in Poland and Catholics in Belarus is what makes them different from the overwhelming majorities in their respective domains, that is, Poland on the one hand, and Belarus plus Russia on the other. Second, at least historically, mainstream Poles' and mainstream Russians' attitudes to Belarusian speakers did not match. One of the most tenacious features of the Polish national mythology has been Poland's civilizing mission among the local population of the *Kresy Wschodnie*, that is, the Polish-Russian borderland.[96] Hand in hand with this myth comes a tradition of looking down on local peasantry as a less-cultured lot that has to be "aided" in its quest to embrace the goods of European civilization. In contrast, the message that Russians used to send to the Belarusian peasantry was "you are us."[97] Consequently, no understanding of the resulting leaning of most Belarusians toward Russia can be achieved without giving thought to these contrasting messages. In the 1920s and 1930s, Polonization was the official policy in western Belarus, and it became overwhelmingly successful among the Belarusian-speaking Catholics. Leopold Skulski, Polish minister of internal affairs in the 1920s, is quoted as saying that within fifty years, one would be able to place all those remaining Belarusians on one sofa.[98] While his prediction certainly has not been realized, the pace of the Polonization of the Belarusian-speaking communities in Poland has been fairly fast considering that, by some accounts, four to five hundred thousand Belarusians remained in Poland after the 1945 demarcation of the Soviet-Polish border.[99]

"Just like other groups," writes Mariusz Kowalski, a Polish scholar, "Belarusian-speaking Catholics faced the imperative of choosing the national option. And it is just in this community that the idea of a separate Belarusian people was born . . . [a community] whose initial orientation was pro-Western.

However, gradually in the Belarusian movement the initiative was wrested by the Orthodox, which followed from their demographic preponderance. This outcome precipitated a shift to closer association with Russian society, and that antagonized Belarusian Catholics. This situation could not help but influence identity. Linguistic (given that the difference between Polish and Belarusian is small), religious, and civilization reasons led not only the upper classes but also Polonized Lithuanian peasants to become intent on associating themselves with the Poles."[100]

Following the example of Janka Kupala's play *Tuteishiya* (see chapter 3), wherein two "scientists," Western and Eastern, intermittently pass their judgments about self-identified Belarusians, the floor should now be given to an Eastern (i.e., Russian) scholar. Sergei Markov, a political scientist, says, "Apparently the members of the Belarusian opposition consider themselves heirs of the Grand Duchy of Lithuania. But the majority of Belarusian people do not. They believe they are Belarusian and Russian, which explains their aspiration to be together with Russia. At the same time, an insignificant minority takes cues from Lithuania and Poland. Herein, not in attitudes toward democracy and freedom, lies the principal schism in Belarus's politics."[101]

The last sentence of Markov's statement has far-reaching implications. If his diagnosis is correct, then the pivotal conflict in Belarus is misread in the West. If the conflict in question is cultural, even civilizational, at its heart, then politicizing it only makes it more difficult to solve, and the national consolidation of Belarusians only becomes more elusive.

It is important to understand that when it comes to ethnic bonds, popular mentality is the only consideration that matters. As Smith notes, "Where . . . meanings, myths and symbols cease to strike a responsive cord— because of other competing ones—there [lie] the cultural boundaries of the nation."[102]

Analyzing the spatial distributions of the three major ethnic groups (Belarusians, Russians, and Poles) allows for additional insight into the identity issue. The comparisons of figures 2.1 to 2.2 reveal not only a high degree of complementarity between Belarusians and Poles (where the share of one of these groups is high, the share of the other is low) but also no complementarity between the distributions of Russians and the two other ethnicities. Whatever the underlying reason, the spatial divide with the most pronounced cultural dimension is between the self-identified Poles and the rest. The concern of Belarusian authorities over external patronage of some grassroots Polish organizations in Belarus is easier to interpret when one takes a look at figure 2.2. The potential for a Kosovo-like separatism and its possible effect on Catholics that identify themselves as Poles do not seem far-fetched.

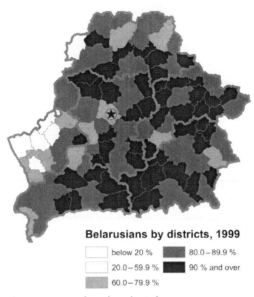

Belarusians by districts, 1999

below 20 %		80.0 – 89.9 %	
20.0 – 59.9 %		90 % and over	
60.0 – 79.9 %			

Figure 2.1.   Belarusians in Belarus.

Source: Calculated by the author on the basis of the 1999 census data contained in *Natsionalnyi Sostav Respubliki Belarus i Rasprostranionnost Yazykov* (Minsk: Ministerstvo Statistiki i Analiza, 2001).

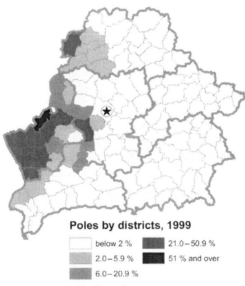

Poles by districts, 1999

below 2 %		21.0 – 50.9 %	
2.0 – 5.9 %		51 % and over	
6.0 – 20.9 %			

Figure 2.2.   Poles in Belarus.

Source: Calculated by the author on the basis of the 1999 census data contained in *Natsionalnyi Sostav Respubliki Belarus i Rasprostranionnost Yazykov* (Minsk: Ministerstvo Statistiki i Analiza, 2001).

Russians by districts, 1999

below 5 %		11.0–15.9 %	
5.0–10.9 %		16 % and over	

Figure 2.3.   Russians in Belarus.

Source: Calculated by the author on the basis of the 1999 census data contained in *Natsionalnyi Sostav Respubliki Belarus i Rasprostranionnost Yazykov* (Minsk: Ministerstvo Statistiki i Analiza, 2001).

A TUG OF WAR

"Passport ethnic awareness" notwithstanding, the existence of a fair number of nationally conscious Belarusians is undeniable. Yet, forces striving to flesh out Belarusian identity have been at war with each other. Who are ethnic Belarusians? Are they Russians' little brothers (whose peculiarity is quite real but falls within the Russian cultural universe)? Or are they proud descendants of the Grand Duchy of Lithuania, whose formative experiences derive from numerous wars *against* Russia?

It is tempting to portray the evolving views on Belarusian identity as a perpetual fight for its meaning. This assertion can be called into question because much of Belarusians' nationally conscious history falls into the Soviet period. However, just as in Russia proper, where the rivalry between the Westernizers and the Slavophiles did not vanish in the communist revolution but was reduced to an undercurrent, so in Belarus calling things by their proper names has been, and still is, an exception. And yet, the ongoing struggle for the meaning of Belarusianness appears to unfold according to the old script, first written in the last quarter of the nineteenth century.

Throughout the twentieth century, Belarusian "Westernizers"[103] seldom rose to a position of power. In fact, this happened three times, and each period was brief and marked by external supervision and controversy. The Westernizers first made a splash in 1918 and 1919 when the Belarusian People's Republic (BPR) was proclaimed under the German military occupation. The BPR introduced the white-red-white flag and a coat of arms in the form of "pursuit" (a knight mounted on a racing horse). "As the emblem of the Grand Duchy of Lithuania, Rus', and Samogitia, the latter represented a link to a proud period" in Belarusian history.[104]

After the Bolsheviks rejected the BPR, Poland reemerged on the political map of Europe (1919), and the war broke out between it and Soviet Russia. The areas populated by Belarusians were in 1921 divided between Poland and Russia in the wake of that war. The BSSR was proclaimed in the eastern section of "ethnographic Belarus." Within the BSSR, the Belarusian Westernizers (a.k.a., nationalists) and the backers of West-Rusism represented two mutually hostile groups. Both with local roots, they were trying to curry favor with the communist regime. Initially the regime favored the nationalists for three reasons. First, Great Russian chauvinism had been given a bad name by Vladimir Lenin himself, and in the early 1920s, fighting it was still on the communist agenda. Second, in order to undo territorial losses, Moscow decided to cast the BSSR as the "true" Belarusian home (as opposed to western Belarus, where Belarusians suffered discrimination by the Poles). Last, but not least, religion was now considered the "opium of the people," and West-Rusism had been a brainchild of the Russian Orthodox Church. As a result, the Westernizers (a.k.a., nationalists) received official support and obtained leverage out of proportion to the size and influence of their group. They even attracted their ideological brethren from Poland, who relocated to the BSSR, and together they launched the linguistic Belarusification campaign reviewed in chapter 1. By the late 1920s, however, the backers of West-Rusism had regrouped. They could no longer appeal to the authority of the Russian Orthodox Church. Instead they appealed to the Soviet state, this bastion of "proletarian internationalism," and labeled Belarusian nationalists as Polish spies. Although nationalists themselves had some success in casting their more numerous opponents as Russian chauvinists and closet Orthodox Church supporters,[105] the Soviet reincarnation of West-Rusism gained the upper hand. Many proponents of the Belarusian national idea were condemned as *natsdems* (national democrats, a code word for an ideological corruption of true Leninism) and were then exiled to the deep interior of Russia. Those arrested or exiled in 1930 and 1931 were, for the most part, subsequently released, but many were imprisoned yet again in 1937 and 1938. This time, Stalinist repressions were more relentless, and most prisoners labeled *natsdems* lost their lives.

The westernizing strand of Belarusian nationalism casts the BPR as a pivotal episode in the national history. However, few people took notice of the BPR in its time. Von Beckeret, the German advisor on Belarusian affairs, reported to the military command of the eastern front that "the Belarusian secessionism, supported by a few Vilna archeologists and journalists, ought to be considered a local matter of no political consequence."[106] Interestingly, the BPR founders became mutually antagonized when several of them reportedly embraced Polonophilia.[107]

The westernizing platform then briefly resurfaced under the supervision of German occupiers, this time the Nazis. When in 1941 Germany invaded the Soviet Union, they treated Belarus as "nothing more than a vague geographical term."[108] Only after the assassination of the general commissar of occupied Belarus,[109] Wilhelm Kube, in September of 1943, and following the overall success of the Soviet-led guerilla activity, did Germans decide to play the card of Belarusian patriotism. The white-red-white flag and the coat of arms of Pahonia were in use again by the local authorities, who were appointed by, and worked under, the close supervision of the occupiers.

Some activity of the Nazi collaborators in Belarus is described by Vakar.[110] More informative is the book by Jerzy (Yury) Turonek, which highlights every aspect of the German occupation, including the uneasy relationship between the most influential Belarusian Nazi collaborators. On many occasions, Turonek shows that the bond between these people (e.g., Fabian Akinchyts, Ivan Yermachenka, Radaslau Astrousky, and Vatslau Ivanovsky) and rank-and-file Belarusians was tenuous at best. For quite some time, the leaders of the Belarusian Central Rada (Council), the organization of the Belarusian Nazi collaborators, resented the fact that Germans used to appoint Poles, not Belarusians, as mayors, policemen, and managers of larger farms. "The Belarusian leaders," writes Turonek, "saw causes of that |situation| not in their weakness but in the all too liberal attitude of the German civilian administration to the Poles."[111] Turonek quotes many German pronouncements, such as the assessments of the *Deutsche Post aus dem Osten*, about the weaknesses of the Belarusian national movement under German occupation.

In 1944, most Nazi collaborators left Belarus with the retreating German army. Many of them in 1945 made it to the American and British occupation zones. In the overall commotion, "it was easy for collaborators to claim that they had worked on their farms until deported by the Germans and had since lost their papers. . . . Despite rules excluding former collaborators from DP |displaced person| status and therefore also from access to emigration under UN regulations, many slipped through the net."[112] For example, out of 342 members of Mir rayon police appointed by the Germans, 104 escaped to the West, and there is no information about the whereabouts of 129 former policemen.[113]

John Loftus has described the successful postwar careers of some former Nazi collaborators from Belarus in U.S. government agencies during the cold war,[114] and an informative website was compiled on the basis of that book.[115] An alternative version of the wartime events is given, very briefly, by Kipel, who writes that "as Germans looked upon the Belarusans as potential allies," it "was only natural that some Belarusans would look upon the Germans as their political allies. This point of view was reinforced with the outbreak of the Soviet-German war when the Germans . . . encountered many Belarusans . . . who had suffered under the Soviets."[116]

Zaprudnik gives a somewhat less straightforward interpretation of those events. In a talk show of the Belarusian Service of Radio Liberty, he said that "a person is morally responsible for his conduct only when he has freedom of choice."[117] Revealing that he had witnessed German-appointed Belarusian police and Germans themselves ("particularly Germans") pursuing and executing Jews, Zaprudnik averred that this atrocity was so obvious, it is unlikely that even 1 percent of the people, including the policemen themselves, approved of what the Germans were doing.[118] While this may be the case, available evidence suggests that in Belarus in 1941 and 1942, local perpetrators of the Holocaust outnumbered Germans in proportions ranging from 5:1 to 10:1, and in 1943 and 1944 the ratio exceeded 10:1.[119] According to Zaprudnik, however, the "question of moral responsibility for what was done under the German occupation is closely linked with the question of moral responsibility of Stalin's collaborators under the Bolsheviks."[120] Zaprudnik conceded that the "responsibility rests on those who shot innocent people, who contributed to the Holocaust, who burned villages, who provoked Germans to burn those villages, who transported villagers to mandatory work assignments, who robbed villages, etc."[121] In other words, the Nazi collaborators and the partisans fighting them share responsibility. Valyantsyn Taras, who as a Belarusian partisan fought "on the other side," disagrees with Zaprudnik. According to Taras, "In those years, deep down the character of the war was not so much conditioned by Stalinism as by popular resistance to foreign invasion, people's fight for not just historical but also physical survival."[122] Also, "the people saw instantaneously . . . who came to Belarus, and resistance to Germans was spontaneous."[123] Under Stalin, "my wife's family was purged and deprived of property," Taras also noted. "In 1937, my father-in-law was arrested and spent one year in a gulag. However, in 1943 he became a partisan. He never joined the party, he hated Stalin, and yet he consciously aided partisans."[124]

To this day, in the minds of quite a few ordinary Belarusians, collaboration with the occupiers remains a stigma—hence the attempts to "rationalize" collaboration. Thus, Turonek claims in the very last paragraph of his book, "the attitude of the German war-time administration toward the Belarusian question was better than the attitude of the Soviet state. This is reflected in the fact that under occupation in the capital of Belarus, only Belarusian-language schools functioned, whereas after its liberation only Russian-language schools did. This qualification cannot be shattered by reference to genocide by the Germans; in Belarus, the number of victims of [Stalinist purges] was no less than the number of crimes committed by the SS."[125]

The last sentence of this verdict may or may not be accurate. In any case, it is alien to Turonek's well-researched book. Certainly Stalinist crimes are worth talking about, but Turonek's book is devoted entirely to Belarus under German occupation. So, his actual, overriding, and verifiable criterion that sets the reigns of Adolf Hitler and Joseph Stalin apart is the language of schooling in Minsk. Naturally, the question as to what Belarusians en masse might think about the importance of this criterion in the overall scheme of things is not even contemplated, a perennial flaw of the strand of Belarusian nationalism Turonek seems to represent.

On a more rational note, Turonek claims that the Soviet assessment of the number of deaths among Belarusian civilians (750,000) is inflated because the estimate in question rests on the enumeration of the population at the end of 1944, by which time not all evacuees (i.e., those who had managed to flee eastern Belarus days before the Germans came) had returned. Incidentally, my family, who returned to Mozyr in the middle of August 1944, was not the last group to return to that town, and Turonek's doubts about the official assessment of civilian deaths merit further analysis. But so does his claim of the German Nazi's benign attitude to Belarusian nationalism. In the words of Zakhar Shybeko, in Belarusian historiography, the interpretation of World War II remains "an ideological barricade."[126] But if this is so, then Turonek's implicit conviction that there is only one strand of Belarusian nationalism defies reality. The ideological battle between the Belarusian Westernizers and the equally Belarusian heirs of West-Rusism is not the figment of someone's imagination. This division does not cease to exist if one side simply decides not to recognize the existence of the other. As Turonek shows in his book, the German Nazis were interested in weakening Russian and Polish influences in the area, as both Soviet partisans and detachments of the Armia Krajowa fought Nazis in Belarus. So, ultimately, the occupiers decided to place their stake on the people who professed no allegiance to either Russians or Poles and claimed to be the sole legitimate representatives of the Belarusians. Turonek's reasoning then is much like "the enemy of my enemy is my friend."

But there is the rub: nobody ever had a monopoly on the political representation of the Belarusian ethnicity.

The following is an excerpt from a book by Yury Shevtsov, a Belarusian historian, much like Turonek, only from the other side of the ideological barricade:

> In Belarus, the war was very brutal and the cultural-political polarization of Belarusians turned out to be tough and across-the-board. During the crushing defeat of the Nazis, the proponents of the non-Soviet version of Belarusian identity were killed or left the country, forming the core of Belarusian emigrant communities in the West. The hatred of the victorious version of Belarusian culture toward the collaborationists is usually automatically transferred to historic Belarusian symbols that those collaborationists used and on everything that is linked with the non-Soviet version of Belarusian identity and ideology including literature and (sometimes) Belarusian language. There is also reciprocal rejection by Belarusian emigrants in the West of all aspects of Belarus's life after the war. This split of the nation has not been overcome.[127]

In Belarus, however, the defeated Nazi collaborators were not as numerous as they were in Ukraine. Very little information on Belarusian collaborationists percolated into Soviet historical writings, in marked contrast with what was divulged to the general public concerning the Baltic states, Ukraine, and, indeed, the occupied section of Russia itself.[128] Apparently, in Belarus, the collaborationist movement had a meager following and was dwarfed by the Soviet-led guerilla movement,[129] which became one of the major epic stories of the Great Patriotic War. Significantly, when in 1947 ethnic Germans were evicted from their homeland in East Prussia, the only non-Russian ethnic group selected to participate en masse in what became the Kaliningrad Oblast's resettlement program were the Belarusians.[130] Apparently, the Moscow authorities did not doubt their loyalty. The late 1940s and early 1950s marked one of the darkest periods of Soviet history, when almost anybody's loyalty could be questioned.

In 1988, Zianon Pazniak discovered a mass grave in Kuropaty, near Minsk, a grave that was traced to the Stalinist terror,[131] not to German occupiers as the authorities of Soviet Belarus strived, but failed, to prove. In the atmosphere of Mikhail Gorbachev's perestroika, this discovery ushered in the third and most recent period of the Westernizers' drive to power. Although their struggle with the Soviet incarnation of West-Rusism did not stop for a moment, the 1992–1995 period was marked by a brief comeback of the white-red-white flag and coat of arms used under German occupation. Yet, once again, the triumph was short-lived, and the backlash was culturally conditioned: most rank-and-file Belarusians simply did not accept these alleged tokens of identity as their own and were swayed overwhelmingly by Lukashenka's 1995 attempt to discredit them. In particular, much was made of the fact that Nazi collaborators had used the same state emblem and flag.

That all three episodes of the Westernizers' triumph were so brief may, of course, be attributed to the ploys of Russian colonialists. Such reasoning, however, appears to be shallow. It shifts attention away from the inherent weaknesses of the Belarusian national movement itself, as well as from the fact that not one but several different and opposing forces have been scrambling to flesh out Belarusian identity.

A CLASH OF MYTHOLOGIES

In his historical account of Belarus, David Marples has written about the challenges that the Belarusian national movement faced from the outset. One of them was that "the national past could only be reconstructed through . . . historical leaps' over centuries of uncertain existence."[132] This terse formula aptly conveys the enormity of the task.

Smith underscores the vital role of myths and symbols as "embodying the corpus of beliefs and sentiments which the guardians of ethnicity preserve, diffuse and transmit to future generations."[133] According to Smith, national myths are "creative recombinations of the past."[134] Although such "novel recombinations are pre-eminently the work of intellectuals in search of their 'roots,'" there are "very clear and very specific limits to their activities." These "are provided by existing criteria of the historiography of the time and by the texture and inner coherence of the myths and motifs themselves."[135]

"Inner coherence," however, may be more important than anything that has to do with "historiography." Although academic historians do play an important role in mythmaking, the principal criterion of success is the acceptance of their activity by the popular audience, not so much its scientifically tested veracity. Even in recent (let alone older) history, one comes across recorded facts that lend themselves to different interpretations. Even so, younger nationalisms have to be careful not to overexploit already known historical facts and cultural icons that other ethnicities have persistently claimed as their own and not to put such twists on those facts that their own constituencies do not find them believable and therefore appealing. At issue, according to Hroch, is "the relation between verbal demands and real interest: the basic condition for any acceptance of national demands [is] that [they] roughly correspond to reality as perceived by those to whom the national agitation [is] directed."[136]

Today, Belarusians face two sets of national symbols. They are profoundly different and backed by different mythologies. The first set of symbols is of

Soviet vintage, and Belarusian officialdom, some prominent historians (e.g., Adam Zalessky) and linguists (Arkady Zhuravsky), and apparently a large portion of rank-and-file Belarusians cling to it.

According to a bitterly ironic pronouncement by an opposition journalist, this set includes Zubrovka, Pesniary, Viskuli, and the 1941–1944 partisan war,[137] or, rather, landmarks, movies, and memories of those years. Zubrovka is a Belarusian brand of vodka featuring a bison (*zubr* in Belarusian and Russian, *zubrz* in Polish) from the Belavezha forest in western Belarus. Pesniary is a Minsk-based rock group extremely popular in the 1970s and 1980s. It drew upon Belarusian musical folklore, performed quite a few songs in Belarusian, and, if anything, contributed just as much, if not more, to Belarus's external recognition than the tractors and heavy trucks produced in the republic. Finally, Viskuli is a government retreat in the Belavezha forest, where in December 1991 Boris Yeltsin, Leonid Kravchuk, and Stanislau Shushkevich terminated the Union Treaty of 1922, and so the Soviet Union ceased to exist.

The anti-Nazi guerrilla war is at the heart of this Russophile variety of Belarusian symbols. It was indeed a major epic story. At least until the late 1970s, all of Soviet Belarus's high-ranking officials had been recruited from the Soviet-led network of the 1941–1944 anti-Nazi underground,[138] a glorified group.

It is little wonder then that the leaders of the BNF, which emerged in the final years of Gorbachev's perestroika, and some intellectuals even before that found these symbols ill suited for stirring up national feelings, particularly those feelings that would draw upon Belarus's alleged affinity to the West. First, based on those symbols, Belarusians appeared as nothing more than Russians' little brothers. Second, Belarusians' knowledge of their own early history was foggy. To me, the entire corpus of the Belarusian history exhibits in the State Historical Museum in Minsk (or, rather, the way they looked in the 1970s) gave the impression of a kitchen garden on hydroponics, wherein roots do not grow down into the soil but somehow dangle in a transparent, man-made solution.

It was only natural for nationally conscious Belarusian Westernizers to be willing to rewrite and retroactively extend the available accounts of Belarusian history. All they had to fall back on was the annals of the national movement that culminated in the 1920s and was then brutally terminated by Stalin's thugs. In accordance with these annals, they began once again to glorify the Grand Duchy of Lithuania as a truly Belarusian state, and they adopted the state symbols that had been used under two successive German military administrations. In 1992, these symbols became the official insignia of independent Belarus, and the Belarusian language was proclaimed the only official language of Belarus. However, as early as 1995, modified versions of Soviet Belarus's flag and national emblem made a comeback. Along with the ruble as the unit of national currency and Russian as one of the official languages of Belarus, these symbols unmistakably reflect Belarus's closeness to Russia, the bulwark of the former Soviet Union. Belarus is the only post-Soviet nation that returned to its Soviet insignia, even as Russia itself disposed of its Soviet-era flag and national emblem.

WHO IS TO BLAME?

In the words of Rainer Lindner, "the neo-Soviet and the opposition memorial cults are in bitter conflict."[139] The fight between the two had been unfolding in the open since the late 1980s, and it culminated in the 1995 referendum on language and state symbols in which 83.3 percent of voters rejected the white-red-white banner and the grand duchy–based national seal and opted for the return of the Soviet national symbols of Belarus. Although nationalists claim that the referendum was anticonstitutional and subject to manipulations or that "every referendum in an authoritarian country is to the satisfaction of its organizers,"[140] it seems that very few people in Belarus had accepted those grand duchy–related symbols as their own. According to Valery Karbalevich, "The white-red-white flag and the emblem Pahonia . . . were perceived not so much as national and state symbols as the insignia of the Belarusian Popular Front."[141]

BNF leader Zianon Pazniak's idea that all the deep-seated underpinnings of the Russophile leanings could be undone forcefully and swiftly through a state-sponsored assault on popular ways of thinking did not materialize. In 1996, Pazniak emigrated to the United States. Having left the country, Pazniak lost his high moral ground even among intellectuals, the only group with which he once had some appeal.

Whereas Pazniak routinely blames all the major setbacks on "carefully crafted" Russification and the perfidious role of Moscow, independent researchers find some flaws with the national movement per se. Thus, Andrei Okara believes that "Belarusian intellectuals developed an understanding of Belarus as non-Poland and non-Russia but failed to rise to the next level, that is, to spell out what Belarus's unique nature and commonly understood historic mission are."[142] Okara points to Ukraine, wherein alongside the westernizing and pro-Moscow ideological blueprints, a "third alternative" is entertained as well, which draws upon "Kiev's unique role as the sacral center of the post-Byzantium cultural realm and a possible geopolitical center of Eastern Europe."[143] No providential role of that or any other kind was ever proposed for Belarus. "Every Orthodox country," writes Okara, "can't help but construe itself as the mystical center of the world, be that the New Rome or the New Jerusalem. As for Belarus, it always saw itself as an advance guard: within the Grand Duchy . . . and Rzeczpospolita it was the eastern forefront of the West; within the Russian Empire, the Soviet Union, the CIS [Commonwealth of Independent States] or the Russia-Belarus Union, it was a 'defense shield' of a large space. Belarus thus is a 'corridor,' 'transit space,' 'a bridge between civilizations'; it is an 'outskirts,' a country located at a 'strategic crossroads.'"[144] These images, according to Okara, are not particularly uplifting. As for Okara's conferring to Belarus the status of an Orthodox country, this, as we know, is not accurate, although most Belarusians have an Orthodox background indeed. This misstatement, however, points to a problem: there is no single Belarusian identity.

Wlodzimierz Pawluczuk echoes Okara as he invokes a contrast between the national ideas of Belarus and Ukraine but highlights a different aspect of the issue. According to Pawluczuk,

> [The] Ukrainian national mythology flows from the religious sources of eastern Christianity and from the Cossack and peasant ethos. . . . As for the Belarusian mythology, it draws from other religious sources and a different ethos. The religion is Catholicism. The ethos is affection of landed gentry for peasants and a moral obligation to embrace peasant cultural values, thus fostering [shared identity] amidst many unrelated people and disassociating them from the Russians. Belarus does not know martyrs of the national cause or heroes like Sagaidachny, Khmielnitsky, or Bandera. The national mystique of Belarus has to do with personalities that are total outsiders with respect to a living and cultural universe of ordinary people. Such a personality from the past is Kastus Kalinowski; a current personality of the same kind is Zianon Pazniak.[145]

Pawluczuk berates Pazniak's 1991 plan of Belarusification of Belarus, described in the 1991 book *Inshadumtsy*,[146] as adventurous, coercive, top down, and elitist. In contrast to Okara, Pawluczuk reaffirms the Catholic roots of Belarusian nationalism, and this points to the same problem: Belarusian identity is Janus-faced, so national consolidation on some commonly accepted principles is badly needed.

TIME FOR NEW PURSUITS:
TEN CENTURIES OF BELARUSIAN HISTORY

After the new and painful setbacks of 1995 and later years, the Belarusian Westernizers have been regrouping. Apparently, a lot of soul-searching has taken place. Now, many prefer to distance themselves from Pazniak and his radicalism.

The newly adopted gradualist approach stems from a renewed awareness of the sheer enormity of the task; and it involves much writing that recasts history in a manner amenable to the westernizing stance. I am not sure that Belarusian authors have scrutinized Western scholarship on nationalism and national movements, but some authors proceed as though aided by a proper road map. For example, in Smith's typology of national myths, one may find a myth of the golden age, a myth of decline, and a myth of rebirth. "A younger nationalism," writes Smith, would portray its respective community as a "Sleeping Beauty, pricked by external forces of evil and put to sleep until the nationalist dawn arrives to restore the community to its true self in a new 'golden age.'"[147]

Some authors have attempted to separate the image of Belarus from that of Russia in the eyes and ears of a foreign audience by linguistic means. Vakar long stated that "as a rallying point of the new nationalism, the term 'Belorussian' presented certain inconveniences. Semantically, it was too close to Russia."[148] When in English the name of the country used to be transliterated as "Belorussia," the aforementioned inconveniences were all too obvious. While "Belarus" sounds "better" in this regard, the adjective "Belarusian" remains treacherous because in English it sounds nearly identical to "Belorussian." In his 1993 book, Zaprudnik attempts to purge the word of its "i" so that the resulting word, "Belarusan," can be traced to Rus' and not by any means to Russia. However, Zaprudnik's lead does not seem to have generated much following.[149]

A more important task focuses on the interpretations of early Belarusian history. According to Lindner's terse formula, "The issue of the ethnic origins of Belarusians has once again become, as during the 1920s, a historiographic question of faith."[150]

The monographs of westernizing nationalist historians, notably Mikola Yermalovich and Gennadz Saganovich, who set out to rewrite Russian renditions of regional history[151] are now available. These books, however, inspire but few sophisticated readers and do not affect the man in the street. Apparently recognizing this, Arlou (Orlov) and Saganovich issued a well-illustrated, two-hundred-page book, *Ten Centuries of Belarusian History, 862–1918*, intended for a mass audience and released in Belarusian and, separately, in Russian by a Vilnius-based publisher. This book is as direct an attempt to lend popular legitimacy to a certain version of Belarus's national mythology as there possibly can be, and it may become a milestone in the Belarusian national movement.

The book's recurring theme is disassociating Belarus from Russia by focusing on their allegedly inborn dissimilarities and on wounds Russia inflicted on the nations of which today's Belarus was part.

Arlou and Saganovich set out to challenge a situation whereby, in the words of Yury Drakokhrust and Dmitry Furman, "Belarusians and Russians do not share any negative historical memories about each other and do not have any negative or hostile stereotypes similar to those that exist, for example, between the peoples of the Baltic States and Russia."[152] The authors try to resolve the monumental problem of Belarusians' lasting anonymity by intermittently applying the token phrase "our country" to (1) a set of tenth- to twelfth-century neighboring princedoms, (2) the Grand Duchy of Lithuania, and (3) Rzeczpospolita.

In such a way, the ancestors of today's Belarusians are placed squarely in the anti-Russian camp. The Grand Duchy's military campaigns against Russia commenced in 1492 and culminated in the September 8, 1514, defeat of the Russian army near Orsha. "In 1992," write Arlou and Saganovich, "on the day of this battle's anniversary the Belarusian military pledged allegiance to their people on the Independence Square in Minsk."[153] In 1517, "Frantsishak Skaryna published the first Belarusian book in Prague thereby introducing Belarus into the fold of pan-European civilization."[154] "Just in the second half of the 16th century, so many books were published in Belarus that their total circulation exceeded that of Muscovy throughout the entire 16th century and the beginning of the 17th century by a factor of ten."[155]

The authors paint a vivid picture of the cruelties that accompanied the 1563 conquest of the enlightened city of Polotsk by the barbarian army of Ivan the Terrible. During his reign, "The bloody dictatorship inundated the country with informants and thugs. Monarchism and megalomania were implanted in the Russian national psyche at that time. It was that Moscow ruler that conferred upon Russia the legacy of a fully accomplished Asiatic autocracy, based on terror against fellow countrymen."[156] The war of 1654 to 1667 between Russia and Rzeczpospolita is characterized as "the most devastating war in our history,"[157] a direct shot at the neo-Soviet mythology that confers this status upon the 1941–1945 Great Patriotic War. According to Arlou and Saganovich, it was actually that seventeenth-century war that "deprived Belarusians of their elite, lower middle class, and entrepreneurs, as these strata suffered most of all. The remaining peasantry could not rise to national consolidation."[158] Broken down by the war with Russians, the region could no longer stage resistance to . . . Polonization.[159]

Other important episodes featured in the book concern the abortive history of the Uniate Church, which was by no means a sellout to Catholics; Peter the Great's unspeakable personal cruelty during his 1710 visit to the Polotsk Uniate Cathedral; an unusually cautious (compared with some other nationalist authors) Belarusization of Tadeusz Kosciuszko, a leader of the 1794 Polish uprising ("the uprising which our compatriot led"); and the horrendous mission of Alexander Suvorov, a Russian commander and yet another icon of Russian history. "For Russia, he was really a great military leader, but for Belarus, he was the commander of the occupiers in the first place."[160] To appreciate the sensitivity of this issue, one has to bear in mind that in the town of Kobrin, Brest Oblast, a Suvorov museum still glorifies the heroic deeds of that commander. And in 2007, a decision was passed to build a memorial architectural ensemble glorifying Suvorov, which will include an Orthodox church to be consecrated in Suvorov's name.

CONCLUSION

Today, roughly one hundred years since the Belarusian idea was packaged for popular consumption, there is still no single Belarusian identity, and the cultural elite of Belarus is split between the Westernizers (the heirs of the Grand Duchy of Lithuania) and the people with a pro-Moscow orientation (the de facto followers of West-Rusism). While these may be construed as political movements, they transcend politics, and so does the difference between them. Correspondingly, there are two competing sets of national symbols and two different mythologies to back them. Whereas the Westernizers nurture national myths that cast Belarus as a country apart from Russia almost from antiquity, others in the elite and many of the officialdom rely upon myths and symbols that evolved throughout more than two centuries of Belarusians and Russians living side by side in a common home, first in the Russian Empire and then in its successor state, the Soviet Union. The two groups celebrate different holidays. For the Westernizers, the major one is Liberty Day on March 25; on this day in 1918, the Belarusian People's Republic was proclaimed. For most Belarusians, however, the major holiday is July 3, on which day in 1944 the Soviet army liberated Minsk from the Nazi invaders.

These two visions of Belarus have not emerged during the postindependence period. Rather, they were articulated anew, but they in fact have lengthy historical roots. The preponderant Russophile orientation in Belarus stems from the Orthodox cultural tradition, Russia being the prime cultural donor of Belarus, and Russia's preeminent role in shaping Belarus's statehood. Still, the Westernizers have been successful in producing their brand of national mythology, and it may yet gain new converts.

Because of this lingering conflict, Belarusians suffer from a collective split-identity disorder. Their identity is Janus-faced, and so is Belarusian nationalism. Each "face" tries hard to pose as the only one, that is, the sole promoter of the Belarusian national cause. It is, however, their ambivalent and uneasy coexistence, their perpetual conflict, that constitutes Belarusian nationalism's hidden agenda. The side effects of this perpetual fight are apathy and cultural confusion among the rank-and-file Belarusians, who remain silent observers of the ongoing contest for their hearts.

NOTES

1. Yann Breault, "Establishing the Borders of the Collective Self: Lukashenka's Belarusian Policy for Foreignness (1994–2007)" (paper presented at the Twelfth Annual World Convention of the Association for the Study of Nationalities, New York, Columbia University, April 14, 2007).

2. Maxim Zhbankov, "Felix, kotoryi vsegda s toboi," *Nashe Mneniye*, June 1, 2006, at www.nmnby.org.

3. The pilot survey of sixty-two secondary school teachers was conducted in May and June 2002 in Minsk (two schools), Grodno (one school), and Vitebsk (one school).

4. Valer Bulgakau, online conference, *Forum*, Belarusian Service of Radio Liberty, May 31, 2006, at www.svaboda.org; by Bulgakau's admission, in the city of Vitebsk (four hundred thousand people), there are no more than twenty steady readers of *Arche*.

5. Nina B. Mečkovskaya, *Belorusskii yazyk: Sotsiolingvisticheskie ocherki* (Munchen: Verlag Otto Sagner, 2003), 22.

6. Miroslav Hroch, *Social Preconditions of National Revival in Europe: A Comparative Analysis of Patriotic Groups among the Smaller European Nations*, 2nd ed. (New York: Columbia University Press, 2000), 9.

7. Anthony D. Smith, *The Ethnic Origins of Nations*, 12th ed. (London: Blackwell, 1999), 36.

8. Viacheslav Nosevich, "Belorusy: Stanovleniye etnosa is 'natsionalnaya ideya,'" in *Belorussiya i Rossiya: Obshchestva i gosudarstva* (Moscow: Prava Cheloveka, 1998), 11–30.

9. Zakhar Shybeko, "Novaya i noveishaya istoriya Belarusi: Vazhneishiye sobytiya i osnovnye tendetntsii," *Russikii Vopros* 2 (2004), at http://russkiivopros.com.

10. Vladimir Orlov (Arlou) and Gennadz Saganovich, *Desiat' vekov belorusskoi istorii* (Vilnius: Nasha Buduchynia, 2001), 165. Some rank-and-file Uniates resisted conversion into Orthodoxy and were persecuted. Interestingly, Felix Dzierzynski, born in 1877 in Dzierzynovo (Oshmiany uyezd, Vilna Gubernia; now Stolbtsovsky Rayon, Minsk Oblast, Belarus), wrote in a letter to his wife that the stories about persecuted and slain Belarusian Uniates conveyed to him by his mother nudged him to become a revolutionary fighter against injustice and evil (an episode related in *Izvestia*, September 11, 2002, in an article pointedly titled "Krasnyi Bin Laden" (The red Bin Laden), at www.izvestia.ru/community/article23734).

11. Nosevich, "Belorusy."

12. This is despite the fact that, officially, Poles account for just 4.64 percent of the Novogrudek *rayon*'s population, according to *Natsional'nyi sostav naseleniya*

Respubliki Belarus i rasprostranionnost' yazykov, vol. 1 (Minsk: Ministerstvo Statistiki I Analiza, 2000), 176.

13. In the words of Valyantsyn Akudovich (V yakim kirunku razvivayetsa religiinaya palitika u Belarusi), *Ekspertiza Svabody*, Belarusian Service of Radio Liberty, April 6, 2007, at www.svaboda.org .

14. Such a church was established in Belarus under Nazi occupation, and all or most of its clerics left Belarus with the occupiers.

15. In 2004, there were 433 Catholic parishes with 410 active churches and 41 churches under construction. Out of 350 available priests, 196 were citizens of foreign countries, mostly Poland ("Etnokonfessionalnaya situatsiya v Respublike Belarus," at www.sovrep.gov.by/index.php/.531.2869...0.0.0.html).

16. Filaret routinely speaks of "our homeland stretching from Brest to Vladivostok."

17. Filaret's office once gained the right to export Belarusian vodka.

18. Personal interview with Stanislau Shushkevich, May 27, 2002.

19. Mečkovskaya, *Belorusskii yazyk*, 61.

20. This is Vladimir Abushenko's remark at the symposium devoted to Belarusian philosophy. Liudmila Rublevskaya, "Dumat Belarus," *Belarus Segodnia*, January 25, 2005.

21. Smith, *The Ethnic Origins of Nations*, 93.

22. V. I. Picheta, *Istoriya belorusskogo naroda* (Minsk: Izdatelskii Tsentr BGU, 2003), 17.

23. Mečkovskaya, *Belorusskii yazyk*, 76.

24. Nosevich, "Belorusy"; Curt Woolhiser, "Constructing National Identities in the Polish-Belarusian Borderlands," *Ab Imperio* (Kazan', Russia) 3 (2003): 293–346.

25. Woolhiser, "Constructing National Identities."

26. Oleg Trubachev, *V poiskakh Yedinstva: Vzgliad filologa na problemu istokov Rusi* (Moscow: Nauka, 1997), 127–29; for Trubachev, other confirmations of this pattern's validity are Akdengis—the Turkish name for the Aegean Sea—meaning White Sea and located west of Turkey, and Russia's White Sea, which for the most part lies west of the mouth of the North Dvina River, the northern outpost of Russian colonization of the European North.

27. See Nicholas Vakar, *Belorussia: The Making of a Nation* (Cambridge: Harvard University Press, 1956), 1–4.

28. R. Skliut, the émigré author of the preface to the 1953 Munich edition of Janka Kupala's play *Tuteishiya*, made a special point of the Polishness of this semianonymous cliché used as a "national pseudonym." The bottom line: even this self-effacing label is of alien origin; in Belarusian, it would rather be rendered as *tutashnii* or *gettashnii* (Janka Kupala, *Tuteishiya* [Munich: Batskaushchyna, 1953], 9).

29. Curt Woolhiser, "Constructing National Identities," 293–346.

30. Orlov and Saganovich, *Desiat' vekov belorusskoi istorii* (Vilnius: Nasha Buduchynia, 2001), 11.

31. M. I. Yermalovich, *Pa sliadakh adnago mifa* (Minsk: Belaruskaya Navuka, 2002), 29.

32. Sergei Markov, "Zachem Rossii nuzhna Belarus," August 24, 2001, at www.strana.ru/print/975679610.html.

33. Vitaut Kipel, *Belarusans in the United States* (Lanham, MD: University Press of America, 1999), 9.

34. Cited in Bazyli Białokozowicz, *Miedzy wschodem a zachodem* (Bialystok: Bialowieza, 1998), 57.

35. Smith, *The Ethnic Origins of Nations*, 93.

36. Hroch, *Social Preconditions*, xiii.

37. Hroch, *Social Preconditions*, 158.

38. Jan Zaprudnik, "Belorussia and the Belorussians," in *Handbook of Major Soviet Nationalities*, ed. Zev Katz, Rosemarie Rogers, and Frederic Harned (New York: The Free Press, 1975), 64.

39. Mečkovskaya, *Belorusskii yazyk*, 52–53.

40. Białokozowicz, *Miedzy wschodem a zachodem* 59.

41. Orlov and Saganovich, *Desiat' vekov Belorusskoi istorii*, 204–205.

42. Alexander Tsvikevich, *Belarus: Politicheskii ocherk* (Berlin: Izdaniye Diplomaticheskoi Missii BNR, 1919), 24–25.

43. Mečkovskaya, *Belorusskii yazyk*, 58.

44. Mečkovskaya, *Belorusskii yazyk*.

45. Jerzy Turonek, *Bialorus pod okupacja niemiecka* (Warsaw: Ksiazka i Wiedza, 1993), 21.

46. Białokozowicz, *Miedzy wschodem a zachodem*, 149.

47. Krivichi is the name of a large East Slavic tribe, the precursors of the Belarusians.

48. Białokozowicz, *Miedzy Wschodem a zachodem*, 61.

49. The ethnic makeup of Vilna, according to the Russian census of 1897, was Jews (40 percent), Poles (30.1 percent), Russians (20.9 percent), Belarusians (4.3 percent), Lithuanians (2.1 percent), etc. See http://en.wikipedia.org/wiki/Ethnic_composition_of_Central_Lithuania#Russian_census_of_1897.

50. Shybeko, "Novaya i noveishaya istoriya Belarusi," 2.

51. Mečkovskaya, *Belorusskii yazyk*, 28.

52. Mečkovskaya, *Belorusskii yazyk*, 58–59.

53. Alyaxander Tsvikevich, *Zapadno-russizm: Narysy s gistoryi gramadskai mysli na Belarusi u 19 i pachatku 20 v* (Mensk: Belaruskaya Dziarzavnaye Vydavetstva, 1929).

54. In the play itself, it is a Polish interrogator who actually calls Taraškevič a man of Polish culture (Sakrat Yanovich, *Arysht*, Kamunikat, at http://kamunikat.net.iig.pl/www/czasopisy/termapily/02/04.htm).

55. Tsvikevich, *Zapadno-russizm*, 332–33.

56. Ivan Lukyanovich Solonevich (1891–1953), *Epoch Times International*, at www.epochtimes.ru (accessed August 1, 2007).

57. Tsvikevich, *Zapadno-russizm*, 182.

58. This 1891 book was published in Cracow, Poland, under the pseudonym Macei Buraczok (Uladzimer Arlou [Vladimir Orlou], "1891, Vyishla u svet kniga Frantsishka Bagushevicha 'dudka belaruskaya,'" at http://knihi.com/10viakou/10v417.html [accessed August 1, 2007]).

59. Ye. F. Karski, *Belorusy*, vol. 1 (Minsk: BelEn, 2006) (reprinted from the 1904 Wilno edition). Two subsequent volumes of Karski's work under the common title *Belorusy* (Belarusians) were published in parts from 1908 to 1912 (volume 2) and from 1916 to 1922 (volume 3) in St. Petersburg.

60. Tsvikevich, *Zapadno-russizm*, 336.

61. Tsvikevich, *Zapadno-russizm*, 286.

62. Tsvikevich, *Zapadno-russizm*, 190.

63. Vasil Bykau, *Dougaya daroga dadomu* (Minsk: Kniga, 2002), 394.

64. Sergei Shapran, "Otets mechtal zhit v svoyei strane i govorit na svoyom yazyke," *Komsomolskaya Pravda v Belarusi*, June 22, 2004, at www.charter97.org/rus/news/2004/06/22/bykov.

65. Fiodor Turuk, *Belorusskoye dvizheniye* (Moscow: Gosizdat, 1921), 12–13.

66. Turuk, *Belorusskoye dvizheniye*, 32.

67. Tsvikevich, *Zapadno-russizm*, 62; *The West Russian Herald* was a journal promoting West-Rusism.

68. Mikola Shkialionek, *Belarus i susedzi* (Bialystok: Belaruskaya Gistarychnaye Tavarystva, 2003), 225–26.

69. T. M. Mikulich, *Mova i etnichnaya samasviadomasts* (Minsk: Navuka i Technika, 1996), 48.

70. A spelling discrepancy, "Belarusan" instead of "Belarusian," is explained on p. 66.

71. Wojtek Kosc, "To Be Belarusan in Bialystok," *Central Europe Review*, September 17, 1999, at www.ce.-review.org/99/13/kosc13.html (accessed July 1, 2001).

72. L. V. Tereshkovich, "Obshchestvennye dvizheniya v sovremennoi Belorussii: kratkii kommentarii k dokumentam," in *Grazhdanskie dvizheniya v Belorussii: dokumenty i materialy, 1989–1991* (Moscow: TSIMO, 1991), 28, 31. Note that the menace of Polonization is brandished 219 years after the incorporation of Belarus into the Russian Empire and 53 years after the unification of Belarus. Apparently, the genuinely Belarusian national movement did not develop much in the meantime.

73. Jan Zaprudnik, *Belarus at a Crossroads in History* (Boulder, CO: Westview Press, 1993), 45.

74. Zaprudnik, *Belarus at a Crossroads*, 66.

75. Zaprudnik, *Belarus at a Crossroads*, 217–18.

76. Zaprudnik, *Belarus at a Crossroads*, 221.

77. Zaprudnik, *Belarus at a Crossroads*, 216.

78. Andrzej Sadowski, *Pogranicze polsko-bialoruskie: Tozsamosc mieskancow* (Bilaystok: Trans Humana, 1995), 118.

79. *Natsional'nyi sostav naseleniya Respubliki Belarus i rasprostranionnost' yazykov* (Minsk: Ministerstvo Statistiki i Analiza, 2001), 16.

80. Calculated on the basis of Robert Kaiser, *The Geography of Nationalism in Russia and the USSR* (Princeton, NJ: Princeton University Press, 1994), 161, and *Natsional'nyi sostav naseleniya Respubliki Belarus i rasprostranionnost yazykov* (Minsk: Ministerstvo Statistiki i Analiza, 2001), 16.

81. Vakar, *Belorussia*, 121.

82. Sadowski, *Pogranicze polsko-bialoruskie*, 73–74.

83. Sadowski, *Pogranicze polsko-bialoruskie*, 119.

84. Mariusz Kowalski, "Bialorusini w Polsce wedlug spisu 2002," *Najwyzszy czas*, May 15, 2004; Krzysztof Goss, "Ilu w ktorej gminie Bialorusinow," *Przaglad Prawoslawny* 1 (2004).

85. Yauhen Miranovich, "Asimilyatsiya belarusau Belastochyny," *Niva*, January 25, 2004.

86. Jan Maksimyuk, "Belarusky narod—shmatmouny i shmatkulturny," Belarusian Service of Radio Liberty, June 23, 2007, at www.svaboda.org.

87. Kowalski, "Bialorusini w Polsce."

88. Kowalski, "Bialorusini w Polsce."

89. Kowalski, "Bialorusini w Polsce"; most college-educated and urban Poles who remained east of the Polish border after the war left for Poland when allowed to do so under Nikita Khrushchev.

90. Although these are just "passport Poles," Polish identity is claimed by a larger group than that of "passport Poles."

91. Kowalski, "Bialorusini w Polsce."

92. Yelena Tusevich, "Zhiviom bez ogliadki na natsionalnost," *Belarus Segodnia*, August 16, 2005.

93. Sadowski, *Pogranicze polsko-bialoruskie*, 120.

94. Sadowski, *Pogranicze polsko-bialoruskie*, 165–66.

95. "Pra zhishchene rezhimam Lukashenki Belaruskai movy i pra neabkhodnast yae abarony," Deklaratsiya Soimu BNF Adradzhene i Kanservatyvno-Khrystsyianskai Partyi—BNF, April 4, 2002.

96. Tomasz Zarzycky, "Uses of Russia: The Role of Russia in the Modern Polish National Identity," *East European Politics and Societies* 18, no. 2 (2004): 1–33; Zbigniew Rykiel, *Podstawy geografii politycznej* (Warsaw: Polskie Wydawnictwo Economiczne, 2006), 135–42.

97. In fact, this is the central message of West-Rusism. Alexander Tsvikevich went to great length criticizing this message in his work *Pagliad P. Bezsonava na belarusskuyu spravu* (Kouna: Drukarnia Baka, 1922).

98. Aleg Latyszonek, "Karysny perapis," *Niva*, January 25, 2004.

99. Jan Czykwin, "My khotim svoyei rabotoi podderzhivat natsionalnoe samosoznanie," *Euramost*, September 7, 2005, at www.euramost.org.

100. Kowalski, "Bialorusini w Polsce."

101. Sergei Markov, "Zachem Rossii nuzhna Belarus," August 24, 2001, at www.strana.ru/print/975679610.html.

102. Smith, *The Ethnic Origins of Nations*, 136.

103. "Westernizers" is a habitual term in the context of Russian culture. It is tempting to adopt exactly the same term with regard to one particular strand of Belarusian nationalism.

104. Zaprudnik, *Belarus at a Crossroads*, 164.

105. The ideological attack on Yevfimii Karski orchestrated by the editor of the Minsk-based daily *Zviazda* in 1927 is just one example of this "success." See Liudmila Rublevskaya and Vital Skalaban, "Okolonauchnyi spor," *Belarus Segodnia*, January 20, 2006.

106. Vakar, *Belorussia*, 246.

107. Nikolai Zen'kovich, *Tainy ukhodiashchego veka* (Moscow: Olma Press, 2000), 258.

108. Vakar, *Belorussia*, 263.

109. According to Vakar, the Weissruthenische Generalbezirk included Smolensk Oblast of Russia and Belarus without Gomel, Pinsk, and Brest Oblasts, which were subordinated to the Reichscommissar of Ukraine, while Bialystok, which in 1939 to 1941 had been part of Soviet Belarus, was included in East Pussia (Vakar, *Belorussia*, 176).

110. Vakar, *Belorussia*, 199–206.

111. Jerzy Turonek, *Bialorus pod okupacja nimiecka* (Warsaw: Ksiazka i Wiedza, 1993), 99.

112. Martin Dean, *Collaboration in the Holocaust: Crimes of the Local Police in Belarus and Ukraine, 1941–1944* (New York: St. Martin's Press, 2000), 155.

113. Dean, *Colloboration*.

114. John Loftus, *The Belarus Secret* (New York: Alfred A. Knopf, 1982).

115. *Belarusian Anti-Communism: Nazi and CIA Connection*, at www.geocities .com/dudar2000/Bcc.htm (accessed September 22, 2007).

116. Kipel, *Belarusans in the United States*, 18.

117. "Partizantka i kalyabaratsiya u Belarusi," *Praski Accent*, a talk show of the Belarusian Service of Radio Liberty, March 28, 2005.

118. "Partizantka i kalyabaratsiya u Belarusi,"

119. Dean, *Collaboration*," 101, 197.

120. "Partizantka i kalyabaratsiya u Belarusi," *Praski Accent*, a talk show of the Belarusian Service of Radio Liberty, March 28, 2005.

121. "Partizantka i kalyabaratsiya u Belarusi."

122. "Partizantka i kalyabaratsiya u Belarusi."

123. "Partizantka i kalyabaratsiya u Belarusi."

124. "Atsenka vainy: Natsiyanalnaya tsi universalnaya," *Prasky Accent*, a talk show of the Belarusian service of Radio Liberty, May 8, 2007, at www.svaboda.org.

125. Turonek, *Bialorus pod okupacja niemiecka*, 241.

126. Shybeko, "Novaya i noveishaya istoriya Belarusi," 5.

127. Yury Shevtsov, *Obyedinionnaya natsiya: Fenomen belarusi* (Moscow: Yevropa, 2005), 75.

128. The most prominent Nazi collaborator, General Andrei Vlasov, was an ethnic Russian.

129. According to a very conservative estimate by Aleg Gardiyenka, in Belarus the ratio of collaborators to partisans was approximately 1:4 ("Belaruskaya kalyabaratsiya: Yakaya yana byla?" *Expertiza Svabody*, a talk show of the Belarusian Service of Radio Liberty, March 28, 2005, at www.svaboda.org).

130. Pavel Polian, *Ne po svoyei vole: Istoriya i geografiya prinuditel'nykh migratsiss v SSSR* (Moscow: OGI, 2001), 135–36.

131. A detailed account can be found in David Marples, *Belarus: A Denationalized Nation* (Amsterdam: Harwood, 1999), 54–60.

132. Marples, *Belarus*, 4.

133. Smith, *The Ethnic Origins of Nations*, 15.

134. Smith, *The Ethnic Origins of Nations*, 16–17.

135. Smith, *The Ethnic Origins of Nations*, 178.

136. Hroch, *Social Preconditions*, xv.

137. Irina Khalip, "Chtoby bylo muchitel'no bol'no," *Belorusskaya Delovaya Gazeta*, November 20, 2001, at http://bdg.press.net.by/2001/11/2001.

138. Michael Urban, *An Algebra of the Soviet Power: Elite Circulation in Belorussian Republic, 1966–1986* (Cambridge: Cambridge University Press, 1989).

139. Rainer Lindner, "Besieged Past: National and Court Historians in Lukashenka's Belarus," *Nationalities Papers* 27, no. 4 (1999): 643.

140. This is Aleh Trusau's exact wording. Personal interview, May 23, 2002.

141. Valery Karbalevich, "Politicheskoye razvitiye i natsionalno-gosudarstvennye interesy respubliki Belarus," *Atkrytaye Gramadstva* 6, no. 1 (1999): 17.

142. Andrei Okara, "Belarus v otsutstvii tret'yei al'ternativy," *Russkii Zhurnal*, November 14, 2001, at www.russ.ru/politics/20011114-oka-pr.html.

143. Okara, "Belarus v otsutstvii tret'yei al'ternativy."

144. Andrei Okara, "Belarus: Severo-Zapadnye Gubernii Rossii ili Wschodnie kresy polski?" *Yevraziiskoye Obozreniye* 3, 2001, at http://eurasia.com.ru/eo/3-12.html.

145. Wlodzimierz Pawluczuk, "Ruskie drogi," *Polityka* 48, no. 2065 (November 30, 1996).

146. Aleksandr Ulitsionak, *Inshadumtsy=mysliashchie inache* (Minsk: Belarus, 1991).

147. Smith, *The Ethnic Origins of Nations*, 191.

148. Vakar, *Belorussia*, 4.

149. Actually, Vitaut Kipel also uses this spelling; I once came across it in *Niva*, a Belarusian-language weekly published in Bialystok, Poland.

150. Lindner, "Besieged Past," 633.

151. Lindner, "Besieged Past," presents a superb analysis of their work, as well as that of their neo-Soviet nemeses.

152. Margarita M. Balmaceda, James Clem, and Lisbeth Tarlow, eds., *Independent Belarus: Domestic Determinants, Regional Dynamics, and Implications for the West* (Cambridge, MA: Harvard University Press, 2002), 232.

153. Orlov and Saganovich, *Desiat' vekov belorusskoi istorii*, 89.

154. Orlov and Saganovich, *Desiat' vekov belorusskoi istorii*, 90.

155. Orlov and Saganovich, *Desiat' vekov belorusskoi istorii*, 109.

156. Orlov and Saganovich, *Desiat' vekov belorusskoi istorii*, 100.

157. Orlov and Saganovich, *Desiat' vekov belorusskoi istorii*, 111.

158. Orlov and Saganovich, *Desiat' vekov belorusskoi istorii*.

159. Orlov and Saganovich, *Desiat' vekov belorusskoi istorii*.

160. Orlov and Saganovich, *Desiat' vekov belorusskoi istorii*, 158.

3

Culture Wars, Soul-searching, and Belarusian Identity

A Belarusian exists, and at the same time he doesn't. Therefore one must either figure him out or track him down. This is always much like going after game.

A person who does not understand who he is, is actually a Belarusian. That, however, does not mean that others have any good understanding of him.

From Belarusians, like from a cocoon, sometimes come out "Russians." These are local silkworms.

—Ales Antsipenka[1]

This chapter deepens our inquiry into a key problem of delayed nation building: the lack of a single consolidating national idea of Belarus. I begin with observations on the Janka Kupala Drama Theater's production of *Tuteishiya*, a quintessential piece on Belarusian identity. The setting of this play,[2] written and performed in Belarusian, is the city of Minsk from 1914 to 1919. The word *tuteishiya* means "locals," but because Jews, Poles, and Russians living in Belarus never identified as *tuteishiya*, this nickname applies to the nationally indifferent, that is, to local Slavs without a clear national identity. Indeed, only three out of fifteen characters in the play refer to themselves, and are referred to by the rest, as Belarusians: Janka, a rural teacher; Alenka, much influenced by Janka's moralizing; and her father, Garoshka. Other characters do not subscribe to this ethnonym. According to Janka, they are all "renegades and degenerates." One of them is Mikita Znosak, whose proclivity to mimic Polish, Russian, German, and, in the end, Belarusian ways, depending on the political convenience of the moment, is scathingly parodied by Kupala. Two comical scientists repeatedly bump into one another, and their identically worded verdicts with regard to Belarus and Belarusians are expressed in Russian and Polish. Both scientists are also *tuteishiya*, but one of them refers to Belarus as Russia's *Severozapadnyi krai* (northwestern fringe) and the other as Poland's *Kresy Wschodnie* (eastern periphery). The play reflects Kupala's satirical attack on his fellow countrymen's lasting anonymity and on Russian and Polish claims on Belarus.

The Janka Kupala Drama Theater's production of *Tuteishiya*, which I watched on May 27, 2005, is superb. It has been on since 1990 (except for a one-and-a-half-year break). The plot unfolds in front of two places of worship, a Polish *kosciól* and a Russian Orthodox *tserkov'*. Both are represented as antinational forces, and Mikita's supposedly Belarusian home is niched right between them. A fixture of the Russian church is a revolving icon, with Jesus Christ on its one side and Karl Marx on the other; so when the moment is ripe the appropriate side is exhibited. In the final episode, which is absent in Kupala's text, Bolsheviks acting as one last incarnation of Russians shoot nationally indifferent and self-identified Belarusians alike.

Following the executions, a white-red-white flag[3] is revealed dangling from a crib. As the crib is lifted above the stage, the flag flutters in the air, signifying that while human bodies can be destroyed, the national spirit of Belarus is indestructible. This cathartic finale captivated the viewers of the May 2005 production, who stood up and kept a minute of silence that gave way to applause. On leaving the theater, however, the first thing that viewers caught sight of was the edifice of the presidential administration across the street, with a red-green banner on its rooftop.

To be sure, encounters with reality began even earlier, when the sales clerk in the box office and the staff selling playbills and working in the snack bar during the intermission all spoke Russian to their customers—in that Belarusian national theater. While I cannot assert that all viewers spoke to their companions in Russian, it is safe to assume that most did.

One's language of communication and one's national identity do not always match, though. In a Minsk-based survey,[4] 61 percent claimed that the ability to speak Belarusian is not an important factor uniting Belarusians into a single community. Yet, 71 percent said that Belarus should remain an independent country, and only 12 percent said it should unite with Russia into a single state. These results reinforce the suspicion that national identity and the ability to speak Belarusian are not in sync. Moreover, they have been evolving in opposite directions. In the past, when Belarus was more rural, more people spoke Belarusian, yet their identity presented a problem for researchers and, as we know, for playwrights as well. Today, however, far fewer people speak Belarusian, but not too many would doubt that Belarus is a separate nation, their nation, and should remain independent.

Belarusians' allegiance to Belarus's statehood is nonetheless tenuous. In Minsk, many more people are associated with national causes than elsewhere around the country. No wonder they value statehood. But when a national survey by the Independent Institute of Socio-Economic and Political Studies (IISEPS) in November 2003 asked, "What is more important to you, economic improvement or national independence?" the result was 62 percent versus 25 percent in favor of economic improvement. Even among the self-proclaimed supporters of the opposition, the ratio was 51.4 percent to 35.9 percent! That a question like this could even be included in a public survey in Russia, Poland, Latvia, or Lithuania is unthinkable because in those countries, statehood, as it is thought of, is of existential importance and not an option to be traded for a better life.[5]

When in May 2002 Vladimir Putin floated the idea that six regions of Belarus be incorporated into Russia one by one, some perceived it as odd, but many remained unruffled, and some even welcomed the idea. Putin's suggestion and the lack of its spontaneous repudiation by Belarusians may have been Alexander Lukashenka's first serious wake-up call during his tenure as president. In the autumn of 2002, after one more run-in between Lukashenka and Putin, all government-controlled media in Belarus began to criticize Russia. Belarusians appeared to be receptive to this change, and the idea of a Belarus-Russia union, let alone a merger with Russia altogether, cooled significantly. When on February 19, 2004, the flow of natural gas into Belarus was cut off for several hours to force Belarus to deliver on its overdue gas payment, Lukashenka did not miss his chance, calling this incident an act of terrorism against the Belarusian people.[6] The incident itself and Lukashenka's rhetoric combined to boost national consolidation in Belarus in an unprecedented way. A shrewd prediction began to materialize, according to which "the Belarus government . . . has no choice but to resort to the national awareness of the population as a sort of barrier against absorption of national sovereignty by Russia."[7] One opposition publisher even suggested that "as long as Lukashenka is certain that by asserting Belarusian sovereignty he is defending himself, he will be doing it 100 times more skillfully than even the most nationalist flank of the opposition."[8]

Having emerged from a contest with Putin as the clear winner, Lukashenka came across to many as a Belarusian nationalist by default, a *kind of* nationalist. Of course, this means that Belarusian nationalism has more than one strand. If a national project is a corpus of normative ideas about Belarus's past, present, and future, then there is more than one such project. I would like to preface my description of those projects by posing a question: do nations shape nationalism, or does nationalism shape nations? As a student in the Soviet Union, I thought the answer obvious: because being determines consciousness, nation comes first. Otherwise, Karl Marx and Friedrich Engels would not have distinguished historical nations from ahistorical ones, and Joseph Stalin, whose teachings influenced Soviet ethnography long after he was declared a thug, would not have come up with his four "objective" criteria for a nation.[9]

Whatever source on the ethnic history of Belarusians you use, be it a book or an article, recent or one hundred years old, you encounter a recurring theme: Belarusians do exist as a separate ethnicity. At first blush, this doesn't seem strange, but when you come across efforts to prove the existence of Belarusians for the umpteenth time, you become intrigued. Whether the refrain in question is couched in neutral terms, is shaped as a disclaimer (e.g., of course, we do not subscribe to those infamous views), or is a fervent rebuttal of somebody's ideas is a different matter, but the refrain itself is a palpable reality. Yury Shevtsov, who recognizes this reality, explains it by pointing to Belarusians' alleged aversion to open manifestation of identity ("Belarusian identity is there to comprehend, not to manifest"[10]). Viacheslav Nosevich, another Belarusian author, writes that Belarusians' ethnic territory was designated by the method of elimination, that is, by pinpointing areas not quite gravitating to Russian, Ukrainian, or Polish national centers.[11] While this may not be a very uplifting image, all efforts at proving Belarusians' existence as a separate ethnicity will prove redundant if we assume that "nationalism is not the awakening of nations to self-consciousness: it invents nations where they do not exist."[12] Embraced by most modern scholars of nationalism, this perspective provides only partial relief to students of Belarus: while no longer required to furnish proofs of the obvious, they ought to focus on a national project with the potential to consolidate Belarusians. But is there such a thing?

In chapter 2, I described the situation of Belarusian identity as a "split-identity disorder" unusual for a modern European ethnic group. I discerned two brands of national mythology: the westernizing brand and the Russophile brand. I observed that these brands are older than the Belarusian idea itself (i.e., the idea that Belarusians are a distinctive ethnic community), and they have been competing for the minds and souls of Belarusians and continue to pull in opposite directions.[13] The notion that three, not two, national projects on Belarus may actually exist took me aback. I believed that even two is one too many, as the perennial fight between them is not conducive to national consolidation. When, however, I began to read the journal *Arche*, a mouthpiece of Belarusian opposition, I found numerous references to three national projects and their respective core communities and descriptive labels. If all three projects are unanimous about one thing, it is the value of the national independence of Belarus.[14] Another shared feature is that the city of Minsk is home to a disproportionately high number of each project's activists.

PROJECT ONE: NATIVIST/PRO-EUROPEAN

Some of this project's framers, such as Valer Bulgakau, Igar Babkou, and Andrei Dynko, christened it as "nativist" and "pro-European." This project is the extension of the Belarusian Revival (*Adradzhennye*) idea envisaging Belarus's liberation from the shackles of Russian colonialism and rediscovering its (Belarus's) true European roots. Those who form a core community of this national project are Belarusian speakers by choice, the so-called *svyadomyya*, or nationally conscious Belarusians. The project has its own codified historical narrative. One of its best expressions, *Ten Centuries of Belarusian History* by Uladzimer Arlou (Orlov) and Gennadz Saganovich, a book earmarked for a popular audience, was discussed in chapter 2. The project sees the precursor of the Belarusian state in the Polatsk princedom, which was more open to Western influences than the Rostov-Suzdal and Vladimir princedoms, which formed the nucleus of Muscovy. Further on, the nucleus of Belarus developed within the Grand Duchy of Lithuania (GDL) and Rzeczpospolita, the European polities that waged wars with Asiatic Russia, and most ancestors of today's Belarusians were fighting not on Russia's side. Eventually, however, Russia's cunning and brute force gained the upper hand, and since 1772 Belarus has been Russia's colonial domain. It is now time to undo Russia's oppressive impact. Politically, the project is represented by the Belarusian Popular Front (BNF), whose founder, Zianon Pazniak, led the way in the nativist project from the late 1980s to his emigration in 1996. The viewpoints of the project's active promoters show up in the *Nasha Niva* weekly and the bimonthly journal *Arche*. The enthusiasts of the project listen to the Belarusian-language Radio Liberty broadcasts and are fixated on anti-Russian sentiment. "For people seeking identity and reinventing ethnicity, enemies are essential,"[15] writes Samuel P. Huntington. This maxim has ample confirmation in various texts authored by the activists of Project One, although the militant Russophobe attitude of Pazniak's vintage is rare these days. Disassociating Belarus from Russia is nevertheless the central idea of the project, whose framers take every opportunity to stress the importance of speaking Belarusian. For them, it is the only legitimate language of national discourse. They perceive the linguistic Belarusification of Belarus as instrumental in fostering a clear-cut national identity, which in turn facilitates democratization, not the other way around. Also, without switching to Belarusian, the monumental task of detaching Belarus from the inherently undemocratic Russia cannot be solved. Language is thought of as not only the means of communication but also a reflection of the soul of the Belarusian people. In that context, the expert opinions of a third party, that is, of someone who is neither Belarusian nor Russian, are particularly appreciated—if, of course, those opinions are in sync with Project One; they are scornfully castigated and disqualified if they are not.

As time goes by, fewer and fewer ideological nativists turn for spiritual guidance to Pazniak, who considers even Alexander Milinkevich (a 2006 presidential candidate from the opposition) and the BNF's leader Vintsuk Viachiorka to be Russian agents of influence. Moreover, Pazniak looks upon the entire segment of the anti-Lukashenka electorate not embracing his views as the cocreation of Russian and German intelligence.[16] Andrei Dynko, editor of the *Nasha Niva*, criticizes Pazniak for his contemptuous attitude toward other opposition leaders. Dynko also faults Pazniak's comrade-in-arms, Siarhei Navumchik, for trivializing economic issues to the point of declaring them completely irrelevant until the national symbols and language gain prominence in society. "Even as a matter of rhetoric, it is not worth declaring the priority of symbols over the economy,"[17] writes Dynko. Bulgakau, who edits the *Arche*, acknowledges that "the cost of acceptance by Belarus of a democratic model of Western type will be a prolonged economic crisis . . . and a decrease in social well-being. In order to withstand this and not roll back into authoritarianism, the society will have to demonstrate a conscious will."[18] Much patience and sacrifice must be put on the altar of a nationalist and democratic future. And because Belarusians are not about to embrace the national idea soon, Belarusian intellectuals ought to be prepared for long and tedious creative work that may take several decades.[19]

PROJECT TWO: MUSCOVITE LIBERAL

Until recently, Project Two was more of a putative or ad hoc intellectual niche, as the existence of its core constituency was far from self-evident. The fact that according to the 1999 census, 77 percent of Belarusian urbanites admitted to speaking predominantly Russian in their homes,[20] while most national surveys reveal an even higher percentage of Russian speakers, does not in and of itself suggest a separate national project. Many Russian-speaking intellectuals developed a habit of issuing public excuses for not conversing or writing in Belarusian. For a long time, the I-am-so-sorry-but-this-is-how-I-was-brought-up disclaimer created the impression that the entire nation-building theme had been farmed out to the nativist camp. At the same time, the self-imposed prerogative of Russian-speaking liberals was to display the abuses of the ruling regime in higher-circulation media outlets of the political opposition (as Belarusian-language publications are not read by many) and to issue pro-democracy statements. Indeed, in Belarus the most obvious mass alternatives to Russia-based media are not by any means the *Arche* or *Nasha Niva* but *Belarusskaya Delovaya Gazeta (BDG)*,[21] the daily *Komsomolskaya Pravda v Belarusi*, and the website Naviny.by, all of which use Russian. The bilingual newspaper *Narodnaya Volya* is also quite popular in Minsk. To be sure, there are many Belarusian-language websites, but sociologist Vladimir Dorokhov, who recorded the frequencies of their use and that of their Russian-language counterparts on a random day in August 2005, has revealed that the Russian-language site Naviny.by was accessed 1,466 times and the *BDG* site, 1,354 times, whereas the Belarusian-language *Nasha Niva*, the de facto major organ of the nativist project, had only thirty-nine visitors.[22]

The rift between two groups of Belarusian intellectuals, the Belarusian-speaking minority and the Russian-speaking majority, is older than the Lukashenka regime. In fact, this is an ideological divide whose origins cannot be reduced to language alone; it is reflected in publications dating back to 1990, if not earlier. For example, Pazniak's 1990 article in *Narodnaya Gazeta*, claiming that though close to each other linguistically, Belarusians and Russians belong in "different races, different cultures, and different value systems, and their historical destinies are different as well,"[23] sparked polemics. A book by Semion Bukchin carefully documents these and other polemics between 1990 and 1994. Bukchin's position suggests that in Belarus, to be critical of Lukashenka and preach democratic values does not spell unanimity on other important issues.

Throughout the 1990s, quite a few self-proclaimed democrats came to resent the BNF-centered nativist community's monopoly on Belarusian nationalism. Aversion to the national radicalism of Pazniak's vintage became widespread, if not overwhelming, in Belarus. At the same time, Russian speakers were reevaluating their ambivalent relationship with Russia on a personal level, and many were concluding, well, I may be a person of Russian culture, but I stand for an independent Belarus, my homeland.

In 1998, Yury Drakokhrust (figure 3.1), a former secretary of the BNF, published an article titled "Belarusian Nationalism Speaks Russian."[24] In it, he shared the results of a 1997 national survey by IISEPS, according to which Russian speakers are on average much less Lukashenka friendly than Belarusian speakers, who are rural villagers for the most part. This conclusion clashed with the iconoclastic nativist message disseminated since the late 1980s, according to which Belarusian speakers form the most dynamic and vividly antiregime group. The entire political opposition and its sympathizers were divided in their reaction to Drakokhrust's article. Those who shared the view that the relatively few Belarusian urbanites who spoke Belarusian ought to renounce their monopoly on Belarusian nationalism began to realize that they were not alone. A community of like-minded people began to form. Among them were such personalities as Svetlana Alexievich, arguably Belarus's best-known living author; Alexander Feduta, a philologist who in 1994 was part of Lukashenka's presidential team and then publicly apologized for his role; Sergei Pankovsky, the editor in chief of the website *Nashe Mneniye*; Leonid Zayiko and Leonid Zlotnikov, both prominent economists, as is Stanislaw Bogdankevich, the first chairman of Belarus's National Bank; Semion Bukchin, Yury Drakokhrust, and a few other well-known people. When in late 2004, the *Arche*, a mouthpiece of the nativist project, rounded up "twelve outstanding Russian-speaking intellectuals of Belarus" for an interview,[25] it effectively defined the core of Project Two's constituency.

In 2005, Drakokhrust published a sequel to his 1998 article. This time, he wrote in Belarusian and published in the *Arche*. The sequel draws from both 1997 and 2004 national polls by IISEPS, which had just been denied registration by the Lukashenka regime. In response to a question from the 2004

Figure 3.1.   Yury Drakakhrust (editor, Belarusian Service of Radio Liberty, Prague).
Photo courtesy of Yury Drakakhrust

national poll, "How would you vote in a possible referendum about the future of Belarus?" twice as many Belarusian speakers opted for unification with Russia than Russian speakers! Obviously, it was mostly, if not exclusively, the voice of rural Belarusian speakers revealing their strong pro-Russia leaning. But this was at odds with their urban counterparts' contention that they are the spokesmen for the Belarusian people. On the contrary, the 2004 national survey confirmed that many more Russian speakers would like to see Belarus in the European Union compared with their Belarusian-speaking compatriots. Also, many more Russian speakers see the precursor of Belarus's statehood in the GDL and fewer in the Belarusian Soviet Socialist Republic (BSSR), as compared with Belarusian speakers.

"Sometimes one can hear," writes Drakakhrust, "that in contemporary Belarus a struggle is under way between two [groups], the one which is simultaneously Belarusian-speaking, pro-independence, and pro-Europe and the one which is simultaneously Russian-speaking, pro-Russia, and anti-West."[26] According to Drakakhrust, this is wrong. "The Russian-speaking-anti-Lukashenka-and-pro-Europe group is here as well. That representatives of this group act on behalf of Russian-speakers may not be quite noticeable today because it would be stupid to fight for their linguistic preferences now that the regime is stifling the Belarusian language and culture, not Russian. But this is not to say that such a fight will not commence under the conditions of free society, particularly if an attempt is made to encroach on the interests of the Russian speakers."[27] The competition between the Belarusian- and Russian-speaking segments of society will then come to a head, the argument goes. It is by no means a product of the Lukashenka regime and will only get more acrimonious and destructive for Belarus when this regime falls. And because Belarus does not have its own equivalent of either Ukraine's Galicia or Crimea, which would ensure a modicum of spatial separation between the diehard linguistic nationalists, this fight threatens to possess the entire country. Knowing this, says Drakakhrust, why do we not sign a kind of Geneva Convention on culture wars in advance, in which we will stipulate mutual recognition and respect and reject either linguistic community's monopoly on Belarusian nationalism?

NATIVISTS VERSUS MUSCOVITE LIBERALS: A SPARRING MATCH

Three ripostes to Drakakhrust's article showed up in the *Arche*. Alongside the view mainstream to the nativist project—that democratization is impossible without joining Europe, Europe is a community of nation states, and without linguistic Belarusification, we cannot become a nation and are doomed to remain a Eurasian satrapy—the ripostes hit below the belt. For example, Bulgakau declared that all that number crunching (Drakakhrust's findings were drawn from cross-tabulated results of the national survey) was not persuasive because, truth be told, Western sociologists normally entrust their Belarusian collaborators only with data collection, not analysis.[28] A more serious argument put forward by Danila Zhukovsky was that Drakakhrust had correlated the actual language use with political and geopolitical preferences. Whereas real-life options are usually limited, however, values by their nature are wider ranging, and Drakakhrust had omitted certain value options. For example, some people are adamantly opposed to Belarusian and hate it.[29] To that argument, Drakakhrust replied that his circle of Russian-speaking acquaintances did not include haters. While these people may in fact exist, the most widespread attitude to Belarusian in Belarusian society is not hatred but well-meaning indifference. To make his case, Drakakhrust prefaced his response to Zhukovsky with an epigraph reproducing a real-life conversation between a correspondent of Radio Liberty and a passerby in a Minsk street.

"Do you speak Belarusian?" asks the reporter.
"Rarely," replies the passerby.
"And why don't Belarusians speak Belarusian?" the reporter asks.
"Apparently they don't have time to," the passerby responds.[30]

This answer, argues Drakakhrust, is an expression of indifference to something that constitutes a deviation from an established societal norm in Belarus, which is to speak Russian. Those who risk violating this norm may be courageous people, but they should not get angry if not too many join their ranks. Otherwise, they will fan the flames of a culture war, which at one point already produced an autocrat whose first widely acclaimed action was to protect his people from "nationalists" (which in Russian is close to a swear word, whose actual meaning is "xenophobes").

Nothing validates the notion of a culture war as convincingly as the August and September 2005 polemics triggered by the decision of Deutsche Welle, a German broadcaster, to begin transmission of its short-wave half-hour roundups of Belarusian news and politics for Belarus's audience. Shortwave receivers are no longer in wide use, and there are other reasons as well why Deutsche Welle's new project was not going to make much of a difference. But the broadcaster's decision to use Russian, not Belarusian, brought about the stormiest public debate ever amid opposition-minded intelligentsia in Belarus. There is no doubt that the skirmish pleased Lukashenka. Those who call it a tempest in a teapot are certainly not Belarus watchers. To me, for example, this public exchange of views confirmed the idea that Project Two exists. The exchange was sparked by Vital Silitski, a Belarusian political scientist who used to be affiliated with the National Endowment for Democracy in Washington, D.C. In an open letter, Silitski claimed that the German broadcaster's decision to use Russian in their new project was "despicable" and a testimony to European bureaucrats' "wholesale support of the politics of annihilation of the Belarusian language and culture."[31] The letter was signed by several people whose engagement with Project One (a.k.a., the nativist/pro-European project) is well known. Silitski's letter contained the caveat that he was not calling for "removal of Russian from Belarus's media space." Rather, he was "protesting removal of Belarusian from that space."[32] However, this disclaimer did not fit the tenor of the letter, which ended up with an appeal to Belarusian politicians, journalists, analysts, and public servants to boycott the new radio project until it changed its language policy.

Publication of Silitski's letter aroused "sound and fury." Scores of individuals went public with their statements. Here are some voices in the debate.

Alexander Feduta

- If they [the nativists] see us as part of the Belarusian context, they would not just bemoan the lack of a Nobel Prize for a pro-democracy Belarusian. They would collect all the pieces by Svetlana Alexievich translated into European languages and begin a lobbying campaign. Would they agree to this, though? No. And if we initiate this, they would say something like "A Nobel for Alexievich is another nail in the coffin for Belarusian." And there will be another brawl like this one about the Deutsche Welle, or worse.[33]

Yury Drakakhrust

- They [the nativists] believed that their Russian-speaking compatriots are beholden to Moscow like Muslims are to Mecca, which they face during their prayers. It turned out, however, that those Russian speakers are also Europeans, and what is particularly troubling is that Europe itself does not deny them that.
- A Russian-language national project on Belarus, the project whose existence [they] doubt, effectively exists. One ought to take off his or her ideological glasses. He or she would then see that in quite a few areas this project is a more serious challenge to the influences of Russia [than the nativists themselves].[34]

Vadim Kaznacheyev

- A remark about the lack of respect to the language of the titular nationality of Belarus does not make sense because the language of the vast majority of this nationality is Russian.
- You [nativists] publish stern statements. But the very tone of your appeals is a problem. What if you come to power? Will you then resist the temptation to resort to forcible methods [of implanting Belarusian]?[35]

Svetlana Alexievich

- Belarusians do not perceive Russian as the language of the occupiers.
- The people from the *Arche* and *Nasha Niva* do not represent Belarusian people. What they represent is their dream about Belarusian people.
- In my books, I convey in Russian my love to Belarus.[36]

Perhaps the most impressive of the nativist responses to "Muscovite Liberals" was by Dynko, editor in chief of the *Nasha Niva* (figure 3.2). "A novel reflecting the Belarusian's pain for his/her language has not been written yet," writes Dynko. Referring to relations between himself and his comrades in arms, on the one hand, and Russian speakers on the other, he poses a question: "Are we going to fight for democratic Belarus shoulder to shoulder, or just side by side?" Shoulder to shoulder is Dynko's own choice. "Whether Russian can become the basis for the national discourse in Belarus requires proof. So, go ahead, prove; but this is risky,"[37] cautions Dynko. And yet, "You are our allies, and you are no Moscow stooges; you are part of our world," says Dynko to Russian-speaking liberals. This was like extending an olive branch, and some on the other side responded in kind. Conciliatory though it is, Dynko's peacemaking is not without qualifications. "My principle," writes Dynko, "is that any new initiative or project must be couched in Belarusian, as Russian-language projects do not need help—they will appear on their own."[38] In Drakakhrust's rendition, this message reads, "Beautiful flowers need to be tended, while useless weeds appear on their own."[39] Dynko ends his letter to *Nashe Mneniye* with an appeal: "Let us proceed together, we know where to go."[40] This self-assured possession of the right knowledge irritated some of Dynko's opponents. Apparently, Dynko meant reconciliation but on his own terms. The message of Dynko's article in the *Nasha Niva* was equally ambivalent. On the one hand, "we remain insensitive to Russophiles; we do not monitor their evolution and do not take their interests into account. . . . It is difficult for us to comprehend how one can be a Moscowphile and at the same time want to build an independent Belarus. Let us leave this behind.

Figure 3.2. Andrei Dynko (editor, *Nasha Niva*, the major opposition-minded newspaper).

. . . By and large they also see themselves as designers of Belarus. Yes, *according to their project*, but on Belarus, not West Russia" (emphasis added).[41] On the other hand, however, "it is difficult to build a bilingual Belarus without a moment of symbolic repentance to the Belarusian language." Also, "Germans [i.e., the Deutsche Welle] give you back to Russian Europe, and you, nationalists—you are Russian-peaking Belarusian nationalists, after all—consent to that." At the end of this article, Dynko admits, "Our discussions about national interests influence the part of the social elite loyal to Lukashenka, *this third side of the Belarusian triangle*"[42] (emphasis added). So, what about that third side?

PROJECT THREE: CREOLE

The third national project on Belarus is labeled Creole. This label was borrowed from Mykola Ryabchuk, a Ukrainian philosopher who spent about ten years calling into question dichotomies like Russians/Ukrainians, Ukrainian speakers/Russian speakers, and nationally conscious/*mankurty*.[43] For

Ryabchuk, Creoles are those Ukrainians who enthusiastically support Ukrainian statehood, yet speak Russian as their primary language and distance themselves from other sociocultural aspects of Ukrainianness.[44]

Uladzimer Abushenka, Valerka Bulgakau, Andrei Dynko, Igar Babkou, and other activists of Project One began to make use of this term in Belarus, which points to a certain evolution in nativist thinking. For much of the 1990s, they repeatedly accused the Belarusian masses of being nationally indifferent *mankurty*. It now appears, however, that many Belarusians who speak *trasianka*, which is phonetically Belarusian and lexically Russian, are quite patriotic and nationalistic. As described by Abushenka, these people are midway in their sociocultural evolution. For them, things Russian no longer belong in "we," but they cannot be assigned to "they" yet. Similar ambiguity typifies their attitude toward things Belarusian. Creole consciousness is a kind of extrapolation of *tuteishasts* (i.e., a Belarusian variety of localism).[45]

Creole is essentially a prenational consciousness. Babkou believes that it has long existed in areas that straddle a kind of cultural divide where the peripheries of adjacent cultural zones come together. Belarus is just such a place.[46] Bulgakau, who until recently was prone to a more politicized, flashy, and straight-arrow language than his philosophic friends, writes, "Russian and Pigeon-speaking Creoles with national passports of the republic of Belarus are . . . the political resource for sustaining the political regime created by Lukashenka. Owing to their sense of cultural inferiority and therefore psychological instability, they appear to be particularly receptive to ideological indoctrination. . . . Lukashenka's 1995 and 1996 referenda removed all the constraints from reproduction of Creole consciousness . . . and made it the major goal of his state policy."[47]

It becomes clear from this declaration not only that the Creole component is dominant in Belarus's population but also that Lukashenka is in fact the president of Creoles. "The Creole masses not so much threaten Belarus's independence as ensure that the authoritarian regime is stable and unassailable."[48] And "Lukashenka's standing is at its weakest not where Russian democratic influence |read Project Two| is at its highest but where Belarusian culture and Catholic anti-imperial ethos survived the best."[49] This last statement is important, as it portrays Projects One and Three as antagonistic but having local roots, whereas Project Two is a mere nuisance not potentially instrumental in getting rid of Lukashenka.

The framers of Project Three (such as Anatoly Rubinov, Eduard Skobelev, Lev Krishtapovich, and Pavel Yakubovich) are associated with Lukashenka's presidential administration. They supervise the development of what is called the "state ideology of the Republic of Belarus," the major components of which are the historic attachment of Belarus to Russia, the role of the Great

Patriotic War of 1941 to 1945 that cemented this bond, a communal and antientrepreneurial ethos, and (however ironic it sounds in conjunction with national ideology) an antinationalist sentiment directed squarely against the nativists. Only in this context can you appreciate one reference to Lukashenka as "the main anti-Belarusian nationalist of Belarus."[50]

Because in Russian "nationalism" is given a bad name, "antinationalist" might be translated as "averse to xenophobia," if in fact the term did not also include aversion to Belarusian nationalists of the nativist strand, whose spiritual mentors, such as Radaslau Astrousky, Fabian Akinchyts, and Yaukhim Kipiel, collaborated with the Nazis.[51] It is little wonder that so much has been made of this collaboration by Lukashenka's staff propagandists. After all, more than one-quarter of Belarus's population perished in World War II.

The "state ideology of the Republic of Belarus" is still under construction, though, and there is no accomplished version of it. If anything, unsteady interpretations pertain more to the past than to the future, which is envisaged as a patrimonial welfare state with elements of a market economy. But there is no codified narrative of the pre-Soviet past. Although some Creole ideologues incorporate historical myths cultivated by Project One, they steer clear of prominent personalities with Catholic roots, such as Tadeusz Kosciuszko and Adam Mickiewicz. There is no clarity about the role of Kastus Kalinowski. Not only is there no accomplished Creole version of Belarusian history, but there is a feeling that the true history of Belarusians somehow begins with the Great October Socialist Revolution of 1917, and the earlier past is not so important. The realization of this weakness led to state funding of a movie epic based on the historic chronicles of the GDL. Whereas nativist authors relish war episodes between the GDL and Russia, the Creole movie project focuses on the GDL struggle with the Crimean Tatars. Anastasiya, Princess of Slutsk, born near the end of the fifteenth century and adept at martial arts, not only presides over her people's success at beating off a Tatar assault on the town of Slutsk but also commits heroic acts herself. She takes the lead after traitors poison her husband, Prince Simeon Olelkovich. In the movie, not all Tatars are "bad guys"; in the town of Slutsk, some local Tatars are peaceful and loyal to the princess, and a few of these get butchered by bad Tatars. Local pagans resisting conversion to Christianity are also good at heart. There is a German and a Balt and even a Jew, who invites everybody to his inn to feast after the military victory, so Slutsk is shown as a truly international, yet cohesive, stronghold, much like the Soviet Union at its best. While the movie *Anastasiya Slutskaya* would not satisfy sophisticated viewers, it was a success with many rank-and-file Belarusians.

The message of Creole nationalism is contained, for example, in Lukashenka's September 23, 2004, speech before a student audience at Brest

State University. In the beginning of that speech, Lukashenka described the confusion and despair that possessed his fellow countrymen in the early 1990s when disruption of supply lines from Russia and a shrinking Russian market brought most Belarusian factories to the verge of closure. He then turned to external influences on Belarus exerted at that time.

> Two outer forces wanted to sway us. On the one hand, Russia was trying to shape Belarus's choice, but it did so in an unpersuasive and unsystematic way because it was itself going through confusion and vacillations. On the other hand, the West that won the cold war was aggressive and businesslike. The West's message to us was: Quickly conduct privatization, unhook yourself from Russia, and jettison the Russian military; then we will accept you and assist you financially. Those were the conditions that the West presented me with. . . . Not only was this influence from without. Also, inside the country a pro-Western party, the Belarusian Popular Front—and it was the only political party at the moment—pushed us in the same direction. Why then didn't Belarus go to Europe? . . . Well, in the first place because in contrast to Poland and the Baltic States, Belarus never—I dare say, never ever—has been part of Western culture and the Western way of life. Yes, we were subjected to the influence of Western culture within Rzeczpospolita and the GDL. That influence, however, was short-lived. They did not succeed in implanting the Western ways then, and they probably cannot succeed today. . . . Yes, we were, are, and will be an inalienable part of pan-European civilization, which is a mosaic of different cultures. But to the Catholic-and-Protestant . . . civilization, Belarus and Belarusians, who are predominantly Orthodox and for centuries coexisted in the same political setting with Russia and Russians, are alien.[52]

Authored by Anatoly Rubinov, deputy chief of the presidential administration, a programmatic text on ideology showed up in July 2006. According to Rubinov, the Republic of Belarus is the first independent Belarusian state ever. Because history is continuous, this state succeeds its immediate predecessor, the BSSR, which in turn owes its emergence to the 1917 communist revolution and the Soviet Union, within which the BSSR was an economic success story. That means that the slogan of Belarusian Revival (*Adradzhen-nye*), the major catchword of the nativist ideology, popular in the early 1990s, is false. "What is there to revive?" exclaims Rubinov. "Poverty, deprivation, illiteracy so vividly described by Janka Kupala in his classic works? Or perhaps even earlier times of bondage? And yet the idea of Revival has already become a kind of cliché."[53]

In his comment to Rubinov's article, Boris Lepeshko, deputy rector of Brest State University (incidentally named after Alexander Pushkin), goes even further. "Many lances have been broken over the national idea. If, however, that idea has not crystallized to this day, it means that it is . . . stillborn.

The national idea is not indispensable for a state, after all."[54] Lepeshko also asserts that "it does not make sense to try to unify all people by one ideology; rather one should talk about the practicality of one specific form of ideology that the state is applying now."[55] This bringing down of a needlessly high-minded notion of ideology echoes the musings of Yury Shevtsov, to whom "Belarusianness is . . . a technology of living in this specific region; sometimes it is the technology of survival."[56]

Alexander Feduta, who analyzed seven books devoted to Belarusian national ideology published between 2004 and 2006, was struck by their lack of clarity in defining it. Perhaps its most tangible aspects, as depicted by some ideologues, are "emphasizing communal-collectivist (Eurasian), not individualistic (West European) values"[57] and a geopolitical leaning toward Russia due to the pull of both Russia's high culture and its energy resources. "A strategic unhooking of Belarus from Russia," claims one of the ideologues, would be "tantamount to the rejection by Belarusians of their civilizational identity."[58]

Persistently appealing to Belarus's Soviet history, while failing to discern anything genuinely Belarusian in it, seems to be a pitfall of Creole nationalism. But if the problem of Belarusian historical self-perception within the Creole project is self-effacing closeness to Russia, it is intriguing to see how Russia, in a way, lends its "helping hand" by pushing Belarus aside from time to time. Disassociating Belarus from Russia gets easier each time Russia threatens to stop subsidizing the Belarusian economy by supplying cheap natural gas. February 19, 2004, was a particular hallmark in this regard. After Russia's Gazprom discontinued the flow of gas into Belarus for several hours to force Belarus to pay off its gas debt, I visited Lukashenka's website (www.president.gov.by) and counted eighteen questions from Belarusians (out of a total of forty-three questions published on that site) with a pronounced anti-Russian streak. For example, "Why should we unite with Russia, which fights wars all the time and cannot put its own house in order? Do we need terrorist attacks and war? We ought to stick to our own independent way. What do you think?" In the winter of 2006–2007, we witnessed yet another increase of tension between Belarus and Russia over the proposed rise in natural gas prices. Here, again, Lukashenka's rhetoric portrays Belarus as an innocent victim of the mercenary and rent-seeking behavior of Russia's tycoons, who are inseparable from Russia's political establishment. "Did you hear that they offered us to buy gas at a higher price than Germany?" Lukashenka exclaimed at a press conference for Russian provincial journalists. "Fifty years ago, this would have been unthinkable. But the generation that fought in the same trenches [with Russians] is not yet entirely gone."[59] This was a very effective way to rally Belarusians around their leader and to detach them mentally from a hostile Russia at the same time.

During the negotiations between Russia and Belarus about the price of natural gas (December 2006) and then about export tariffs on crude and refined oil (January 2007), Lukashenka reinforced his symbolic capital as a Belarusian nationalist even more. For the first time, the official Belarusian media put it plainly: Belarusian independence is at stake, and it is the president of Belarus, not by any means the Belarusian-speaking opposition, who is defending the statehood of Belarus.

By all accounts, Creole nationalism, Belarusian style, is on the offensive; its mobilization potential in Belarus is second to none, which appears to be more important than critical remarks about the unsophisticated nature of Lukashenka's court ideologues. On the one hand, surveys show that Russia tops the list of Belarus's friends as perceived by ordinary Belarusians. On the other hand, fewer and fewer of them want to be incorporated into Russia, and more and more are aware of Russia's expansionist bent.

"Ironically, it may be that fostering the Russia-Belarus Union may eventually help promote the pro-Western ideological blueprint for Belarus," I wrote in 2003. "The likelihood of this outcome would increase if Belarus is somehow mistreated in that Union, which seems plausible. The only way to promote the vision of Belarus as a nation apart from Russia is through opposition to Russia's real and/or perceived actions."[60] It appears that this prediction is materializing, and there is poignant irony in the fact that this is happening under the tutelage of the supposedly pro-Russia national project and has no connection at all to the activity of the overtly anti-Russian nativist group.

THE STRENGTHS AND WEAKNESSES OF THE NATIONAL PROJECTS

Although the idea of three national projects on Belarus was conceived by pundits representing just one of them (Project One), it proves a useful abstraction. Indeed, most, if not all, Belarusian intellectuals concerned about the future of their country can be assigned to one of the three projects described above. This is not to say that the borderlines between the projects are set once and for all. For example, some activists of Project Two (Muscovite Liberals) have expressed concern about the possibility of collusion between the two other national projects behind the Muscovite Liberals' back. Grigory Minenkov, a dean of philosophy at the European Humanities University, has expressed this concern most eloquently. Minenkov has predicted that Lukashenka will soon switch to Belarusian and that traditional ethnolinguistic nationalism will be "the last frontier of Lukashenka's defense from the rest of the world."[61] The ideologues of Project One have expressed similar concerns that somehow Lukashenka in befriending Russian-speaking liberals behind their, nativists', backs. By the same token, one may also speculate about some common ground between Projects Two and Three.

Taken separately, however, each project has strengths and weaknesses. The principal strength of Project One is its tight-knit community united by conscious choice of the Belarusian language, devotion to it, and an anticolonial national liberation ethos, including the fight against Russian cultural colonialism. Given the overall deficiency of traits by which to tell Belarusians from Russians, language may indeed be viewed as an important agent of nation building.

Some of the weaknesses of Project One are the extensions of its strength. The project's community resembles a sect insulated from the country's ambient environment. If "nationalism is essentially the general imposition of high culture on society,"[62] then one may say that Project One performs this function superbly, considering the unfriendly political climate. The *Arche* and *Nasha Niva* set standards of high culture, Belarusian style. The problem of the nativist cultural elite, however, is in its constituency, which still leaves much to be desired in terms of sheer numbers. To some extent, this is the case because the members of the elite come across as arrogant; they claim a monopoly on Belarusian patriotism and are prone to accusing all those who speak Russian or disagree with their version of history of having ulterior motives. The legacy of three unsuccessful Belarusification campaigns[63] also works against Project One, as does its wholesale negativism with regard to the Soviet period, which is the longest period of Belarusians' nationally conscious existence to date.

Valyantsyn Akudovich, one of the most respected critical intellectuals in the nativist community, came up with a stunningly bitter criticism of the entire project. In his essay pointedly titled "Without Us" published on April 28, 2003, in conjunction with the tenth anniversary of the *Nasha Niva* weekly, he writes,

> The Revival [*Adradzhennye*] movement denied any value whatsoever to real Belarus. Lurking behind the need to return to the historical legacy, language, and cultural experiences of the past is a rigid ideological construction that does not sit well with the achievements and values of contemporary Belarusian society, because all its triumphs, accomplishments, and delights are either of communist or colonial origin. . . . We have remained lonely not because somebody abandoned us but because in their absolute majority the denizens of [this] state . . . do not even budge to take a trip to the "new land" that we discovered for them. Even if they were pushed towards us by tommy gun barrels on Lukashenka's orders, even then they would flee to their comfy quarters. . . . It does not make sense to think that the situation will change if there is somebody other than Lukashenka at the helm of power. It is not us but the "Belarusian people" who

elected him, and the same "people" will throw him out (sooner or later), and then again they will elect not our but their own president; and we will again write about Belarus as a hostile territory.[64]

Akudovich's impressive essay elicits a mixed reaction. On the one hand, his is the harshest criticism possible, suggesting that the nativist national project has been a complete failure. On the other hand, just because his criticism is inwardly directed, the nativist community may be able to sustain itself through refreshing change. The prescription for such change is unclear, though. In his later essay, Akudovich writes that Belarusians have been too late with their "national revival" and that in a qualitatively new, information-based society, the declared goals of that revival can no longer be achieved. Openness to communication is something that even totalitarian regimes cannot escape. But cultures whose formative experience is not yet over are the first to fall victim to this openness.[65]

A strength of Project Two is its embrace of the language of the overwhelming majority of Belarusians. In Belarus, all bureaucratic, scientific, technological, and economic, as well as much interpersonal, communication is in Russian, so using Russian presents itself as a cultural norm. Another strength of Project Two is that it is not as elitist as Project One and is less insulated from larger society. A weakness of Project Two is its lack of its own historical narrative and a detailed formulation of its blueprint for the future that goes beyond the mere statement that Belarus should maintain its statehood and be a democratic country. Also missing is a cohesive explanation of Belarusians' differences from Russians. In many ways, the national project of Russian-speaking liberals remains putative. Its backers seem to form a community when there is a commonly shared sense of threat, and they become atomized when it recedes. Silitski's letter protesting a Western Russian-language radio project had such mobilizing potential because it purported to use the language of ultimatum. But because a mobilizing sense of threat is not always incited by another brand of self-proclaimed democrats (only by the Lukashenka regime), the Muscovite Liberals, as they are called by their nativist/pro-European counterparts, remain blissfully disorganized. Their evolution into a tight-knit community will most probably intensify if Lukashenka indeed forges an alliance with the nativists, as some Russian-speaking liberals fear, or if Lukashenka is gone.

An obvious strength of Project Three is that its social base is broader than that of the other projects. Its other strength is its sponsorship by the ruling regime. The economic success of post-1995 Belarus, all doubts about which should have evaporated after the 2005 reports by the World Bank and the International Monetary Fund, can also be attributed to national mobilization techniques within the so-called Creole project, and so can the loyal, professional, and disciplined cadre of Belarusian bureaucrats and their relatively low level of corruption. Apparently, Lukashenka's management style and his charisma of a peasant-born upstart have been, and still are, to the liking of many Belarusians. In their own way, even devout Lukashenka haters recognize his bond with the people. In December 2003, Victor Ivashkevich, an opposition journalist, was released from jail. Accused of publishing a libel about Belarus's president, he had been sentenced to a two-year term but was released after one year due to intense international scrutiny of his case. While in jail, he was visited by two foreign ambassadors (U.S. and Czech) and by the members of Parliament of several countries; the Organization for Security and Cooperation in Europe and the U.S. government made statements on his behalf. "I got out of prison more tolerant and sober-minded than before," said Ivashkevich upon his release. "The problem is not Lukashenka. . . . Lukashenka did not fall from the sky, his coming was not accidental. He embodies the worst traits of our people, which is why he comes across to people as their man."[66]

While most observers recognize Lukashenka's bond with many of his fellow countrymen, not everybody is as emotional as a former prisoner and a victim of the regime. According to Drakokhrust, "Much of what we attribute exclusively to Lukashenka's ill will pertains to Belarusian society regardless of who presides over it."[67] Andrei Pankin admonishes Russian liberal democrats that their common interest with Putin outweighs the contradictions; Pankin sees that common interest in not letting a Lukashenka-like spokesman for real people seize power. Pankin's article is pointedly titled "*Demos* and *Cratos* in Belarus and in Russia."[68] Clearly, he makes a point of avoiding idealizing *demos* in either of these countries. Yet, another confirmation of Lukashenka's bond with his numerous supporters can be seen in his deliberate 2002–2003 campaign to discredit Russia's political establishment, which worsened the public attitude toward a close union with Russia, a fact recorded by independent pollsters.

The continuing glorification of Soviet Belarus's role in the Great Patriotic War and constant appeals to the socioeconomic success of Belarus throughout the period between that war and the breakup of the Soviet Union are among other strengths of Project Three because, on these matters, Lukashenka is very much in sync with the vast majority of Belarusians. It is unclear, though, how long the mobilization potential of the war and the postwar success will last. Definitely among the project's strengths is its maintenance of close ties with Russia, with which most Belarusians feel a strong bond, yet not to the point of giving up on Belarusian statehood.

The project's major weakness is its low appeal to highly skilled and educated Belarusians. In a way, Creole nationalism helps sustain Belarusians as a *demotic ethnie* (i.e., an ethnic group devoid of high culture and its promoters).

IS BELARUS ON THE ROAD TO NATIONAL CONSOLIDATION?

Whether or not the above account of culture wars in Belarus is illuminating, one may find it somewhat depressing. Today, a hundred years after the Belarusian idea was first popularized and even longer since it was conceived, national consolidation of Belarusians is still in the balance. Held up against Miroslav Hroch's influential three-phase model of nation formation (the scholarly phase A, the national agitation phase B, and the national movement phase C),[69] Belarusians are still somewhere in the beginning of phase B. As a result, Belarus is deficient as a nation, even while having a state of its own. "The internal group around which the nation coalesces and the external groups to which the nation is contrasted and compared have historical and cultural experiences and associations with particular modes of political and economic development,"[70] writes a researcher of nationalism.

Belarus presents two major deviations from this normative pattern. First, there is no single internal group around which to "coalesce." Second, in Belarus, the outward-looking dimensions of identity apparently overshadow its inward-looking dimensions. Each concept of Belarusianness is more specific in stressing whom Belarusians lean to or away from outside of Belarus (Russia or Europe) and more vague in asserting who they are. Drakokhrust calls this situation "blissfully medieval,"[71] and Ales Chobat warns that "no nation which has not resolved its inner problems has a chance for political independence and survival of its culture and distinctiveness."[72] In light of this nation-building morass, the statement of Yury Shevtsov that "Belarusian identity is there to comprehend, not to manifest" sheds an aura of mysticism and acquires down-to-earth meaning: Belarusian identity would certainly be manifested just as any other, if only Belarusians knew what to manifest, which they apparently do not. Instead, they are confused.

One mitigating circumstance, though, objectively speaking, has always stood in the way of national consolidation in Belarus. The country straddles a cultural divide that Huntington calls a civilizational fault line, and cultural geographers have long been fascinated with it. Piotr Eberhardt attempted to mark out this cultural divide more accurately than Huntington did in his seminal book about the clash of civilizations. According to Eberhardt's version (figure 3.3), the divide leaves a strip along the northwestern border of Belarus (at the crossroads between the Grodno, Minsk, and Vitebsk regions) on the side of

Figure 3.3.   A civilizational fault line.

Source: Grey line: Samuel Huntington, *The Clash of Civilizations* (New York: Simon and Shuster, 1996). Black line, partially dashed (where the border is somewhat debatable): Piotr Eberhardt, "The Concept of Boundary between Latin and Byzantine Civilization in Europe," *Przegląd Geograficzny* 76, no. 2 (2004): 169–88.

"Western civilization," while the rest of Belarus gets assigned to the Byzantine Orthodox.[73]

If this is the case, then Western individualism and attachment to personal freedom should have been waging war with Oriental communalism inside Belarus, undermining cultural homogeneity. One traffic policeman in Minsk inadvertently familiarized me with his take on that clash of civilizations. When he learned that I was from the United States, he asked what I was doing in Minsk. When I said that I was gathering material for a book about

Belarus, he stunned me with the following exclamation: "A book about Belarus? To be put out in America? Then let it be known to everybody in America that the president of Belarus ought to be selected from Grodno or Brest and not from Vitebsk or Mogilev." While such a blueprint for Belarusian elections may be found too rigid, it is no more rigid than Huntington's pronouncements about the dismal prospects for democracy and markets outside the Western world. And yet, in a mysterious way, the overall situations in Eastern Europe seem to vindicate Huntington's projections. For example, in Ukraine, another country straddling the cultural divide, the triumph of pro-Western forces is not a foregone conclusion.

Igor Bobkov, a Belarusian author who has been researching the impact of the major cultural divide on Belarusian identity, concludes that this identity can develop only as transcultural. Moreover, he sees the civilizational divide as potentially the major organizing principle of Belarusian culture. In this transcultural tradition, "Adam Mickiewicz is a native alien, whereas Alexander Lukashenka is an alien native."[74] Bobkov envisages Belarus's eventually waking up to consciously embrace its inborn transculturalism, so his entire account of the Belarusian idea's genealogy reads like an implicit appeal to synthesize the available national projects, perhaps under some civic nationalist umbrella. Drakakhrust also realizes the need for such a synthesis.[75] Akudovich says that he sees Belarus as "the original combination of different linguistic and cultural models. Here, the Russian culture and language will never be displaced, and the analogous Polish influence will not disappear either, and in the nearest future the English-language culture will play an enormous role."[76]

Yet, there is quite a distance between recognition of the idea of cultural synthesis and its implementation. While theoretically speaking it is within the realm of possibility, pitfalls are equally obvious. Huntington deftly distinguishes between torn and cleft countries. According to him, "A torn country has a single predominant culture, which places it in one civilization, but its leaders want to shift it to another civilization. They say in effect 'we are one people and belong together in one place, but we want to change that place.'"[77] For Huntington, Russia is a classic torn country, by which he probably means Russia proper without its numerous and compactly settled Muslims. "In a cleft country, major groups from two or more civilizations say in effect 'We are different people and belong in different places.' The forces of repulsion drive them apart, and they gravitate toward civilization magnets in other societies."[78] Belarus seems more cleft than torn, which curbs my optimism with regard to its national consolidation. Yet, hope remains that the ongoing existence of Belarusian statehood will sooner or later generate demand for national unity, and new generations of Belarusians will be up to that task.

NOTES

This chapter was first published in *East European Politics and Societies* 21, no. 2 (2007): 348–81; © 2007 American Council of Learned Societies.

1. Ales Antsipenka, "Zatsemki na paliakh belaruskai mentalnastsi," *Nashe Mneniye*, September 23, 2005, at www.mnnby.org.

2. Janka Kupala, *Tuteishiya* (Munich: Batskaushchyna, 1953), 22.

3. This flag was a symbol of the Belarusian People's Republic declared by the enthusiasts of the Belarusian idea in 1918 under German military occupation. The white-red-white flag was also used under another German occupation, particularly in its final 1943–1944 phase. In 1991, it became the official flag of independent Belarus. In 1995, the country returned to a slightly modified Soviet insignia, including a red-green flag with a strip of Belarusian folk ornament. Belarus is the only post-Soviet country to resort to Soviet-era symbols.

4. A survey of two hundred randomly selected adult residents of Minsk was conducted in July 2005 by the Novak firm. The random-route method was used in the study. To realize interviews with "difficult-of-access respondents," at the end of each route, quotas were used that made it possible to reach the required level of conformity between the universe and the sample. Respondents' genders and ages were used as quota criteria. The main criterion was age. The correlation by gender was controlled during the study by each interviewer independently (~50/50). When using quota by age, the following age groups were used: 18 to 24, 25 to 34, 35 to 44, 45 to 54, 55 to 64, and 65 and older. The number of respondents in each age group was proportional to their numbers in the general population.

5. As for Ukraine, yet another of Belarus's neighbors, the responses to the same question would likely be different from those obtained in Belarus as well, although some regions of eastern and southern Ukraine may actually harbor similar reactions.

6. See, for example, Alexander Bekker, "Lukashenko otstupil," *Vedomosti*, February 20, 2004.

7. Jan Zaprudnik, "Belarus: In Search of National Identity between 1986 and 2000," in *Contemporary Belarus: Between Democracy and Dictatorship*, ed. Elena A. Korosteleva, Colin W. Lawson, and Rosalind Marsh (London and New York: Routledge/Curzon, 2003), 112–24.

8. Piotr Martsev, "Prezident v kotle," *Belorusskaya Delovaya Gazeta,* February 25, 2004.

9. J. V. Stalin, "Marxism i natsional'nyi vopros," *Prosveshcheniye* 3–5 (March–May 1913), at www2.unil.ch/slav/ling/textes/Stalin13.html.

10. Yury Shevtsov, *Obyedinionnaya natsiya: Fenomen Belarusi* (Moscow: Yevropa, 2005), 71.

11. Viacheslav Nosevich, "Belorusy: Stanovleniye etnosa is 'natsionalnaya ideya'" in *Belorussiya i Rossiya: obshchestva i gosudarstva* (Moscow: Prava Cheloveka, 1998), 11–30, at http://vn.belinter.net/vkl/17.html.

12. Ernest Gellner (1964) as quoted by Benedict Anderson, *Imagined Communities* (London: Verso, 1991), 6.

13. These observations were first published in Grigory Ioffe, "Understanding Belarus: Belarusian Identity," *Europe-Asia Studies* 55, no. 8 (2003): 1241–71.

14. While some Belarusians still favor merging into one state with Russia, there are fewer of them today than before February 2004 and decidedly fewer than before May 2002. In 1998, their political affiliation did not even apply for requisite government reregistration. Either they failed to round up one thousand followers required by law or the government gently advised them to dematerialize. (Yury Drakokhrust, "'Pamiarkounasts' zhiviot i pobezhdayet," *Kuriyer* 2 [2002]).

15. Samuel P. Huntington, *The Clash of Civilizations* (New York: Simon and Schuster, 1996), 20.

16. "Zianon Pazniak: Ya budu udzelnichat u prezidentskikh vybarakh 2006 godu," Belarusian Service of Radio Liberty, October 5, 2005, at www.svaboda.org.

17. Andrei Dynko, "Patrabuyu nemagchymaga—budzte realistami," *Nashe Mneniye*, September 4, 2006, at www.nmnby.org.

18. Dynko, "Patrabuyu nemagchymaga."

19. "Tsi maye prademakratychnaya menshasts shans na pospekh?" *Prasky Accent*, a talk show of the Belarusian Service of Radio Liberty, May 18, 2006, at www.svaboda.org.

20. *National Composition of Population of the Republic of Belarus and Languages Used by the Population* (Minsk: Ministry of Statistics and Analysis, 2001), 326.

21. Discontinued in March 2006, it now exists only online at www.bdg.by.

22. Vladimir Dorokhov, "Trusovskaya logika," *Belorusskaya Delovaya Gazeta*, August 12, 2005.

23. Semion Bukchin, *Khronika suverennogo bolota* (Minsk: Yevropeiskoye Vremia, 1996), 106.

24. Yury Drakokhrust, "Belorusskii natsionalism govorit po-russki," *Belorusskaya Delovaya Gazeta*, January 19, 1998.

25. "Na pytan'ni *Arche* adkazvayuts viadomyya raseiskamounyye intelectualy Belarusi," *Arche* 5 (2004): 7–27.

26. Yury Drakakhrust, "Zhaneuskaya kanventsiya dlya vainy kul'turau," *Arche* 3 (2004), at Arche.home.by/2004-3/drakakhrust304.htm.

27. Drakakhrust, "Zhaneuskaya kanventsiya."

28. Valer Bulgakau, "Chamu Belarus nia Austrya, a yeuraziiskaya satrapiya," *Arche* 5 (2004): 33.

29. Danila Zhukousky, "Pax vobiscum," *Arche* 5 (2004): 49.

30. Yury Drakakhrust, "Vayennaya khitrasts," *Arche* 5 (2004): 54.

31. Obrashcheniye Vitaliya Silitskogo, *Nashe Mneniye*, August 10, 2005, at www.mnnby.org.

32. Obrashcheniye Vitaliya Silitskogo, *Nashe Mneniye.*

33. Alexander Feduta, "Bol'noi zub," *Nashe Mneniye*, August 12, 2005, at www.nmnby.org.

34. Yury Drakakhrust, "Yashche raz pra zhaneuskuyu kanventsiyu," *Nashe Mneniye*, August 23, 2005 www.nmnby.org.

35. Vadim Kaznacheyev, "Voina i pena," *Nashe Mneniye*, August 31, 2005, at www.mnnby.org.

36. "Sprechki vakol movy novai pragramy Niametskoi Khvali dlia Belarusi" (dialogue between Svetlana Alexievich and Gennadz Buraukin), *Prasky Accent*, a talk show of the Belarusian Service of Radio Liberty, September 24, 2005, at www.svaboda.org.

37. Andrei Dynko, "Poplech tsi pobach?" *Nashe Mneniye*, August 12, 2005, at www.nmnby.org.

38. Dynko, "Poplech tsi pobach?"

39. Yury Drakakhrust, "Yashche raz pra zhaneuskuyu kanventsiyu," *Nashe Mneniye*, August 23, 2005, ww.nmnby.org.

40. Dynko, "Poplech tsi pobach?"

41. Andrei Dynko, "Deutsche Welle, braty-rusafily," *Nasha Niva*, September 2, 2005.

42. Dynko, "Deutcshe Welle, braty-rusafily"

43. These are fictional creatures whose historical memory was surgically removed from their brain; they are pictured by Chingiz Aitmatov in his 1980 hallmark novel *The Day Lasts More Than a Hundred Years*.

44. Mykola Ryabchuk, *Vid Malorossii do Ukrayiny* (Kyiv: Kritika, 2000).

45. Uladzimer Abushenka, "Mickiewicz kak 'kreol': Ot 'tuteishikh geneologii' k geneologii Tuteshastsi," 2002, at www.lib.by/frahmenty/sem-abuszenka.htm (accessed September 22, 2007).

46. Igar Babkou, "Genealyogiya belaruskai idei," *Arche* 3 (2005): 136–65.

47. Valerka Bulgakau, "Vybary prezydenta kreolau," *Arche* 4 (2001), at Arche.home.by/2001-4/bulha401.htm.

48. Bulgakau, "Vybary prezydenta kreolau."

49. Bulgakau, "Vybary prezydenta kreolau."

50. Alexander Feduta, "Nedoliot," *Nashe Mneniye*, August 3, 2005, at www.nmnby.org.

51. See John Loftus, *The Belarus Secret* (New York: Alfred A. Knopf, 1982); see also *Belarusian Nazis during World War II and Their Work for the Cold War*, at www.geocities.com/dudar2000/Bcc.htm (accessed September 22, 2007). A few alleged collaborators who found themselves in the West were tried and convicted. Anton (Andrei) Savoniuk, who in 1999 was given two life sentences for his role in a 1942 massacre of Jews, died in a British prison in November 2005.

52. Alexander Lukashenka, "Stenogramma vystupleniya pered studencheskoi molodiozh'yu Brestchiny," September 23, 2004, at www.president.gov.by.

53. Anatoly Rubinov, "Yeschio raz ob ideologii," *Belarus Segodnia*, July 28, 2006.

54. Boris Lepeshko, "Traditsiya i avtoritet," *Belarus Segodnia*, August 9, 2006.

55. Lepeshko, "Traditsiya i avtoritet."

56. Yury Shevtsov, *Obyedinionnaya natsiya: Fenomen Belarusi*, 72.

57. Alexander Feduta, "Kollektivnyi politinformator i agitator. Izbrannye mesta iz uchebnikov po gosudarstvennoi ideologii Respubliki Belarus," *Neprikosnovennyi Zapas* 47 (2006).

58. Feduta, "Kollektivnyi politinformator i agitator."

59. Alexander Lukashenka, "Press Conference for Russia's Provincial Media," September 29, 2006, at www.president.gov.by/press31104.html.

60. Ioffe, "Understanding Belarus: Belarusian Identity," 1267.

61. Grigory Minenkov, "Zametki o yazyke, znanii puti i prochem," *Nashe Mneniye*, August 23, 2005, at www.nmnby.org.

62. Ernest Gellner, *Nations and Nationalism* (Ithaca: Cornell University Press, 1983), 57.

63. See Chapter 1.

64. Valyantslyin Akudovich, "Bez nas," *Nasha Niva*, March 28, 2003, at www.litara.net.

65. Valyantslyin Akudovich, "Vaina kulturau ili pramida Kheopsu za muram Mirskaga Zamku," 2005, at www.knihi.com.

66. Sergei Nekhamkin, "Na put' ispravleniya nie vstal," *Izvestia*, December 17, 2003, at www.izvestia.ru/world/article42249.

67. Yury Drakokhrust, "Sapega i masherov," *Svobodnyye Novosti* 33 (August 31, 2001), at www.bymedia.net/press/gazeta.article.php?articleID=146193.

68. Alexei Pankin, "Demos i kratos v Belorussii i v Rossii," *Izvestia*, November 3, 2004, at www.izvestia.ru/comment/629774_print.

69. Miroslav Hroch, *Social Preconditions of National Revival in Europe: A Comparative Analysis of Patriotic Groups among the Smaller European Nations*, 2nd ed. (New York: Columbia University Press: 2000).

70. Stephen Shulman, "National Identity and Public Support for Political and Economic Reform in Ukraine," *Slavic Review* 64, no. 1 (2005): 59–87.

71. Yury Drakokhrust, "Velikoye kniazhestvo belorusskoye," *Belorusskiye Novosti*, August 15, 2003, at www.naviny.bu/ru/print/?id=18242.

72. Ales Chobat, "Tlum dziatsei," *Nasha Niva*, 2001, at http://gw.longwo.minsk.by/nn/2001/35/10.htm.

73. Piotr Eberhardt, "The Concept of Boundary between Latin and Byzantine Civilization in Europe," *Przegląd Geograficzny* 76, no. 2 (2004): 169–88.

74. Igor Bobkov, "Etika pogranich'ya: Transkul'turnost kak belorusskii opyt," *Perekriostki* 3–4 (2005): 130.

75. Drakakhrust, "Zhaneuskaya kanventsiya."

76. Valentin Akudovich, "Belorusy—strashno ambitsioznyye liudi," *Turizm i Otdykh* 39 (September 27, 2001).

77. Huntington, *The Clash of Civilizations*, 138–39.

78. Huntington, *The Clash of Civilizations*, 139.

4

Belarusian Economy

> In the case of Belarus we are dealing with such a deviation from the norm that it amounts to a miracle. And miracles do not call for condescension.
>
> —Ergaly Gher[1]

Before the communist revolution, Belarus was one of the poorest regions of European Russia. Belarus had meager manufacturing and was beset with rural overpopulation. In agriculture, yields were paltry, in part due to acidic and poorly drained soils. The first industrialization wave (1880s) that affected many regions of European Russia largely skirted Belarus. Only a few large enterprises were born, such as the iron foundry Yacobson, Lifshits, and Company and the machine-building firm Tekhnolog in Minsk; a flax mill and an optical factory in Vitebsk; three wood-processing factories (producing plywood and matches), a foundry, and a cigarette-wrapper factory in Pinsk; a brewery in Mogilev; and a cigarette factory in Grodno.[2] In the first decade of the twentieth century, in Belarus eight hundred industrial establishments employed twenty-five thousand workers. Most of these production units were small and primitive wood and food processors.[3] Still, in 1912, they contributed 24.4 percent of Russia's output of oak sleepers for railway lines, 23.5 percent of plywood, 44.8 percent of matchwood, and 14.5 percent of wallpaper. Despite this evidently high level of specialization in wood processing, the output of alcoholic beverages was the number-one contributor to local revenues, with wood processing being number two. And the per capita industrial output in Belarus was one-half that of Russia as a whole.[4]

Several sizable manufacturing plants emerged in Belarus as a result of the implementation of the first two Soviet five-year plans, including Minsk,

Vitebsk, and Gomel machine-tool factories, as well as an agricultural machinery plant in Gomel.[5] Yet, the scope of Ukraine's and the Russian Federation's prewar industrialization dwarfed that of Belarus, and correspondingly the pull of urban centers was small. In 1940, only 21 percent of Belarus's population lived in cities and towns, compared with 34 percent in Russia and Ukraine.[6] By all accounts, Belarus's location along the western frontier of the Soviet Union was deemed strategically vulnerable.

From 1941 to 1945, Belarus experienced arguably more devastation than any other country affected by World War II. At least one-quarter of the entire population perished. On the eve of the war, the population of Belarus was 9.2 million; in 1945, it was only 6.3 million. Out of 270 towns and *rayon* centers, 209 were demolished, including Minsk, Gomel, and Vitebsk, in which 80 to 90 percent of the entire stock of prewar buildings was destroyed.[7] According to Soviet monetary assessments of the war-inflicted damage, Ukraine sustained the largest destruction.[8] However, prewar industrial investment in Ukraine had been more significant than in Belarus by far, which must have heightened the value of what was then exposed to destruction. In per capita terms, the war-inflicted loss of property appears to be higher in investment-poor Belarus, which underscores the extraordinary scale of its devastation.

Belarus's industrial spurt began with postwar reconstruction. The newly obtained *cordon sanitaire* of satellite states along the western border of the Soviet Union changed Moscow's perception of Belarus's location. It was no longer vulnerable. Belarus was now the locus of the major transit routes linking Russia with Eastern and Central Europe. Later on, the significance of these routes increased even more as the Soviet Union began to sell its oil and gas to the West, receiving consumer goods and food in return. From the late 1950s on, Belarus emerged as one of the major Soviet manufacturing regions, emphasizing tractors, heavy trucks, oil processing, metal-cutting lathes, synthetic fibers, TV sets, semiconductors, and microchips. Much of Belarus's high-tech industry was military oriented.

A detailed account of Belarus's growth under the Soviets is contained in my earlier publication.[9] It follows from that account that despite the ingrained flaws of the Soviet economic model, Belarus was an undeniable Soviet success story. In 1990, accounting for just 3.6 percent of the Soviet Union's population and 0.9 percent of its land area, Belarus contributed 30.7 percent of synthetic fibers, 21.2 percent of flax, 20.3 percent of tractors, 18.9 percent of mineral fertilizers, 13.5 percent of potatoes, 12.3 percent of TV sets, 9.8 percent of metal-cutting lathes, 6.9 percent of milk, 5.9 percent of meat, and 5.4 percent of trucks produced in the Soviet Union.[10] All the impulses and driving forces of Belarus's achievements, as well as their side effects, have been of Soviet vintage. On the eve of the 1990s, Belarus had one of the better-managed regional economies, with an unusually high share of export-oriented enterprises: more than 80 percent of industrial output was exported to other republics or foreign countries. In all the other Soviet republics and "socialist" countries, this share did not exceed 60 percent.[11] Belarus's industry was the most technologically advanced in the entire Soviet Union. The worn-out phrase that Belarus was an assembly workshop of the Soviet Union is not exactly accurate. Belarus's specialization was in research and development (R&D), as well as assembling high-tech products. The important feature was that almost all the personnel for R&D were trained within Belarus, which among other things explains why there are so few migrants in Belarus and, therefore, why the share of ethnic Belarusians is so high. In 1986, Belarus, which seventy years ago had no institutions of higher learning at all, was second only to Russia in the number of college students per one thousand residents.[12]

In the 1980s, more than half of the industrial personnel of Belarus worked for enterprises with over five hundred employees. Most of the large-scale processing and assembly operations were located in Minsk and the eastern part of the republic.

The industrial core of eastern Belarus took shape due to its transit location. Three transportation axes crossed in this region: between Moscow and the most economically advanced of the East European satellites of the Soviet Union, between Leningrad and Ukraine, and between the Baltic ports and Ukraine. The physical distance from eastern Belarus to Moscow also proved optimal: close enough to be within Moscow's sight, it was not too close so that Moscow could siphon off all the best and brightest, as it did from all its immediate neighbors. To be within Moscow's sight proved important, though, as no industrial enterprise in eastern Belarus was placed there on local initiatives; all resulted from the federal blueprints adopted by the congresses of the Communist Party of the Soviet Union.

Ten manufacturing giants and dozens of their smaller subsidiaries form the industrial core of eastern Belarus. These enterprises fall into four branches: mechanical engineering, petrochemical, radioelectronic, and ferrous metallurgy. Mechanical engineering is represented by six giants: MTZ (Minsk; tractors), MAZ (Minsk; trucks), MoAz (Mogilev; self-propelled scrapers and earth movers and trailers for underground works), Gomsel'mash (Gomel; harvesting combines, mowers, and sowing machines), MZKT (Minsk; an offspring of MAZ; heavy-duty tractor trailers), and BELAZ (Zhodino, Minsk region; heavy trucks for mining operations). The technological cycles of all these factories are entwined.

The petrochemical industry is based on two refineries: NAFTAN, based in Novopolotsk, Vitebsk region, and Mozyr NPZ in Mozyr, Gomel region.

NAFTAN is the largest refinery in Europe, with a processing capacity of twenty million tons of crude oil a year, while Mozyr NPZ can process up to twelve million tons a year. The refineries are located on two different pipelines from Russia. The products of NAFTAN are further transported through pipelines from Novopolotsk to Ventspils suited for gasoline and diesel fuel. So, the Latvian port of Ventspils appears to be the major trans-shipment site for NAFTAN. The Mozyr NPZ receives crude oil from the pipeline Drouzhba; gasoline and other products are then delivered to Central Europe by tank trucks and rail. The combined capacity of the two refineries exceeds domestic demand by a factor of three, and so export has been the major function of Belarus's refineries from the outset. Several chemical plants connected to the major refineries by local pipelines operate in Novopolotsk, Polotsk, Mozyr, Mogilev, and Grodno.

Fuel produced from Russia's oil makes it to Western Europe also through Ukraine. The capacity of Ukrainian refineries does not exceed sixty million tons of crude oil, but Ukraine's domestic demand is much higher than that of Belarus. The capacity of Poland's refineries is about the same as those of Belarus, but again, Poland has higher domestic demand. In all three Baltic States, only one sizable refinery in Mažeikiai, Lithuania, has the same capacity as Mozyr NPZ. Belarus thus appears to be the key producer of fuel for export to Europe.

The leading enterprise in radioelectronics in Belarus is Minsk-based Integral, offering a broad array of automotive and power electronic products (e.g., monochip voltage regulators and temperature sensors), timers, sensors, microcontrollers, LCD drivers, plasma-panel drivers, and integrated circuits for electronic contact cards, transporters, and consumer electronics, including watches, thermometers, and TV sets. Integral is technologically linked with other enterprises like Minsk-based Gorizont, the largest producer of TV and radio sets in the Commonwealth of Independent States (CIS) and also a producer of systems for satellite and cable TV.

Yet another industrial giant is the free-standing Belarusian Metallurgic Plant in Zhlobin, Gomel region, whose principal products are steel cord and steel wire.

Other components of Belarusian industry, mostly based in eastern Belarus, include textiles and the production of potassium fertilizers. The latter represents the only production cycle located in, and controlled by, Belarus in its entirety as Soligorsk district in the Minsk region is where potassium is mined. All industries other than production of potassium are deeply integrated with Russia and, to some extent, Ukraine. They either process raw materials from Russia (petrochemical industries) or depend on parts and semifinished products from Russia and Ukraine (as do all plants in the mechanical-engineering sector, which receive up to 80 percent of all their parts from outside Belarus). Some Belarus industries are attached to major consumers in Russia, as are factories producing electronic and optic devices for the Russian army and enterprises producing household appliances like refrigerators and TV sets.

According to the Soviet plans, the industrialization of western Belarus was to pick up during the last decade of the twentieth century, when new electronic and petrochemical factories were to be built in Grodno and Brest. Prior to that time, western Belarus contributed labor to manufacturing in the East and developed into an advanced agricultural region. The postwar collectivization in western Belarus was not nearly as destructive of rural communities as the prewar collectivization had been in eastern Belarus, and the survival rate of locals during the war was higher as well. The West even had a postwar baby boom, a rarity in the non-Muslim regions of the Soviet Union. In western Belarus, rural population decline commenced only in the 1980s, decades later than in the East.

For a long time, the main obstacle to agricultural development in the southern part of the republic (both West and East) was the prevalence of marshes in the poorly drained Polesie lowland, which accounts for 40 percent of the entire land area of Belarus. Straddling the border between Belarus and Ukraine, this is Europe's largest concentration of marshes. Here, the patches of dry land on the few elevated areas between the tributaries of the Pripet River (the axis of the entire lowland) used to shrink significantly during high-water periods. A costly state program of land improvement was launched in the 1960s. A massive artificial drainage system proved to be particularly successful in the western part, in the region of Brest, because the land-reclamation projects were implemented in areas that still had vibrant rural communities.

In the Brest region, wherein land reclamation schemes proved most successful, and in the Grodno region, with a much smaller scale of land improvement (but with the highest natural fertility of the soil in Belarus), sixteen giant cattle-fattening and pig farms were built in the late 1970s and the 1980s. A large segment of the local population became used to supporting this highly centralized animal husbandry, which resembled rhythmic industrial operations more than traditionally seasonal peasant farming. In terms of quality of life in the countryside, intensity of land use, and output per unit of land, western Belarus in the 1980s did not yield to the Baltic republics (the all-Soviet leaders in agriculture).

In summary, a country of dismal workshops and unproductive wetlands in the beginning of the twentieth century, Belarus seventy years later was dominated by large-scale industry and vastly modernized agriculture. The capital city of Minsk became the symbol of Soviet Belarus's success. It demonstrated an astounding pace of population growth: 509,000 people in 1959, 917,000 in 1970, 1,331,000 in 1980, and 1,613,000 in 1989.[13] No other large city in the entire Soviet Union grew this fast.

POST-SOVIET DEVELOPMENTS

Despite the fact that one of the three cosigners of the Belovezh agreement, which was a death sentence to the Soviet Union, was a Belarusian (Stanislau Shushkevich), most of his fellow countrymen were ill prepared for independence. While a few Minsk-based intellectuals were able to convert the newly emerging freedom into some sort of social capital that materialized in contacts with the West and in its financial support, most Belarusians saw their lifelong savings evaporate and their quality of life plummet. By 1994, most industrial enterprises in Belarus were about to discontinue their operations because of the disruption of Russia-controlled supply lines. In 1995, Belarus's gross domestic product (GDP) was 33.9 percent lower than in 1991. Predictably, it had decreased by about the same degree as Russia's, whose GDP was 34.6 percent lower.[14] By all accounts, Russia's robust economic growth since 2001 has been due to the high international prices of oil and gas, while Belarus demonstrated on average a 7.5 percent growth of GDP from 2001 to 2005[15] despite being a net importer of both fuels. In both countries, most people disapproved intensely of privatization, but in Russia it proceeded anyway. As early as 1992, 40 percent of Russia's GDP was produced in the private sector, and by 2006, 65 percent was. In contrast, in Belarus, the share of GDP contributed by the private sector was 10 percent in 1992, and since that time it has increased to just 25 percent.[16]

Since 1996, Belarus has arguably been the world's leader in terms of the sheer number of published pronouncements of its imminent economic collapse. Yet economic growth has been impressive: 7 percent in 2003, 11.4 percent in 2004, 9.4 percent in 2005, and 9.9 percent in 2006.[17]

Back in 1994, when the transition paths of Russia and Belarus began to diverge, stoppages of factories, empty grocery stores, and a steep rise in the cost of living resulted in huge rallies in usually calm Minsk. Because industry stopped due to severed supply lines from Russia, people demanded that these ties be restored. Unlike Russia, though, where the elites and "ordinary people" have been far apart on many issues, Belarusian attitudes have been more harmonious across the board. In the words of Andrew Wilson and Clelia Rontoyani, "To the overwhelming majority of the Belarusian political elite, the costs of an economic strategy aimed at reducing interaction with Russia were immediate, certain, and of such a magnitude as to make such a choice unthinkable."[18] Therefore, the premonition of impending chaos and doom, preponderant in Belarusian society, was largely responsible for bringing to power a strongman, Alexander Lukashenka, formerly director of a state farm in Mogilev Oblast and a self-proclaimed crusader against corruption. While I characterize this leader in chapter 6, a few points are in order now. Lukashenka stopped voucher privatization (which had barely begun) and secured subsidized transport and utilities, as well as free health care and education. By that time (1995), most industrial workers worked barely two to three days a week (as plants ran out of supplies and could not dispose of their output), but they could perhaps eke out a living for a year or so at the most with the aid of their own kitchen gardens. By 1996, most industrial giants resumed their full-capacity work schedule, mostly due to the restored ties with Russia. Lukashenka had been voted in for that purpose in 1994, and he made good on his campaign promise. Since 1996, Belarus has been experiencing economic growth.

DOOM AND GLOOM OVERSTATED

Up until 2005, Western media and a large part of the Russian media assessed Belarus's economic situation as abysmal. The phraseology used by academics included "the myth of economic revival,"[19] and the "'shampoo paradise' of Brezhnev's 1980s"[20] (to which Belarus of the late 1990s was likened). My attempt to implant a modicum of objectivity into the analysis of economic growth in Belarus was referred to as painting "a picture of an economic utopia."[21] Because no alternative analysis was offered, one could discern only one reason to maintain requisite skepticism: Lukashenka was a bad guy, and so everything under him was supposed to be bad. Assessments of corruption in Belarus are a case in point. From 1998 to 2002, Transparency International (TI) considered Belarus to be one of fifty countries with the least corruption. More specifically, the 2002 ranking of 102 world nations on "perceived corruption" had Belarus as number 36, tied with Lithuania and less corrupt than Poland (ranked 45), not to mention Russia (71) and Ukraine (85). This complies with a wealth of anecdotal evidence, according to which Belarusian officials are significantly less corrupt than their Russian and Ukrainian counterparts. However, in 2003, when the Belarus Democracy Act was in the works, the country was ranked 53; in 2004 (when the act was adopted) Belarus's rank was within the range of 74 to 78; and in 2005, it was within the range of 107 to 116. A change of this magnitude within just three unremarkable years defies objective explanation and allows one to suspect regrettable corruption of TI's criteria, that is, their infusion with politics. This suspicion finds tentative confirmation in the October 25, 2005, broadcast of *Prasky Accent*, a talk show of the Belarusian Service of Radio Liberty. "What happened? Did they begin to steal more in Belarus?" asks the talk show's host. Says Yaroslaw Romanchuk, an opposition-minded philologist turned economist,

> The authors justly call this index [TI's corruption index] a perception index—this is how corruption is perceived by different personalities and institutions. Belarus's rating of 2.6 [on the 0–10 scale, where 10 stands for the total lack of corruption] was assigned on the basis of responses to five questions given by ... the Economist Intelligence Unit, Freedom House, and UN. The presence of these organizations in Belarus is not wide enough to monitor all changes in our legislation and practical relationships between business and state. I met with TI's experts and explained to them the methodological differences between corruption estimates in market and nonmarket countries. And two years of those discussions and explanations brought about the result which led to an essential methodological correction.[22]

At about the same time, however, the World Bank and the International Monetary Fund (IMF) published their Belarus reports. While critical of Belarus's economic policies, the reports disposed of any suspicion that economic growth in Belarus may have been contrived. The IMF report upholds Belarusian statistics: "The overall size of the statistical measurement biases ... appear not to fundamentally alter the picture conveyed by official national account statistics pointing to strong output growth in recent years."[23] Several revealing statements describe nine years of uninterrupted growth. "The rapid growth has occurred from a relatively high base, since Belarus suffered a smaller drop in output in the early 1990s than most other CIS countries."[24] It is obvious that registering growth from a low base, as was the case in Uzbekistan or Azerbaijan, would have been easier. "In contrast to some other CIS countries, the patterns of growth in Belarus have been much more beneficial for labor" as "benefits from recent growth were broadly shared by [the] population. Growth in labor earnings amounted to about 53 percent of the total GDP growth over 1996–2003. Poverty rates declined substantially, while inequality remained rather stable and moderate. The poverty head-count ratio ... was more than halved—from 28.6 percent of the population in 1996 to 17.8 percent in 2004, which meant that about 2 million people moved out of poverty."[25] One statement in the IMF report caught my attention due to its unusual syntax: "The IMF's growth forecasts in past years have been below those of the authorities, as well as the eventual outcomes."[26] I took this as a somewhat Byzantine admission of the IMF's own biases.

To be sure, the economic situation in Belarus is far from serene. One problem is a considerable depreciation of capital stock in the absence of any significant foreign direct investment, a usual source of modernization for transition economies. A related problem is a high level of energy intensity, whereby Belarus burns three times more fuel per dollar of its GDP compared with Western Europe, and this high level of consumption takes place in an economy that is crucially dependent on one external (Russian) source of energy. It is also unlikely that recent growth in real wages (by 18 to 20 percent in both 2005 and 2006!) is sustainable even under the current robust economic growth simply because that growth exceeded the increase in labor productivity by a factor of two. As for the sustainability of economic growth itself, too much depends on special relationships with Russia. In the winter of 2006–2007, these relationships underwent the toughest trial ever (discussed later in this chapter). Regardless of this trial's eventual outcome, being solely dependent on one foreign market for selling Belarusian industrial products is a cause for concern. Even more worrisome is Belarus's almost 100 percent dependency on Russia for natural gas and 90 percent dependency on Russia for oil.

Throughout the post-Soviet period, the Republic of Belarus has retained the industrial emphasis in its economy. The share of industry in overall employment, 26.7 percent, is second to none in the CIS, with services only accounting for 55.2 percent[27]; moreover, industry accounts for 32 percent of national income, second only to Azerbaijan's exorbitant 51 percent.[28] Within industry, the superlarge enterprises still prevail with 90 percent of industrial output produced by 350 production units and 55 percent by just 113 units, which also generate 75 percent of all exports.[29]

In 2004, Belarus's GDP was 117.2 percent of its 1992 level; Russia was far behind with 89.5 percent, and Ukraine was even further behind with 66.7 percent.[30] In the CIS, Belarus's share in the overall production of tractors is 73 percent. Belarus produces 54 percent of all TV sets in the CIS and 26 percent of all refrigerators.[31] In the early years of the twenty-first century, Belarus produced 48 percent of the world output of electronic microchips for watches, 30 percent of microchips for calculators, 10 to 15 percent of heavy trucks for mining operations, 7 percent of tractors, and 7 percent of metallic cord.[32] Some of Belarus's products, notably shoes and refrigerators, occupy an important niche in Russia's provincial markets: those products are not as expensive as their Western counterparts and not as unattractive as the Russian made.

Last, but not least, Belarus is the only post-Soviet country in which the number of users of the state-, enterprise-, and trade union–sponsored health and recreation centers and rest homes (a fixture of the late Soviet period) has actually increased since the Soviet times.

"In some respects," writes Mario Nuti, "the Belarusian economy has performed better than its Russian counterpart. Belarus has not squandered state capital through debt-for-equity swaps or insider privatization; it has little domestic and foreign indebtedness; . . . the government collects taxes and pays for most of its purchases and for wages and pensions; inter-enterprise arrears are low, though fluctuating; and barter is limited to trade with Russia. Criminality—economic and its other forms—has been kept in check, as a by-product of a zero-tolerance approach."[33]

In summary, if the reference line is sought within the CIS, Belarus's economic standing appears to be favorable, which is in stark contrast to the picture routinely painted by the Western media and some Russian media alike. According to the 2001 United Nations Human Development Report, Belarus was also ahead of all the other CIS countries and some East European countries on the Human Development Index. It was ranked fifty-third, whereas Russia was fifty-fifth, and Ukraine was seventy-fourth.[34] By 2006, Belarus's relative position had nevertheless worsened; it was only sixty-seventh, slightly below Russia (sixty-fifth), whose relative gain was entirely due to the monetary (GDP) component of the Human Development Index (which in turn was exclusively due to high oil prices). Still, Belarus was above all the other CIS countries, including Ukraine (seventy-seventh).[35] Importantly, in Belarus, life expectancy at birth is three years longer among women and four years longer among men than in Russia.[36] Although gross national product per capita is about $3,000 less in Belarus than in Russia, those Belarusians who believe that life in their country is better than life in Russia are now almost five times as numerous as those who believe the opposite (table 4.1). Arguably, this preference has less to do with satisfaction with achieved living standards—in both Russia and Belarus, there are little grounds for that—than with adamant rejection of social stratification, Russian style. Whereas total earnings of the 10 percent wealthiest Belarusians exceed those of the 10 per-

Table 4.1. Percentage Distribution of the Answers to the Question "Where Is Life Better Now, in Belarus or in Russia?"

	December 2002 (%)	*March 2003 (%)*	*March 2004 (%)*	*June 2006 (%)*	*January 2007 (%)*
Life better in Belarus	35.1	34.2	34.1	46.4	51.0
Life better in Russia	44.0	39.5	30.4	12.1	11.8
Life is the same in both countries	20.9	26.3	28.3	36.2	30.3

Source: National surveys by IISEPS; www.iiseps.org.

cent poorest Belarusians by a factor of 6.9, in Russia the corresponding ratio is 12.7.[37]

Belarus is the only country in the entire post-Soviet space (i.e., the CIS and Baltic countries) that has experienced incoming migration from each and every other post-Soviet country in excess of the outgoing migration to each and every other country during every year from 1996 to 2005. To be sure, the actual net influx is not overly significant and is declining, but the steadily positive net migration speaks for itself. Overall, from 1996 to 2003, 201,000 people migrated to Belarus from the other republics of the former Soviet Union, whereas 71,000 left for those republics. The bulk of those newcomers (86 percent) were from Russia, Ukraine, and Kazakhstan.[38]

Needless to say, migrants streaming into Belarus from other segments of the post-Soviet space do not read the CIS statistical yearbooks, much less the United Nations documents, yet they vote with their feet, thus lending legitimacy to the data obtainable from these sources. Apparently, among the prospective migrants, Belarus ranks favorably on many counts, including relatively good infrastructure, social benefits, and lack of tension, among others. Most probably, the fact that Belarus does not have a strong sense of nationalism matters as well, as ethnic aliens appear to be more welcome (or, rather, less unwelcome) in Belarus than elsewhere in the post-Soviet space.

FOREIGN TRADE AND ECONOMIC GROWTH

Belarus is unique within the CIS in terms of export and import operations. First, Belarus's economy is unusually open: in 2005, export accounted for 54 percent of the GDP.[39] For comparison, in Russia, this indicator stands at 18 percent.[40] The ratio of export to GDP normally tends to be higher for economically advanced countries of smaller size,[41] and it is noteworthy that Belarus fits the pattern.

Second, as recently as 2000, no other CIS country emphasized links within the CIS as much as Belarus. In 2000, 60 percent of all export went to CIS countries, and 70 percent of all import came from CIS countries. By 2005, this situation had changed: only 44 percent of Belarus's export was to the CIS, whereas the CIS share in imports had declined only slightly to 67 percent. Belarus's trade connections with the CIS remain tighter than those of Russia (14 percent of exports and 19 percent of imports) and Ukraine (31 percent and 47 percent, respectively).[42] In 2005, Russia alone accounted for 48.4 percent of Belarus's foreign trade,[43] down from 58.7 percent in 1999.[44] In 2005, in the overall Belarusian export to the CIS, Russia accounted for 80.6

percent, and in the overall import from the CIS, Russia's share was even higher at 90.8 percent.[45]

Third, in 2000 Belarus was second to none in the CIS in the per capita value of export.[46] By 2005, the monetary value of exports from Russia had been boosted due to the exorbitant world price of oil; even so, Belarus's per capita export was only slightly below Russia's ($1,630 versus $1,676).

Fourth, in Belarus's exchange with Russia, the former looks like a more economically advanced country than the latter. Indeed, in 2000, over 60 percent of imports to Belarus from Russia were raw materials. In contrast, such value-added products as vehicles, equipment, machinery, textiles, and plastics account for 62 percent of Belarus's exports to Russia. Among the most notable export articles from Belarus to Russia are tractors and heavy trucks, refrigerators, TV sets, and footwear: 86 percent of refrigerators, 55 percent of tractors, 73 percent of trucks, and 77 percent of furniture exported from Belarus in 2004 were sold in Russia,[47] and 90 percent of all TV sets and more than 80 percent of all furniture produced in Belarus is exported to Russia. Furthermore, up to 70 percent of the production costs of Belarusian tractors and trucks involve parts and semifinished products received from Russia.[48] While refrigerators and TV sets made in Belarus are hard to come by in Moscow, which is awash with TV sets of the world's renowned brands assembled in China and Southeast Asia, they sell well in Russia's provincial centers.

Given that Belarus's value-added products are much less competitive in the West than they are in Russia, there appears to be no immediate incentive for Belarusian authorities to attach high priority to the reorientation of its trade connections. According to Valery Tsepkalo, though, export connections with Russia allow Belarus to acquire scale economy that would facilitate Belarus's activity on Western markets. The case in point is the production of Belaz superheavy trucks for the mining industry. Belaz is the world's third-ranked producer of these trucks (after Caterpillar and Kamatsu). The minimum acceptable profit margin for Belaz is sustained by the company's producing no less than four hundred heavy trucks a year. Maintaining production capacity above this level is possible only due to purchases by the Russians. As a result, Belaz has been establishing its presence in Latin America.

However, Belarus is also active on Western and Asian markets on its own. For instance, potassium fertilizers account for only a small share of Belarus's exports to Russia and Ukraine. This is because the output of the Soligorsk Potassium Combine (Minsk Oblast) is for the most part sold in Brazil, China, and Poland.[49] This enterprise is the third major contributor to the national budget of Belarus, the first and the second being NAFTAN and Mozyr NPZ, the two Belarusian refineries mentioned above, which process Russian oil.

TRADE IN OIL AND GAS AND ECONOMIC GROWTH

Russia transports 50 percent of its oil export and 20 percent of its natural gas export to the European Union (EU) through Belarus. Besides being a transit country, Belarus consumes a fair amount of both fuels sold by Russia at a discount.

According to the 1995 custom union agreement, Belarusian oil processors were supposed to pay export tariffs, 85 percent of which was to accrue in the Russian budget and the remaining 15 percent in the budget of the Republic of Belarus. This stipulation was abided by until 2001. Thereafter, Belarusians stopped transferring any proceeds from export tariffs to the Russian budget. There is at least one reason why the Russian government did not retaliate for a long time by imposing export tariffs of its own on oil exported to Belarus: Russian oil companies, relieved from export tariffs at home, used Belarus as a sort of offshore haven. These companies likely paid kickbacks to Belarusian authorities and were able to lobby for the retention of a zero-tariff situation in Moscow. With the passage of time, the gap between the price at which oil is sold by Russia to Belarus and the price at which Russia sells its oil in the EU has been steadily widening (table 4.2). In 2005, this gap amounted to a net gain to the tune of 4.2 percent of Belarus's GDP. Leonid Zlotnikov estimates that in 2006, the said gain increased 1.6 times.[50] In 2006, Belarus bought more than twenty million tons of Russian oil, nine million of which was for domestic consumption; the balance was exported mostly as refined oil.[51]

Interesting changes began to occur to the commodity and geographic structure (table 4.3) of Belarus's export as a result of its increased emphasis on refined oil. In the first half of 2006, refined oil accounted for 53 percent of all Belarus's export to the EU. Together with potassium fertilizers and ferrous metals, it accounted for 75 percent of Belarus's export to the EU and 42.6 percent of its total exports, and at the same time, the share of mechanical-engineering exports declined.[52] Geographically, export to the Netherlands (of all places!) skyrocketed, and export to France increased 3.8 times (table 4.3). The Netherlands and the United Kingdom became the second and third largest importers of Belarusian products. In 2006, these countries still retained their second and third

Table 4.2. Price Differential between Crude Oil Sold by Russia to the European Union and to Belarus

	2001	2003	2004	2005	2006
Price per ton of crude oil sold to Belarus	$116	$133	$182	$218	$268
Price per ton of crude oil sold to the EU	$156	$181	$233	$350	$470

Source: Leonid Zlotnikov, "Nado bezhat," *Belorusy i Rynok,* December 25–January 1, 2007.

Table 4.3. Change in Belarus's Exports and Imports, 2004–2005

	Export		Import	
	January to June 2005 ($ millions)	*As a Percentage of That from January to June 2004*	*January to June 2005 ($ millions)*	*As a Percentage of That from January to June 2004*
Total	**7,381.7**	**119.6**	**7,087.3**	**101.7**
Russia	2,656.4	91.3	4,289.3	90.9
Netherlands	1,052.0	330	66.1	129.0
United Kingdom	500.6	83.3	68.2	134.7
Poland	419.6	138.7	257.9	124.4
Ukraine	403.8	177.7	383.0	159.7
Germany	327.9	138.8	431.1	100.2
China	208.1	135.0	112.8	202.2
Lithuania	155.7	134.2	57.5	62.5
Latvia	148.6	95.7	43.1	101.6
France	141.9	380	81.0	122.2
United States	104.8	149.1	96.8	137.2
Sweden	101.9	160.7	30.4	55.0
Italy	75.7	99.6	165.5	129.9
Hungary	75.2	118.9	32.3	152.4
Brazil	73.5	104.6	87.5	133.7

Source: Leonid Zayiko, "Konvergentnaya divergentsiya: paranormalnaya normalnaya integratsiya," *Nashe Mneniye*, September 19, 2005, at www.nmnby.org.

positions; moreover, Belarusian export to the former grew by 83.7 percent. Almost all of the Belarusian export to the Netherlands and United Kingdom is gasoline and diesel fuel.[53] "Which political declarations of the Western countries can be taken seriously after that?" asks an opposition-minded Belarusian economist. "These countries are investing in support of the current political regime of Belarus. One has to recognize this quite frankly."[54]

In the area of natural gas, in 2006 Belarus facilitated the transit of 30 billion cubic meters through the Russian Gazprom-owned pipeline Yamal-Europe and 14.5 billion cubic meters through the Belarus-owned Beltransgaz network.[55] Overall, this is only 20 percent of Russian gas in transit to Europe; unlike oil, the bulk of natural gas goes through Ukraine. There are technological connectors between Beltransgaz and Yamal-Europe, but so far they have been kept sealed. In 2006, Belarus's own import of Russian gas amounted to twenty-two billion cubic meters. The price of it to Belarus was $46.7 per thousand cubic meters. For comparison, Armenia paid $100, Ukraine $230,[56] and EU countries $265 and more per thousand cubic meters.[57]

Low pricing of natural gas for Belarus was stipulated by a 2002 bilateral agreement, according to which the Beltransgaz network was to become a

Russian-Belarusian joint-stock company, with Russian Gazprom acquiring half of its shares no later than July 1, 2003. This deal was never realized, and bickering over the actual price of the Beltransgaz lingered on, culminating in the hiring of a Dutch appraising firm, ABN-AMRO, to arrive at an independent judgment.

Virtually all Belarusian economists not working for the government[58] concur that the preferential treatment of Belarus by Russia in the areas of oil and natural gas has been the cornerstone of Belarusian economic success, although some of them (notably Stanislaw Bogdankevich) concede that they underestimated the effect of enforced managerial discipline, while others (notably Leonid Zayiko) appreciate the sanity of governmental policies when writing about the homegrown investment boom.

UNEXPECTED INVESTMENT BOOM

Earlier I mentioned that the depreciation of capital stock in Belarusian industry is a major problem. Moreover, if Lukashenka detractors and his fans alike point out one problem, it is indeed the wear and tear on equipment and the slow pace of its modernization. Traditionally, most experts see foreign direct investors as the remedy. However, the investment climate in Belarus is not inviting for political reasons and due to the unrealistic requirements that Belarusian authorities set for potential investors, such as a commitment to refrain from laying off workers and/or to invest in the "social sphere" (e.g., to build a stadium in a company town) above and beyond investment in capital stock. Nobody expected that sources of investment could be found within Belarus itself. But in 2006, $7 billion was invested in Belarus, up from less than $900 million in 2001 and 31.9 percent more than in 2005. Note that in 2006, Belarus's GDP was about $39 billion. Remarkably, foreign sources accounted for no more than $200 million, that is, less than 3 percent of the total investment. About 55 percent of new investment has been into services, from hypermarkets (gigantic retail facilities that carry an enormous range of products under one roof, including full lines of groceries and general merchandise) to mobile phone systems, and 45 percent into production. Only 7.3 percent of new investment came from the national budget, whereas about half of it came from the financial means of enterprises themselves. The fastest growth (a 50 percent gain in 2006 compared with 2005) was registered in the public sector. The Belarusian banks ($600 million) and population ($340 million) have made a significant amount of new investment.[59] In 2005, Belarusians bought $12 billion worth of goods and services,[60] not bad at all for a mid-level economy with a population of less than ten million. "The conclusion is simple," writes Leonid Zayiko, who was the first independent expert to publicize the investment boom in Belarus. "Belarus set itself on the Japanese path. This is when money is not borrowed but earned. Our investment boom is our own national phenomenon, and one has to take guidance from it when predicting the future."[61]

The lion's share of the fraction of the investment total (7.3 percent) that came from the national budget was directed to the countryside, where a system of Soviet-era collective and state farms lingers. There is a seeming paradox: though in western Belarus the entrepreneurial spirit among the peasantry is more alive than in the East, individual family farming is more widespread in the East. This is because in the West, people became supportive of generally successful Soviet-style socialized farming operations, and they see their interest in preserving them; hence, there is no vacant land other than that on household farms, which are not registered as independent businesses. In contrast, the sociodemographic erosion of rural communities in the East, much like in the non-Chernozem zone of Russia, transformed local collective farms into almshouses and wards of the state. Here, land abandonment is rampant, so those willing to set up a registered family farm have an opportunity to do so.

RUSSIA-BELARUS TRADE WAR

The flow of investment, however, is conditional on the continuation of Russia's direct and indirect subsidies, although their actual contribution to the economic success of Belarus is subject to wide-ranging estimates, depending on the political views of the expert. Some Russian analysts, for example, believe that those subsidies amount to as much as $10 billion, which is more than one-quarter of the Belarusian GDP.[62] Other Russian experts are less definitive and assess subsidies to Belarus in terms of opportunity costs: how much could the Russian state budget and/or Russian businesses have gained if they had treated Belarus as a "normal" foreign country. Such estimates are not particularly revealing, if only because Belarusian authorities readily invoke reciprocal charges. For example, as much as forty thousand hectares have been assigned to the Yamal-Europe pipeline, an area equivalent to two *rayony* of Belarus, with self-imposed land-use restrictions, and Russia was not charged for that. Also, two important military facilities occupy land in Belarus, and Russia is not charged for that either. Belarus spends disproportionately more funds than Russia on maintaining what essentially is the common Russia-Belarus western frontier. Because of that, Russia is not expected to spend on safeguarding its actual western border, which remains transparent.

Independent Belarusian experts all agree nonetheless that Russia's subsidies are significant, though not nearly as high as $10 billion a year, but from 30 percent to 40 percent of that sum.

Be that as it may, in December 2006, Russia made a political decision to cut back on those subsidies with the ostensible aim of eliminating them altogether. The most widely publicized reasons behind this decision have been President Lukashenka's lingering strategy of repeatedly trading empty promises for tangible financial aid. In Russia, there are different viewpoints on subsidizing the Belarusian economy. According to the geopolitical school of thought,[63] Belarus ought to be subsidized regardless of net economic loss for Russia in the name of maintaining and protecting the identity of East Slavic civilization against the onslaught of both Atlantic and Islamic geopolitical centers. According to economic purists, most of which are Russian economists of the neoliberal school (such as Yegor Gaidar, who has long believed that supporting "unreformed" Belarus is a self-imposed burden,[64] as well as Vladimir Putin's ministers Alexei Kudrin and German Gref), Lukashenka's refraining from turning in the controlling shares of Beltransgaz to Russia's Gazprom, preventing Russian businesses (e.g., the Russian brewery Baltika) from buying up Belarusian enterprises, and subjecting Russian merchandise imports to quotas are sufficient reasons to consider Russian financial support of Belarus unwarranted. An influential group of Russians, most probably including President Putin himself, are more than irritated by Belarus's stalling not only the introduction of Russian currency as the common currency of Russia and Belarus (with only one emission center in Russia) but also the adoption of the Russian rendition of the Constitutional Act of the Russia-Belarus Union, two developments that combined have the potential to bring about Belarus's de facto incorporation into Russia.

Apparently, due to the lack of political will under the presidency of Boris Yeltsin (and for a couple of years thereafter), as well as, strangely enough, a lack of understanding of the Belarusian political landscape, Russia passed up the opportunity to incorporate its western neighbor at a time when this would not have generated serious resistance in Belarus. Based on reliable public opinion polls (see the discussion in chapter 7), this time ended around 2002; by early 2004, the consolidation of the Belarusian political elite had made incorporation difficult to achieve, if possible at all. The realization of this mishap might have led to frustration for Russia. This time, however, Russia counted on what it saw as economic and political imperatives: economically, Belarus is dependent on Russian energy and cannot easily compensate for it, and politically, Lukashenka is cornered because he cannot reconcile with the West, or so it is believed. This sort of reasoning seems to underlie Russia's latest effort to force the Belarusian leadership to agree to a Belarus-Russia union on Russia's terms. To this end, a double blow was dealt to Belarus, and the "brotherly spirit" between the two countries all but vanished in the winter of 2006–2007.

First, Russia announced that it would begin to charge Belarus $200 per thousand cubic meters of natural gas come January 1, 2007, but the ultimate decision about transferring 50 percent of Beltransgaz' shares to Russia's Gazprom might lessen the price somewhat. It must be taken into account, though, that according to the deal signed with the EU in conjunction with Russia's pending accession to the World Trade Organization, Russia is expected to charge market prices on natural gas to its own consumers as early as 2011, so price hikes for Belarus were inevitable one way or another. The Belarusian authorities contended that they were not against those hikes in principle but that such hikes should be equally applied to Belarusian and Russian customers in the spirit of a custom union and other bilateral agreements harmonizing economic conditions within the emerging interstate union. Intense bargaining followed, accompanied by a mutually hostile media campaign in both countries, and a definitive deal was reached only at 11:58 p.m. on December 31, 2006.

According to the new contract between Gazprom and the Belarusian government, in 2007, the price of natural gas sold to Belarus was to be $100 per thousand cubic meters, 2.14 times higher than in 2006, and the entire payment was to be received in cash. At the same time, Gazprom agreed with a Dutch financial firm's appraisal of Beltransgaz and will pay Belarus $2.5 billion over four years (in equal installments) for 50 percent of Beltransgaz's shares. By 2011, the price of natural gas for Belarus will reach the "European" level, whatever that might be. According to the signed agreement, the transit tariff on natural gas was to increase from $0.75 to $1.45 per thousand cubic meters per hundred kilometers.[65] According to Zayiko, in 2007, additional natural gas expenses would amount to $500 million and would be unsustainable for the Belarusian economy.[66]

The nature of the second blow is more difficult to grasp, at least for me. As was mentioned, the gap between prices at which Russia sells crude oil to Europe and to Belarus has been steadily on the rise. In addition, until 2007, Russia did not levy an export tariff on oil sold to Belarus, and Belarus's own export tariff on refined oil was one-half of that charged by Russia. So, for Russian petroleum oligarchs, Belarus was like a tax haven, and they most probably paid kickbacks to officials in both countries. In late 2006, Russia announced that it was going to charge an export tariff of $180 per ton of crude oil obtained by Belarus, the same amount levied on oil sold by Russia to Europe.[67] So, yet another tough negotiation commenced after the first day of 2007 and ended on January 12 with the announcement that the size of the export tariff levied by Russia on its oil obtained by Belarus would be determined by multiplying the tariff applied to oil sold to the EU by a certain co-efficient. For 2007, this coefficient was set at 0.293. Multiplying $180 by 0.293 comes to $52.7. This is the tariff Russia is now applying to oil obtained by Belarus. In 2008, the coefficient will be 0.335.[68] Part of the same agreement is the stipulation that Belarus must increase its tariff on the fuel oil exported from Belarus. Up until the end of 2006, Russia levied $138 on a ton of high-quality fuel oil, whereas Belarus only charged $75.80. Together, both aspects of the oil trade agreement have done away with Belarus as a tax haven for Russian oil oligarchs, who are being deprived of exorbitant profits. So, if every aspect of the bilateral trade in oil were transparent, then the only losers would appear to be Russian oligarchs. The Russian budget gains $1 billion, and the Belarusian budget gains an additional $1.65 billion. However, everything in the bilateral oil trade has most probably not been transparent, and more oil was probably transported through Belarus than the books show. Furthermore, part of it was reexported as crude, not as fuel oil. It is this illicit part that has been removed from the equation.

To complicate matters further, there are two ways in which Belarus obtains Russian crude oil. Out of twenty-one million tons of it, only about half is purchased, whereas the other half makes it to Belarus through so-called give-and-take schemes under which no cash is paid for crude oil. Belarusian refineries process crude oil that belongs to their Russian partners, and they get paid by appropriating a fraction of that crude. The rest is exported to the West by the offshoots of Russian oil companies registered in Belarus. In February 2007, three out of six Russian oil suppliers announced that under the new conditions, give-and-take schemes no longer made sense to them, so they would terminate that part of the supply. This is interesting: if one takes into account that Russia's export tariff on oil to Belarus is $53, and Belarus is expected to impose $108 per ton of fuel oil on average, the sum of these two tariffs is still short of $180, which is Russia's own export tariff on crude oil to the EU. So, although give-and-take schemes are no longer wildly profitable, they are still profitable nonetheless. The Belarus government sounded an alarm and decided to subsidize give-and-take schemes.

Leonid Zayiko, an independent Belarusian expert whose judgments are usually least politicized, believes that Belarus is facing a political decision by the Kremlin bent on extracting two major concessions from Lukashenka: the unification of currency systems and the signing of the Constitutional Act of Belarus-Russia Union on Russia's terms.[69] If this is the case, some far-reaching consequences are to be expected, but most probably political and economic bargaining will soon resume.

At this writing, it is too early to judge which side's concessions were more significant and what kind of damage has been done to Russia's life-support of the Belarusian economy. It appears obvious that under the newly negotiated conditions, no reexport of Russian oil from Belarus is possible any longer, at least officially. In addition to the price of crude oil, Belarusian buyers will now be required to recover the export tariff of $53 per ton and $180.7 for its reexport. Definitely, some damage has been done in addition to eliminating the reexport of Russian oil, and already Yaroslaw Romanchuk, invariably the first to herald the demise of Lukashenka's economic model no matter what stumbling block it has hit at the time, has delivered his dire prediction, according to which Belarus will lose $2.5 billion (17.8 percent of its budget and 8.3 percent of its GDP).[70] However, other usual Cassandras have not been equally damning. For example, Zayiko stated that under the negotiated conditions, all sides—the Russian state bureaucracy, Russian oligarchs, and the Belarusian state and oil refineries—will make money, and neither the export of refined oil (worth $6 billion) nor employment in Belarus's petrochemical industry is in danger.[71] Earlier Leonid Zlotnikov had averred that two measures could cushion the double blow dealt by Russia. The first is radical market reform, which would create conditions attractive to foreign banks and investors. The second entails cutting back on unreasonably high infusions of money into Belarusian agriculture. Currently $2 billion is spent for that purpose, which is about the same amount that gigantic Russia spends to subsidize its farmers.[72] Definitely, the Belarusian economy is at a crossroads, and it remains to be seen how and whether it will survive its arguably most crucial test. In February 2007, Belarus officially asked Russia for a $1.5 billion loan to offset the price hikes.

At the same time, though, the negotiated results of the Russia-Belarus trade war are decidedly more sparing for Belarus than anticipated by every Russian commentator and all independent Belarusian commentators who weighed in on the subject. Belarus will continue to pay significantly less for oil and gas than any other buyer; it thus remains on Russia's life-support, although, granted, it is not as generous as before. According to President Putin of Russia, in 2007 Belarus's savings as a result of buying natural gas at a discount will amount to $3.3 billion, and Belarus's savings as a result of buying crude oil at a discount will amount to $2.5 billion. The total savings thus account for 41 percent of Belarus's budget.[73] Even if these data constitute an exaggeration as they do not include the appraisal of benefits that Russia itself extracts from Belarus, such as free-of-charge land allotted to the Russia-owned pipeline Yamal-Europe, it still appears that Russia's support continues to be integral to Belarus's economic model and explains its vitality, if only in part. So, what kind of economy exists in Belarus, or in Marxist terms, what is its formational identity?

BELARUSIAN ECONOMIC MODEL: FORMATIONAL IDENTITY

It might seem that the Russia-Belarus trade war of the winter of 2006–2007 made the above question senseless or obsolete. In the media accompaniment of the bilateral negotiations, particularly from the Russian side, there was no shortage of scathing metaphors depicting ties between the two economies. "Belorussia wants a union with Russia as . . . an intestinal worm wants a union with a stomach," said one Russian liberal journalist during a talk show on the *Echo Moskvy* radio channel. "That is the ideal image that we used to have of a union between the Batska [Lukashenka's nickname, meaning "father"] and Russia."[74] Another Russian commentator likened Russia's treatment of Belarus to parents who stop giving their son change for ice cream when he reaches maturity.[75] Even earlier, some opposition-minded Belarusian economists appealed to the Russian government to stop subsidizing a totalitarian regime. This was the message of an article titled "Asymmetrical Unity" that Yaroslaw Romanchuk coauthored with Nikita Belykh, the leader of Russian liberal Union of Right Forces party.[76] If those metaphors and appeals were taken seriously, then whatever the Belarusian economic model was, its days were numbered. Indeed, it seemed that Russia's double blow would subject the Belarusian economy to such an existential test that the outcome might be either drastic liberalization or incorporation into Russia and liberalization, Russian style.

Yet, something was undercutting this sort of certainty, even when the Belarus-Russia spat over gas and oil was still underway. First, the Belarusian model had survived for ten straight years, and it suited many people in Belarus. Second, powerful forces in Russia are in favor of keeping Belarus on Russia's life-support. Also, considering that the negotiated outcome of the Russia-Belarus trade war was more favorable for Belarus than most commentators predicted, posing the question as to whether Belarus's economic model is sustainable might be reasonable after all.

The Belarusian authorities call their economic model a "socially oriented market economy."[77] They claim that they "reject the extremes of liberalism and statism and choose to build an economic system characterized by a strong state, effective market mechanism, and its social orientation."[78] This, they claim, is a mixed economy in transition. Because the experiences of "landslide privatization" in Russia and Poland were perceived as negative, Belarus took a more evolutionary path. It is recognized, though, that this evolution has not been overly successful due to an "insufficiently favorable business environment, weak state support of entrepreneurial activity, low pull of foreign investment, lack of a broad stratum of efficient proprietors bent on long-term development of their enterprises . . . and their low level of responsibility for the results of their activity."[79] Yet, the very idea of market transition has not been discarded.

Since 1994, the European Bank for Reconstruction and Development (EBRD) has been releasing its annual transition reports. "In addition to the private sector share of GDP, estimated by the EBRD taking into account the 'informal' economy and reflecting the private or public nature of enterprise governance, transition scores covering other aspects of the economy range from 1 (little or no change) to 4 (OECD [Organization for Economic Cooperation and Development] standards)."[80] For Belarus, transition indicators are above two only on price liberalization and also, more recently, on small-scale privatization. All of the EBRD scores, though, as well as almost all qualitative characteristics of the Belarusian economy tracked by Western Belarus watchers, are part and parcel of the neoliberal discourse, "which has been the hegemonic mode of discourse" from as early as 1978.[81] "The assumption that individual freedoms are guaranteed by freedom of the market and of trade is a cardinal feature of neoliberal thinking, and it has long dominated the U.S. stance toward the rest of the world."[82]

Since the late 1980s, the most committed neoliberal scholars of postcommunist transition, such as Anders Aslund and Jeffrey Sachs, advocated speedy and sweeping privatization and "shock therapy" through decontrolling all prices. By now, however, neoliberal recipes for transition have been subjected to abundant and versatile criticism. One important critical argument suggests that preaching about the building of civil society and applying shock therapy at the same time is an artifice at best because shock therapy boosts social stratification and thereby undermines efforts at building civil society. "Western advisers made economic transformation a priority, but wherever their advice was followed it was poverty, not pluralism that resulted. Across the old communist block 'shock therapy' enriched a few dozen oligarchs and their foreign economic advisers, but the mass unemployment it caused and the collapse of public spending it demanded smashed the foundations of the civil society emerging under Gorbachev."[83] Mark Almond, an Oxford University lecturer in modern history and the author of the above comment, caused a stir when he suggested that "by protecting Belarus from the ravages of free-market fundamentalists and delivering economic growth . . . for the masses of Belarusians, Lukashenka has sown seeds of a pluralistic society far better than by handing the state's assets over to half a dozen cronies of Western advisers."[84] As it turns out, an analysis of the recent dynamics of personal consumption in Belarus by economist Zayiko, a fierce Lukashenka basher, effectively upholds Almond's view. Since 2004, personal incomes in Belarus have been growing at a fast pace, and "with growing income we will be also demanding political wares of higher quality,"[85] Zayiko writes. In other words, favorable political change in Belarus is now viewed as resulting from the current regime's economic success, not from overt democracy promotion.

In his doctoral thesis defended in England, Viacheslau Yarashevich, a Belarusian scholar, reviewed almost two hundred Western publications critical of the neoliberal perspective on postcommunist transition.[86] The very fact that such a broad literature exists reflects deep dissatisfaction with neoliberal recipes, some of which are informed by dubious convictions, such as "the people of the former Soviet Empire desire democracy rather than bread."[87] Critics of such views maintain that some postsocialist societies have adopted a "primitive" model of capitalism based on the "mythologized histories of . . . the free market paragons, Britain and the United States."[88] Instead, the argument goes, they might have learned from the experience of late industrializing economies, particularly in East Asia, and aimed at creating a corporatist social order, where the state would provide a "more visible hand than neoliberalism envisioned."[89] This social order is indeed quite similar to the one that has emerged in Belarus.

But if the neoliberal orthodoxy—fast privatization, cutting back on social expenditures, and a preponderance of monetary regulations of economic activities—is no longer a mantra even among Western-trained scholars, what is the opinion about the formational identity of Belarus's economy among homegrown economists critical of Lukashenka?

All of them agree that Belarus has taken extraordinary advantage of ties with Russia and that by doing so, Belarus extracted short- and medium-term benefits but squandered time that might have been best spent on the liberalization of its economy. According to the late Valery Dashkevich, the residual socialist features of the Belarusian economy are (1) the significant role of the public sector in all economic activities; (2) the fact that purely political decisions impact monetary income and prices on necessities; (3) retention of the social safety net, which is worth about 55 percent of the GDP; (4) maintaining near-full employment through state production orders and bans on firing personnel; and (5) precluding bankruptcies through soft budget constraints.[90]

Zayiko agrees with the official label of the Belarusian economy as a mixed or double-track economy. He thereby denies that the Belarusian economy is entirely socialist and observes that, alongside legitimate private businesses, creeping privatization of working capital is taking place in Belarus in tacit anticipation of the privatization of large state-owned firms. Scores of private businesses are emerging as go-betweens in procuring the input and selling the output of those large firms. These auxiliary businesses do not boast a large profit margin, but gradually they will accumulate the financial means necessary to buy up Belarus's major industrial plants when privatization is given the green light. Those waiting on the sidelines are local political elites eager to complete their transformation into Belarus's economic elites.[91]

This observation has to do with the sustainability of the Belarusian economy in the long run. It is likely that what the neoliberal paradigm has long insisted on doing is going to be accomplished anyway, only gradually. The unique possibility of this gradualist approach is afforded by Belarus's strategic position as a transit country. Due to its transit position in exporting Russia's hydrocarbons to Europe, Belarus has been able to extract concessions from Russia. Accomplishing this and at the same time staving off incorporation into Russia may be nothing short of a political feat that many generations of Belarusians will owe to Lukashenka. So, when some analysts recognize Belarus's economic success but reason that it cannot be sustained because "economic theory and practice would predict a number of less-welcome effects"[92] associated with Lukashenka's economic policy, it is hard for me to be swayed by such reasoning.

First, until recently the idea that Belarus even had a positive economic dynamic was discounted as a myth. Second, and more importantly, any prediction of economic sustainability makes sense only for an entity that performs its vital functions on its own, with only marginal outside aid. However, there is little to suggest that Lukashenka's vision of Belarus fits this template. Because in times of need his homeland stretches from Brest to Vladivostok, he clearly counts on the continuation of Russia's subsidies, direct and indirect, and he views his transit location and industrial assets as bargaining chips. Under this scenario, sustaining positive trends in the relatively small entity that Lukashenka presides over may prove possible.

While the Russia-Belarus tussle of December 2006 to January 2007 called this conclusion into question, it did not shatter it altogether. Moreover, signs have appeared that not just Russia but the EU itself may begin to turn a blind eye on "Europe's last dictator" and help him lessen the dependency on Russia. With the EU potentially entering the fray, it is not unthinkable that Belarus, much like the German Democratic Republic of the 1980s, will milk its strategic neighbors both to the east and west in accordance with a pithy American commercial: "When banks compete, you win!"

In 2006, the EU had already extended an offer of aid to Belarus, contingent on progress in the area of free press, elections, and human rights. In early 2007, it appeared that these preconditions might be rendered more "flexible" and that Poland was likely to play the role of promoting tighter links between Belarus and the EU. When the Russia-Belarus oil conflict was in full swing, Pawel Zalewski, chairman of the Foreign Affairs Committee of the Polish Seim (parliament) and a veteran Lukashenka basher, wrote that the EU should "support the structures of an independent Belarusian state. . . . Paradoxically,

Belarus's withdrawal from the Russian price zone opens for Minsk a chance for reform and economic modernization. To enable this, significant economic and financial support is necessary. Considering the EU's potential, rendering such support is entirely within the EU's possibilities."[93] According to a realistic assessment by Zalewski, "Even if Lukashenka is gone and the opposition takes power, the political elites of Belarus are not going to change, and so Poland and the EU are to talk to them in the future anyway."[94] Moreover, "Poland and Europe as a whole ought to significantly broaden their contacts with Belarus . . . even if hopes for the Ukrainian scenario of an orange revolution prove to be false."[95] It may well be that the chairman of the Polish parliamentary committee was not the only influential Westerner who expressed those views. Anyway, on January 14, 2007, when the trade war was officially over, Lukashenka made an interesting statement: "During the oil conflict between Belarus and Russia, Europe and the USA acted decently. They offered us their help and support in case the state and people of Belarus need them. That, we will never forget."[96] Ironically, this statement was made just a couple of days after George W. Bush signed the extension of his Belarus Democracy Act. News that surfaced soon thereafter about the possible opening of the European Commission's office in Minsk and the initiation of the energy dialogue between the EU and Belarus did not come as a surprise.[97] At the same time, Russia's supreme policy makers rest in their conviction that because Lukashenka's reputation in Europe cannot be worse than it currently is, Belarus has nowhere to go. To be sure, there is much truth to this opinion, just as there is much truth to what America's Belarus Democracy Act says. Amazing, though, is how inflexible the foreign policies of the two cold war enemies, Russia and America, are: proudly set in their great-power ways, tone-deaf, and blind to nuances. Given this inflexibility, Lukashenka may once again wriggle his way through.

In summary, Belarus's economic growth has been robust. Special relationships with Russia have been an important growth factor, but apparently not the only one. Implications of the trade war with Russia are going to be serious but not cataclysmic. It may well be that Belarus will be able to sustain its peculiar economic model, which can only be understood in the context of Belarus's transit location between Europe and its "poorly illuminated periphery,"[98] Russia.

NOTES

1. Ergaly Gher, "Belorusskoye zerkalo," *Znamya* 1 (2007), at http://magazines.russ.ru/znamia/20071/ger8-pr.html.

2. V. I. Golubovich, ed., *Ekonomicheskaya istoriya Belarusi*, 3rd ed. (Minsk: UP Ecoperspectiva, 2004), 156.

3. "Belorusskaya Sovetskaya Sotsialisticheskaya Respublika," *Bol'shaya Sovetskaya Entsyklopedia*, Moscow 1969–1978, at www.rubicon.ru/bse.

4. Golubovich, ed., *Ekonomicheskaya istoriya Belarusi*, 3rd ed., 169.

5. Golubovich, *Ekonomicheskaya istoriya Belarusi*.

6. *Naseleniye SSSR 1987* (Moscow: Finansy I Statistika, 1988), 16.

7. "Posledstviya Velikoi Otechestvennoi voiny dlya Belarusi," at www.president.gov.by/gosarchives/vov/spravpos.htm.

8. *Narodnoye khoziaistvo SSSR za 70 let* (Moscow: Finansy i Statistika, 1987) contains the following monetary estimates of damage: Ukraine, 285 billion rubles and Belarus, 75 billion rubles in 1941 prices. According to *Naseleniye SSSR* (Moscow: Finansy i Statistika, 1987), the 1940 population of Ukraine was 41 million people, and Belarus was home to 9 million people.

9. Grigory Ioffe, "Understanding Belarus: Economy and Political Landscape," *Europe-Asia Studies* 56, no. 1 (2004): 85–118.

10. Alexei Smolsky, "Izderzhki ekonomicheskogo razvitiya Belorussii," *Materik*, February 2007, at http://materik.ru.

11. Yuri Guraliuk, "Novyi Lukashenko: schastlivaya obrechionnost' pobezhdat'," *Yevraziiskoye Obozreniye* 3 (2001), at http://eurasia.com.ru/eo/3-12.html.

12. Calculated on the basis of *Narodnoye khoziaistvo SSSR: Yubileinyi statisticheskii ezhegodnik* (Moscow: Finansy i Statistika, 1987), 548, 389–92; in 1986, in Russia there were 20 college students per one thousand of the population; in Ukraine, there were 16.6, whereas in Belarus, there were 17.9.

13. *Natsional'nyi sostav naseleniya Respubliki Belarus i rasprostranionnost' yazykov* (Minsk: Ministerstvo Statistiki i Analiza, 2001), 37.

14. *CIS in 2004* (Moscow: Interstate Statistical Committee of the CIS, 2005), 25.

15. *CIS in 2004*, 26.

16. EBRD Transition Report: Structural Indicators, at www.ebrd.com/country/sector/econo/stats/sci.xls (accessed January 3, 2007).

17. Ministerstvo Statistiki i Analiza, at http://belstat.gov.by/homep/ru/indicators/svodn_2000-2005.php.

18. Andrew Wilson and Clelia Rontoyani, "Security or Prosperity: Belarusian and Ukrainian Choices," in *Swords and Sustenance: The Economics of Security in Belarus and Ukraine,* ed. Robert Legvold and Celleste Wallander (Cambridge, MA: MIT Press, 2004), 43.

19. David Marples, *Belarus: A Denationalized Nation* (Amsterdam: Harwood, 1999), 40.

20. Margarita M. Balmaceda, "Myth and Reality in the Belarusian-Russian Relationship," *Problems of Post-Communism* 46, no. 3 (1999): 12.

21. David Marples, "Europe's Last Dictatorship: The Roots and Perspectives of Authoritarianism in 'White Russia,'" *Europe-Asia Studies* 57, no. 6 (September 2005): 896.

22. *Praski Accent*, talk show of the Belarusian Service of Radio Liberty, October 25, 2005 at www.svaboda.org/textarticlesprograms/pragueaccent/2005/10/27.

23. "IMF Country Report No. 05/217, June 2005," in *Republic of Belarus: Selected Issues* (IMF: Washington, DC, 2005), 4.

24. "IMF Country Report," 2.

25. *Belarus: Window of Opportunity to Enhance Competitiveness and Sustain Economic Growth* (Washington, DC: The World Bank, 2005), at http://web.worldbank.org/wbsite/external/countries/ecaext/belarusextn.

26. "IMF Country Report No. 05/217, June 2005," in *Republic of Belarus: Selected Issues* (IMF: Washington DC, 2005), 7.

27. *CIS in 2005* (Moscow: Interstate Statistical Committee of the CIS, 2006), 144.

28. *CIS in 2005*, 39.

29. Alexei Smolsky, "Izderzhki ekonomicheskogo razvitiya Belorussii," *Materik*, February 2007, at http://materik.ru.

30. *CIS in 2004*, 25.

31. *CIS in 2005*, 203–21.

32. *Natsionalnaya ekonomika Belarusi* (Minsk: BGEU, 2005), 137.

33. D. Mario Nuti, "The Belarus Economy: Suspended Animation between State and Markets," in *Post-Communist Belarus*, ed. Stephen White, Elena Korosteleva, and John Lowenhardt (Lanham, MD: Rowman & Littlefield, 2005), 98.

34. *Human Development Report 2001*, "Human Development Indicators," 2002, 210–12, at www.undp.org/hdr2001/back.pdf.

35. http://hdr.undp.org/hdr2006/statistics.

36. *2007 World Population Data Sheet* (Washington, DC: Population Reference Bureau, 2007). In 2006, life expectancies in Russia and Belarus were seventy-two and seventy-five years among women and fifty-nine and sixty-three years among men, respectively.

37. *Human Development Report 2006*, at http://hdr.undp.org/hdr2006/statistics/indicators/145.html.

38. "Belarus sokhraniyayet polozhitelnoye saldo migratsii so vsemi stranami SNG i Baltii," *BDG*, August 30, 2004, at www.bdg.by.

39. Calculated on the basis of *CIS in 2005*, 114, and http://hdr.undp.org/hdr2006/statistics.

40. *CIA World Fact Book*, 2006, at https://www.cia.gov/cia/publications/factbook/geos/rs.html#Econ.

41. Dean M. Hanink, *Principles and Applications of Economic Geography* (New York: John Wiley and Sons, 1996), 341–42.

42. *CIS in 2005*, 118, 119.

43. See http://belstat.gov.by/homep/ru/indicators/ftrade.php.

44. See http://belstat.gov.by/homep/ru/indicators/ftrade.php.

45. *CIS in 2005*, 122, 123.

46. *CIS in 2005*, 114, 135.

47. Leonid Zayiko, "Ot zhelayemogo k deistvitelnomu," *Rossiya v Globalnoi Politike* 1 (2006), at http://library.by/portalus/modules/beleconomics.

48. Aidyn Mekhtiyev and Alexei Shcheglov, "Opasnye slova," *Strana Ru*, January 29, 2007, at www.strana.ru.

49. Galina Muzlova, "Belarus na fone stran tsentral'noi i vostochnoi Yevropy: Spetsifika regionalizatsii vneshnei torgovli," in *Regionalizatsiya i tsentralizm v territorial'noi organizatsii obshchestva i regional'nom razvitii* (Moscow: IGRAN, 2001), 167; Zayiko, "Ot zhelayemogo k deistvitelnomu."

50. Leonid Zlotnikov, "Nado bezhat," *Belorusy i Rynok*, December 25, 2006–January 1, 2007.

51. Yelena Novozhilova, "S neft'yu, kak i s gazom, tozhe nichego ne yasno," *Belorusskie Novosti*, December 29, 2006, at www.naviny.by.

52. Leonid Zlotnikov, "Nado bezhat," *Belorusy i Rynok*, December 25, 2006–January 1, 2007.

53. *Polugodiye oschutimykh peremen. Vneshniya torgovlia v pervoi polovine 2006 g.* (Minsk: Mises Center, 2006), 3, at http://liberty-belarus.info/content/view/1382/50.

54. Leonid Zayiko, "Konvergentnaya divergentsiya: Paranormalnaya normalnaya integratsiya," *Nashe Mneniye*, September 19, 2005, at www.nmnby.org.

55. "Gazprom obespechit transit gaza v Yevropu v polnom ob'yome," December 28, 2006, at http://top.rbc.ru/index.shtml?/news/policy/2006/12/28/28171741_bod.shtml.

56. Actually Ukraine paid much less per thousand cubic meters of natural gas because of the high share of cheaper Central Asian (Turkmen) gas in its 2006 consumption; but the $230 price reportedly applied to the Russian share of gas imports. But even "much less" was not below $100, twice the price of gas sold to Belarus.

57. "Gazprom idiot na posledniuyu ustupku Belarusi," *Belorusskie Novosti*, December 27, 2006, at www.naviny.by.

58. The most published of these experts are Stanislaw Bogdankevich, Valery Dashkevich, Stanislaw Romanchuk, Leonid Zayiko, and Leonid Zlotnikov.

59. Leonid Zayiko, "Investitsionny bum Belarusi—natsionalnyi fenomen," *Belorusskie Novosti*, December 9, 2006, at www.naviny.by.

60. Leonid Zayiko, "Luchshii god novogo stoletiya," *Nashe Mneniye*, January 4, 2007, at www.nmnby.org.

61. Zayiko, "Luchshii god novogo stoletiya."

62. Alexander Fadeyev, "Rossiya i RB: Na poroge neftegazovoi voiny," *Materik: Informatsionno-analiticheskii portal post-sovetskogo prostranstva*, December 2006, at http://materik.ru.

63. See, for example, Sergei Mikheyev, "Perspektivy integratsii: Elity protiv ob'yektivnykh predposylok," *Politcom.Ru*, December 20, 2006, at www.politcom.ru; Yury Shevtsov, "Soyuz Moskvy i Minska raspadayetsia?" *Rosbalt*, October 20, 2006, at www.rosbalt.ru/2006/10/20/271898.html.

64. "Bumazhnyi korol," *Belorusskaya Delovaya Gazeta*, August 29, 2002, 1.

65. "Yest' kontrakt: 100 dollarov za tysiachu kubometrov," January 2, 2007, at www.naviny.by.

66. Zayiko, "Luchshii god novogo stoletiya."

67. "Rossiya vvodit poshlinu na export nefti v Belorussiyu," Strana.Ru, December 12, 2006, at www.strana.ru.

68. "Pobedila 'druzhba,'" *Beloruskie Novosti*, January 13, 2007, at www.naviny .by.

69. Leanid Zayiko, "Galounaye shto zberagutsa patoki nafty," Belarusian Service of Radio Liberty, January 12, 2007, at www.svaboda.org.

70. "Yaroslau Ramanchuk: Belaruskaya ekanomika stratsits kalia $2.5 billion," Belarusian Service of Radio Liberty, January 12, 2007, at www.svaboda.org.

71. Zayiko, "Galounaye shto zberagutsa patoki nafty."

72. Leonid Zlotnikov, "Mozhno li smiagchit posledstviya rosta tsen na neft I gaz?" *Belorusskie Novosti*, December 19, 2006, at www.naviny.by.

73. "Vladimir Putin: Podderzhka Rossiyei belorusskoi ekonomiki nachinaya s etogo goda znachitelno sokratitsia," *Belorusskie Novosti*, January 15, 2007, at www .naviny.by.

74. *Ekho Moskvy*, daily evening interactive program, January 9, 2007, at www .echo.msk.ru/programs/razvorot_evening/48788/index.phtml.

75. "Gurnov: Nikakoi ustanovki po osveshcheniyu konflikta s Belarusyu i byt ne moglo," *Belorusskie Novosti*, January 12, 2007, at www.naviny.by.

76. Nikita Belykh and Yaroslaw Romanchuk, "Assimetrichnoye yedinstvo," *Nezavisimaya Gazeta*, June 26, 2006.

77. *Natsionalnaya ekonomika Belarusi* (Uchebnoye posoibiye edited by Vladimir Shimov) (Minsk: BGEU, 2005), 465.

78. *Natsionalnaya ekonomika Belarusi*, 466.

79. *Natsionalnaya ekonomika Belarusi*, 456.

80. D. Mario Nuti, "The Belarus Economy: Suspended Animation between State and Markets," in *Post-Communist Belarus*, ed. Stephen White, Elena Korosteleva, and John Lowenhardt, 98.

81. David Harvey, *A Brief History of Neoliberalism* (New York: Oxford University Press, 2005), 3.

82. Harvey, *A Brief History of Neoliberalism*, 7.

83. Mark Almond, "Less Bizarre Than It Seems: The Landslide in Belarus Reflects Its Demonized Leader's Refusal to Back Market Fundamentalism," *The Guardian*, March 21, 2006.

84. Almond, "Less Bizarre Than It Seems."

85. Leonid Zayiko, "Na porsche between Brusselem i Moskvoi," *Nashe Mneniye*, September 11, 2006, at www.nmnby.org.

86. Viachaslau Yarashevich, *Political Economy of Modern Belarus in the Context of Post-Socialist Transformation Discourse* (PhD diss., University of Kingston, Kingston-upon-Thames, United Kingdom, 2006).

87. Joseph Brada, "A Critique of the Evolutionary Approach to the Economic Transition from Communism to Capitalism," in *The Evolutionary Transition to Capitalism*, ed. Kazimierz Poznanski (Boulder, CO: Westview Press, 1995), 201, 203.

88. Alice Amsden et al., *The Market Meets Its Match: Restructuring the Economics of Eastern Europe* (Cambridge, MA: Harvard University Press, 1994), 3.

89. Amsden et al., *The Market Meets Its Match*.

90. Valery Dashkevich, "Belorusskaya ekonomichskaya model: Razlichiye i povtoreniye," *Nashe Mneniye*, July 27, 2005, at www.nmnby.org.

91. Leonid Zayiko, "Vybor prezidenta: Kliuch situatsii v ekonomicheskoi pobede nad nomenklaturoi," *Nashe Mneniye*, November 11, 2005, at www.nmnby.org.

92. Patricia Brukoff, "The Belarusian Economy: Is It Sustainable?" in *Independent Belarus: Domestic Determinants, Regional Dynamics, and Implications for the West*, ed. Margarita M. Balmaceda, James Clem, and Lisbeth Tarlow (Cambridge, MA: Harvard University Press, 2002), 113.

93. Pawel Zalewski, "Nie otdawać Bialorusi walkowerem," *Rzeczpospolita*, January 7, 2007.

94. Zalewski, "Nie otdawać Bialorusi walkowerem."

95. Zalewski, "Nie otdawać Bialorusi walkowerem."

96. "Alexander Lukashenka: Belarus ne priyemlet otnosheniya k sebe s pozitsii sily," press conference of January 14, 2007, BELTA, at www.belta.by, January 15, 2007.

97. "Rashiriayetsia dialog ES i Belarusi po kanalam PASE i Yevrokomissii po energetike," *Belorusskiye Novosti*, January 16, 2007, at www.naviny.by.

98. These are words of Vladislav Surkov, deputy chair of Russia's Presidential Administration, at http://russdom.ru/2005/200512i/20051205.html.

5

Belarusian Political Landscape

Anyone who tells you that it is easy to change the way groups of people do things is either a liar, a management consultant, or both. Change is hard for individuals; for groups it is next to impossible.

—The Economist[1]

If there is another trait, aside from the vague sense of separate identity, that has a similar potential to influence the sociopolitical situation in Belarus, it is arguably the delayed, but impulsive, urbanization. Because the urbanization of Belarus only occurred during the latter part of its two-hundred-year-long coexistence in one polity with Russia, I invoke works on Russian and Soviet urbanization in the following analysis.

In his classic research on the Soviet *nomenklatura*, Mikhail Voslensky points to the high percentage of the rural-born among the higher echelon of Soviet leaders. Among others, he cites the example of Minsk Oblast, where in 1946, 855 people were in leadership positions, 709 of whom were former peasants.[2] Anatoly Vishnevsky notes that the share of urban-born Soviet leaders was at its highest during the first years after the 1917 communist revolution. This circumstance reflects the fact that the leading Bolsheviks recruited from the intellectual elite. Further on, the share of rural-born leaders began to grow, thus beginning to match more accurately the overall composition of the Soviet Union's population. Yet, as urbanization progressed, the tradition of promoting former rural villagers to positions of prominence did not subside.[3] This tradition may be a surface reflection of a deeper trend. When Marxism—Western in origin and staked on the vanguard role of the urban proletariat—"stepped out of the elitist circles and got in touch with peasant masses or, still worse, masses of the outcasts already no longer rural, yet not quite urban, this revolutionary school of thought could not help but regenerate into something else."[4] Vishnevsky believes that the communist revolution in Russia matched Oswald Spengler's notion of a "conservative revolution" that set out to modernize Russia by medieval means. The Russian peasantry, with its primitive communal instincts and redistributive ethos, could not help but impact the Soviet pattern of development in a most crucial way. Russia's rural communal ethos is thus the true cradle of Russian communism (apart from Karl Marx's creative mind), and its many facets have been thoroughly researched. Among these facets are a tradition of patience; a proclivity to tolerate inherited inequality rather than inequality resulting from individual contrasts in ingenuity, talent, and work ethic; a cult of a strong leader who would make decisions for the rank and file and thus relieve them from making personal choices; a Manichaean worldview in which the utmost evil wages a perennial tug-of-war with the utmost virtue without a sense of anything whatsoever in between those poles; and a belief in abiding by moral reasoning rather than legal norms. Soviet urbanization was accomplished in record time, too quickly for the acculturation of the archaic peasant masses gushing into the cities. It is these masses whose communal cultural codes gained the upper hand in the Soviet Union, and the rural origin of most Soviet leaders was instrumental in that.

The above stance falls into a school of thought founded by Nikolai Berdiaev. In his book *The Origin of Russian Communism*,[5] Berdiaev attributes communism's most essential features to Russia's Oriental affinities (among which he included communal collectivism), not to Marxism. Whereas the latter had come to be the source of communist symbolism, the former provided human capital susceptible to social engineering and made it possible to muster the energy of the entire nation.[6] "In the USSR, the family is forming, the close-knit circle of relatives, the household teaming with children, with Stalin as the father or the elder brother to all of them,"[7] wrote Andrei Platonov in 1935.

The school of thought that promoted this perspective was off to a bumpy start because the ideologically indoctrinated audience was not ready to listen. When Nicholas Vakar, the same scholar who earlier authored the still unsurpassed volume on Belarus, published *The Taproot of Soviet Society*, in which he showed that the Soviet polity was essentially a reincarnation of the Russian peasantry's traditional arrangements now extended over the entire society under a smoke screen of Marxist symbols,[8] the audience was impressed even less. Published in 1962, Vakar's book was deemed eccentric and fell into oblivion. The cold war was in full swing, and it came to a head during the 1962 Cuban missile crisis. At that time, touting some shadowy cultural roots for communism was too much for the politically agitated reader. Not only did communism look ominous from afar, but the Western agitprop viewed it entirely as a product of erroneous and misleading theory. The fact that Marxism swayed quite a few people in the West aggravated ideological excitement. It was only much later, when communism had retreated from the forefront of international affairs, that Berdiaev's cultural approach began to gain ground; in fact, it now carries the day in the intellectual discourse on the liberal side of Russia's political spectrum among the descendants of Russia's Westernizers.[9] By the mid-1990s, for Russian communists, history had come full circle; at that time, their most ardent supporters were peasants from Russia's South, not industrial workers.[10]

It follows logically from the peasant theory that the Soviet order did not collapse under the burden of economic and political problems endemic to it. Communism came to an end when the tenacious mentality nurtured by the redistributive peasant commune had weakened its grip over the majority of people in a few principal urban areas, notably Moscow and St. Petersburg, which became the loci of the crucial constituency for the change in regime.[11] For the far-flung Soviet regions, change of this nature could not be expected to occur at once. In 1990, when urbanites made up 66 percent of the entire Soviet population, only 15 to 17 percent of those who were sixty and over had been born in urban areas; of those in their forties, about 40 percent had. Only among those aged twenty-two and younger did the percentage of urban-born exceed 50 percent.[12]

What has been just said about the Soviet Union in general pertains especially to Belarus. The urbanization of Belarus was even more delayed than that of Russia and even more impetuous (table 5.1). In Belarus, the redistributive peasant commune existed up to the late 1920s, although Catholics in Belarus's West had disposed of it several generations earlier. Yet, the peasant roots of the infamous Belarusian conservatism are as apparent as they are in the provinces of the so-called Red Belt of southern Russia. And in both cases,

Table 5.1. Percentage of Urban Population

	1800 (%)	1900 (%)	1950 (%)	1970 (%)	1990 (%)	1999/2000 (%)
Western Europe	12	41	59	67	79	79
United States	5	42	57	66	74	75
Euro-Russia	6	13	42	62	74	75
Belarus	6	13	21	43	65	67

Sources: Paul Bairoch, *Cities and Economic Development* (Chicago: University of Chicago Press, 1988), 221, 290; Population Reference Bureau: World Population Data Sheets; *The Demographic Yearbook of Russia 2000* (Moscow: Goskomstat, 2000); Ministerstvo Statistiki i Analiza Respubliki Belarus.

the first economic success took place under the traditional-turned-Soviet forms of collectivism.

Aleh Trusau called my attention to the fact that authoritarianism is inherent in peasant tradition and that "all peasant countries initially promoted dictators to the helm of power. Look at Hungary's Horti, Portugal's Salazar, and Poland's Pilsudski."[13] When in the late 1980s, Ales Adamovich, a Belarusian author turned Moscow-based publicist, called his native country the "Vendee of Perestroika,"[14] the crux of the matter was deeply entrenched rural conservatism.

In addition to the peasant communal background of the majority of today's Belarusians, an acute deficit of entrepreneurial culture within Belarusian ethnicity ought to be mentioned, a feature that sets Belarus apart from all its neighbors. In eastern Belarus prior to the communist revolution of 1917 and in western Belarus prior to its 1939 incorporation into the Soviet Union, the majority of businessmen were Jews and Poles. Both Jewish and Polish communities were largely eliminated during World War II (Jews) and shortly thereafter (Poles[15]). That was, according to some Belarusian scholars, a revolutionary change, as the gates of vertical mobility were thrust open for ethnic Belarusians for the first time in modern history.[16] Yet, nobody could possibly succeed as a businessman in the Soviet Union after World War II. Belarusians thus got stuck between primitive peasant communalism and the more "advanced" Soviet-style collectivism.

This formative legacy ought to be taken into account when analyzing the mass attitudes of today's Belarusians to various facets of the market economy. "There are no obstacles for [market] reform in Belarus," writes Leonid Zayiko, "but there is no perceived necessity in it either, if one takes cues from mass social values. Belarusians invariably choose social equity, not economic freedom. People are afraid of economic freedom, assuming that it brings about economic responsibility."[17] Sergei Nikoliuk makes a related point in his critique of the worldview of the Belarusian opposition. According to Nikoliuk, the popular idea that there are some committed supporters of Alexander Lukashenka, some committed supporters of the opposition, and some undecided electorate in the middle whose support is up for grabs should be taken with the grain of salt. This is because most of those who dislike Lukashenka merely want another father figure, one more to their liking. To Nikoliuk, not enough Belarusians are willing to take the risk of no longer being the wards of the state.[18]

One of the earliest Belarusian entrepreneurs, Yevgenii Budinas, views Belarus as a lingering peasant-communal universe in harmony with its own progeny at the helm of power and as having weak national identity. "Do you expect any change in Belarus on March 19, 2006?" an interviewer from a nonpolitical journal asked Budinas one month prior to the last presidential election. "No, I do not," Budinas responded.

> Nothing is going to happen at all. Get used to the current situation; it is here for a long haul. What, you don't like this life? But the people do! You don't like the people? So, go ahead and enlighten them. . . . While we keep on thinking that we'll begin to live our life to the fullest only when the regime changes, life itself will come to an end. . . . Our people do not appreciate those self-proclaimed Europeans who work tirelessly to make sure all services and utilities are provided for a fee. Ours is an entirely different life, which is impossible to make over. Or perhaps it is possible, but for that you need a different people."[19]

JUST LOOK AT WHAT HAPPENED IN RUSSIA

In Russia, however, the egalitarian mentality nurtured by the redistributive peasant commune is by no means weaker than in Belarus. So, why is it that Russians nevertheless live under an admittedly imperfect, but still market, economy, a fact recognized by some of the same trendsetting Western agencies that assign low scores to postcommunist "transition" in Belarus?

One of the reasons may be the availability of a robust westernizing minority that took over in Russia during the late 1980s and early 1990s and had no match in Belarus. Although Boris Yeltsin presided over the entire country of Russia, his de facto constituency that "called the tune" was the cities of Moscow and, to some extent, St. Petersburg, where most politically active people belonged to the Westernizers' camp (to an incomparably higher degree than now, incidentally). For the entire Soviet Union minus the Baltic states, that was a truly unique constituency. Muscovites subsequently came to possess the lion's share of personal fortunes created in the early 1990s. In no other part of Russia and the Commonwealth of Independent States (CIS) at large were people willing to endure hardships in exchange for something as obscure as democracy and market economy.

By now, there are plenty of accounts of how several self-made and brazen entrepreneurs "privatized" Russia in the early 1990s. In an unusually candid interview with Piotr Aven, now a billionaire who used to be a minister in the government led by Yegor Gaidar, some light is cast on the human side of the political support of the whole privatization affair in Russia.[20] Aven portrays a group of young and committed conspirators who managed to fill the political vacuum that ensued after Mikhail Gorbachev was sidelined by Yeltsin and did their best to transform the economic system of Russia irretrievably. Aven's description reminded me of the episodes and characters from Fyodor Dostoyevsky's novel *The Devils*, only those devils of the 1860s were preoccupied with installing the regime that the group led by Gaidar and Anatoly Chubais set out to dismantle in the early 1990s. But the two groups match each other in arrogance, zealotry, and secretiveness. Firm believers in the ideas of Milton Friedman's school, the Gaidar-led "Chicago boys" knew that they should stay away from any homegrown economic managers because contacts with them might compromise the tough stand of the reformers and mitigate their zeal. Throughout the two years preceding his 1991 ministerial appointment, Aven did not live in Russia and was stationed in Laxenburg, Austria, at the International Institute of Applied Systems Analysis, and prior to that he was a PhD student. In his interview, Aven acknowledges that the group he became a part of did not engage in any dialogue with Russian society but did transform the entire fabric of Russia's economy. Aven recognizes that he and his comrades in arms will never be appreciated by their fellow countrymen, most of whom believe (unduly as far as Aven is concerned) that their lives worsened as a result. Indeed, according to the January 2007 national survey by the Russian polling firm VTSIOM, 27 percent of Russians have a decidedly negative opinion of the accomplishments of the Gaidar-led government, and 31 percent evaluate those accomplishments as "rather negative." Only 6 percent credit that government with staving off Russia's ultimate ruin (Aven's view). Considering the direction taken by the Gaidar government, only 18 percent believe in retrospect that it was generally right, but nothing much was achieved; 28 percent said that the government led the country in the wrong direction; and 25 percent subscribed to the view that the reformers consciously destroyed the economy. One-half of Russians are sure that "shock therapy" was not the only way to go, and a less painful alternative was possible; only 19 percent are of the opinion that there was no other way.[21] In its eulogy to Yeltsin, the Associated Press pointedly stated that many Russians "were outraged . . . by his sale of the nation's industrial might and natural resources in shadowy auctions, by the disintegration of the public health care system and by pensions that turned to cinders in the fires of raging inflation."[22]

The above account of popular Russian attitudes toward Russian reform is not intended to convey my personal value judgment. Rather, my point is that popular attitudes are significant in and of themselves, regardless of what anybody thinks about them. Now, fifteen years after the start of reform, these attitudes allow me to label the economically successful Muscovites and Peterburgers (not only those who struck it as rich as Aven) as the market-dominated minority, which succeeded in imposing its ways on the silent majority. "Market-dominated minority" is a term Amy Chua uses in her now famous book, *The World on Fire*. While I am not inclined to read as much into the ethnic makeup of this minority as Chua does, the percentage share of ethnic Russians within it is indeed below that in the general population, and many Russians see this as a problem.

Yet another argument put forward in the aforementioned book by Chua, an argument I take issue with, is that the "United States has been promoting throughout the non-Western world raw, laissez-faire capitalism—a form of markets that the West abandoned long ago."[23] It is extremely unlikely that the capitalism that emerged in Russia—and might have emerged in Belarus had it been in possession of a consolidated market-dominated minority of its own—could possibly be anything but raw with or without American stewardship. For that, I see two major reasons. First, the Western capitalism of today is an outgrowth of lasting development, whereas Russian (and would-be Belarusian) capitalism is in its early stage. Today's Russian oligarchs might not think and act altogether differently from the American robber barons of the nineteenth century. The second reason, however, preoccupies me the most in conjunction with political economic options for Belarus. Russia, as well as much of Ukraine and all of Belarus, does not have any lasting democratic tradition, and the civic attitudes dominant in Russian/Soviet society were, and still are, far from refined. Ambient attitudes have been in line with Western authors' descriptions of the Western world's "own" more backward environments. Invoking the Western world is important in this context as this suggests that no deliberate demonization of Russia is implied.

Robert Putnam wrote the following about the southern Italy of the early 1970s:

> Public life . . . is organized hierarchically rather than horizontally. The very concept of "citizen" here is stunted. From the point of view of the individual inhabitant, public affairs is the business of somebody else—*i notabli,* "the bosses," "the politicians"—but not me. Few people aspire to partake in deliberations about the commonweal, and few such opportunities present themselves. Political participation is triggered by personal dependency or private greed, not by collective purpose. Engagement in social and cultural associations is meager. Private piety stands in for public purpose. Corruption is widely regarded as the norm, even by politicians themselves, and they are cynical about democratic principles. "Compromise" has only negative overtones. Laws (almost everyone agrees) are made to be broken, *but fearing others' lawlessness, people demand sterner discipline* (emphasis added).[24]

I spent the first thirty-eight years of my life in Soviet Russia, visiting Belarus at least once a year, and I find that the above description fits both segments of Soviet society almost impeccably. One ought only to replace "piety" with "paternalism." I italicized the last sentence of the above quote because it casts some light on what many Americans have a problem understanding, that is, why people in much of the former Soviet Union, and in fact in all non-Western environments, want order in the first place, not liberty, let alone markets. If only in part, this need for order is due to a well-grounded fear of evil behavior on the part of other members of the same society, a problem so pivotal that everything else pales beside it. Consequently, everybody who shares that fear is in need of protection.

When Saddam Hussein was deposed in Iraq, sectarian violence erupted, which Hussein, or anyone else governing with an iron fist, would not have allowed. And when the communist order was removed in Russia, its market-dominated minority seized state-owned assets and left most ordinary people out in the cold. Under such conditions, only a lunatic would harbor regrets about lacking democracy. For most people, "democracy" becomes a swear word. In the words of Robert Kaplan, "Democracy loses meaning if both rulers and ruled cease to be part of the community tied to a specific territory."[25] The much-reviled behavior of the so-called New Russians is a case in point. The sundry jokes about them pivot on their combination of social arrogance and uncouth ways. They flaunt their wealth, engage in brazen behavior, breed corruption by bribing bureaucrats, and wholeheartedly despise their less successful compatriots.

Just at this writing, one of the news items widely discussed in Russia and beyond is that the Russian oligarch Vladimir Potanin paid George Michael, a British pop singer, $3 million to perform at his New Year's Eve party (on December 31, 2006) twenty miles outside Moscow. Another Russian oligarch, Boris Prokhorov, was arrested at an exquisite ski resort in Courchevel, France, and held for three days by the French police on a suspicion of ties with illicit prostitution networks.

The magnitude of income disparity aggravated by the collapse of the health-care system and other Soviet-era entitlements in the post-1991 Russia repels many Russians born and raised under the Soviets, but to those versed in Russia's earlier history, this is a déjà vu. "One hardly needs to be reminded," notes Nicholas Riasanovsky, "that the division between the elite and the masses in Russia paralleled similar divisions in other countries. Still, the Russian split was not quite like the others, or at least it represented a more extreme species of the same genus. In this, as in so many other cases, the evolution of Russia seems to offer a sharper and cruder version of what happened to the west of it."[26]

A social contrast of this magnitude is much like a "separation of charge." Once in a while, it leads to an unusually mighty release of the accumulated tension through sociopolitical equivalents of lightning and thunder. "God save me from witnessing a Russian rebellion, senseless and unrelenting," wrote Alexander Pushkin in his *History of Pugachev's Rebellion*. The social discontent that emerged in Russia early in the twentieth century was on a scale unseen anywhere in Europe, where the upper classes had understood their vested interest in contributing to the well-being of the masses through organized charities and negotiations with trade unions. The Russian elite failed to develop a similar mechanism of self-preservation.

This failure makes anybody preoccupied with social stability worry when he or she witnesses the restoration of profound social contrasts in post-Soviet Russia. On the one hand, there are fifty-three U.S.-dollar billionaires, and at the same time, the officially reported national average salary was 11,410 rubles or $436 a month, according to a January 2007 report by the Russian Ministry of Economic Development.[27]

In the above-mentioned account of Russian privatization by Aven, a sobering confession is triggered by the following question by his interviewer: "By now, has your worldview changed compared to the one you embraced at the start of [Russian] reform?" Aven responded, "I began to think more about integrity and fairness. This is number one. Secondly, I began to think more about protecting people who do not understand what is going on, and about the factor of trust and attitude toward those reforms . . . not just about the mechanism of reform itself, but about its perception and trust—these are fundamental parts of reform. This is what I would emphasize today. Next in importance is everything that pertains to the fight against corruption. The problem of corruption and its psychological and institutional causes have been entirely neglected by us, but they turned out to be the most important."[28]

Let us now turn to Belarusian society. How might its various strata react to the changes unfolding in Russia, the country most Belarusians have the most thorough knowledge of? After all, most people in both countries speak one and the same language; more than half of all Belarusians either have relatives in Russia or have been in various other contacts with it. There is no impenetrable border between Russia and Belarus, and most of the Russian media are still in circulation in Belarus. Whereas by now Lukashenka has created his own propaganda machine, up until 2002, there was no alternative to the stranglehold of Russian information channels on Belarus. Some Belarusians even complained that they acquired more information about Russia than about their own country. A significant portion of that information was from the left flank of Russia's political scene or produced by apolitical newsmakers who were nevertheless shocked by the onslaught of the New Russians. Looking at what transpired in Russia, even the potential business elite of Belarus was likely to take a pause. This is because most personal fortunes in Russia were initially made in extractive industries such as oil, gas, and nonferrous metals after the state foreign-trade monopoly had been removed. These fortunes subsequently boosted privatization of other economic sectors. In Belarus, however, there was only one commercially rewarding substance, potassium, and it did not compare with Russia's wealth of oil, gas, and metallic ores. And upon seeing how the pendulum had shifted from the extreme of totalitarian control to the opposite extreme of free-for-all, the rest of the Belarusian public, those without entrepreneurial skills, was nothing short of terrified. When giving thought to the emergent mental images of "market reform," it is worth remembering that even East Germans, whose transition was cushioned by the world's most generous welfare system, used to say, "What the GDR authorities told us about socialism was false, but what they told us about capitalism turned out to be true." Nobody cushioned the transition in Russia; and nobody would have in Belarus.

To that situation, one should add the debilitating effect of the Chernobyl disaster, with Belarus receiving 70 percent of the radioactive fallout. If there is some truth to the observation that in every society a limited number of people has inborn entrepreneurial skills, while some others are congenital dependents, and the rest are activists and dependents to a degree, then the effect of Chernobyl could not but significantly boost dependency as the prevalent mode of social expectation.[29] This is because so many people became displaced, and many more became immersed in constant fear of being affected by the invisible enemy, so they had to depend on various state agencies most of the time. One author observes that "an almost pathetic reliance on the aid of the state . . . has become part of the national psyche."[30] Another author writes about "the complex of a victim whereby everybody is guilty of one's misery and the responsibility for one's fate is shifted to . . . state, foundations, health care, and one's entire life becomes the expectation of humanitarian aid."[31] The joint report of seven United Nations agencies and the World Bank on the legacy of Chernobyl also mentions "the dependency culture that has developed over the past two decades."[32] Strangely enough, this side effect of Chernobyl is almost exclusively reflected upon in conjunction with the environmental catastrophe as such, not in the context of postcommunist transition, to which the prevalent mode of dependency is in fact even more relevant.

LESS BIZARRE THAN IT SEEMS

Evaluating the path that Belarus took under Lukashenka is an exercise in concurrent causation. Russia's scary example, a drop in the standard of living in Belarus due to Russia's new masters' cutting back on supplies to Belarusian industrial plants, the Chernobyl-related proliferation of the spirit of dependency (in addition to the legacy of peasant communalism and Soviet communism already in place), and a still lacking ability of many Belarusians to think of themselves as a community apart from Russia—each of these factors and their combined effects must be taken into account. From that perspective, Lukashenka's course deserves more empathy and less censure. From the same perspective, what current propaganda executives in Belarus say and write about markets cannot be dismissed easily. Predictably, they no longer turn for inspiration to Russia because "today's Russia is no longer a country with which we lived together. In Russia, the order of things, the priorities, have changed, and they are subject to different influences. . . . Powerful corporate structures exert influence there; they have narrow and self-serving financial concerns, and their interest in Belarus is quite pragmatic. The major interests of some of Russia's political and financial groups are in the West."[33] But if Russia is no longer the source of inspiration, who is? After all, regardless of what some devout Lukashenka bashers may claim, Belarus is not turning out a pristine ideological product along the lines of the North Korean *Chuch'e*. On the contrary, it appears that for Lukashenka's ideologues, the arrangements of Western European welfare states are the pattern to emulate. Unfortunately, though, "it is not possible to transfer their experiences to [Belarus] directly and immediately because our tradition, mentality, and economic base are too different."[34] What actually is different is of interest as well, in light of some previous arguments in this chapter. "The Western system was being built for centuries . . . It is not just ideology that has been instrumental in it, it is a certain level of civilization that cannot be achieved in one day or even in two or three decades."[35] And because we, Belarusians, have not yet stopped littering our forests and still tolerate filth, theft, corruption, and lack of respect for other human beings, privatization would lead to chaos and destruction. Moreover, "the example of Russia shows vividly what one-time distribution of property and self-removal of the state from economic regulation lead to."[36]

Those unimpressed by this message of Anatoly Rubinov, a physicist by training and a recently appointed ideological guru of Belarus, may well be missing the point. Invoking a feature shared by Belarus and Russia, Rubinov in the same breath contrives to set them apart. The shared feature is the traditional inferiority complex vis-à-vis "more cultured" (Western) Europe.[37] What separates Belarus and Russia is how their governments treat their respective uncivilized masses. Whereas Russian leaders appear to have recklessly overstepped the bounds of the national character, the Belarusian ruling elite has been more circumspect. As Pushkin once noted, "The government is our sole European"[38]; that is, it is the sole agency that effectively promotes European values despite resistance from the uncultured masses. "It is just the efforts of the government and the president that nudge us to extricate ourselves from filth and bigotry," writes Rubinov.

Indeed, as Lukashenka once observed, "Belarusians are Russians, only with the quality logo." Back in the early 1990s, the prevalent public mood in both Russia and Belarus demanded a popular leader who would act in the interest of those genuinely appalled and sidelined by Russian privatization. In Russia, Gennady Zyuganov and his communist colleagues tried their best to position themselves as defenders of the downtrodden. Despite his questionable charisma, in 1996, Zyuganov was one inch from the electoral victory, and some commentators even believe that if the ballots had been counted carefully, he would have become the Russian president. It took a well-funded effort to prevent Zyuganov's victory. Thereafter, his political star has been slowly declining, in part because petrodollars have finally begun to trickle down the social ladder and spread around, and in part because nationalist and populist demagogues, first Vladimir Zhirinovsky, then Dmitry Rogozin, and now Sergei Mironov, have been dispatched by the Kremlin to make inroads into the communist territory. In Belarus, Lukashenka responded to the same call of wounded justice and became successful without any aid from local nationalism. So, what is the nature of the political system that became associated with his name?

IS THE LUKASHENKA REGIME A DICTATORSHIP?

A habitual label attached to the Belarusian political regime in the Western media is "Europe's last dictatorship." Arguably, this is one of the few successful clichés of the American foreign policy agitprop. With few people able to identify Belarus on a map but many more capable of pinpointing Europe, a quality sound bite is all that matters. On a more serious note, however, "Dictatorship refers to an autocratic form of absolute rule by leadership unrestricted by law, constitutions, or other social and political factors within the state."[39] The most frequent names on the dictators' list are Joseph Stalin, Adolf Hitler, Idi Amin, and Augusto Pinochet. The Soviet leaders of the post-Stalin era are not usually referred to as dictators despite sundry restrictions imposed on Soviet citizens during their tenures, like a ban on emigrating or even traveling abroad at will, the lack of political affiliations other than the Communist Party and its subsidiaries, the lack of true elections, purges of dissidents, and so forth. Just from this perspective, affixing the "dictatorship" label to the current Belarusian regime appears to be a hyperbole, as some of the above-mentioned Soviet constraints do not seem to exist in Belarus. By no means is the political situation in Belarus serene, however. Here is a brief list of the gravest violations of decent political behavior by the Lukashenka regime:

- May 1995: Presidential security guards forcibly evict MPs who declared a hunger strike from the parliamentary building.
- April 1996: Police and security forces forcibly disperse a rally devoted to the tenth anniversary of the Chernobyl disaster.
- November 1996: Lukashenka dismisses the Parliament and replaces it with a hand-picked one, and he extends his first presidential term on what is believed to be the flimsy basis of the 1996 constitutional referendum.
- April 1997: Protesters against the Belarus-Russia union treaty are forcibly dismissed, and several journalists are beaten.
- Summer 1998: Several Western ambassadors are evicted from their residences in Drozdy, a suburb of Minsk.
- May 1999: Former interior minister Yuri Zakharenka disappears in Minsk.
- September 1999: Former Central Election Commission head Victor Gonchar and his friend Anatoly Krasovsky disappear in Minsk.
- October 2004: Voter fraud is suspected in a referendum designed to change the constitution to give Lukashenka the right to become president for the third time.
- March 2006: A week-long protest against the perceived electoral fraud on Oktyabrskaya Square in Minsk is forcibly dispersed, and one presidential candidate is arrested and charged with violation of public order. Subsequently, this candidate (Alexander Kozulin) receives a five-and-a-half-year sentence.

By all accounts, the regime's actions with regard to the people actively opposing its policies toughen during the run-ups to the presidential elections. This was particularly obvious in early 2006 (see chapter 7). And yet, somehow the best-informed western Belarus watchers and even some opposition-minded Belarusians themselves hesitate to call the Lukashenka regime a dictatorship. Whereas some question the notion that Belarus is a dictatorship up front, others resort to qualifications that have the same effect. David Marples, for example, has written that Lukashenka "failed manifestly to establish a dictatorship despite the general use of this appellation in the international media."[40] Marples was upset by my reference to the above statement[41] but still averred that Belarus is "an incomplete dictatorship with several outstanding loopholes for free expression."[42] As stated on behalf of the entire group of authors of the multiauthor collection *Contemporary Belarus*, "The consensus of this volume is that [Belarus] is not a total dictatorship, since it retains some aspects of a democratic state, but that it could be described as an 'elected dictatorship.'"[43] A German Belarus watcher, Heinz Timmermann, writes that "to

describe the Lukashenka regime as a totalitarian dictatorship, which is sometimes done in the West, would be incorrect"[44] if only because this would trivialize the creations of Stalin and Hitler. To Yaroslav Shimov, a Prague-based
scholar who spent most of his life in Minsk, the Lukashenka regime is much
closer to the "soft authoritarianism of a Pilsudski, Salazar, or latter-day Tito
than to the totalitarian tyrannies of Hitler and Stalin."[45] "I do not really think
we have a dictatorship in the same sense we talk about Hitler, Mussolini or
some other monsters," says Elena Gapova, an opposition-minded scholar.
"We have really got something else."[46]

Because, however, the dictatorship label has stuck, a Pyrrhic victory of the
George W. Bush administration, calling it into question is a risky business,
certain to be construed as defending the above-mentioned improprieties of the
Lukashenka regime. Out of 441 panels and roundtables at the 2006 annual
meeting of the American Association for the Advancement of Slavic Studies
held in Washington, D.C., only one was devoted to Belarus entirely. The
roundtable in question touched on the issue of dictatorship only marginally.
Apparently, this was enough to generate the following question from the audience: "I have just returned from Poland where I spent my sabbatical. There,
I ran into dozens of students from Belarus accepted by Polish universities after they were dismissed by Belarusian schools for political reasons. These students go from Poland to Belarus and back several times a semester. If Belarus
is a dictatorship, why are students allowed to go back and forth?" After the
chair of the roundtable discussion touched upon Belarusian officials' reluctance to send Belarusian scholars to the West, a woman in her early thirties
got up and said that she was a scholar from the Belarusian Economic University in Minsk on exchange at Columbia University. "While Belarusian officials are in no position to facilitate exchange with the West," she observed,
"nobody prevents one from going to the West if one is able to procure an in-
vitation." It turned out that prior to the roundtable in question, Elena, as the
exchange scholar's first name turned out to be, had attended a panel devoted
to understanding the Soviet media. A member of that panel observed that because the Belarus of today has recreated the Soviet atmosphere, he certainly
did not expect anybody from Minsk to attend this convention. After Elena
cautiously revealed her presence in the room, three men with stern faces
abruptly left. "Could it be that they wanted to use a restroom?" I asked Elena.
"All three at the same time?" she replied. "To me, this came across as a
protest. Apparently they thought that because I am from Minsk, I was dele-
gated by the dictatorial regime."

On a more serious note, there are signs that some Belarus watchers find the
Western agitprop's stranglehold on Belarusian studies annoying. Thus, a
Japanese author writes about Belarusian nongovernmental organizations as a

"colonial civic enclave" cursed by incompetence and "tactless intervention by the international community in Belarusian politics."[47] And a respectable 2002 West European book on Belarus broaches the question of "whether the opposition in Belarus is past resuscitation and whether Western agencies should continue wasting their taxpayers' money *on the client-based policies* that have proved so ineffective" (emphasis added).[48]

In light of these observations, it makes sense to steer clear of clichés and preconceived notions of any kind, as well as from attempts to frame crude geopolitical concerns for democracy and human rights. In February 2007, I found it disingenuous that Western interest in Belarus significantly increased in the immediate aftermath of the trade war with Russia. It's not that criticism of the Belarusian regime was silenced, but it was noticeably muffled for a while. Rene Van Der Linden, chairman of the Parliamentary Assembly of Europe, unexpectedly showed up in Minsk amid muted protests by the Belarusian opposition and held talks with the leaders of two chambers of the Belarusian parliament. Shortly thereafter, Uta Zapf, head of the Belarusian Working Group of the Organization for Security and Cooperation in Europe arrived as well and held a conference in which both the government and the opposition were represented. Lukashenka, whose interviews for many years were not solicited by Western media outlets, suddenly gave a lengthy interview to *Die Welt*, a major German daily (published on January 25, 2007).[49] "Throughout more than ten years of my presidency," said Lukashenka, "I do not recall Germany and other countries being as interested in what really is going on in Belarus as during this crisis in Belarus-Russia relationships. They began to visit, look, ask questions, receive information. [And when they published it,] for the first time it was close to objective. Belarusians appreciated this right away and momentarily reacted to it. But note, this was for the first time in history."[50] Lukashenka's interview with *Die Welt* was followed by another one with Reuters, and as one Belarusian author reported in early February of 2007, Western reporters were lining up on Lukashenka's premises, eager to ask him a question. On February 14, 2007, Radio Liberty reported that Valdas Adamkus, Lithuania's president, said at a press conference on the last day of his visit to America that Belarus could rely on Lithuania's rail and on the oil terminal in Klaipeda to transport oil from alternative (read non-Russian) sources. Adamkus added that he had conferred with Vice President Dick Cheney and Secretary of Energy Samuel Bodman about aiding Belarus in the area of energy supply. The last sentence of Radio Liberty's message was, "Such an aid would not mean support of Belarus's regime, but it will be Lithuania's response to the needs of the Belarusian people."[51] To me, the hypocrisy conveyed by this quote exceeds the carrying capacity of a sentence. One ought to wonder whether the public officials referenced in the above message have "the needs of the Belarusian people" on their agendas at all.

This question of motives, however, is of little help in categorizing the ruling regime of Belarus. On the one hand, its treatment of any organized opposition and any non-government-sponsored press is clearly objectionable. Yet, on the other hand, the dictatorship cliché does not stand up to close analysis

First, Belarus is too open a country, not just to Russia and Ukraine but to its Western neighbors as well. To travel to the West, Belarusian citizens must get an okay stamp in their passports, but this measure does not seem to have deterred those trips; otherwise, we would have long learned about this from the Belarusian opposition. Numerous critics of the regime routinely travel to the West and come back, as do many rank-and-file Belarusians. About 22 percent of Belarusian adults have traveled to Poland and Germany.[52] In summer, the Lithuanian consulate in Minsk issues about thirteen hundred visas a day. Many children from Chernobyl-affected areas have spent their vacations in the West, particularly in Germany. In June 2005, just weeks after the Belarusian leader expressed concern that too many Belarusian children were traveling to the West and coming back ideologically indoctrinated, I met a group of thirty ten- to twelve-year-old children from Gomel at the Sheremetyevo Airport in Moscow. Accompanied by three teachers, they were heading to a scout camp in New Jersey. The teachers discounted the importance of appeals by the government to curb trips to the West and opined that as long as those trips continued to be funded by the Western sponsors, they would continue undeterred. Personally, I know several Belarusians working and living in the West who spend their summer vacations in Belarus. All of them come and go without a problem. In Virginia Beach, Virginia, I routinely meet Belarusian students in work-study programs toiling at the ice cream outlets and nearby amusement parks. They leave Minsk and, for the most part, return. If there are obstacles to travel, they are of an economic nature, and some of them are erected by Western governments. For example, when Poland introduced a $20 visa, the number of Belarusians traveling to Poland declined. As mentioned in an interpretative 2006 document by an opposition think tank, "Throughout the last twelve years, public opinion in regard to the West was under the influence of open borders on the one hand and of powerful state propaganda on the other."[53] While acknowledging the reality of propaganda, one ought to acknowledge the open borders as well.

The second reason I do not believe Belarus is a dictatorship is that despite assaults on media freedom and the closure of independent newspapers, there has never been a time without public outlets for dissident opinions inside Belarus, even when Western media reported the closure of "one last independent voice." Presently, antiregime opinions show up in newspapers like *Belarusy i*

Rynok, *Narodnaya Volya* (both in Russian), and *Nasha Niva* (in Belarusian). To be sure, only the first of these newspapers is now available at kiosks or can be subscribed to at the post offices. The two other newspapers can be obtained through private channels. For example, copies of the *Nasha Niva* are mailed out to the subscribers by the editorial staff. The opinions reflected in those newspapers often include personal attacks on Lukashenka. In the western-most part of Belarus, Polish TV highly critical of Lukashenka's politics is easily received, and the same goes for Russian TV in the eastern part of Belarus. RTVI (a Russian-language cable network owned by the rogue oligarch Vladimir Gusinsky), *Euronews* in Russian, and several English-language channels, including CNN, are available to those able to pay for them, and to my knowledge, many Minsk residents have these channels in their homes—a far cry from Soviet conditions. Close to 28 percent of Belarusians now use the Internet as a source of news at least several times a month, including 12 percent who use it regularly,[54] and on the World Wide Web the number of anti-Lukashenka sites in Russian and Belarusian exceeds the number of pro-Lukashenka sites by at least a factor of ten. Most informative sites critical of Lukashenka are funded by Western grants. Of those, the most frequently visited sites are Belorusskiye Novosti (www.naviny.by), Nashe Mneniye (www.nmnby.org), Belorussky Partizan (www.belaruspartisan.org), Telegraf (www.telegraf.by), Salidarnasts, (www.gazetaby.com), AFN (www.afn.by), and Charter 97 (www.charter97.org). These sites predominantly use Russian. The most elaborate and well-informed Belarusian-language site is that of the Belarusian Service of Radio Liberty (www.svaboda.org.), courtesy of the American government.

POLITICAL PARTIES

My third reason for disagreeing with the dictatorship cliché is the multiplicity of political parties, some of which have been harassed but never banned. At this writing, seventeen political parties are registered with the Belarusian Ministry of Justice.[55] To be sure, the parties are weak. During the parliamentary elections of 2004, a national survey revealed that no party received more than a 2 percent rating, and 90 percent of respondents could not even name a political party they knew.[56] Reporting this fact, the opposition-minded *Belarusian Yearbook 2004*, published in Vilnius, Lithuania, mentions several instances of harassment of parties by the Belarusian state. However, "orientation of the political culture of the population to strong personal power" is the first in the list of factors of the political parties' weakness.[57] According to the same source, the habitual division of political parties into "Left" and "Right" is not topical for Belarus. More relevant discriminating features are attitudes to the Belarusian language and to the ruling regime (and the degree of being co-opted by it). As for the first of these features, only two parties, the successors of what once was a single party, the Belarusian Popular Front, communicate and publish only in Belarusian as a matter of principle. Other parties use that language occasionally and do not insist on linguistic Belarusification as the first order of business for Belarus.

Regarding the second feature, only three parties have been co-opted by the ruling regime: the Belarusian Communist Party, which boasts eight members of Parliament (MPs) and supports Lukashenka; the Agrarian Party, represented by three MPs; and the Liberal Democratic Party, whose leader Sergei Gaidukevich is an MP who recently acquired a government post as a special representative in charge of relations with the European Union.[58]

Among the antiregime or opposition parties, the most visible are the United Civic Party led by Anatoly Lebedko, the splinter Communist Party led by Sergei Kaliakin, and one of the successors of the Belarusian Popular Front led by Vintsuk Viachiorka. Other known opposition affiliations, among others, are two Social Democratic parties calling themselves Hramada, in reference to early-twentieth-century political groups, and the Party of Women.

Observing the relationships within and between parties to the extent that those relations are reflected by the opposition media and the Belarusian Service of Radio Liberty, one cannot but get the impression that the struggle within the opposition for visibility and favors from the West is more important for the party leaders than the grand idea of unseating Lukashenka. This impression is particularly hard to discard now as the party bosses are questioning the overall political leadership of Alexander Milinkevich, one of two 2006 opposition presidential candidates and the darling of some Western dignitaries.[59] Part of the problem is that most of those bosses have held their positions for years, whereas Milinkevich is not even affiliated with any party. Speaking at a Kiev-based conference, "Towards the New Vision for Belarus," Alexander Feduta observed that under Lukashenka even *rayon* administrators have changed three times, but there does not seem to be any rotation at all at the helm of the opposition parties. Turning to some of party dignitaries in the audience, Feduta exclaimed, "Only Filaret [the supreme Orthodox leader of Belarus] has served in his capacity longer than you have in yours, but it is God himself who speaks through him, and on whose behalf do you speak?"[60] Kidding aside, it seems unlikely that most, if any, Belarusian party leaders would survive the test of unfettered political life. In a peculiar way, they are both suppressed and legitimized by one and the same agency, the ruling regime of President Lukashenka.

IN SYNC WITH THE PEOPLE?

The fourth and arguably most important reason I do not believe Belarus is a dictatorship is best worded by the Belarusian political commentator Vital Silitski. Affiliated for some time with the Washington, D.C.–based National Endowment for Democracy (NED), Silitski published a well-substantiated critique of the Belarusian regime in English. His Belarusian-language texts, however, are more nuanced and less definitive in assigning blame. Among the nuances I find revealing is that Lukashenka's regime "placed the outlook and political culture of the average Belarusian into its own foundation."[61] This fact, according to Silitski, has been one of the major reasons this regime is sustained. This is the same as saying that a great deal of harmony exists between the regime and a broad strata of Belarus's population, so much so that even the former NED associates and sworn enemies of that regime find it hard to avoid talking about this intimate relationship when facing domestic audiences. Dictatorship by its very nature is oppressive, but for most Belarusians, the Lukashenka regime is anything but. Acknowledging this fact does not cast a shadow on those who do find that regime oppressive. Their reaction is justified, and no society can be expected to agree unanimously on crucial issues confronting it. But there is no need to go over the top about a difference in opinion. Yury Shevtsov, for example, claims that the conflict between the majority of Belarusians and the West is not political at its core; rather, it is a culture conflict about values.[62] Yann Breault, a Canadian researcher, echoes Shevtsov: "The gap could hardly be wider between the American and Belarusian political cosmologies."[63] Yaroslav Shimov cites a statement by his Belarus-based acquaintance: "The opposition and Europe say that we need freedom. But we *are* free—in our own way. Europe and America simply do not understand that; they think that freedom can only be the way *they* know it."[64]

I find these three remarks more meaningful than the righteous indignation invariably conveyed by some Western commentators about Belarus. Upon discovering that their homemade templates do not match the attitudes of ordinary Belarusians, these commentators never blame themselves. Instead, they blame Lukashenka supporters who are reportedly "blinkered"[65]; that is, they do not understand their own good.

PIGEONHOLING THE LUKASHENKA REGIME

Despite the overall sense of bewilderment that modern Belarus elicits among Western politicians and academics, there have been at least three attempts to categorize the political regime in Belarus by applying certain "isms" and justifying them by a set of normative-looking criteria. Thus, Steven Eke and Taras Kuzio labeled the Belarusian regime sultanistic[66] and Stanislau Shushkevich labeled it neocommunist.[67] I have critiqued both labels in an earlier publication.[68] The third, and in my view most successful, attempt to categorize the political regime of Belarus has been by Kamitaka Matsuzato, a Japanese scholar, who described this regime as authoritarian populism.[69] In Matsuzato's two-tier classification of postcommunist political regimes, countries of East Central Europe and the Baltic states are set apart from the CIS countries based on several criteria, including parliamentary systems (in the states of the European Community and the Baltic states) versus superpresidentialism (in the CIS); full-fledged political parties versus underdeveloped political parties and the dominance of client-patron relations therein; compliance versus noncompliance with "European" norms of political behavior; and pure market versus patrimonial capitalism. Although Belarus belongs in the CIS group, according to Matsuzato, it differs from other CIS countries, notably from Russia and Ukraine, in that those countries have multiple clans that reign supreme and compete for influence, whereas Belarus has a single dominant clan with a strong antielite bias. Matsuzato admits that Lukashenka chose to communicate with Belarusians directly over the heads of the elite and their representative structures like the Parliament, parties, and affiliations. In choosing this mode of communication, Lukashenka acts much like a Russian tsar appealing to the masses and sidelining the boyars. This is a populist mode that involves putting high-level managers on trial for show, reshuffling regional leaders to prevent them from consolidating local power bases, relying on referenda, and issuing presidential fiats. To this list Matsuzato might have added that Lukashenka's populism includes projecting himself as a father figure and micromanager who gets personally involved in every facet of Belarus's economy and social well-being. Matsuzato likens Lukashenka's populism to its Latin American counterpart and admits that Lukashenka's populism is even more antielite than Latin America's.

While Matsuzato's attempt at categorizing the Belarusian political regime is eminently more convincing than all the other attempts that I know of, his explanation of how such a regime came about and what sustains it is less impressive. In the triad of Belarus's formative features—weak identity, delayed urbanization, and status as a former Soviet success story—Matsuzato only acknowledges the significance of the latter. Because "Belarusians lacked the sense of stagnation even in the late socialist period," they, according to Matsuzato, became "vulnerable to populist nostalgic slogans in the postcommunist era."[70] They simply could not agree to the significant slump in living standards that others around them experienced in early postcommunist times.

This "vulnerability" was reportedly reinforced by some features of the Belarusian mentality, such as servility and a "lack of self-satirizing humor."[71] Most certainly, the latter is not lacking at all as I intended to show in chapter 1 by citing Belarusians' good-natured and self-critical jokes about their notorious patience and moderation.

Not only does Matsuzato neglect to attribute Belarusian egalitarianism to the lingering legacy of the peasant commune, but one of his passing remarks clearly points to another lapse in his analysis. Specifically, he notes that "Belarusian scholars enjoy more freedom in teaching and writing than their Ukrainian counterparts, who are obliged to teach students, for example, that 'Kievan Rus' was already a Ukrainian state."[72] While I cannot rule out that some Ukrainian scholars are indeed "obliged" to impose that historical perspective on their students, it seems obvious that many have embraced it with enthusiasm. This is because the perspective in question derives from Mikhailo Krushevsky's theory, which was banned under the Soviets and allows those embracing it to set the "civilized and consistently European" Ukraine apart from the "Eurasian horde of uncivilized Russians." By the same token, most Belarusian scholars do not willingly endorse the idea that their country has consistently Western European roots, and this fact does not allow them to set their country apart from Russia and to embrace, if only in theory, the so-called European values. It is doubtful, though, that this failure on the part of Belarusian scholars can be interpreted as academic freedom, as Matsuzato alleges. Be that as it may, coupled with the legacy of peasant communalism, this inability to separate themselves from what is, and has been for quite some time, another country casts Belarusians as a group that is even more proverbially "Russian" in their outlook than Russians themselves. After all, Russians surrendered to the "evil forces" of capitalism, and Belarusians have so far eschewed that. It then appears that Lukashenka's one-time assertion that "Belarusians are Russians, only with the quality logo" is more meaningful than it is given credit for, and Matsuzato's keen observations confirm that. "If we consider Western values such as diligence, courtesy, neatness, and devotion to technological developments, Belarus looks even better than the Baltic countries," exclaims Matsuzato. "Minsk is one of the cleanest cities in Eastern Europe."[73] He later observes that "Belarusian taxi drivers address clients with professional courtesy, not familiarity. . . . Belarusian train conductors do not yell at passengers. . . . Minsk citizens do not swear at each other on public transport. These virtues are particularly pleasant for those who have had the experience of staying in Russia and Ukraine."[74] More of the same can be added to the list favoring conditions in Belarus over their Russian counterparts, including better roads and better upkeep of provincial towns, a more humane attitude of emergency health-care professionals toward their patients, a more caring response by local bureaucrats to sundry people's needs, easier and cheaper public access to the Internet, and so forth.

Concluding my brief analysis of an attempt to categorize the Belarusian political regime, I have to sound a note of caution. Belarus and its ruling regime are not easy to categorize. It may be that no such attempt can succeed in principle until and unless Belarus becomes a self-sustained cultural and political entity that can be understood in and of itself, external influences notwithstanding. This entity may (and probably will) materialize in the future, but so far it has not, which makes me believe that the Belarus of today simply cannot be understood and categorized on its own. To be sure, it does possess some defining sociocultural features, but it only makes sense to discuss each of them in conjunction with Russia, which for Belarus appears to be much more than just its eastern neighbor. Although Belarus's relations with Russia were recently (December 2006 to January 2007) subjected to a tough test by the trade war, resulting in an unprecedented level of mutual alienation between the ruling elites of the two countries and sundry predictions of the "worst" as yet to come, nothing is preordained, and ties between Russia and Belarus are still above and beyond any other bilateral ties in the contemporary world. Thus, an inquiry into Belarus-Russia relations is in order.

ON THE ROAD TO A BELARUS-RUSSIA (DIS)UNION?

The issue of Russia-Belarus reintegration is not easy to categorize either. On the one hand, signs of togetherness are conspicuous. There is a transparent border between Russia and Belarus (at least for individuals and groups), and nobody checks IDs on trains between Moscow and Minsk. To cross the mutual border, citizens of Russia and Belarus do not need to obtain the external passports required if those same citizens go to most other countries. To foreigners from any third country visiting Russia and/or Belarus, a single Russian-and-Belarusian immigration card is now issued. On their personal and business trips to Belarus, people from Russia do not normally get a sense of being abroad. Economic and interpersonal ties between Russians and Belarusians are strong. On both sides of the transparent border between the two countries, one and the same language is spoken. On numerous occasions, both national presidents, Vladimir Putin and Alexander Lukashenka, have noted that Russians and Belarusians are "effectively one people." There is a strong military cooperation between the two countries and a multifaceted similarity between the two national armies. Russia owns two military bases in Belarus. One of them, in Gantsevichi (in the eastern part of Brest Oblast), is an early missile detection station whose perceived significance increased after the breakup of the Soviet Union and the subsequent loss of an identical military installation in Skrunda, Latvia. Another base is a submarine monitoring station in Vileika, Minsk Oblast (one hundred kilometers to the northwest of Minsk). Scores of Belarusian military personnel study in Russian schools, and all of the Belarusian army's ammunition is either Russian made or a product of Russia-Belarus industrial cooperation.

Yet, on the other hand, since December 1991, Russia and Belarus have been separate countries. They have different ruling elites and different political economic preferences. "Belarusian" and "Russian" are names for closely related, yet supposedly separate, ethnicities. Although relatively few people in Belarus speak Belarusian, there is widespread recognition that it is in fact Belarus's native language. Also, Russia and Belarus are polities of very different size, with Belarus being fourteen times smaller than Russia in terms of population and eighty-one times smaller in terms of land area.

Since as early as 1995, however, the two countries have been going through some sort of reintegration. The term "reintegration" makes sense considering that for more than two hundred years, Belarus was a part of the same polity as Russia. What is more, rightly or not, "Russia" was the broadly recognized name of that polity, even when the "Soviet Union" was the official name. The overt hallmarks of Russia-Belarus reintegration are well known: the treaty on neighborly ties and cooperation signed by Yeltsin and Lukashenka on February 21, 1995; the solemn removal of a short-lived border pole near the Belarusian village Rechka on May 26, 1995; and the December 8, 1999, treaty on the creation of a union state signed by the same political actors. Since that time, though, even the overt signs of reintegration have begun to wane.

For example, according to Article 13 of the union state treaty, Russia and Belarus were to adopt a single currency, not just in name but by unifying their monetary systems into one, with a single authority controlling the supply and production of the currency.[75] According to the Program of Activities entitled to implement the 1999 treaty (and signed into law simultaneously with that treaty), the common currency should have been introduced in 2005; this was then postponed until 2006, and then postponed indefinitely. Also, the treaty of 1999 stipulated that the Constitutional Act of the Union State be developed and endorsed by the joint Russia-Belarus parliament by the autumn of 2000, submitted to broad public discussion by the winter of 2001, and subjected to referenda in both Russia and Belarus by the spring of 2001.[76] But neither has the common currency been introduced, nor has the constitutional act been developed to the mutual satisfaction of the power elites of Russia and Belarus, so no draft of that document has even been published, let alone subjected to its planned approval by the parliaments. And while the national leaders and their subordinates have never totally abandoned the rhetoric referencing the union state—on the contrary, in Belarus it peaked on the eve of both the 2001 and 2006 presidential elections—even that rhetoric had already been losing momentum when the winter 2006–2007 trade war between Russia and Belarus threatened to sentence it to oblivion. Yet, surprisingly, even amid mutual acrimony following the oil-and-gas dispute, both Putin and Lukashenka continued to refer to the promise of the union state. Only for Lukashenka, it is now the Kremlin that has undermined it, whereas for Putin, the two-state union is still a possibility, despite "someone's" being unduly hysterical about the long-announced price hikes.

So, what is the undercurrent or hidden agenda of this never-ending reintegration saga? And why is it that both would-be members of an interstate union or commonwealth fail either to impart any finality to its form and substance or to abandon it altogether?

A systematic effort to respond to these questions was undertaken by Alex Danilovich, who published a reference book on the Russia-Belarus union. It subjects every step taken on the road to that union to penetrating analysis involving sundry personalities and events, as well as the political and economic interests at stake.[77] Danilovich shows that Russia's and Belarus's leaders have exploited the slogan of integration for domestic gain, particularly when their popularity at home has needed propping up. In the late 1990s, Yeltsin's rating plunged to single digits, and he exploited the union rhetoric to the fullest. Even at that time, though, the strongest promoter of reintegration was Lukashenka, who wanted complete unification of the two countries whereby the president of Russia would initially become president of the commonwealth and the president of Belarus would become vice president of the commonwealth. That solution reportedly suited Lukashenka, who was certain of his ability to unseat or defeat the ailing and unpopular Yeltsin in a potential contest. Indeed, from 1997 to 1999 many liberals in Moscow were leery that Lukashenka might become their president. Because at that time Russia was going through the most painful stage of postcommunist transition, while Belarus reversed privatization, secured full employment, and paid most salaries on time, Lukashenka's popularity in Russia was on the rise everywhere outside Moscow and St. Petersburg. In October 1997, the Kremlin had even banned the airports of Yaroslavl and Lipetsk from accepting any plane with Lukashenka on board. Yet, he continued his frequent visits to Russian regions until 2000. The Russian side continued to play along, if only not to surrender the popular slogan to the nationalist and communist opposition. The December 8, 1999, treaty about the creation of the union state containing the articles about the common currency and the constitutional act thus became the pinnacle of mutual integration efforts. Yeltsin soon resigned, and thereafter the entire integration gambit began to gain a different quality.

In Russia, the first sign of the lowering priority of the reintegration project was the entrusting of its supervision to Pavel Borodin, Yeltsin's former bursar, or superintendent of the entire real estate in the Kremlin area. With Yeltsin's departure, Borodin's de facto status plunged. He was later (in early 2001) charged with corruption and arrested upon arrival in the United States and held in a prison cell, first in Brooklyn, New York, and then in Switzerland, for a total of three months. Borodin became the secretary of the union state and has been effervescent about its prospects ever since, even in those situations least conducive to optimism.

In Belarus, Lukashenka continued his pro-integration rhetoric, which played a huge role in his second bid to win the presidency in 2001. However, he became reticent with regard to the actual steps being taken toward integration. This showed up not only in the failure to endorse a common currency but also in the prevention of any large Russian businesses from acquiring Belarusian industrial assets. Repeatedly promising, then stonewalling, the creation of a joint venture on the basis of Beltransgaz (see chapter 4) was the most publicized of Lukashenka's actions, but there have been many more stories of the same kind. These include the recalled acquisition of a Belarusian brewery by the Russian firm Baltika after the latter declined to build a stadium in Belarus and the negotiated, then recalled, sale of four petrochemical plants to the Russian corporate group Surgutneftegaz.

By some accounts, it was after the 2001 elections that Lukashenka switched to a more defensive mode, even as his rhetoric continued to push for a close union with Russia for several more years. There seem to be two reasons behind this switch, one of which has been more publicized than the other. The more publicized reason, particularly in Russia's liberal and centrist press, is Putin's success in the court of Russian public opinion and in taming Russian oligarchs. Putin did not leave any chance whatsoever for Lukashenka to enter and victoriously perform on the Russian political scene within the plausible framework of a union state. From the very beginning, Lukashenka did not get along with Putin, at least this is what the Russian liberal press suggested time and again. Scores of commentators emphasized that whereas Lukashenka is a rustic man, a *kolkhoznik*, Putin is a European. Even if interpersonal relationships were not nearly as bad as insinuated, repeated comments like that were expressly designed to poison them.

A somewhat less publicized, but, in my judgment, more important reason, for Lukashenka's "change of heart" is that the Belarusian ruling elite eventually became accustomed to their role. Lukashenka is by no means alone, as his image as the last dictator of Europe implies. Under his stewardship, a fairly strong and, by some accounts, professional ruling apparatus has evolved. Members of the ruling elite have strong mutual commitments and discipline, almost like the military at a time of war. Ministers, members of Parliament, ambassadors, and generals no longer want to give up their power and national standing to become provincial administrators. Belarusian statehood has actually taken root. It also appears that despite seemingly irreconcilable mutual differences, the ruling elite and the opposition are impeccably united on the issue of restraining Russia's influence in Belarus.

The Russian side found itself in a more ambivalent position. On the one hand, it felt obliged to support Lukashenka in both the 2001 and 2006 elections out of fear that the victory of any alternative candidate would result in a shift in the geopolitical orientation of Belarus to the West. In 2005 and 2006, the possibility of yet another "orange revolution" scenario could not be discarded. It took a bit more time to realize that the revolutionary events in Kiev could not possibly undo the East-West schism in Ukraine quickly, if at all. On the other hand, the Kremlin was becoming exceedingly irritated with Lukashenka's intransigence on the single-currency issue, Beltransgaz, and other botched deals. This irritation was reinforced by Lukashenka's reluctance to follow the Russian line in the formulation of the constitutional act. As ardently as he had been pushing for a merger of Russia and Belarus prior to 2000, he was now defending Belarusian statehood. Even though no draft of the constitutional act has ever been published, a significant body of literature emerged, courtesy of the Belarusian power elite, that sees the would-be constitutional act as an international agreement, not a merger of two states into one.[78] The desire to wring at least something from Lukashenka in exchange for low-priced energy supplies and the utter inability to do so led to a conflict that came to a head in December 2006, as a result of which the entire reintegration agenda is currently at a crossroads.

In my judgment, the above situation raises more questions on the Russian side than on the Belarusian side. Lukashenka's Belarus has managed to extract crucial benefits from Russia during the most fragile nascent period of Belarusian statehood. It managed to obtain those benefits in exchange for assurances of eternal friendship and willingness to create a union state. Once a designation for the merger, "union state" is now a term for a bilateral structure, a two-state solution, at least as far as the Belarusian side is concerned. There is even a scientific-looking theory rationalizing Belarus's stand on the issue. Because both personally and as a group Belarusians used to achieve success as part of the larger and multiethnic polity—be it the Grand Duchy, Rzeczpospolita, Russia, or the Soviet Union—they, according to this theory, developed what is called *uniinost'*, that is, a proclivity to enter into alliances with outsiders to achieve their own goals without getting diluted by those alliances. From this perspective, Lukashenka's drive to integrate with Russia and yet retain independence is construed as entirely natural in the "Belarusian political tradition." At the same time, mutual integration without the smaller partner's giving up its statehood is unnatural for the imperial tradition of Russia. From Belarus's side, however, integration exclusively with Russia is not imperative but, rather, situational and rooted in a common industrial legacy and an understanding of Belarus's own national interests at the moment.[79]

It is, I think, much harder to understand why Russia failed—and failed persistently—to cultivate a Belarusian leadership that would be more inclined to play according to Russia's rules. Understanding this is all the more difficult if one considers the genuine, not contrived, cultural affinity between Russia and Belarus and the close ties between the Belarusian economic-management elite and Russian oligarchs. Because this book is not about Russia, I am not researching this issue in any depth, but my hypothesis is that Russia's failure has three ingredients. First, it is the inborn defect of imperial thinking, according to which smaller and more dependent states and groups within the imperial reach should remain forever grateful for the big brother's benevolence. According to this line of thought, many in Russia genuinely believe that if Lukashenka, cranky and perfidious as he is, were somehow sidelined, many others in Belarus would opt for a merger with Russia. This, however, is a delusion, which was slow to be acknowledged as such. Nothing could be further from the truth. The second ingredient of Russia's myopic behavior is, strangely enough, Russia's "transition" along the neoliberal path. As much as Putin has tamed Russian oligarchs, they still have vital interests far apart from his or any other government. Lukashenka was quick to recognize that; hence, for many years in a row, the Russian "oil sheikhs" used Belarus as a tax haven. From that arrangement, they extracted enormous benefits and could not care less about Russia's national interest, however one understands that term. This is what brings us to the third ingredient of Russia's failure, Lukashenka's political savvy in simply outmaneuvering and outsmarting Russia's elites. He used Russia when Belarus needed Russia most, and now he may try to milk two cows, Russia and the European Union, at the same time. Even if he does not succeed in that and his political star begins to decline, he will come down in history as the true father of Belarus's independence for what he has already done.

In summary, slowly but surely, Belarus is emerging as a nation of its own. Belarus's ruling regime, most accurately categorized as authoritarian-populist, derives from a combination of such formative features as vestigial peasant communalism, popular rejection of Russian-style raw market, and the lack of a consolidated market-dominated minority. The biggest achievement of Belarus's regime has been turning incredibly close ties with Russia to the benefit of Belarus, while at the same time, slowly but surely, curtailing Russia's pervasive influence.

NOTES

1. "Information Technology Survey," *The Economist*, June 16, 1990, 11.

2. Mikhail Voslensky, *Nomenklatura: Gospodstvuyushchii klass sovetskogo soyuza* (Moscow: MP Oktyabr, 1991), 140–41.

3. A. G. Vishnevsky, *Serp i rubl* (Moscow: OGI, 1999), 98–99.

4. Vishnevsky, *Serp i rubl*, 97.

5. Nikolai Berdiaev, *The Origin of Russian Communism* (London: The Centenary Press, 1937).

6. In David Harvey's critique (see chapter 4) of neoliberalism, a stridently anticommunist school of thought, the point is made that neoliberalism is established in the name of freedom, whereas freedom appears to be just a word or, rather, "a button that elites can press to open the door to the masses to justify almost anything" for the American people. In this regard, Harvey quotes Antonio Gramsci, according to whom "political questions become insoluble when disguised as cultural ones" (Harvey, *A Brief History of Neoliberalism* [New York: Oxford University Press, 2005], 39). It is interesting that the opposite also appears to be true: cultural questions like the pursuit of the peasant ideal of equality become insoluble when disguised as political questions like the scramble for a classless society.

7. Andrei Platonov, *Zapisnye knizhki: Materialy k biografii* (Moscow: Naslediye, 2000), 157.

8. Nicholas Vakar, *The Taproot of Soviet Society* (New York: Harper and Brothers, 1962).

9. The most influential books written in a corresponding tradition are A. S. Akhiezer, *Rossiya: Kritika istoricheskogo opyta* (Moscow: FO, 1991); A. G. Vishnevsky, *Serp i rubl* (Moscow: OGI, 1999); A. S. Akhiezer, et al., *Sotsio-kul'turnye osnovaniya i smysl bol'shevizma* (Novosibirsk: Sibirskii Khronograf, 2002).

10. This situation began to change only when political centrists led by Vladimir Putin made inroads into communists' power base.

11. The driving forces for regime change in the Baltics were different: anti-Russian sentiment and the awareness of once being cut off by the Russians from the Western civilization to which Lithuanians, Latvians, and Estonians rightfully belong.

12. Vishnevsky, *Serp i rubl*, 94.

13. Personal interview with Aleh Trusau, May 23, 2002.

14. I do not know when this pithy formulation was coined; however, it has been frequently referred to. See, for example, *Ad tuteshasci do natsianal'nai dziarzhaunasti* (Warsaw: Embassy of the Netherlands to Poland, 1999), 12.

15. Actually, many Poles in entrepreneurial positions had been exiled to Siberia in 1940. Around 1945, many educated Poles who had not been exiled left for Poland. A

fair number of those who did not take that opportunity left under Nikita Khrushchev in the late 1950s. Among the remaining people with Polish identity, peasants prevailed.

16. Yury Shevtsov, *Strana bazirovatiya* (Minsk: Belyi Svet, 2001), at http://zvezda .ru/geopolitics/data/belarus.htm.

17. "Na voprosy otvechayut experty," *Nashe Mneniye*, November 9, 2005, at www.nmnby.org.

18. Sergei Nikoliuk, "Azbuka politologii," *Nasha Belarus*, September 8, 2006, at http://ourbelarus.org.

19. Yevgenii Budinas, "Nashei 'fishkoi' mozhet stat 'Dictatur,'" *Turizm i Otdykh* 7 (February 23, 2006).

20. "Piotr Aven: My zalozhili fundament dalneishei zhizni," *PolitRu*, www.polit .ru/analytics/2006/12/20/aven.html.

21. Yelena Yakovleva, "Shok—eto ne po-nashemu: Reformam Gaidara 15 let," *Rossiiskaya Gazeta*, January 25, 2007, at www.rg.ru/2007/01/25/gajdar.html.

22. "Russians Bid Farewell to Yeltsin," Associated Press, April 25, 2007, at www.msnbc.msn.com/id/18304207/print/displaymode/1098.

23. Amy Chua, *World on Fire: How Exporting Free Market Democracy Breeds Ethnic Hatred and Global Instability* (New York: Anchor Books, 2004), 14.

24. Robert Putnam, *Making Democracy Work: Civic Traditions in Modern Italy* (Princeton: Princeton University Press, 1993), 115.

25. Robert Kaplan, "Was Democracy Just a Moment?" *The Atlantic Online*, December 1997, 18, at www.theatlantic.com/issues/97dec/democ.htm.

26. Nicholas Riasanovsky, "Afterword: The Problem of the Peasant," in *The Peasant in Nineteenth-Century Russia*, ed. Wayne S. Vuchinich (Palo Alto, CA: Stanford University Press, 1968), 263.

27. Anna Kaledina, "Kto men'she rabotayet, tot bol'she yest," *Izvestia*, March 9, 2007.

28. "Piotr Aven: My zalozhili fundament dalneishei zhizni," *PolitRu*, December 20, 2006.

29. Grigory Ioffe, "Belarus and Chernobyl: Separating Seeds from Chaff," *Post-Soviet Affairs* 23, no. 4 (2007).

30. This quote is by Gennady Grushevoi in David Marples, *Belarus from Soviet Rule to Nuclear Catastrophe* (New York: St. Martin's Press, 1996), 112.

31. Yury Shevtsov, *Obyedinionnaya natsiya: Fenomen Belarusi* (Moscow: Yevropa, 2005), 170.

32. *Chernobyl's Legacy: Health, Environmental and Socio-Economic Impacts and Recommendations to the Governments of Belarus, the Russian Federation and Ukraine* (New York: United Nations, 2005), 37.

33. Anatoly Rubinov, "Toupiki krestovogo pokhoda za demokratiyu," *Belarus Segodnia*, October 27, 2006, at www.sb.by/article.php?articleID=54844.

34. Anatoly Rubinov, "Yeschio raz ob ideologii," *Belarus Segodnia*, July 28, 2006.

35. Rubinov, "Yeschio raz ob ideologii."

36. Rubinov, "Yeschio raz ob ideologii."

37. Many authors have elaborated on that issue. "Our political elite," writes, for example, Andrei Konchalovsky, an acclaimed Russian film director, "is unable to tell the truth: there is no democracy in Russia, and it is unlikely to materialize in the nearest future. . . . This, however, does not mean that one has to sit idly. . . . I think that we will not develop a successful economy . . . until we feel the need to work on the most grandiose of the national projects, the project of reforming the national mindset. . . . One cannot overemphasize what a colossal shift in the mind-set of the new generation would be . . . the realization of a simple truth that in a school toilet one should pee into the urinal, not past it" (Andrei Konchalovsky, "Verit ili razmyshliat'?" *Moskovskiye Novosti*, September 27, 2006).

38. Alexander Pushkin, *Dnevniki. Zapiski* (St. Petersburg: Nauka, 1995): 701.

39. Rubinov, "Yeschio raz ob ideologii."

40. David Marples, "Europe's Last Dictatorship: The Roots and Perspectives of Authoritarianism in 'White Russia,'" *Europe-Asia Studies* 57, no. 6 (2005): 905.

41. Grigory Ioffe, "Unfinished Nation-Building in Belarus and the 2006 Presidential Election," *Eurasian Geography and Economics* 48, no. 1 (2007): 44.

42. David Marples, "Elections and Nation-Building in Belarus: A Comment on Ioffe," *Eurasian Geography and Economics* 48, no. 1 (2007): 65.

43. Elena A. Korosteleva, Colin W. Lawson, and Rosalind Marsh, eds., *Contemporary Belarus: Between Democracy and Dictatorship* (London: Routledge, 2003), 16.

44. Heinz Timmermann, "Belorussiya, Rossiya i ES: Problema dlia obshcheyevropeiskoi bezopasnosti," *Nashe Mneniye*, October 31, 2005, at http://nmnby .org/print311005/timmermann_prn.html.

45. Yaroslav Shimov, "Belorussiya: Vostochnoyevropeiskii paradox," *Neprikosnovennyi Zapas*, no. 47 and no. 3 (2006), at www.nz-online.ru/print.phtml?aid= 80011752.

46. "Tsi maye prademakratychnaya menshasts shans na pospekh?" *Prasky Accent*, a talk show of the Belarusian Service of Radio Liberty, May 18, 2006, at www .svaboda.org.

47. Kamitaka Matsuzato, "A Populist Island in an Ocean of Clan Politics: The Lukashenka Regime as an Exception among CIS Countries," *Europe-Asia Studies* 56, no. 2 (2004): 255.

48. Ann Lewis, ed., *The EU and Belarus: Between Moscow and Brussels* (London: Federal Trust of Education and Research, 2002), 61.

49. Alexander Rahr, "Lukaschenka: Die Opposition ist in Weißrussland keineswegs verboten," *Die Welt*, January 25, 2007, at www.welt.de/data/2007/01/25/ 1188208.html.

50. "Tsitaty iz interview prezidenta Belarusi nemetskoi gazette, ostavshiyesia 'za kadrom,'" *BELTA*, January 27, 2007, at www.belta.by/ru/print?id=134252.

51. "Prezident Litvy prapanuye Belarusi energetychnuyu dapamogu," *Belarusian Service, Radio Liberty*, February 14, 2007, at www.svaboda.org.

52. IISEPS's national survey of March 2005, at www.iiseps.org.

53. IISEPS's national survey of June 2006, at www.iiseps.org.

54. Online interview with Oleg Manayev, *Gosts na Svabodzie*, the Belarusian Service of Radio Liberty, May 14, 2006, at www.svaboda.org.

55. "Min'yust: V Belarusi zaregistrirovano 17 politicheskikh partii," *Novosti OpenBy* at http://news.by/333/2007-02-06/26668.

56. *Belorussky yezhegodnik 2004* (Vilnius: Institut Belarusi, 2005), 313.

57. *Belorussky yezhegodnik 2004*, 312.

58. Gaidukevich seems to be a comical political figure representing what was initially the Belarusian arm of Russia's Liberal Democrats. The latter, as many allege, is also led by a comical figure (Vladimir Zhirinovsky), but one of much higher visibility and caliber than his Belarusian clone.

59. See the account of elections and the aftermath in chapter 7.

60. Alexander Feduta, "Parliamentary Elections 2008: Possible Scenarios," International Conference "Towards the New Vision for Belarus," Kiev, Ukraine, September 12, 2007.

61. Vital Silitski, "Pamiatats, shto dyktatyry ruinuyutsa," *Arche* 7 (2006), at http://arche.bymedia.net/2006-7/silicki706.htm.

62. Yury Shevtsov, *Obyedinionnaya natsiya: Fenomen Belarusi*.

63. Yann Breault, "Establishing the Borders of the Collective Self: Lukashenka's Policy of Foreigness" (paper presented at the Twelfth Annual World Convention of the Association for the Study of Nationalities, Columbia University, New York, April 14, 2007, 7, quoted with the author's permission).

64. Yaroslav Shimov, "Belorussiya: vostochnoyevropeiskii paradox," *Neprikosnovennyi Zapas,* 2006, at www.nz-online.ru/print.phtml?aid=80011752.

65. Marples, "Elections and Nation-Building in Belarus: A Comment on Ioffe," 65.

66. Steven Eke and Taras Kuzio, "Sultanism in Eastern Europe: The Socio-Political Roots of Authoritarian Populism in Belarus," *Europe-Asia Studies* 52, no. 3 (2000).

67. Stanislau Shushkevich, *Neo-Communism in Belarus* (Smolensk: Skif, 2002).

68. Grigory Ioffe, "Understanding Belarus: Economy and Political Landscape," *Europe-Asia Studies* 56, no. 1 (2004): 85–118.

69. Matsuzato, "A Populist Island," 235–61.

70. Matsuzato, "A Populist Island," 243.

71. Matsuzato, "A Populist Island," 242.

72. Matsuzato, "A Populist Island," 241.

73. Matsuzato, "A Populist Island," 240.

74. Matsuzato, "A Populist Island," 241.

75. *Dogovor o sozdanii soyuznogo gosudarstva*, December 8, 1999, at www.soyuz.by/second.aspx?uid=101.

76. Yanina Bolonskaya, "Soyuznaya saga," *Belorusskaya Delovaya Gazeta*, December 13, 2005, at www.bdg.by.

77. Alex Danilovich, *Russian-Belarusian Integration: Playing Games behind the Kremlin Wall* (Aldershot, UK: Ashgate, 2006).

78. See, for example, Andrei Kozik, "Pravovye aspekty razrabotki konstitut-sionnogo akta soyuznogo gosudarstva," *Belorussky Zhurnal Mezhdunarodnogo Prava i Mezhdunarodnykh Otoshenii* 1 (2003), at http://evolutio.info/index2.php?option=com_content&task=view&id=604&itemid=54.

79. Yury Shevtsov, *Obyedinionnaya natsiya: Fenomen Belarusi.*

6

Alexander Lukashenka and His Detractors

No other politician in Belarus—in either the elite or the opposition—has ever had such a forceful, almost hypnotizing, grip on an audience as Lukashenka.

—Jan Maksymiuk[1]

We are an unaccomplished nation and our president mirrors that. He is successful because he reflects the condition of the electorate.

—Piotra Sadouskii[2]

Who is Alexander Lukashenka (figure 6.1)? The answer depends on whom you ask. For Western politicians, he is "the last dictator of Europe." The opinions of Western Belarus watchers from among social scientists are more nuanced than those of politicians. For example, David Marples professes "little doubt that the incumbent president [of Belarus] would have led by a considerable margin in a free election with an accurate vote count"[3] because "the degree of popular support for Lukashenka is quite impressive."[4] And Ronald Hill recognizes that "Lukashenka reflects popular values and aspirations."[5] More often than not, however, Lukashenka's popularity is seen as a nuisance: his supporters are just unable to see their own good, hence the assertion by Marples that Lukashenka's electorate is "blinkered."[6] Jan Maksymiuk, Radio Liberty's analyst, notes that "Lukashenka came over as a fantastic hero-leader, brandishing a sword of retribution over the head of those [whom Belarusians] see as their oppressors. . . . His tough-guy approach to politics [has] strong appeal for a society craving authority and a firm hand—the same society that had been overwhelmingly rural and patriarchal only half a century

Figure 6.1. Alexander Lukashenka visiting an elementary school in Petrikov (2006).

Photo courtesy of Nasha Niva

ago."[7] "When Lukashenka designates himself as 'father' (*bats'ka*)," observes Rainer Lindner, "we note the presence of the family unit of the Russian village."[8]

In Russia, Lukashenka is a "divider, not a uniter." National patriots idolize him, while liberals despise him and tirelessly ridicule his pronunciation. Andrei Okara attributes Lukashenka's popularity to the fact that "his rhetoric, behavior, and politics match a Belarusian-peasant archetype."[9] While ethnologists would probably point to some differences between the "peasant archetypes" of Russia and Belarus, these do not appear significant in the larger scheme of things, at least as far as Belarus's Orthodox majority is concerned. Other authors analyzing Lukashenka's personality also attribute Lukashenka's mannerisms, particularly his habit of thrashing members of his government in front of TV cameras, to a communal peasant ethos. For example, Yury Bogomolov likens Lukashenka to a buffoon character from a satirical short story by the late Vassily Shukshyn, a legendary connoisseur of peasant life. The character in question is a hillbilly upstart who sets out to snub and frustrate a lecturer, an urban outsider, by barraging him with a string of essentially senseless, but provocative, questions. The goal is to distract the lecturer and publicly humiliate him. According to Bogomolov, when Lukashenka snubs prominent foreigners, as in his infamous 1998 treatment of Western ambassadors,[10] he resorts to the same pattern of self-assertion in the eyes of his fellow countrymen that Shukshyn's character did. By doing so, he appeals to the basic instincts of the inferiority-ridden peasant mindset: Look, people, how I slapped this reputable guy. Look and gloat, as we are every bit as important as him.[11] In his column titled "Our son," Maxim Sokolov criticizes Russian authorities for failing to cultivate "mentally sound" opposition in Belarus. Instead, they throw their support behind a buffoon on the assumption that though he is in fact a "son-of-a-bitch," he is "our son-of-a bitch." Further substantiating his point, Sokolov reasons that such support is shortsighted and miscalculated: "A political pendulum, once swung to an extreme, may swing to the opposite extreme, compared with which even Zianon Pazniak will look like the utmost Russophile."[12]

From 2003 to 2006, however, reviling Lukashenka was not fair game in major Russian media outlets; only the most liberal of them, like the radio channel Echo Moskvy, did not toe the line. By the end of 2006, the mainstream Russian media had resumed the innuendos. Thus, the *Moskovsky Komsomolets* daily published a muckraking article about Lukashenka's relatives: reportedly they drink heavily and live in squalor in their godforsaken village, abandoned by their man at the helm of power.[13] When the Russia-Belarus trade war was in full swing, an article in *Izvestia* called Lukashenka a "conceited parasite."[14]

To me, the nature of this publicity reveals that neither Russia nor the West is prone to taking Lukashenka for what he most likely is: a national leader whose policies have something to do with his nation's circumstances and mind-set. This makes me think that an examination of the phenomenon of Lukashenka as part and parcel of the Belarusian context, not a straw man or cartoon character, is long overdue. In a book intended for a Russian audience, Yury Shevtsov points out that as a leader, Lukashenka "cannot but be part of his people's culture and local political tradition. This is particularly so when it comes to a personality who has led the state for more than ten years and ensured its successful development despite intense counteraction by some powerful forces."[15] So far, however, clichés and facts about Lukashenka, just like those about Belarus at large, are not so much in conflict; rather, they are like parallel worlds. Below is the line of established facts about Belarus's leader.

Not all of them constitute primary evidence, but the amount of spin is held to a feasible minimum.

- Born (1954) and raised by a single mother in a nondescript Belarusian village, he earns two college degrees and becomes director of a state farm (1987). From that unremarkable position, he enters a race to become a member of Belarus's parliament and wins that race (1990).
- As a member of Parliament (MP), he heads an anticorruption committee (1993–1994). He delivers a speech containing only trivial charges against well-known officials but wins public support as a crusader against corruption at a time when the living standards of Belarusians are sagging.
- Having entered the first presidential race in Belarus's history (1994), he defeats scores of candidates, including the acting prime minister, the former speaker of the Parliament, and the leader of Belarus's then largest political party.
- Lukashenka consolidates his power through popular referenda (1995 and 1996) by soliciting the direct support of the people. He thereby undercuts the role of the Parliament and courts.
- While Lukashenka "connects" best with people with a low level of education, many technocrats and some intellectuals support him as well. In 2001 he wins his second presidential race. While many in the opposition believe that the results have been rigged, there is consensus that he would have won the support of more than half of the electorate anyway.
- Lukashenka plays to Russia's imperial complexes. For example, he manages to get Russia to sell its natural gas to Belarus for about one-third to one-half of the price that four of Belarus's neighbors pay. At the same time, Lukashenka steers clear from those formulae of a union with Russia that call into question Belarus's statehood.
- Lukashenka succeeds in marginalizing both pro-Western Belarusian nationalists and ardent supporters of unification with Russia. Slowly but steadily, Lukashenka's consolidating role becomes evident to many Belarusians, including those who dislike him. This role is obvious after February 19, 2004, when Russia cuts off the flow of natural gas into Belarus, and Lukashenka labels this "an act of terrorism on the highest level." This role is even more obvious during the Russia-Belarus trade war of the winter of 2006–2007.
- From 2001 to 2004, Vladimir Putin's popularity rating in Belarus is higher than Lukashenka's. After February 2004, Lukashenka's popularity in Belarus is ahead Putin's.

- The tenure of the Russian ambassador to Belarus expires in the summer of 2005. Russians designate a former regional governor to be his successor. At a press conference in his hometown, the ex-governor takes the liberty of speaking disparagingly about Lukashenka. The seat of the Russian ambassador in Minsk is vacant until February 2006.
- Since 1996, Lukashenka presides over steady, socially equitable economic growth. There is no income disparity on the scale of Russia, to which Belarusians tend to compare their own country.
- In 2004, Lukashenka stages and, by the official count, wins a referendum designed to change the constitution so that he can run for president for the third time.
- From 2004 to 2006, Lukashenka presides over a steep increase in Belarus's trade with the West.
- Speaking at the Third All-Belarusian Convention in March 2006, on the eve of the presidential election, Lukashenka states that the country has already extracted all it can from its Soviet industrial legacy. Therefore, the cardinal tasks for the future are modernization of industry and the establishment of reliable networks to promote Belarusian goods on foreign markets. The investment boom of 2006 thus comes about as a planned surprise.
- In 2006, Lukashenka wins his third presidential term. Once again, voter fraud is suspected, but as in 2001, the consensus is that Lukashenka would have won the election anyway, only with a smaller margin.
- Despite Lukashenka's lasting ostracism (since 1996) by the West, his regime is by no means less stable today than at any other time since 1994, when he was first elected president. The Belarus Democracy Act, signed by George W. Bush in October 2004, authorizes the U.S. administration to locate and freeze Lukashenka's bank accounts in the West by January 2005, which, however, is not done. In December 2005, Lukashenka refers to this promise as doomed due to the nonexistence of his Western bank accounts. In March 2006, Bush finally passes some relevant information to Congress, but its factual content is strikingly unimpressive. The text of the letter of March 16, 2006, from the U.S. president to House and Senate Committees on International/Foreign Relations uses harsh wording like "a repressive dictatorship on the doorstep of the EU and NATO." However, it rehashes some old information from the international media, including muckraking articles from the Russian daily *Moskovsky Komsomolets* and another Russian daily, *Kommersant*. The ending paragraph of Bush's letter reads, "Given the lack of transparency in state property ownership and the Presidential Administration's role in the economy in general, it is difficult to know how much of the income

and revenue generated by state organizations (many of them beneficiaries of subsidized prices on energy from Russia) flows into accounts available for the personal use of Lukashenka, his family, his associates, and members of his government. Though Lukashenka is not known for an ostentatious lifestyle, information from former associates like Vinnikova[16] and Titenkov[17] points to extensive abuses of public resources by the president and those around him."[18] Given the noncommittal and compromised nature of these sources, it is little wonder that Lukashenka keeps ridiculing Bush's attempt to locate his American bank account.

Has Lukashenka had any failures? In my judgment, Lukashenka's most serious failure has been his inability to co-opt many Belarusian intellectuals. At this writing, it would nevertheless be fair to endorse Shevtsov's view that Lukashenka has confronted powerful interests inside and outside Belarus and has come out victorious.

The West accuses Lukashenka of stifling the independent media, harassing political parties and nongovernmental organizations, taking political prisoners, changing the constitution to extend power, and rigging the 2004 referendum, as well as of possible complicity in the disappearance of five prominent Belarusians. While Western criticism of abuses in Belarus has been loud and clear, identical abuses in many other countries have been at least as grave as those in Belarus, but they have not elicited a similar response. If, however, criticism of Lukashenka's domestic policies is taken at face value and found, as it has been by many, justifiable on most counts, it would still be far-fetched to claim that he treats Belarusian society as a perpetrator treats his victim.

There is a personal aspect to this assertion. Most Belarusians that I know are not Lukashenka's fans. If I lived in Belarus—quite a possibility considering that all my ancestors from my mother's side are from there—I might not be a Lukashenka fan either. Arguably the Lukashenka haters represent one side of an irreconcilable divide, the spatial and cultural dimensions of which this book has reflected on. This divide is deep-seated; Belarusians from each side of it are unwilling to listen, and this lack of communication deters nation building. One of the advantages of being a distant observer is that I am able to maintain sensitivity to both sides. The following analysis of three books about Lukashenka is easily a testing ground for that sensitivity. Books by Lukashenka critics are particularly useful in that regard; by striving to make their case against the Belarusian leader, they furnish valuable information about him and inadvertently about themselves.

Three books about Lukashenka—*Invasion*,[19] *An Accidental President*,[20] and *Alexander Lukashenka: A Political Biography*[21]—were all written in Russian, published in Russia, and brought to Belarus by volunteers. So that numerous Belarusians on business trips or in transit can obtain them, they have been routinely available in kiosks at the Belorussky Railway Terminal in Moscow. Two of the books' authors are well known in Belarus, and the books are released by registered publishers; as a result, they carry International Standard Book Numbers (ISBNs). The publication of *Invasion* is a conspiracy enterprise: the author's real name is hidden under a pseudonym, the publisher is unknown, and there is no ISBN.[22]

INVASION BY VLADIMIR MATIKEVICH

A brief preface to *Invasion* reads, "For several years the officers of Belarus's KGB [State Security Committee] clandestinely collected materials about the life and activity of Alexander Lukashenka. The investigative work of these honest and valiant people laid the foundation for this book, which fuses the concepts of fiction and documentary." *Invasion* reads like a thriller, laid out as a succession of episodes interspersed by their participants' dossiers and appended by one prison diary. Seemingly discrete episodes of Lukashenka's personal and political life build up an overall impression about what has been accomplished in Belarus under his guidance. To call this impression negative is an understatement: more accurate adjectives would include "ominous," "criminal," "horrifying," and "sickening."

Lukashenka's allegedly pathologic personality takes center stage. In medical terms, the pathology's name is mosaic psychosis (*mozaichnaya psikhopatiya* in Russian), a combination of "malignant narcissism, inferiority complex, and a syndrome of priceless ideas."[23] According to the text, a person with that kind of diagnosis[24] can live next to you, and you would not notice anything extraordinary about him except some reticence and aggressiveness. But as soon as such a person acquires decision-making and controlling powers, then he or she begins to pose a real danger to other people. The more commonly known disease that the book also attributes to Lukashenka is epilepsy.

A deep-rooted moral pathology adds to the above diagnosis. As a child, Alexander reportedly had outbursts of unprovoked anger, was hated by people in his native village, and loved to torture and kill cats. His anger was in part caused by growing up without a father. According to the book, Lukashenka's prodigal father was a Gypsy who never married Alexander's mother and only temporarily stayed in her village. Other reprehensible features of Lukashenka's character include an insatiable sexual appetite, deviant sexual practices, beating his women, informing on his coworkers, beating a

drunk tractor operator into unconsciousness (while he was a state farm director), beating his chief of staff (as president), and being a power-hungry ma-
niac. Most dialogues with Lukashenka's participation are awash with obscene
language. On several occasions, it is mentioned that Lukashenka has fat, female-looking thighs. The body parts of some other people are not spared
attention either. For example, Alexander Feduta, whose book is discussed
below, is mentioned as having a fat behind.

Lukashenka's activities portrayed in the book are as ominous as his personality. Handpicked to be the future president by the Russian Federal Security Service (Federalnaya Sluzhba Bezopasnosti, or FSB),[25] he received con-
gratulations and guidelines from his handlers at a secret rendezvous at 19
Korol Street in Minsk.

Besides his coming to power as a protégé of the FSB, Lukashenka's
other accomplishments described in *Invasion* are conspiring with former
Soviet citizens, now in the West, in order to create shadowy accounts for
money laundering; exporting precious metals as scrap iron and amassing
the true profits in extrabudget funds; exporting weaponry to sub-Saharan
Africa and rogue regimes all around the world; facilitating drug traffick-
ing; plotting to abduct and kill his former comrades in arms, Victor Gonchar and Yury Zakharenko; and protecting the immediate perpetrators of
that crime despite an attempt by the prosecutor general and the boss of the
Belarusian KGB to arrest and persecute them. The most ominous role in
the alleged crimes of the Lukashenka regime is attributed to his sidekick,
Victor Sheiman,[26] an Afghan war veteran described as a tight-lipped, cynical, and calculating monster. When Lukashenka was a presidential hopeful, Sheiman reportedly staged a fake shooting of Lukashenka's vehicle in
order to boost his popularity as a tested fighter of corruption. The alleged
assassination of Gonchar is described in chilling detail, with the killer lis-
tening to Beethoven afterwards.

On many occasions, the author of *Invasion* plays on ethnic stereotypes.
Thus, Ural Latypov, an FSB-KGB spook and a long-time member of
Lukashenka's administration, is described as placing a goodbye kiss on Pavel
Yakubovich's moustache and then spitting with disgust. It appears that
whereas Yakubovich, editor in chief of the *Sovetskaya Belorussiya* daily, is a
Jew, Latypov is a Muslim, and "Muslims are not supposed to kiss Jews."[27]

Several times Lukashenka is described as referring to his fellow countrymen as *bydlo* (cattle). Ironically, as the plot unfolds, it becomes disturbingly
clear that the author's own opinion of the intellectual ammunition and, indeed, the literary taste of his or her readers is no more flattering than
Lukashenka's alleged opinion of Belarusians.

AN ACCIDENTAL PRESIDENT
BY PAVEL SHEREMET AND SVETLANA KALINKINA

In terms of the authors' de facto attitude toward the reader, this book is a notch above *Invasion*. The authors do not hide behind pseudonyms: Svetlana Kalinkina is a well-known opposition journalist,[28] and Pavel Sheremet is a TV producer, currently with the Russian ORT channel. The book carries two endorsements by prominent Russians, one by the late Alexander N. Yakovlev, the father of perestroika, and the other by Boris Nemtsov, a former leader of the liberal Union of Right Forces party. While praising the book, Yakovlev objects to its title. For him, Lukashenka's presidency is not accidental at all — he is a legitimate child of the Soviet system. Nemtsov endorses the title but admits that the Belarusian dictator came to power as a direct result of the adoption of a democratic constitution and truly democratic elections. This, according to Nemtsov, amounts not so much to a mistake as to a mockery of history.

The book dwells on much the same episodes of Lukashenka's activity as *Invasion*. In addition, *An Accidental President* uncovers repeated inaccuracies in Lukashenka's official employment record and depicts Lukashenka's marriage to Galina Zhelnerovich (his estranged wife) as his first serious career booster because Zhelnerovich's parents were teachers. Galina Lukashenka still lives and works in the town of Shklov, Mogilev region, the initial power base of her husband, who reportedly changed about ten jobs in that town. Whereas *Invasion* offers only one version of the origin of Lukashenka's father, *An Accidental President* considers three: a Gypsy, a Jew, and a Belarusian. The first two versions are referred to as still popular amid the Belarusian opposition. In contrast to *Invasion*, whose blanket condemnation of Lukashenka does not spare his childhood and later years in the town of Shklov, some of Sheremet and Kalinkina's Shklov-based interviewees evince respect for and praise Lukashenka.

Another interesting detail furnished by the book is that during Lukashenka's 1990 electoral campaign for the Belarusian parliament, the members of his team were instructed to record words and phrases in Lukashenka's speeches that were taken positively and negatively by the audience. This technique looks fairly advanced for the early stage at which political image making was in post-Soviet countries at the time. The observation, though, is essential because if there is one thing that Lukashenka's sympathizers and his critics and haters agree on is that he is charismatic and adept at working the crowd. This quality helped Lukashenka in his 1994 campaign against Viacheslav Kebich, the prime minister and the presidential candidate of Belarus's *nomenklatura*, at a time when living standards took a dive after the breakup of the Soviet Union, and the people wanted to penalize those responsible.

> People adored Lukashenka. He was their man, from the low rung of the ladder, brave and ready to unabashedly fight the *nomenklatura*. His campaign rallies drew thousands. He could talk for hours about any topic and could shed a tear where appropriate. . . . People were instinctively drawn to him, they tried to touch him, and brought their babies [so he could share parents' delight at them]. This resembled mass psychosis, whose secret was entirely simple: he could speak with people in the language they could understand.[29]

Lukashenka's early (1991–1994) activity in Minsk in the capacity of an MP is described as opportunistic. While he later claimed he was the only MP who voted against the endorsement of the Belovezh agreement, which invalidated the Soviet Union, "in reality" (or so the book says) he did not cast any vote at all. When the white-red-white flag was solemnly brought into the Parliament's hall, Lukashenka made sure he was visible in proximity to the flag only to denounce it four years later. Lukashenka reportedly tried to ingratiate himself to the mutually antagonistic factions of the Popular Front and the Communist Party at the same time.

After Lukashenka won the 1994 presidential election, few foreign delegations honored Lukashenka's inauguration by their presence, and the ones who did were headed by officials whose rank did not exceed deputy prime minister. Legends still circulate in Minsk about the governmental reception given in conjunction with the 1994 inauguration.

> Oh, what a spectacle it was! The "New Belarusians" . . . from a collective farm. They were arriving as if at a rural wedding. Ladies with Babbeta [i.e., outdated] hair styles; gentlemen in suits, neckties, and sandals. . . . It was a doomsday! Since that time many people in Belarus feel uncomfortable and ashamed when they hear the responses of foreign observers about the "Belarusian political beau monde." Its personae now look more genteel and wear expensive neckties and jackets. But one cannot hide one's inferiority complex behind an expensive pin.[30]

This description, particularly the notion of shame it conveys, resonates with a publication by Belarusian sociologist Elena Gapova. In it, she depicts a habit that is not endemically Belarusian but that pertains to countries of recent urbanization: educated people, themselves children or grandchildren of peasants, all too often hold today's peasants in contempt. Here is how Gapova relates the emotions of a college-educated Belarusian who is waiting at the Polish-Belarusian border crossing amid his or her less-educated compatriots:

You understand only too well why our Western neighbors do not like "our folks." Who could ever like them: their vodka may cause health problems, and their cigarettes have a nasty smell. They are cynical, have lost visible sexual features, do not take care of their looks. They curse and speak loudly. . . . They are "second rate" people: that's how the locals take them. By the way, it seems to me that when "our folks" return home (to Slonim, Lida, or Baranovichi), they turn—in some miraculous way—into the local elite. Affluent, owning estates, cars and property that they got through decades of hard market work. . . . But listen, there are your compatriots! They should be closer to you than local Poles, who look at this horde of peddlers from the East with fear and disgust. So why do you feel belonging with the Poles, and not with our folks, why are you ashamed?[31]

My feeling is that both quotes—from Sheremet and Kalinkina and from Gapova—may hold a key to the lingering bond Lukashenka has with many rank-and-file Belarusians and to their consistent estrangement from the opposition. A remark by Oleg Manayev made during a talk show of the Belarusian Service of Radio Liberty comes in handy: "Fifteen years ago, Prime Minister Viacheslav Kebich had real power in the country," said Manayev. "But did anybody use to refer to him as 'our Slava' [Slava is a diminutive of Viacheslav]? No. But 'our Sashka' [Sashka is a diminutive of Alexander] they did say and keep on saying all the time. This is a regularity: people have a gut feeling that [Lukashenka] is their man."[32]

An Accidental President, however, finds fault with this bond: Lukashenka is a rustic man from the social bottom, and this is no good at all. One of the book's chapters is even titled "President from a Trash Can" whereas "How Does One Become a Dictator?" is a subtitle. Indeed, how? The authors paint a picture of Lukashenka as consistently getting rid of the brighter people in his team, some of whom, like Victor Gonchar, would later (1999) fall victim to abduction and assassination. Loyalty to the new leader becomes more important than professionalism, and loyal mediocrities fill the vacuum left by professionals.

Just like *Invasion*, this book charges Lukashenka with selling weaponry and not giving an official account of revenues, with reexporting undocumented hard liquor to Russia through rogue tax-exempt firms relieved of paying tariffs, and with spreading "lies" that lands contaminated by Chernobyl are now safe "to live on, grow grain, and give birth to children."

"Money and repressions are what his power rests on," write Sheremet and Kalinkina. By their own account, however, money and repressions do not tell the full story. Tamara Vinnikova, Lukashenka's deposed chief banker, is quoted as saying, "It is now easy for me to talk; I have a right to do so, as Lukashenka mistreated me so much. A solitary cell, torture, and even meetings and correspondence with my family were forbidden. I was not allowed to consult my attorneys without supervision, and, most importantly, for two years I was not allowed to undergo urgent surgery. He knew everything. But at the same time, here's what persistently torments me. When I fault Lukashenka, doesn't this hurt the honor of ordinary Belarusians, who have chosen him as their idol? This is what constantly restrains me."[33] Sheremet and Kalinkina do not offer insights into the lingering bond between Lukashenka and at least half of his nation. Apparently, much like Gapova's intellectual at a border crossing, the authors do not think that the views of uneducated people deserve much attention.

Yet, one more skill that Lukashenka has honed to perfection is playing to Russia's imperial instincts and former-great-power complexes. Until recently, this skill allowed Lukashenka to exchange real benefits for promises that have never materialized. Lukashenka's 1999 speech at Russia's Duma session, abundantly quoted in *An Accidental President*, is an example of his winning strategy with Russia. Lukashenka's ambitions, though, allegedly reached further. According to a widespread view, he allegedly wanted to become an independent player on the Russian political scene and possibly win the greatest prize, the Kremlin. According to Sheremet and Kalinkina, Lukashenka was close to achieving this goal in 1997. Anatoly Chubais, however, reportedly thwarted Lukashenka's attempt, and the subsequent enthronement of Putin put an end to Lukashenka's pursuits.

An Accidental President contains a detailed account of what is known about the disappearance of four prominent Belarusians—Victor Gonchar, Anatoly Krasovsky, Yury Zakharenko, and Dmitry Zavadsky—as well as about the suspicious sudden death of Victor Karpenko (former vice speaker of Belarus's parliament). Like *Invasion*, the book attributes the masterminding of the alleged crimes to Victor Sheiman and also to Yury Sivakov (former minister of internal affairs), whose last post, from which he was fired in 2005 by Lukashenka, was as Belarus's minister of sports.

Also, like *Invasion*, *An Accidental President* takes up the alleged psychiatric diagnosis of Lukashenka. Whereas *Invasion* traces this diagnosis to Lukashenka's medical record, which was destroyed by the hospital boss on orders from above, Sheremet and Kalinkina attribute the same verdict to the psychiatrist Dmitry Shchigelsky, who repeatedly observed Lukashenka on TV and shared his extramural findings in his electronic messages to several Belarusian and Russian periodicals.[34] The book's verdict on Lukashenka is that he "is a person who arose from the social bottom. His threshold of moral permissiveness is low: what is unacceptable for an ordinary person, for him is a way to achieve his goals." He "believes that he is infallible and that he is the chosen man. He divides all the people surrounding him into supporters and opponents and the latter are to be dealt with according to the stipulations of martial law. He is sick and healthy at the same time. And the name of his illness is power. This is why he should not be allowed to rule the people."[35]

Because Sheremet and Kalinkina identify with this verdict, one admission strikes me as dissonant with the entire book's letter and spirit. All of a sudden, on their book's last page, the authors profess "no doubt that Lukashenka loves Belarus and his people."[36] Literally nothing in the entire book allows one to suspect any such virtue on Lukashenka's part. And this may be one of the book's problems. While Sheremet and Kalinkina hold their readers in somewhat higher esteem than the undercover author of *Invasion*, the difference is small, and the indiscriminately accusatory tone does not help to build up the case against Lukashenka.

ALEXANDER LUKASHENKA: A POLITICAL BIOGRAPHY BY ALEXANDER FEDUTA

Alexander Feduta (figure 6.2) is a native of Grodno, one of the two provincial centers of western Belarus and, culturally, the westernmost one, with significant Polish influence. After graduating in 1986 from Grodno State University, Feduta taught Russian literature at a secondary school in Grodno and was active in Komsomol (the Young Communist League) during Gorbachev's perestroika. In 1991, the Soviet Union's last year, Feduta joined the Communist Party and became the last boss of Belarus's Komsomol. After December 1991, with the Soviet Union gone, the organization purged the word "communist" from its name and continued to exist. By 1994, Feduta was still its boss, in charge of a spacious building in downtown Minsk. By that time, however, the Soviet-born spheres of institutional influence had been shattered. Feduta figured that he would soon lose a coveted piece of real estate in downtown Minsk anyway, and so he decided to use it as a trump card to ally himself with someone whose political star was on the rise. At that time, the first-ever presidential race in Belarus was in full swing. Feduta decided to place his stake on Lukashenka, who positioned himself as an antiestablishment candidate. Unlike his two powerful rivals, Prime Minister Kebich, and the leader of the Belarusian Popular Front, Zianon Pazniak, Lukashenka lacked premises for his campaign staff. Feduta approached the members of the Lukashenka team and offered to share the Young League's premises with Lukashenka's campaign headquarters.

Upon winning the race, Lukashenka returned the favor and made Feduta his press attaché. Feduta's tenure, however, lasted only from June to December 1994. He quit because the revival of censorship was becoming associated

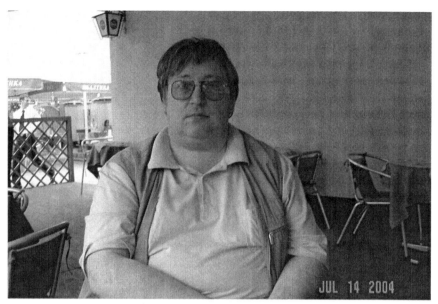

Figure 6.2. Alexander Feduta (political commentator, former press attaché of Alexander Lukashenka).

with his name. Upon quitting, Feduta became an opposition journalist. He also defended his doctoral thesis on the beloved Russian poet Alexander Pushkin (1799–1837), entitled "The Reader in Creative Consciousness of Alexander Pushkin," and he published articles and books on Pushkin and on Fadei Bulgarin, one of Pushkin's foes with roots in Belarus.

It takes just a few pages to realize that compared to *Invasion* and *An Accidental President*, Feduta's book is in a different weight category. This may be taken literally, as the book is almost seven hundred pages long, but even more so figuratively. With so much room at his disposal and no attempt to hide his negative attitude toward Lukashenka, Feduta nevertheless avoids speculations about the ethnic origin of his former boss's prodigal father. No inquiry into the young Lukashenka's habit of torturing cats is offered either. Still harder to believe, the much rumored psychiatric diagnosis of Lukashenka is absent in Feduta's book.

When reading the two previous books, I had the feeling that I was kept on a short leash and ridden roughshod through an uninterrupted sequence of harrowing episodes out of the authors' apparent concern that, left to my own devices, I might weaken and go soft on Lukashenka. Feduta's treatment of his reader is noticeably more humane. The book's opening episode is a true attention getter. In it, Feduta describes Lukashenka's 1998 visit to Nagano,

Japan, the site of the winter Olympics. Lukashenka decided to go to Japan on the spur of the moment and gave only two day's notice to everybody involved. Among those inconvenienced were Belarus's newly appointed ambassador to Japan, who had taken over just days ago; Japan's and Russia's Ministries of Foreign Affairs; and Russian and Japanese air traffic controllers. By Feduta's description, Lukashenka behaved in Japan like an elephant in a china shop. To the consternation of rural landowners, he and his entourage took a cross-country skiing trip across privately owned land. During the intermission of an ice hockey match, Lukashenka rushed into the locker room to personally encourage his country's national team, despite the fact that such contacts were not allowed. The stadium associates, however, were dispersed by Lukashenka's more muscular bodyguards. It was next to impossible to organize an official meeting for Lukashenka in Japan on two days' notice, but Yevgeny Primakov, then Russia's foreign minister, went out of his way to facilitate a meeting with the speaker of the Japanese parliament. After the appointment had been scheduled, Lukashenka declined to show up because the rank of the Japanese official seemed too low to him as president. On his departure from a Japanese hotel, Lukashenka had his chief of staff pay for the hotel rooms in cash from a flat briefcase full of greenbacks. Many people who happened to be involved or just ran into Lukashenka during his impromptu trip were stunned, wondering who on earth that man was—as are Feduta's readers. Indeed, who is that man?

To that question, no simple answer is offered, but Feduta pictures several of Lukashenka's leadership qualities. It appears that throughout his political career, Lukashenka has, on most occasions, evinced an unmistaken political instinct: sensing what ordinary people think and what they want to hear, he proceeds to make statements that are not just in tune with their mood but one step ahead of it. For example, not only was Lukashenka quick to grasp how people thought about the economic downturn of the early 1990s, but he also sensed that his fellow countrymen opted for simple solutions. One such solution was to penalize allegedly corrupt officials. One of them, Stanislau Shushkevich, used a government firm to make low-cost repairs at his dacha, then paid for those repairs. This was a minor misdemeanor, if a crime at all. But the people wanted somebody punished for worsening their lives. In the end however, Shushkevich lost his post as parliamentary speaker not because he allegedly stole "a box of nails," as the opposition media wrote more than once, mocking the pettiness of the peasant-born political beau monde, but because of his role in the breakup of the Soviet Union. Of course, his utter inability to muster public support mattered as well. For all his intellect, Shushkevich never won popular elections. In contrast to him, as a presidential hopeful, Lukashenka gained more support with each public appearance.

The effect of Lukashenka's public appearances was stunning. I remember accompanying him to Gomel [a provincial center in Belarus's south and the second largest city of Belarus]. During that trip he made a speech at a covered stadium before 2,500 people. He was standing at the center of the playing field and relating his favorite "epic story" of how he fought the hydra of corruption. This lasted close to two hours, and then for more than two hours the speaker responded to questions. . . . When he took off his jacket, the back of his shirt was dripping wet. . . . He sat down with no expression on his pale, tired face. . . . And the people gushed down the amphitheater. It seems that they did not get to the isles first but just stepped over the front rows of seats and flowed down the playing field as a mass of molten rock. While this lava moved closer and closer to its hero, hands stretched out to him. They were handing over some scraps of paper, notepads, books—only to get his signature. Somebody handed over a passport; and somebody else—in a country so wretchedly poor at the time—a $100 bill! He attracted them not as a popular idol but as a saint. . . . Three months earlier I saw the eyes of Minsk residents widened at the appearance of Bill Clinton: theirs, however, was an interest in somebody exotic, whereas here it was about genuine belief in miracles.[37]

After the quality of life in Belarus plunged in the early 1990s, due to disrupted economic ties with Russia and the subsequent closing of most manufacturing plants, Lukashenka made a passionate speech at the 1997 Minsk-held Congress of the Peoples of the USSR, bemoaning the lost union and pledging to recreate it in some form. Those in the West who cannot bring themselves to understand, much less accept, Putin's 2005 statement that the demise of the Soviet Union has been the "biggest geopolitical catastrophe of our time" may likewise be baffled as to why Lukashenka finds a receptive audience at home when he emphasizes order over democracy and civil liberties. To those willing to understand, Feduta's book makes this clear. Just yesterday, life in Belarus was orderly, and there was food on the table, perhaps not as plentiful as in the West but decidedly more plentiful than it was in Belarus ten, twenty, and certainly thirty years ago. Then, following all those hard-earned improvements, some politicians created a dangerous mess in the name of freedom. Work and food vanished as a result.

Six years after Lukashenka's speech at the Congress of the Peoples of the USSR, I received a rare chance to observe Lukashenka's debating skills. Here in America, I cannot watch Belarus State TV, and during my regular summer trips to Minsk, I was never fortunate enough to watch Belarus's president in action. But on March 11, 2003, courtesy of Dishnetwork of America, a Russian NTV channel broadcasted a verbal duel between Lukashenka and Anatoly Chubais, the ideologue and enforcer of Russia's privatization program. The duel was aired as part of NTV's now canceled show *Svoboda Slova* (Freedom of Speech). Himself a seasoned polemist, Chubais lost pitifully to

Lukashenka. Writing about this duel, Feduta claims that whereas "Chubais appealed to commonsense and economic logic, Lukashenka appealed to the emotions and feelings of 'ordinary people.'"[38] While this assertion is not off the mark, saying that Lukashenka merely plays to raw emotion does not, I am afraid, do him justice. Here is an excerpt from one of Lukashenka's statements as conveyed by Feduta:

> People need money, but they also need calm . . . which is why one should not say "give property away." Who should we give it to? The electric grid and power-generating capacities to Chubais? Pipelines to Miller [Gazprom's boss]? Or maybe to Khodorkovsky? But haven't you just put him in jail? So, who will that property now belong to? . . . As for us, we do not even raise the question of passing property on to somebody, particularly if it works and meets people's demand. We could have toyed with that giving-away experiment, if we had as much oil and gas as you do. If we scupper, there is nothing we can patch the hole with. You have billions that are flowing from the Almighty God, all this money you are receiving for oil and gas. As a matter of fact, in Russia's electric power grid, which Anatoly Borisovich Chubais heads, as well as in oil and gas, there is an enormous contribution by Belarusians; we also built cities in those regions. However, you threw us away, and we do not get anything from there and we do not even ask.[39]

Clearly, the above monologue reflects Lukashenka's political instinct. First, he knows exactly what people want to hear. Second, he never stops his brinkmanship with Russia; he depends on it for survival, yet he distances himself from its hugely unpopular privatization schemes and skillfully forges his us-versus-them line of attack.

There are, of course, many inspirational speakers. One may succeed in that capacity as a corporate manager or as a college professor. But to endear yourself to a significant part of an entire nation, you have to connect with a lot of people who never attended a college, which brings us to yet another selling point of Lukashenka as a leader, his humble origin. In fact, Lukashenka's charisma is that of a peasant-born upstart in a country that only a generation ago was a peasant universe. In this context, Lukashenka's language appears to be important. That language is disparagingly called *trasianka* (see chapter 1). But this is precisely how less-educated Belarusians talk. While using *trasianka* made Lukashenka the butt of jokes in the Russian media, his ability and willingness to speak the way most of his fellow countrymen do has a more important implication. Quite a few Belarusians identify and feel comfortable with Lukashenka.[40]

It seems to be common knowledge that first-generation intellectuals evince more arrogance toward common folk than do "hereditary" intellectuals. One

Russian saying, *iz griazi v kniazi* (literally, "from dirt to princes") aptly re-flects this habit. Of all political actors in Belarus from 1990 to this day, Lukashenka is least prone to that sort of conceit. In contrast, Lukashenka's former ally turned foe, Victor Gonchar believed that "power should belong to intellectuals."[41] Interestingly, Gonchar and yet another such intellectual, Dmitry Bulakhov, planned to use Lukashenka as a battering ram. With his peasant charisma, he was thought of as the one who would only win power, then throw it at the feet of those truly anointed to exercise it.

Looking down on ordinary people remains both a pet peeve and a malady of the Belarusian opposition. The integral part of its message to the outside world is that people vote for Lukashenka because of their limited under-standing of political and socioeconomic reality. They are either semiliterate or blinded by propaganda, or both.[42] Feduta's book contains information to the contrary: people voting for Lukashenka make a rational choice. For ex-ample, a leader of Chernobyl public initiatives, Gennadii Grushevoi, is quoted as saying that the retirees and those affected by the Chernobyl disas-ter collectively account for more than half of the Belarusian electorate, and these people are the most loyal Lukashenka supporters precisely because they understand that they depend on the state[43] and stand to lose in the more competitive economic environment that the opposition is likely to promote in Belarus.

While Feduta takes "ordinary people" more seriously than the authors of the two books about Lukashenka that I have just reviewed, he is not immune to intellectual chutzpah. For example, he calls the (now former) speaker of Belarus's parliament, Vladimir Konoplev, a Neanderthal[44] because of his hill-billy demeanor. At one point, Feduta expresses the view that with the quality of life in Belarus turning for the worse in the early 1990s, the number of the lumpen (that is, underclass) increased,[45] and they were the nourishing envi-ronment for a leader like Lukashenka. However, two hundred pages later, Fe-duta attributes popular support for Lukashenka to the fact that wages were now growing, and pensions were being paid on time, which is what people appreciate most, and so they turn a deaf ear to loftier matters.[46] It therefore appears that either way, the ordinary people side with Lukashenka, not with his bashers, when life is getting worse, as in the early 1990s, and also when it is getting better, as it has been since 1996.

Yet, one more selling point of Lukashenka's leadership in the eyes of the Belarusian public has been his attempt to reintegrate Belarus with Russia, but not to the point of giving up national independence. On that score, Lukashenka appears to be in sync with most of his fellow countrymen. For many of them, though, seeing Belarus as a country apart from Russia contin-ues to be problematic, although it is reasonable to assume that the longer Belarus exists as a formally independent country, the easier it will be to get rid of Russia's spell.

Feduta writes in his biography of Lukashenka, "Sinitsyn[47] looked at me. . . . The second Presidential Elections were drawing close. Commotion pervaded the government apparatus, as bureaucrats were pricking their ears in order to detect any audible noise from Moscow. Any [Russian] TV show with a message somehow related to Belarus was being perceived as something that the destiny of the country depended upon."[48] Note that at the time of this observation, Belarus had enjoyed statehood for ten years. Leonid Sinitsyn, who wanted to enter the presidential race, changed his mind after he realized that Moscow did not support his candidacy. And so did Natalya Masherova, the daughter of the most beloved communist leader of Belarus, who died in a car crash in 1980. With no sanction from Moscow, there is no presidential ambition—even trying is not advisable. Whether this is a reflection of Moscow's actual power to determine political outcomes in Minsk or "just" Moscow's sway on the Belarusian mentality is not addressed, but my feeling is that there is a little bit of both.

"Our economy was closely linked with Russia's," writes Feduta "so much so that this link may be likened to the umbilical cord that connects an infant to the mother's organism. The August putsch of 1991 acted as a midwife who, however, neglected to cut that cord, so a child was now developing separately as it were, and yet the mother's organism kept on supplying requisite nutrients."[49] This description is clearly on target. What is questionable is whether it applies only to economy. By Feduta's own account, the Belarus-Russia connection runs deeper.

DISCUSSION

Even after twelve years at the helm of Belarusian power and despite understandable Lukashenka fatigue on the part of some of the Belarusian electorate, Lukashenka is still in sync with half of it—at the very least. Consequently, regardless of what his detractors say, Lukashenka is a genuinely Belarusian leader, the most successful leader in Belarusian history. One vintage formula used by this leader in reference to his problem-solving strategy is *my shli ot zhizni*. Literally, this means that in developing an independent Belarus, "we" proceed from life as "we" know it and from folk wisdom that "we" tirelessly contrast to the perfidy of the Western advisors. They wanted us to privatize industry, but we disobeyed. In the end, however, even the World Bank and the International Monetary Fund recognized Lukashenka's success. Of course, this recognition is not without qualifications, one of which is that the salary increases of 2004 and 2005 cannot be sustained under the current growth of labor productivity. That is, considering the country's financial means, Belarusian workers are overpaid! More importantly, special deals on Russian oil and gas prop up Belarus's success. There is no doubt that these special deals matter. However, on their usual mission to castigate Lukashenka, his critics overlook the obvious. Observing that Belarus's "impressive economic statistics derive primarily from Russian 'benevolence' and the withdrawal of that largesse—in the long run—was only to be expected,"[50] those critics turn a blind eye to the fact that no country in Belarus's neighborhood, not even those hostile to Russia, has come up with alternative energy supplies, and Poland is utterly enraged by Russia's and Germany's joint decision to build a pipeline circumventing Poland (as well as, obviously, Lithuania, Belarus, and Ukraine). In the foreseeable future, no reasonable alternative to Russian oil and gas is available for Belarus. And from this perspective, that someone has been able to keep the selling price at its lowest in exchange for promises of eternal friendship, and to do so for years, is no small feat! As one shrewd author noted, Lukashenka's integration game with Russia is a "brilliant sham."[51] Accentuating this brilliance is the May 2, 2007, *Manifesto of Russia-Belarus Unification* issued by two members of the Belarusian opposition, Leonid Parfenovich (an Olympic champion in boat racing and a former MP) and the above-quoted Leonid Sinitsyn.[52] These two enemies of Lukashenka are in favor of Belarus's becoming an associated member of the Russian Federation, something along the lines of Puerto Rico vis-à-vis the United States.

Measured against this proposition, Lukashenka comes across as a national hero. In my 2002 report on my International Research and Exchanges Board–funded short-term trip to Minsk, I noted that "if a goal of the U.S. policy is to prevent Belarus from being reunited with Russia, then, however paradoxical this may sound, Lukashenka is the only hope."[53] Today, I stand by this statement, only I no longer discern a paradox: Lukashenka is the sole reliable defender of Belarusian statehood; nobody else even comes close. Surely, he is no Thomas Jefferson. But he is no Augusto Pinochet either. In a Radio Liberty online conference, Andrei Dynko, editor of the *Nasha Niva*, the most blatantly antiregime newspaper published in Belarus, was offered a question: "Are there any positive aspects of Lukashenka for Belarus?" "Lukashenka is a rational leader," said Dynko, "who does not like bloodletting and has not allowed a power vacuum. Under the colonial elites, the abysmally poor education, and the conformism of the intelligentsia that we had in the early 1990s, it could be worse—a total idiot could have seized power."[54] Note that Dynko has a spotless reputation as a Belarusian nationalist of the traditional (nativist and westernizing) strand, and he was one of those briefly jailed after the dispersal of a tent camp on October Square in Minsk in March 2006 (see chapter 7). Particularly valuable about Dynko's remarks is that they contain some reference points—such as colonial and Russified elites, conformism, and so forth—that are quite different from those implicitly used by most Western commentators in their pronouncements on the Belarusian regime. If these reference points make any sense at all, then many critics of Lukashenka should pause and reflect: Belarus is no Sweden, England, France, or "even" Poland, and so judgments about the way political power is exercised in Belarus must take this into account. Apparently, what Lukashenka has been doing is working. One does not judge a person based on a contest he did not take part in: Lukashenka has not been trying to win Western applause, but he has earned the approval of his compatriots. According to the January 2007 national survey taken by an opposition polling firm right after the trade war with Russia, 64.1 percent of the respondents subscribed to the notion that Lukashenka has been successful in installing order in Belarus, and 61.3 percent named building an independent Belarus as a hallmark of Lukashenka's success.[55]

In light of public approval of this magnitude, Lukashenka may feel safe at the helm of power. He maintains his image as a popular, charismatic leader, despite being assailed by the West, and now the East as well, and despite being surrounded, annoyed, and often obstructed by high-ranking public servants. As a leader who solicits direct authority from his people, the authority to act decisively and mercilessly on their behalf and for their own good, Lukashenka may retain his position for the foreseeable future. It is true that his practices subvert habitual Western arrangements, but they succeed because, in Belarus, people invest more trust in the leader than in the Parliament, constitution, and courts. One variety of this tradition, known as the "tsar and the people versus the boyars," has been called for quite a number of times in Russian history. A milder strain of the same tradition is actually practiced in Russia today, with Putin's popularity exceeding that of his government and MPs by a huge margin. The Latin American varieties of the same tradition seem to be associated with the likes of Hugo Chávez of Venezuela, Evo Morales of Bolivia, and Ollanta Humalla of Peru.

It is to Lukashenka's benefit that the United States continues its policy of verbal innuendos and travel sanctions and that the European Union (EU) half-heartedly toes the same line. Harmless in practical terms, this policy is immensely helpful in cultivating Lukashenka's image as a rare national leader not beholden to either Washington, Brussels, or Moscow.[56] Yet, at the same time, he proudly reports to his nation that "despite all the problems in our relationships with the EU, its countries account for almost half of our export, and our export to the EU grew 28 percent in 2006. And our export to the

United States has grown almost 80 percent."[57] Definitely there is some disconnect—on the part of the West—between words and actions, and I am not certain at all that it is the actions that are wrong. It may well be that the words are, particularly when they are awkward, inconsistent, and confusing. Examples are many. The above-quoted letter from Bush to Congress regarding Lukashenka is one of them. Just one day after the Belarusian elections, a CNN correspondent asked Alexander Lukashuk, the director of the Belarusian Service of Radio Liberty, whether or not it was true that under Lukashenka wages had trebled and that there had been economic growth and no unemployment. Almost a namesake of Belarus's president, yet his ideological nemesis, Lukashuk said, "In truth, we don't know for sure. The parliamentary and presidential elections and referenda throughout twelve years of Lukashenka's presidency have been considered unfair and dishonest by the Organization for Security and Cooperation in Europe. Prior to yesterday's elections, surveys taken by different sociological firms stated that Lukashenka enjoys the support of more than 50 percent of the population. But by the same token, one can judge that Stalin also enjoyed the genuine support of the majority of the Soviet people."[58] However inadvertently, Lukashuk added a serious dimension to the problem. Surely, Stalin was genuinely supported, and so is Lukashenka, but the realization of this does not make the task of unseating an authoritarian leader any easier or any more legitimate. Just the opposite: if people themselves do not care for Western-style democracy, making them adopt it against their will is strikingly undemocratic. As Vladimir Litvin, former chairman of the Ukrainian Supreme Rada (Parliament) said three days after the Belarusian elections, "One should not teach people democracy when one is awash in one's own problems."[59]

Fortunately, Lukashenka is no Stalin, not even close. And the underpinnings of his popularity are possible to grasp, provided there is willingness to do so, which means that politically biased judgments ought to be kept at bay, if only for the time being. My analysis suggests that Lukashenka and many of his fellow countrymen see eye to eye on some critical issues defining Belarus as a country and Belarusians as a community. Lukashenka is a person of humble origin and peasant upbringing, and so are many Belarusians. Most Belarusians speak *trasianka*, a mixture of Russian and Belarusian, and so does Lukashenka. Most Belarusians have found it problematic to see themselves as a community apart from Russia, and so did Lukashenka. Yet, the country and its leader have made important steps in the direction of psychological (not yet economic) independence from Russia. Significantly, they have done this in unison, without any attempt on the part of the leader to push it along, get ahead of his fellow countrymen, or preach historical myths that do not strike a chord with Belarusians. A further strengthening of the Belarusian economy and the positioning of Belarus vis-à-vis major global challenges with little regard to Russia's stand on them are likely to rid Belarus of Russia's spell. As Lukashenka's charisma appeals to Belarusians, so do his policies, particularly his emphasis on communalism, a social safety net, and staying away from privatization Russian and Ukrainian style. With all his policies and with Russian energy supplies at a discounted price, Lukashenka has managed to deliver 8 to 10 percent economic growth annually since 2001 and significantly boost real wages. Nowhere in the world do leaders who accomplish this get booted.

NOTES

1. Jan Maksymiuk, "Belarus: Father of the Nation or Fatherless Son?" *Radio Liberty*, February 8, 2007, at www.rferl.org/featuresarticle/2007/02/d22a8d8e-95a3-48f5-a3fd-cf11f7536421.html.

2. *Praski Accent*, talk show of the Belarusian Service of Radio Liberty, July 12, 2007, at www.svaboda.org.

3. David Marples, "Color Revolutions: The Belarus Case," *Communist and Post-Communist Studies* 39, no. 3 (2006): 363.

4. Marples, "Color Revolutions," 361.

5. Ronald Hill, "Post-Soviet Belarus: In Search of Direction," in *Post-Communist Belarus*, ed. Stephen White, Elena Korosteleva, and John Lowenhardt (Lanham, MD: Rowman & Littlefield Publishers, 2005), 1–16.

6. David Marples, "Elections and Nation-Building in Belarus: A Comment on Ioffe," *Eurasian Geography and Economics* 48, no. 1 (2007): 65.

7. Jan Maksymiuk, "Belarus: Father of the Nation or Fatherless Son?" *Radio Liberty*, February 8, 2007.

8. Margarita M. Balmaceda, James Clem, and Lisbeth Tarlow, eds., *Independent Belarus: Domestic Determinants, Regional Dynamics, and Implications for the West* (Cambridge, MA: Harvard University Press, 2002), 98.

9. Andrei Okara, "Belarus v otsutstvii tret'yei al'ternativy," *Russkii Zhurnal*, November 14, 2001, at www.russ.ru/politics/20011114-oka-pr.html.

10. In June and July 1998, the Lukashenka administration waged the so-called sewage war against the U.S. and EU ambassadors, seeking to evict them from their residences at a government compound near Minsk under the pretext that a local sewage system required an overhaul. The EU and the United States retaliated by prohibiting some thirty ministers and senior officials in Lukashenka's government from entering their countries, thus inaugurating a longer series of travel bans on Belarusian officials in subsequent years (*Post-Soviet Belarus: A Timeline*, RFE/RL, February 24, 2006).

11. The Shukshyn episode occurred in a rural club to which local authorities invite urban lecturers to enlighten the local community about the achievements of modern

science. Yuri Bogomolov, "Narodnyi pomazannik," *Izvestia*, October 9, 2001, at www.izvestia.ru/rubr.cgi.

12. Maxim Sokolov, "Our Son," *Izvestia*, September 7, 2001.

13. Irina Bobrova, "U lukomotya zmii zelionyi," *Moskovsky Komsomolets*, November 10, 2006.

14. Vitaly Ivanov, "Ne nuzhno zabluzhdadtsia naschiot Belorussii," *Izvestia*, January 18, 2007, at www.izvestia.ru/comment/article3100239/index.html.

15. Yury Shevtsov, *Obyedinionnaya natsiya: Fenomen Belarusi* (Moscow: Yevropa, 2005), 9.

16. From 1995 to 1997, Tamara Vinnikova was chair of Belarus's Central Bank; she was fired and jailed, then surfaced in London where she currently resides.

17. From 1994 to 1999, Ivan Titenkov served as a real estate manager of Lukashenka's presidential administration; he currently lives and conducts business in Moscow, Russia.

18. "Report on Belarus, the Last Dictatorship in Europe, Including Arms Sales and Leadership Assets," White House Press Release, Office of the Press Secretary, Washington, DC, March 16, 2006.

19. Vladimir Matikevich, *Nashestviye* (Moscow, 2004).

20. Pavel Sheremet and Svetlana Kalinkina, *Sluchainyi prezident* (St. Petersburg: Limbus Press, 2004).

21. Alexander Feduta, *Lukashenko: Politicheskaya biografiya* (Moscow: Referendum, 2005).

22. It is normal for Russian books to identify not only the publisher but also the printing house; even the advent of computer-designed camera-ready copy has not changed this routine. Where *Invasion* was printed is not disclosed, however. Perhaps for these reasons, that book has not been seen in the respectable bookstores of Moscow, whereas the other two books have. *Invasion,* however, is widely available in its Internet version. Links to it exist, for example, at www.ucpb.org, the site of the United Civic Party of Belarus, and at www.batke.net (which literally means "No to Batska," that is, to the national father figure, Alexander Lukashenka), and at the Russian fiction site at http://lib.ru.

23. Matikevich, *Nashestviye*, 30.

24. Not a medical doctor, I was unable to find an English equivalent of this diagnosis. If, however, if one Googles in (мозаичная психопатия) (that is, conducts a Russian-language Google search using the above-mentioned phrase), close to one hundred Internet files are unearthed, all of which are devoted to a single patient with this diagnosis, Alexander Lukashenka.

25. The FSB is one of the descendants of the KGB.

26. Sheiman was prosecutor general, chief of staff, and chief of Lukashenka's electoral campaign; at this writing, he is the chair of Belarus's Security Council.

27. Matikevich, *Nashestviye*, 40.

28. Interestingly, in an article vaguely reminiscent of one of the refrains of *Invasion*, Kalinkina makes a point that Lukashenka's bodily frame is not really that of the sportsman he pretends to be because of his female-looking thighs (Svetlana Kalink-

ina, "Maski-shou," *Belorusskii Partizan*, February 19, 2006, at http://belaruspartizan .org).

29. Pavel Sheremet and Svetlana Kalinkina, *Sluchainyi prezident*, 23.

30. Sheremet and Kalinkina, *Sluchainyi prezident*, 27.

31. Elena Gapova, "The Nation in Between, or Why Intellectuals Do Things with Words," in *Over the Wall/After the Fall: Post-Communist Cultures through the East-West Gaze*, ed. Sibelan Forrester, Magdalena Zaborowska, and Elena Gapova (Bloomington: Indiana University Press, 2004).

32. Aleg Manayev, "U Belarusi yest' satsialnaya baza dlia vertaniya v Yevropu," *Gosts na Svabodzie*, a talk show of the Belarusian Service of Radio Liberty, May 14, 2006, at www.svaboda.org.

33. Sheremet and Kalinkina, *Sluchainyi prezident*, 66.

34. The analogy may be drawn between this case and a March 2005 statement by Bill Frist, a medical doctor and U.S. Senate majority leader. After observing Terri Schiavo, a comatose patient who had suffered devastating brain damage, on television, Bill Frist said publicly that she was "not somebody in a persistent vegetative state." According to most American commentators, Frist's statement was inappropriate.

35. Sheremet and Kalinkina, *Sluchainyi prezident*, 236.

36. Sheremet and Kalinkina, *Sluchainyi prezident*, 237.

37. Alexander Feduta, *Lukashenko: Politicheskaya biografiya*, 127.

38. Feduta, *Lukashenko*, 608.

39. Feduta, *Lukashenko*, 607.

40. Incidentally, during George W. Bush's presidential campaigns, many people in the American South and Midwest were quoted as saying "W speaks like my neighbor," while that other guy comes across as a kind of an aloof aristocrat. In Lukashenka's and probably in Bush's case as well, a rustic manner of speaking veils the man's political savvy. Indeed, most, if not all, political actors in Russia and Belarus underestimated Lukashenka initially, taking him for someone less smart than themselves.

41. Feduta, *Lukashenko*, 305.

42. Because most Western Belarus watchers get cues from their contacts in the opposition, they for the most part "share" the same view.

43. Feduta, *Lukashenko*, 399, 645.

44. Feduta, *Lukashenko*, 134.

45. Feduta, *Lukashenko*, 126.

46. Feduta, *Lukashenko*, 342.

47. From 1994 to 1995, Leonid Sinitsyn served as Lukashenka's chief of staff; he then worked as deputy prime minister of Belarus (until 1996).

48. Feduta, *Lukashenko*, 463.

49. Feduta, *Lukashenko*, 338.

50. Marples, "Elections and Nation-Building in Belarus: A Comment on Ioffe," 61.

51. Nina B. Mečkovskaya, *Belorusskii yazyk: Sotsiolingvisticheskie ocherki* (Munchen: Verlag Otto Sagner, 2003), 140.

52. "Leonid Sinitsyn: Dalucheniye da Rasei—eta zaichyk u matrioshtsy," Belarusian Service of Radio Liberty, May 2, 2007, at www.svaboda.org.

53. See www.irex.org/programs/stg/research/02/ioffe.pdf.

54. Andrei Dynko, "Responses to Questions," *Forum*, the Belarusian Service of Radio Liberty, November 29, 2006, at www.svaboda.org.

55. IISEPS's national survey of January 2007, at www.iiseps.org.

56. Natalia Leshchenko, "The National Foundation of the 'Last European Dictatorship'" (paper presented at the Twelfth World Convention of the Association for the Study of Nationalities, Columbia University, New York, April 14, 2007).

57. Alexander Lukashenka, "Poslaniye belorusskomu narodu i natsionalnomu sobraniyu Respubliki Belarus," *Belarus Segodnia*, April 25, 2007, at www.sb.by.

58. "Alexander Lukashuk u interview CNN: Stalina tak samo padtrymlivala bolshasts," Belarusian Service of Radio Liberty, March 20, 2006, at www.svaboda.org.

59. "Litvin: Ukraina ne dolzhna uchastvovat' v sanktsiyakh protiv Belarusi," *Belorusskie Novosti*, March 22, 2006, at www.naviny.by/ru/print/?id=60916.

Opinion Polls and Presidential Elections

The Lukashenka regime has managed to achieve a certain equilibrium between itself and society by . . . placing the outlook and political culture of
the average Belarusian into the regime's own foundation.

—Vital Silitski[1]

Stability of the system of governance created by Lukashenka is based on
rational choice by Belarusians: a redistribution-based populist model converts all those who would be the first to lose from liberal economic reform
into beneficiaries. Hence the perceived cost of sustaining the regime is
dwarfed by the perceived costs of change.

—Alexei Pikulik[2]

Throughout this chapter, for the most part I use polling results obtained by the
Independent Institute of Socio-Economic and Political Studies (IISEPS) and regularly featured on its Russian-language website (www.iiseps.org). IISEPS is an
opposition-minded Minsk-based think tank and polling firm headed by Dr. Oleg
Manayev (figure 7.1), a sociologist with an international reputation. At this writing, he is a visiting Fulbright scholar at the University of Tennessee. IISEPS was
subjected to harassment by the Belarusian KGB in December 2004. On December 27, 2004, the U.S. ambassador visited IISEPS as a sign of support for beleaguered Belarusian nongovernmental organizations (NGOs). On April 15, 2005,
the Supreme Court of Belarus ruled to close down the institute. It is currently active as a nonprofit organization registered in neighboring Lithuania. Manayev
has been repeatedly warned by the General Prosecutor's Office that the continuation of polling in Belarus by an institution not registered in Belarus is a criminal offence. To keep himself out of trouble, Manayev recently issued a public

statement that he no longer directs a "Lithuanian" polling firm. Instead, polling is conducted by a group of private citizens. Whatever it is, the entity in question has indeed managed to sustain its reputation for evenhandedness. While the authorities are always displeased by the outcomes of its surveys, on many occasions the opposition is equally displeased. In each national survey, about fifteen hundred randomly selected Belarusian adults are interviewed, distributed between age groups and settlements of Belarus in proportion to their populations. The sample error is within 3 percent.

Figure 7.1.   Oleg Manayev (major independent sociologist of Belarus).
Photo courtesy of Yury Drakakhrust

WHERE DO BELARUSIANS GET INFORMATION?

The descending order of news sources ranked in terms of the percentage of people using each source is as follows: Belarusian TV (69.7 percent), Russian TV (66.8 percent), radio (34.2 percent), state newspapers (33.7 percent), relatives and friends (25.5 percent), independent newspapers (17.1 percent), and foreign media (11.7 percent).[3] Interestingly, the wording used in this survey does not qualify Russian TV as foreign: "Russian TV" and "foreign media" mean two different, nonoverlapping things. Although the kind of "radio" listened to is not identified, most probably, this is Belarusian state radio for the most part. Foreign radio broadcasts do not have a large audience in Belarus. The Belarusian Service of Radio Liberty (BS RL), for example, is listened to by 5 percent of Belarusian adults, for the most part living in Minsk and western regions of Belarus.[4] One may suggest, on the basis of the above ranking, that Belarusians are influenced mainly by Belarusian state propaganda. This impression gets reinforced if one takes into account that according to March and April 2006 national surveys, only from 4.7 to 5 percent of Belarusian adults use the Internet on a daily basis, 8 to 8.8 percent use it several times a week, and 69 to 71 percent have never used it at all.[5]

It is then all the more important to acknowledge that not all pronouncements or actions of the Belarusian authorities earn the support of Belarusians. For example, a national survey from December 2005 asked Belarusians to express their attitude toward the statement by Alexander Lukashenka that children from Chernobyl-affected areas should no longer be sent abroad to improve their health. Only 23.8 percent of all respondents supported that statement, whereas 53.3 percent did not.[6] Three days before the March 2006 presidential elections, Stepan Sukhorenko, in charge of the Belarusian KGB, stated somewhat hysterically that "under the cover of presidential elections, a coup is being prepared." To the question "Do you agree with this statement?" posed in the end-of-March 2006 national survey, 30.9 percent of respondents said yes, whereas 49.1 percent said no. Another statement by Sukhorenko, that "active participation in street protests will be perceived as an act of terrorism," was rejected by an even bigger margin: 58.1 percent versus 26.8 percent. Yet another question in the same survey read, "When Kozulin, the former rector of the Belarusian State University, attempted to participate in the All-Belarusian People's Convention, he was beaten by the secret service's associates, and two suits were brought against him on the grounds of criminal offense. What's your attitude to that?" Slightly more than 30 percent commended the authorities, and 38 percent faulted them.[7]

WHAT DO BELARUSIANS VALUE?

"What is more important to you, economic improvement or national independence?" read one question in the November 2003 national survey by IISEPS. As noted in chapter 3, the result was 62 percent versus 25 percent in favor of economic improvement. Even among the self-proclaimed supporters of the opposition, the ratio was 51.4 percent versus 35.9 percent.[8] Yet, as time goes by Belarusians are warming up to the idea of independent statehood. When in October 2006, the identical question was posed, 48.5 percent opted for economic improvement and 41.9 percent for national independence, a significant change in the ratio.[9]

That said, in all available surveys, Belarusians steadily demonstrate that they care more about economy than about politics. When asked whether Belarus ought to maintain the status quo as far as its path of development is concerned, 51.1 percent said yes, and 48 percent opted for change. However, of those who opted for change, 48.6 percent assigned priority to the economy (with such options included as raising quality of life, stopping inflation, and improving the state of the economy), and only 16.8 percent meant political change (e.g., changing people in power, making sure human rights are honored).[10] Table 7.1 lists, in order of importance, the problems that a typical Belarusian family faces. This order points to the high degree of primacy attached to material problems and the low priority of human rights.

Most Belarusians are people of modest means. In June 2006, 55.1 percent of them said their earnings were barely enough to obtain the necessary food

Table 7.1. Distribution of Responses to the Question "What Problems Does Your Family Face?" (This Is an Open Question, and More Than One Response Is Possible)

Option	Percentage
Material problems (not enough money, low level of living, price hikes, etc.)	87
Health care and medical service problems (bad health, high prices, and low quality of medical care)	26.5
Residential and utility problems (inadequate living space, bad communal utility services)	25.2
Unemployment	15.6
Interpersonal relations (family problems, problems with children, etc.)	9.2
Corruption and crime	6.7
Education problems (low quality, high price, etc.)	6.7
Violation of human rights	4.3
Other problems	6.6
My family faces no problems	6.6

Source: IISEPS's May 2005 national survey, at www.iiseps.org.

and clothing; 14.9 percent said that even this they could not afford, whereas only 25 percent said they could afford high-quality and versatile food and clothing. Only 1.2 percent could afford a new car, while a cheap, used car could be obtained by 22.9 percent.[11] This modest level of well-being explains, if only in part, the insignificant attention paid to problems of a loftier, noneconomic nature, such as human rights. But one cannot rule out that there is more to this than simply a modest living standard, as many Belarusians simply do not see that their rights are violated and do not perceive the anti-Lukashenka opposition as their genuine defender.

Paval Sevyarynets, a prominent opposition leader sentenced to two years of compulsory work for his role in organizing street rallies in October 2004, wrote a letter from a remote rural village in Vitebsk region, where he was toiling for a tree-felling enterprise. In that letter, published on the website of the Malady Front (Young Front), the unregistered NGO that Sevyarynets heads, he shares ten questions that local villagers asked him when they found out that he represented a group hostile to Lukashenka and was sentenced for political reasons. Below are questions 3 to 10 in my verbatim translation:

3. We (Belarusians) don't have resources. We are paupers. Where will you take resources from? Oil, gas, and metal?

4. Are you still for the Belarusian Popular Front (BNF)? When will you finally calm down? Where is your Pazniak? And where is your Shushkevich? No, we will not get duped by the BNF.

5. Why are you stirring people up? Factories are working and pensions are being paid. We may not be well-to-do, but it's fine and calm. So, why all this whipping up? Only war and blood can come from this.

6. What are you going to give us [if your people win the elections]? Suppose we will vote for you, what is going to happen to us? Will you give us money or bring a tank car with alcohol?

7. One can't read about you people anywhere or get a feel for what you want. You can't get anything done. So, how are you going to win?

8. Really, what is your program? Point by point? About the flag and language we already know. Anything else?

9. What, do you want to make it like they have in Ukraine? The orange revolution, a crowd in the square, and bedlam thereafter? You'll start bickering and getting each other by the throat, and you'll bring the economy to a halt. Another crisis?

10. Or do you want to make it like they have in Poland? So we are unemployed as they are? Or like in the Baltics where the retirees became beggars? Or like in Russia with its mafia, oligarchs, and tough life for an ordinary man?

Sevyarynets concludes that only when the opposition has responded to all these questions, so that even in the sticks there is a clear sense of the answers, will the opposition win.[12]

REACTION TO PERCEIVED CHANGE

Even though democracy and human rights are not high on Belarusians' priority list, they do not seem to embellish the actual situation if and when asked to reveal their attitude to perceived change in those specific areas. Thus, according to the December 2005 national survey, the situation with democracy and human rights actually got worse during Lukashenka's reign. Not on all counts, therefore, does the opinion of Belarusians depart from the "mainstream" international opinion.

However, positive changes have been recorded in the areas that Belarusians value most. In this regard, a comparison of June 2004 and June 2006 responses to the question "What are the most acute problems that the country and its citizens face?" (see table 7.2) is especially revealing. Of particular importance is the steep reduction (from 58 to 19.5 percent) in the share of those naming pauperization as the most acute problem. At the same time, few people are concerned about the international isolation of Belarus and the decline of national culture.

Table 7.2. "What Are the Most Acute Problems That the Country and Its Citizens Face?" (Percentage of Responses Pointing to Each Problem as Most Acute)

Problem	June 2004 (%)	June 2006 (%)
Price hikes	73.2	60.1
Unemployment	49.7	37.0
Corruption, bribes	35.6	27.6
Overcoming consequences of Chernobyl	21.1	25.5
Crime	37.3	23.2
Lack of law and order	32.9	22.1
Violation of human rights	30.4	22.1
Depopulation	19.8	21.9
Pauperization	58.0	19.5
Decline in production	22.2	18.7
Threat posed by the West	7.7	18.2
International isolation	14.7	14.4
Decline in national culture	13.8	10.8
Threat of losing national independence	7.2	8.3
Divisions in society	8.9	7.3

Source: Sergei Nikolyuk, "Navedeniye poryadka," *Nashe Mneniye,* August 18, 2006, at www.nmn.by.org. Based on the national surveys of IISEPS, with close to fifteen hundred randomly sampled respondents; sample error is within 3 percent.

Most Belarusians agree that throughout the past fifteen years (1991–2006), Belarus has become a truly independent country. Close to 69 percent of respondents endorse that view, and only 20 percent disagree. Among the self-proclaimed supporters of the Lukashenka regime (47.8 percent of the entire sample probed in October 2006), the ratio of firm believers in independence is even higher than among the general public; whereas people opposed to the regime (15.5 percent of those probed) are tied on the issue; and the ratio among the politically indifferent (26.2 percent of those probed) is 60 percent versus 25 percent.[13] Not only do most believe that Belarus is now a fully fledged independent country, but most also believe that they have personally gained from that independence, and the numerical advantage of gainers versus losers is particularly high among the self-proclaimed supporters of Lukashenka.

PROTEST POTENTIAL

In 2005, IISEPS assessed the likelihood of Belarusians to protest and potentially overthrow the regime, an assessment in large measure motivated by the so-called color revolutions in Ukraine, Georgia, and Kyrgyzstan. The official stand of the Belarusian authorities with regard to those events is threefold: in the above-mentioned countries, power structures were weak, quality of life was low, and Western political technologies proved efficient under those conditions. IISEPS's analysts disagreed with this diagnosis. First, neither Leonid Kuchma of Ukraine nor Askar Akaev of Kyrgyzstan had been seen as particularly weak. Second, quality of life in Ukraine may be lower than in Belarus, but not much lower. Third, Western support of Belarusian opposition is by no means less generous than, say, of Kyrgyz opposition. Hence, the hypothesis that bearing a grudge against people in power—in other words, the popular feeling of being mistreated by them—was instrumental in color revolutions in the first place. With this in mind, Belarusians were asked in March 2005 whether they felt that the authorities had mistreated them: 74 percent responded that they had not been mistreated, and 26 percent said that they had. The mass attitudes of these two groups were profoundly different. For example, whereas more than half of the latter group repeatedly encountered corruption, only 19 percent of the former did. Whereas one group agreed with the current course of the government's policy and preferred the status quo, the other disagreed and opted for change. Overall, the sociologists concluded that in Belarus, the limit of people's patience was far from exhausted.[14] Indeed, few Belarusians believe that events like the "orange revolution" are even possible in their country. Among those supporting Lukashenka, 71 percent identified with this view. Even among Lukashenka bashers, 50.7 percent thought that such events were impossible in Belarus, whereas only 35 percent deemed them possible.[15]

In May 2005, 56 percent of Belarusians probed by a national survey said that life in Belarus is generally fine for people like them, whereas 36.8 percent said that it is not. In response to the question "Who does the solution to your problems depend upon?" 71 percent pointed to the Belarusian authorities, 29.6 percent to themselves, 5.9 percent to the opposition, 3.9 percent to Russia, and 2.4 percent to the West. More than one answer was possible, so the sum exceeds 100 percent.[16] In late March and early April 2006, right after the presidential elections, 38.9 percent of Belarusians believed that since 2001 life had changed for the better, 15.9 percent believed that it had changed for the worse, and 44 percent did not record any noticeable change.[17] Also, at the time of the elections, 35.9 percent of Belarusians felt that there was no tension in Belarusian society, 39 percent felt that there was some tension but significantly less than in Russia, and only 17.1 percent believed that tension was quite real and on the rise.[18] And the overwhelming majority did not feel like participating in various forms of active protest.

ATTITUDE TO FOREIGNERS, FOREIGN COUNTRIES, AND WESTERN ALLIANCES

In several national surveys Belarusians were asked to name the five countries most friendly and the five countries least friendly to Belarus. Table 7.3 contains responses received in late April 2006. The last column of the table contains the so-called index of friendliness, computed as the difference between the percentages of respondents who named a country in two polar categories (friendliest and least friendly) divided by one hundred. The pattern table 7.3 reveals may be construed as a throwback to the cold war, only the "iron curtain" has shifted further east, which is reflected in negative evaluations of all the new North Atlantic Treaty Organization (NATO) and European Union (EU) members. The highly positive rating of China apparently derives from the fact that the leaders of China and Belarus exchanged visits, and the state-run media lavishly praised this exchange and its potential significance for Belarus. The negative rating of Poland is not matched by a negative rating of the Poles: table 7.4 shows that the "social distance" between Poles and residents of Belarus is the third shortest. Note that the ABCDE succession of columns in table 7.4 reflects the descending order of commitments, from readiness to become a relative to readiness just to live in one country, hence the coefficients attached to these commitments in the computational formula for the index of social distance (see note underneath table

7.4). As both tables 7.3 and 7.4 testify, relationships with Russia and Russians are deemed especially close.

It is noteworthy that the degree of closeness has little, if anything, to do with how Belarusians evaluate quality of life in foreign countries. For example, in late April 2006, Belarusians for the most part believed that life in Poland, Latvia, and Lithuania was better than in Belarus. However, Belarusians do not seem to take any guidance from that belief. Even before Poland, Latvia, and Lithuania became members of both NATO and the EU, they used

Table 7.3. Responses to the Question "Name Five Countries Which in Your Opinion Treat Belarus in the Friendliest Way and Five Countries That Treat Belarus in the Least Friendly Way" (Percentage of Responses Mentioning Each Country in Each of the Two Categories and the Index of Friendliness)

	Friendly (%)	Unfriendly (%)	Index*
Russia	85.1	1.4	0.837
China	43.1	2.1	0.420
Kazakhstan	23.2	2.3	0.209
Cuba	20.3	2.4	0.179
Ukraine	24.9	13.5	0.114
Bulgaria	10.0	1.2	0.088
Kyrgyzstan	6.4	1.7	0.047
Moldova	9.2	4.5	0.047
Italy	11.4	6.8	0.046
Iran	13.3	9.8	0.035
Armenia	5.3	1.9	0.034
Israel	6.2	3.4	0.028
Uzbekistan	4.6	2.1	0.025
Turkmenistan	3.5	1.2	0.023
Azerbaijan	4.4	2.2	0.022
Germany	16.8	15.2	0.016
Turkey	2.3	2.3	0
Slovakia	3.6	4.9	−0.013
Czech Republic	2.4	4.0	−0.016
Serbia and Montenegro	2.6	5.0	−0.024
Sweden	1.3	4.1	−0.028
Poland	19.9	23.3	−0.034
France	3.0	11.6	−0.086
Lithuania	10.6	19.5	−0.089
Estonia	0.7	11.9	−0.112
Latvia	9.2	23.4	−0.142
UK	2.6	21.6	−0.190
Georgia	4.2	23.8	−0.196
USA	4.1	74.3	−0.702

Note: *Index is calculated as the percentage of "friendly" responses minus the percentage of "unfriendly" responses divided by one hundred.
Source: IISEPS's national survey of April 2006, at www.iiseps.org.

Table 7.4.   Percentage Distribution of Response to the Question "To What Extent Do You Tolerate Representatives of the Following Groups?"

Group	Ready to Become a Relative (%)	Ready to Work Together (%)	Ready to Be a Neighbor (%)	Ready to Live in One Town (%)	Ready to Live in One Country (%)	Index*
	A	B	C	D	E	
Russians	50.9	14.9	19.8	8.6	8.6	2.051
Ukrainians	32.8	19.2	28.5	10.4	10.4	2.439
Poles	31.1	21.7	25.9	11.0	11.0	2.464
West Europeans	21.6	26.1	24.2	16.9	16.9	2.743
Central Europeans	14.2	26.1	27.5	18.5	18.5	2.953
Jews	10.7	23.4	24.5	23.9	23.9	2.984
Lithuanians	12.6	24.4	31.3	19.2	19.2	3.000
Latvians	11.5	23.1	32.2	20.2	20.2	3.059
Americans	16.2	23.4	23.1	27.5	27.5	3.076
Central Asians	4.0	18.9	28.9	31.6	31.6	3.523
People from the Caucasus	2.4	14.6	26.7	44.1	44.1	3.806
Arabs	2.3	14.5	26.9	44.0	44.0	3.809
East and Southeast Asians	1.5	16.3	24.1	44.6	44.6	3.831
Africans	1.9	13.1	28.4	44.6	44.6	3.834

Note: *This is an index of social distance; it is calculated as (A + 2B +3C + 4D + 5E) ÷ (A + B + C + D + E). The index ranges from 1 (when all respondents expressed readiness to become a relative of a member of a certain group) to 5 (when all respondents can tolerate a member of a certain group only as another resident of Belarus).
Source: IISEPS's national survey of April 2006, at www.iiseps.org.

to be physically close, yet faraway countries (i.e., belonging in a different civilization). In contrast, Russia and Ukraine have always been close to Belarus in every respect. This is almost like the difference between immediate family and third cousins. In this regard, the ambivalent assessment of life in Russia (where gross domestic product per capita is now significantly higher than in Belarus, but social inequality is glaring) and the decidedly negative assessment of quality of life in the fresh-from-the-orange-revolution Ukraine (both revealed by the national poll of April 2006) matter a lot, as they help us to better understand why quality of life in Belarus is deemed decent.

When asked whether they would like to move to a foreign country for good and, if so, what their preferred destination would be, 62.3 percent opted to stay put. Among the prospective destinations, Germany was number one with 9.6 percent of respondents, and the United States was number two with 7.3 percent. Only 2.2 percent would consider moving to Russia, and only 1.7 percent to Poland.[19] Note that the percentage of those willing to move abroad among people below thirty is close to 50 percent, which is significantly higher than among the general population. While no survey probed the reasoning behind Belarusian youths' willingness to leave Belarus, Valyantsyn Akudovich hypothesizes that should such a survey be conducted, lack of democracy in the country would be the least important reason, whereas economic reasons would top the list.[20]

An interesting attempt at parallel Belarus-Ukraine polling brought about some expected and some counterintuitive outcomes with regard to Ukrainians' and Belarusians' stand vis-à-vis NATO and the EU. The national survey in Ukraine was conducted in December 2005 by the Kiev-based International Institute of Sociology.[21] In December 2005, the leaders of the orange revolution were still in power; this was seven months prior to Victor Yanukovich's comeback as prime minister. A national survey containing the same questions was conducted in Belarus by IISEPS in April 2006, that is, after the presidential elections in Belarus, which—at least initially (up until the trade war with Russia broke out in December 2006)—solidified the pro-Russia geopolitical orientation of Belarus. The comparative results of the two polls became available on the IISEPS website in June 2006.

Despite qualitatively different political situations in the two countries at the times of those polls, the popular attitudes of their citizens to the prospect of joining the EU and NATO did not differ much. In both Ukraine and Belarus, roughly the same numbers favored joining the EU (32.4 percent in Belarus and 33 percent in Ukraine) and NATO (14.4 percent in Belarus and 16 percent in Ukraine).[22] Also, as the above numbers in parentheses indicate, in both Belarus and Ukraine the hypothetical readiness to join NATO was significantly lower than the readiness to join the EU. But even with regard to the EU, proponents and opponents were almost equally numerous in both countries (one-third versus one-third). Despite the seemingly reasonable assumption that the situation in Belarus is less conducive to candid expression of one's views, somewhat more Belarusians (than Ukrainians) agreed to give a definitive response to the questions about joining NATO and the EU. Those in favor of integration into NATO and the EU were relatively more numerous in Ukraine, which complies with the observation that, in Ukraine, joining the two Western structures is perceived as not just a purely theoretical possibility. Counterintuitively, though, in Belarus the *opponents* of joining NATO and the EU were somewhat less numerous than in Ukraine: 33.8 percent of Belarusians and 39 percent of Ukrainians were against joining the EU; 46.2 percent of Belarusians and 57 percent of Ukrainians were against joining NATO.[23] "Belarusians' retaining about the same degree of commitment to the European idea in a situation seemingly less conducive to it than that in Ukraine," hypothesize IISEPS's associates, "may suggest that Belarusians are genuinely more European in their outlook than Ukrainians."[24] Interestingly, Julia Korosteleva and Stephen White drew the same conclusion from their own comparative survey conducted in Belarus, Ukraine, and Russia: Belarusians turned out to be the most pro-European, or, considering that pro-Europeans are minorities in their respective countries, the least anti-European of the three communities.[25] From this assertion, it would be logical to turn to Belarusians' views about themselves.

WHO ARE WE?

When asked abroad, "Who are you in your perception?" 44.3 percent of Belarusians would say "a citizen of Belarus" and 43.7 percent would say "Belarusian." Only 4.1 percent said they would introduce themselves as Russians, well below the actual percentage of ethnic Russians in the population of Belarus.

Identity, however, is usually multilayered and polyvalent, so it was worth posing a question about people's attachment to a larger cultural niche. Two national polls faced Belarusians with a rather rigid choice: "Do you consider yourself a contemporary European or a Soviet person?" Although this wording casts "Soviet person" as a less appealing option by legitimately depriving it of the attribute "contemporary"—after all, it had been fifteen years since the Soviet Union's demise at the time of the polls—more Belarusians identified with the Soviet (46.1 percent) than with the European (41.3 percent) niche,[26] thus lending credence to a popular idea that Belarus was, and still is, the most Soviet of the former republics.

In June 2006, a national poll asked Belarusians to relate to Vladimir Putin's statement that "we and Belarusians are by and large one and the same nation." To be sure, similar statements were made by Alexander Lukashenka, but because Putin is the president of another country, posing a question on his assertion made perfect sense in a Belarusian poll. More than half (54 percent) of all respondents identified with Putin's statement, only 7 percent were insulted by it, and 29 percent said that they disagreed but did not feel badly about Putin's assertion.[27] This result raises the question of whether Belarusians have managed to detach themselves from Russia mentally or it continues to be a part of Belarusians' sense of self.

This question is taken up by Yury Drakokhrust, who invokes Akudovich's pronouncement about the Belarusians' ambivalent attitude toward their great eastern neighbor: for Belarusians, "Russia is not *to the east of* Belarus—rather, Russia is *the east of* Belarus."[28] In other words, spatial continuity may be inherent in Belarus's self-perception; because the ethnic frontiers have not

Table 7.5. The Relationship between Comparative Assessments of Quality of Life and Geopolitical Preferences

If You Were to Choose between Joining Russia and Joining the EU, What Would You Choose?	*Where Is Life Better, in Belarus or in Russia?*	
	In Belarus (67.8%)	*In Russia (14.7%)*
Joining Russia (51.6%)	58.5	40.6
Joining the EU (24.8%)	21.1	38.1
Should Belarus Become an EU Member?		
Yes (36.7%)	33.3	56.9

This is a cross-reference table compiled on the basis of a December 2005 national survey by IISEPS (a random sample of fifteen hundred adults; sample error within 3 percent). For example, 58.5 percent of all respondents prefer joining Russia *and* believe that life in Belarus is better.
Source: Yury Drakokhrust, "Gde konchayetsia Belorussiya?" *Neprikosnovennyi Zapas* 47 (2006).

been distinct, at least part of Russia's space has always been within Belarusians' mental map, and so has part of Poland, albeit to a lesser extent. With this hypothesis in mind, Drakokhrust interprets the relationship between the geopolitical leanings of Belarusians and their comparative assessments of quality of life as revealed by a December 2005 IISEPS national survey. Unless one factors in the above-mentioned spatiality, the relationship reflected in table 7.5 seems counterintuitive—to the point that one might suspect the two columns of the table had been switched by mistake. Indeed, according to table 7.5, those who believe that life in Russia is better than life in Belarus evince a stronger leaning toward Europe than toward Russia. Conversely, those who believe that life in Belarus is better than life in Russia make a geopolitical choice in favor of Russia, not Europe. Drakokhrust's reading of this relationship is that the traditional attitude of Belarusians to Russia is not by any means mercenary, as the "domestic nationalists" (read those embracing the nativist/pro-European national project discussed in chapter 3) repeatedly allege; rather, it is value laden. For those who think that life in Russia is better, Russia is *to the east of* Belarus, but for the majority (67 percent according to table 7.5) for whom life in Belarus is better, Russia *is the east of* Belarus. You just cannot get rid of your own East; you can only try your best to make it (Russia) as good as Belarus already is.

EARLIER ELECTIONS

The preceding chapters and the foregoing sections of this chapter have cast light on some critical underpinnings of the political process in Belarus. A lingering collectivist mentality, a live memory of Belarus's Soviet roots and achievements, a tortuous quest for separate identity from Russia amid an endless and, at times, acrimonious divorce from it, and little taste for fighting for anything beyond narrowly defined economic goals—this is how the admittedly unfinished list of these underpinnings might look.

As was pointed out in chapter 4, Lukashenka was propelled to power by a premonition of impending chaos and doom when the reins of centralized control over the Belarusian economy were suddenly left hanging in the air, no pro-reform constituency or market-dominated minority was available to seize them, and high-ranking bureaucrats were so accustomed to receiving orders from Moscow that they did not know what to do when those orders stopped coming.

Given that atmosphere, the 1994 presidential elections in Belarus were arguably the most free and fair. At least, nobody has ever challenged this view. Moreover, throughout the first round of elections, Lukashenka did not enjoy support from any powerful clan, much less from the entire political establishment. He ran as the prime antiestablishment candidate, and in the second round, he won in a landslide.

By the end of his first presidential term, Lukashenka had become a bogeyman in the West but had much to boast of to his constituency at home. He had reestablished economic ties with Russia and moved toward reunification with it, he had consolidated his power and defeated the opposition without banning it, and he had presided over five years of resumed economic growth.

According to the official count, in 2001 Lukashenka got 75.65 percent of the electoral vote in his second presidential contest. The opposition cried foul, but its Western sponsors did not have much time even to launch an anti-Lukashenka campaign in the international media. This is because the elections in question occurred on September 9, 2001. Two days later, the world had a truly big event on its hands, which definitely eclipsed the elections in the little-known country of Belarus. Lukashenka's principal contender, a trade union leader named Vladimir Goncharik got 15.65 percent. The opposition had initially put forward five candidates, out of which only one (Siamion Domash) could speak fluent Belarusian. However, to better the electoral chances of Goncharik, deemed the most electable contender, the four other opposition candidates collectively withdrew from the race.

The widespread view of the September 2001 presidential election is that it was falsified, even though about one thousand international observers did not furnish definitive evidence to this effect. The media organs controlled by the Belarusian opposition did not call Lukashenka's popularity into question, yet they still maintained that the electoral results were rigged. The most detailed and matter-of-fact analysis leading to that conclusion was published by the *Belorussky Rynok* weekly. The analysis was based on two polls using different methodologies, conducted by IISEPS in cooperation with *Wirthlin World-*

wide, a Washington-based consulting firm. The first methodology involved a small, stratified, random sample of two to three hundred people and daily polling from July 1 to September 16, 2001. For each polling, a new random sample was put together, and the ensuing trends were analyzed. The second methodology involved one-time postelection polling of 1,465 people at least eighteen years old (the sample error was within 3 percent). Both methodologies led to similar results: Lukashenka was favored by 57 to 58 percent of the electorate, and Goncharik by 28 to 29 percent.[29] The authors of the IISEPS analysis believe that the official election results (75.65 percent for Lukashenka versus 15.65 percent for Goncharik) were doctored out of a desire to avoid a second round of voting, which would have been conducted had no one gained at least 50 percent of the vote in the first round. However, no doubt is expressed with regard to the eventual Lukashenka victory one way or another. The authoritative *Economist* magazine concurred, stating that "Mr. Lukashenka could perhaps have won the election without cheating."[30]

According to the IISEPS analysis, Lukashenka actually received 60 percent of the rural vote; also, 78 percent of retirees and 55 percent of women voted for him. In Minsk, where the opposition candidate by all accounts had enjoyed the friendliest electorate, 36.3 percent voted for Lukashenka and 34 percent for Goncharik. The dominant groups in the pro-Goncharik constituency were eighteen- to twenty-year-olds (39.3 percent of which voted for Goncharik versus 23.4 percent for Lukashenka), students (35.4 percent versus 21.1 percent), and small businessmen (37.5 percent versus 16.7 percent). Among those who favored Lukashenka, 71 percent believed that their families' economic situations either had not changed or had improved during his first term, whereas 61 percent of those in favor of Goncharik said their situations had worsened.[31] According to the IISEPS analysts, "The explanation is simple: $50 per family member is being earned through hard work by Goncharik voters, who compare their situation with that of their European neighbors, whereas the overwhelming majority of Lukashenka voters receive their $40 from the state in the form of pensions and various allowances."[32]

SOUL-SEARCHING AFTER THE 2001 ELECTION

Another insightful piece of postelection analysis, titled "Learning from Mistakes," showed up in the *Belorusskaya Delovaya Gazeta*. Published by the daily whose stand vis-à-vis Lukashenka could not possibly be more negative, this material is inward looking: it is about learning from *one's own* mistakes. The authors' interpretation of the distribution of the electoral preferences is, most certainly, arbitrary. It is based on the results of unnamed sociological surveys conducted in the winter of 2000, well in advance of the elections. According to those surveys, Lukashenka had the guaranteed support of only 30 to 35 percent, whereas the potential opposition candidate (not yet named at the time) could count on 15 percent (which is what Goncharik ultimately got in September 2001). The share of those completely or partially dissatisfied with the ruling regime was reportedly about 40 percent, and the rest were undecided. According to the authors, for the opposition candidate to win, he would have to muster a majority comprising those loyal 15 percent plus those dissatisfied 40 percent and at least part of the undecided—altogether a minimum 60 percent of the vote.[33] Inconsistent preelection statistics notwithstanding,[34] the narrative is particularly revealing when it comes to the perceived causes of the opposition's defeat in the 2001 presidential elections. Not a word is mentioned about tampering with ballot boxes—the first battle cry of the opposition immediately after its defeat. Instead, it offers a list of the opposition's perceived weaknesses.

- In the eyes of Belarusian society, the opposition looks too belligerent and is simply feared; boycott and blanket rejection are its major tools.
- The opposition propagates a black-white vision of society; this sort of vision is proclaimed valiant and democratic.
- Instead of acting on behalf of the electoral majority, the opposition creates the impression that it acts on behalf of a special caste of the initiated and is in no way connected with the majority of the people on the grounds that this majority comprises the "nationally indifferent" [literally, *nieswiadomyya*, which is the opposite to *swiadomyya*, a code word designating all those in favor of promoting Belarusian language and Belarusian ethnic and national identity in opposition to those of the Russians].
- The potentially undecided voters perceive Belarusian politics through the prism of Russian TV channels and pay special respect to the Russian president; these voters are intensely irritated by the rhetoric of the return to Belarusian national symbols [like the white-red-white flag and emblem "inherited" from the Grand Duchy of Lithuania], the Belarusian language, and NATO expansion.[35]

The analysis of the election results, however, would be incomplete without focusing on the fate of Vladimir Goncharik, Lukashenka's electoral rival. After all, even the official 15.65 percent vote was no small achievement on Goncharik's part. This result might have made him the potential leader of the united opposition, a leader that Europe and Russia could treat seriously and even cultivate as Lukashenka's potential replacement come the next elections. At least in Russia, this was not out of the question at all, as asserted by Gleb Pavlovsky, a political commentator and operator with close ties to the Kremlin.[36] Instead, however, Goncharik fell into oblivion. For some time, he was rumored to have gone to Moscow and worked in construction industry, and then every trace of him was lost. In February 2007, an interview with Goncharik suddenly appeared on one of the opposition websites. In it, Goncharik ruefully admitted that "throughout the last five years nobody from the opposition [had] even called to ask how [he] was doing."[37] Why was Goncharik sidelined by the leaders of the opposition parties? The answer to this question is disturbingly simple. Goncharik was not a member of any party. Soon after the elections, the party leaders switched to their habitual mode: jockeying for visibility and the attention of Western sponsors. Goncharik was seen as an extra rival in that fascinating and self-absorbing game, so without much ado, he was trashed.

THE 2004 REFERENDUM AND 2006 PRESIDENTIAL RACE

In May 2004, the date of the constitutional referendum was set for October 17 of that year, the same day as the parliamentary elections. The referendum queried Belarusians about whether they would allow Lukashenka to participate in the upcoming presidential race and accept a new version of Article 81 of the Belarus constitution disposing of the presidential maximum of two consecutive five-year terms. More than 50 percent of the vote was required to adopt the constitutional amendment. In any event, official statistics indicated that 79.4 percent of the registered voters approved the measure as opposed to the 48.4 percent approval rating indicated by exit polls administered by the Lithuanian arm of the Gallup Institution.[38] To be sure, at the time of the referendum, not a single opposition figure enjoyed the support of more than 1.5 percent of the electorate.[39]

Contrary to rumors and expectations that the congress of the united opposition would have to be held outside Belarus, as no premises spacious enough to host eight hundred people would be provided by Belarusian authorities, the meeting actually took place in Minsk in the Palace of Culture of the Truck Factory. On October 2, 2005, Alexander Milinkevich was elected the united opposition candidate. The congress was attended by the members of five parties, including the Belarusian Popular Front, the United Civic Party, and a splinter Communist Party. Milinkevich, who has a doctorate in physics, served as vice mayor of Grodno responsible for culture and education from 1990 to 1996. During his tenure, many Belarusian-language schools were opened in the city. In 2001, Milinkevich headed the staff of Siamion Domash, the only opposition-minded presidential hopeful (out of five) who spoke fluent Belarusian.

The date of the presidential elections was determined in early December 2005 following a parliamentary vote held on short notice. This date (March 19, 2006) took the Belarusian opposition by surprise, as it was set almost six months prior to the expiration of Lukashenka's second term in office. This provided limited time for the opposition to campaign on behalf of its candidate. Nonetheless, Milinkevich traveled to all oblast capitals and many larger *rayon* centers of Belarus, and by mid- to late December 2005, his name recognition had increased significantly. According to a December 2005 IISEPS poll, given a choice between Lukashenka and Milinkevich, 55 percent of Belarusians would have voted for Lukashenka and 18 percent for Milinkevich. According to the Baltic arm of the Gallup Institute, the ratio was 53 to 21 percent, the highest rating Milinkevich obtained in any poll. When Gallup posed the open question "Who will you vote in as president" with respondents inserting the candidates' names, 53.1 percent named Lukashenka, and only 10 percent Milinkevich.[40] By all accounts, however, Milinkevich was more successful in his public relations campaign outside Belarus, which was undertaken to enlist support and demonstrate the acceptance of Belarusian opposition in Western capitals where Lukashenka and members of his team are non grata. Many European dignitaries met with Milinkevich before the elections, including the chairman of the European Commission, president of the European Parliament, secretary general of the Council of the EU, the chancellor of Germany, the presidents of Poland and Lithuania, and the French minister of foreign affairs. Milinkevich spoke at the meeting of the Parliamentary Assembly of Europe and in the Polish Seim (Parliament). However, attempts to organize a high-level reception of the united opposition candidate in Moscow failed despite Milinkevich's repeated claims that in Belarus, an anti-Russian politician has no chance, which was why he was not such a politician.

Cerebral, soft-spoken, and versed in Belarusian, Russian, Polish, French, and English, Milinkevich was a sharp contrast to Lukashenka, a firebrand with a peasant background and folksy demeanor. By his own admission, Milinkevich was "a Belarusian whereas Lukashenka is a Soviet man."[41] Indeed, whereas Lukashenka speaks *trasianka*, a dialect that is lexically Russian and phonetically Belarusian, Milinkevich speaks good Russian and Belarusian and does not mix them. One of Milinkevich's two fifteen-minute TV speeches that I got a chance to watch (courtesy of the website http://by .milinkevich.org) exposed a lamentable lack of charisma, in which, by all accounts, Lukashenka excels. Milinkevich looked strained and rarely raised his eyes from the text. Most of his speech was in Russian, but when he read excerpts from several letters that people had written to him in Belarusian, he responded in kind. Addressing the question of why Milinkevich spoke Russian on TV, his press secretary Pavel Mazheika, noted, "A multitude of our supporters from the regions begged us tearfully that the major part of the speech be in Russian. This was to prevent the state propaganda from affixing the tag of fascist and nationalist [read "xenophobe"] on Milinkevich."[42] Intriguing about this remark is not so much the assertion that the state propaganda would label someone in this way but the well-grounded suspicion that doing so would strike a chord with many Belarusians.

Although Milinkevich was not a member of any party, the official media and Lukashenka personally portrayed him as a *beneefovets*, a member of the Belarusian Popular Front, to which so many Belarusians are allergic. Indeed, prior to the October 2005 congress of the united opposition, Milinkevich noted, in his interview to the *Nasha Niva*, that he was in favor of giving official status only to the Belarusian language in the Republic of Belarus.[43] In many interviews, Milinkevich observed that one of his major accomplishments had been the discovery of the gravesite of the last king of Rzeczpospolita (in Grodno Oblast). During a tiff about the language of the Deutsche Welle newscasts (see chapter 3), Milinkevich signed a petition urging the use of Belarusian, not Russian. In Belarus, all of the above unequivocally assigns a person to a certain ideological camp, one that I earlier called national Project One (see chapter 3). Five months after the elections, the deputy chairman of the BNF, Yury Khodyko, stated point-blank that "Milinkevich had been a creature [*vydvizhenets*] of the BNF."[44] The official propaganda also made much of the fact that Milinkevich had adopted his mother's maiden name because his father's name was Baran, meaning "male sheep." The country's leading official daily, *Belarus Segodnia*, did not, to my knowledge, publish overtly negative or libelous materials demeaning Milinkevich. The tone set in a few articles, wherein Milinkevich was mentioned at all, was rather condescending: "Milinkevich is an ordinary middle-aged man, probably a decent family man and nice to talk to. What I cannot fathom, though, is what nudges those pleasant people to take part in a presidential election. After all, presidency in Belarus is not a safe haven like a department at the University of Grodno. . . . One has to at least know what the difference is between a tractor and a silage cutter and have a clear understanding that potato pancakes do not grow on trees."[45] Yet another refrain of the state propaganda message on Milinkevich was that he was a wimp whom his second wife, Inna Kulei, kept under her thumb.

Perhaps the most intriguing theme in preelection portrayals of Milinkevich was that he was a Catholic and had overly close relations to the Poles. This ran contrary to Milinkevich's own assertions that he is from an Orthodox family, and some of his ancestors fought for the Belarusian national cause. The issue of putative belonging to a neighboring ethnicity is a delicate one.

Unlike Janka Kupala in his early 1920s play, I would fail to articulate how a typical Pole looks these days. And yet the idea of the allegedly Polish appearance of Milinkevich did not strike me as entirely bizarre. Apparently, I was not the only one with whom the idea resonated. "The only thing that worries me," said Svetlana Alexievich,[46] "and I trust that this would worry a significant part of our society, is that Milinkevich is of a Polish type, and with this some historic injustices and complexities are associated that stand between us and the Polish society and Catholicism. I am afraid that this will harm [Milinkevich] to some extent."[47] Reinforcing the same image of Polishness, Pavel Starodub (possibly a pseudonym of Pavel Yakubovich, editor in chief of *Belarus Segodnia*) mentions in an article that seasoned sports fans may still remember "Jerzy Kulej, a famous Polish boxer nicknamed Bull. He was possessed by eagerness to strike first and beat his rival into unconsciousness. I don't know whether Inna Kulei [Milinkevich's wife] is his relative or just a namesake, but hers is a similar character."[48]

During the run-up to the elections, Lukashenka opined that because the opposition was bedeviled by a perennial fight for outside money (Western grants), as many as ten "single" candidates might eventually emerge. Although that prediction proved wrong, one person did in fact break the united opposition front to register as a candidate—Alexander Kozulin, former rector of Belarusian State University and former minister of education. Kozulin had been fired as rector amid accusations of corruption, which, however, were not upheld in court. Announcing his candidacy, Kozulin claimed that whereas Milinkevich was a pro-American and pro-Western candidate, he (Kozulin) was for a balanced foreign policy, maintaining good relations with both Russia and the West. Kozulin apparently assumed that Milinkevich's base of support in Russia was slim and that the Russian political elite, who were wary of Lukashenka's brinkmanship, might decide to focus their support on someone who would maintain ties with Russia but prove to be a more reliable and predictable partner. Further, it was clear to Kozulin that while many Belarusians disapproved of Lukashenka's policies, very few supported the pet ideas of the Belarusian Popular Front (such as eliminating Russian as an official language of Belarus), with which Milinkevich was associated. By his own admission, Kozulin did not even speak Belarusian, but in order to broaden his base as a potential national leader, he hired a language tutor. Finally, Kozulin might have thought that he could outperform Lukashenka by resorting to Lukashenka-like rhetorical skills.

Watching one of Kozulin's two fifteen-minute speeches broadcasted by Belarusian State TV, I noticed that Kozulin had learned a lot from his former boss. Though a former professor, Kozulin looked and sounded much less professorial than Milinkevich. Kozulin's was the rough talk of an authoritarian Soviet-style bureaucrat, the so-called *khoziaistvennik* with a military background. But while every bit as forceful as Lukashenka's, Kozulin's speech was not nearly as folksy and revealed no tinge of Belarusian phonetics. Kozulin came across as an angry man eager to avenge his humiliation and return to power. His two megamistakes were publicly disclosing some widely rumored facts of Lukashenka's personal life (assuring all those still in doubt that his quest for the presidency was a personal vendetta) and accusing his former boss of ruling the country in the manner of a *kolkhoznik* (a collective farmer).

While no reliable preelection forecast predicted a decent showing, much less a victory for either of the opposition candidates, the fact that Milinkevich and Kozulin effectively split the protest vote made Lukashenka's victory all the more inevitable.

POPULARITY ESTIMATES OF PRESIDENTIAL CANDIDATES

Regular national IISEPS surveys allow one to follow the dynamics of Lukashenka's popularity rating (table 7.6). Peaks are evident in 2001 (the year of the second presidential election) and in 2005 (on the eve of the third election). A comparison of the above peak ratings with the annual dynamics of salaries and pensions reveals that the steepest raises coincided with presidential elections. Average wages shot up by 18 percent and 16 percent in 2001 and 2005, respectively; average pensions exhibited similar peaks of 26 percent and 22 percent. Nonelection year changes in wages and pensions typically

Table 7.6. Time Series of Responses to the Question "If Presidential Elections Were Tomorrow, Whom Would You Vote For?" (in Percentage of All Responses)

	Oct. 2001 (%)	Apr. 2002 (%)	Sept. 2002 (%)	Dec. 2002 (%)	Mar. 2003 (%)	Sept. 2003 (%)	June 2004 (%)	Nov. 2004 (%)	Mar. 2005 (%)	May 2005 (%)	Sept. 2005 (%)
Lukashena	46.0	30.9	27.0	30.5	26.2	31.7	34.2	47.7	46.4	41.7	47.3
Other candidate*	11.8	8.3	6.5	5.0	2.6	4.0	3.0	1.5	1.4	2.0	3.5
Stumped for an answer	24.1	15.7	25.5	18.7	31.9	25.0	23.1	16.5	17.6	22.3	18.1
No response	11.7	16.8	16.2	17.0	14.0	11.2	16.5	18.5	15.0	12.2	10.5

Note: *Refers to the alternative candidate with the highest rating among the candidates named by the respondents.
Source: Pavliuk Bykovsky, "Reiting Lukashenko i yego konkurentov," *Belarusian Elections,* at http://ru .belaruselections.info/current/2006/sociology/0022756. National surveys of IISEPS; N = 1,500 randomly sampled respondents; sample error is within 3 percent.

exhibited low, but positive, growth rates (single digits) or negative rates.[49] Indeed, most Belarusians assert that quality of life is improving.

"Buying" the people's vote, however, is only part of the story. First, the positive dynamics of salaries and pensions would not have been possible but for the uninterrupted economic growth of Belarus since 1996. Second, although Belarusians did indicate that they value economy over independence, they have definitely warmed up to the latter as well. In December 2005, only 12 percent of surveyed Belarusians opted for Belarus and Russia becoming one state, whereas just two years prior to that, twice as many did.[50]

Third, to an ever-increasing extent, Belarusians associate their separate-from-Russia existence with Lukashenka. Even experts who are the least sympathetic to the president of Belarus come to that conclusion. "My friends in Belorussia hate it when I tell them that Lukashenka has become the true father of Belorussian independence . . . as during the years of his rule, the national identity which simply had not existed developed amongst both the rank and file and the elite,"[51] says one of the most avowedly pro-Western Russian analysts and a frequent guest of American think tanks.

Not long ago, however, even Belarusians with warm feelings toward Lukashenka used to like Putin better. To the question "If the position of president of Belarus-and-Russia were instituted, whom would you rather vote for in the corresponding election?" most people used to respond "for Putin." This began to change (table 7.7) after the memorable February 19, 2004, suspension of the inflow of Russia's natural gas to Belarus. This change should be attributed to the propaganda campaign directed squarely against the political establishment of Russia and to the replacement of newscasts broadcasted from Moscow via major Russian TV channels by newscasts produced in Minsk.

In summary, to anyone versed in developments in Belarus (not just what the Western media had said about Belarus), the prospects of a Lukashenka landslide in the 2006 presidential elections appeared certain. Indeed, a national survey conducted in early March 2006 by VTSIOM, a Russian polling

Table 7.7. Time Series of Responses to the Question "If the Position of President of Belarus and Russia Were Instituted, Whom Would You Rather Vote for in the Corresponding Election?" (in Percentage of All Responses)

	Nov. 1999 (%)	Apr. 2000 (%)	Apr. 2001 (%)	Apr. 2002 (%)	Dec. 2002 (%)	Sept. 2003 (%)	Mar. 2004 (%)	Nov. 2004 (%)	Sept. 2005 (%)	Dec. 2005 (%)
Lukashenka	31.0	22.3	24.4	14.0	20.5	21.1	28.7	29.8	33.2	38.8
Putin	13.2	31.1	40.3	50.5	46.9	45.2	35.9	24.3	25.7	19.8

Source: Yury Drakokhrust, "Gde konchayetsia Belorussiya?" *Neprikosnovennyi Zapas* 47 (2006); based on the national surveys by IISEPS.

Table 7.8.   The Official Count versus IISEPS Polls in the 2006 Presidential Elections in Belarus

	Official Count on Mar. 19, 2006 (%)	IISEPS Poll Feb. 10 to 20, 2006 (%)	IISEPS Poll Mar. 27 to Apr. 6, 2006 (%)	IISEPS Poll Apr. 16 to 29, 2006 (%)
Lukashenka	83.0	64.7	64.9	63.1
Milinkevich	6.1	18.3	21.4	18.8
Kozulin	2.2	7.0	5.0	7.3
Gaidukevich*	3.5	5.0	2.2	5.2

Note: *Gaidukevich is a comical political figure representing what was initially the Belarusian arm of Russia's Liberal Democrats. The latter, as many allege, are also led by a comical figure (Vladimir Zhirinovsky) but one of much higher visibility and caliber than his Belarusian clone.
Sources: www.iiseps.org/4-06-7.html; "Okonchatel'nye itogi prezidentskikh vyborov," *Belorusskie Novosti,* March 23, 2006, at www.naviny.by.

firm, showed that 60 percent of Belarusians were willing to vote for Lukashenka, 11 percent for Milinkevich, and 5 percent for Kozulin.[52] Olga Abramova, the only Belarusian member of Parliament (MP) who allows herself to publicly criticize some of Lukashenka's policies, said eleven days prior to the elections that, in her judgment, the range of the president's support had remained steadily within 60 to 63 percent, whereas 25 to 30 percent of the electorate disagreed with Lukashenka (and that latter range also included those voting against all candidates). If the turnout were to reach 80 percent, Abramova predicted, then Lukashenka would probably win 75 percent of the vote owing to the fact that his electorate was more committed and disciplined than that of his opponents.[53]

In hindsight, the most impressive forecast was issued by Alexander Potupa, chairman of Belarus's Union of Entrepreneurs. In his interview with the Latvian Russian-language newspaper *Telegraf* on September 14, 2005 (a fairly early date!), Potupa indicated that "in 2006, Lukashenka's victory is as assured as it was in 2001. He will win no less than 80 percent of the vote. But one has to understand that he would win 2:1 (or about two-thirds of the vote) even without sneaky fiddling technologies. . . . There is no indication at all that the actual split of the electorate goes beyond 1:6 or even 1:7."[54] As will become clear from what follows, Potupa's forecast proved impeccable not only in terms of the official count (table 7.8) but also, most probably, in terms of the degree of distortion of the actually cast vote.

AFTERMATH OF THE ELECTION

In the evening of March 19, several thousand opposition-minded youths gathered on Oktyabrskaya (*Kastrychninskaya* in Belarusian) Square in downtown

Minsk. They were convinced that the election results were rigged; they just did not know to what extent. At one point, Milinkevich, for whose arrival in the square the protesters had waited for two hours, announced that he had won about 30 percent of the vote. A commotion ensued, as neither Milinkevich nor Kozulin, who had joined the protesters earlier, seemed to know how (or whether) to continue the rally. The two opposition leaders could not reach any consensus: whereas Milinkevich called upon the youths to go home and return the next evening, Kozulin first seconded that appeal, then reportedly was motivated by the steadfastness of the protesters to change his mind. Because the orange revolution in Ukraine was on everybody's mind, some volunteers set up tents, and a miniature and less-spirited replica of the December 2004 events in Kiev followed, with thirty-five tents being forcibly removed by police in the early morning hours of March 24. Throughout the entire ordeal, the protesters who spent nights in tents referred to Oktyabrskaya Square as Kalinowski Square, after Kastus Kalinowski, one of the leaders of the 1863 Polish uprising (Polish and Belarusian, according to an alternative interpretation) against Russia. On March 23, 2006, *Belarus Segodnia* reported that the events on Oktyabrskaya Square were directed over cell phone by Pawel Kazaniecki, president of the Polish branch of the Washington-based Institute for Democracy in Eastern Europe. Lengthy excerpts from his allegedly intercepted conversations (from his base in Warsaw) with Victor Korneyenko, vice chair of Milinkevich's staff, were broadcasted by the Belarusian state TV and published by the *Belarus Segodnia*.[55]

Besides the removal of the tents, the denouement of the postelection rallies in Minsk included the arrest of Kozulin, who on March 25, 2006, led a group of protesters to the jail in which the youths captured the day before by police on Oktyabrskaya Square were being kept. Even before the elections, Kozulin, a former marine, had a fistfight with police when he tried (on March 2, 2006) to enter the Palace of the Republic in which the meeting of the Third All-Belarusian People's Convention was taking place. Kozulin attempted to enter the meeting and make a speech, but security guards prevented him. I have a feeling that, having failed to muster support both at home and abroad, Kozulin staked his political future on a spectacular act of personal bravery so that he could later capitalize on it and be set apart from the indecisive Milinkevich. Kozulin may have miscalculated. On June 13, 2006, he was sentenced to five and a half years in prison for disrupting public order and clashing with police. A national survey held in September 2006 showed that 44 percent of Belarusians did not even know Kozulin was in prison.[56]

Throughout the elections and in the aftermath, one of the best sources of information and dialogue about the events in Minsk was the BS RL. While in hindsight some of the opinions reported by BS RL seem overly emotional and more than tinged by wishful thinking, many have withstood the test of time. For example, on March 21, 2006, in response to a question about differences and parallels between the Belarusian 2006 and Ukrainian 2004–2005 elections, Jan Maksymiuk, a Prague-based political analyst and ethnic Belarusian, had this to say: "The situation [in Belarus] is psychologically different because in 2004 people in Kiev were convinced: Yushchenko won the elections, but the victory was stolen from him. The situation of Milinkevich is different. Naturally, the results were falsified, and nobody doubts this. But at the same time, people have a feeling that Milinkevich would not have been able to win these elections even if they were honest and free."[57]

Aleg Grudzilovich, a BS RL correspondent, related a conversation with a sergeant in charge of a military unit dispatched to Oktyabrskaya Square to separate the protesters from passersby. "If you managed to gather a fifty-to-one-hundred-thousand-strong crowd, then we would switch to your side, whereas now we are with the people but not with you because there are so few of you,"[58] the sergeant reportedly said.

Victar Ivashkevich, deputy chairman of the Belarusian Popular Front, noted that "[the official figure of] 83 percent infuriated everybody. People would have agreed if they had been told that Lukashenka won 55 to 60 percent, but 83 percent revealed that those in power do not take people seriously and just lie."[59] What is indeed revealing in this statement is the de facto admission that Lukashenka would have won the elections even without falsification.[60]

Olga Abramova, the already-mentioned MP, observed that Lukashenka again outperformed both the opposition and the West. To all people able to think rationally, his victory was beyond doubt. "Several days before the elections," Abramova said on a BS RL talk show, "I predicted that the united opposition would be able to bring from five to ten thousand people to the square. This is exactly what happened despite what your radio said."[61] But the biggest disgrace of the opposition, according to Abramova, was not even its inability to mobilize people; it was that the opposition was ill prepared for peaceful protests. They did not procure biotoilets and did not designate those responsible for removal of waste. "Two years ago," noted Abramova, "I asked the leaders of the opposition what they would do two years from now when Belarusians would have gotten used to the idea that their leader is irreplaceable. And now I have two more questions. Incidentally, the same questions were posed to Secretary Rice by the congressmen from the Democratic Party after the electoral victory by Hamas in Palestine. *Why is such an unfounded significance attached to the very act of elections? And why is it then that if the election is unequivocally won by whoever is not ideologically close to you that you reject the idea of a dialogue with the winner?*" (emphasis added).[62]

During a roundtable debate on the BS RL, Ivashkevich tried to shrug off Abramova's criticism on the grounds that she "consciously serves Lukashenka." In response, Abramova complained that she routinely receives symmetrical accusations from her fellow MPs whenever she demands liberalization of the economy or defends some opposition activists. It becomes clear from that exchange that someone with lines of communication open to both the Lukashenka team and the opposition does not have a chance to build a bridge between them, and it is far from certain that only the government side ought to be blamed for that. According to Abramova, to initiate a dialogue about the national consensus, the opposition ought to (1) recognize the election results, (2) send an unequivocal message to Western sponsors that economic sanctions on Belarus should not be pursued, and (3) select representatives for talks with the government. Abramova also thinks that indiscriminately using words like "dictatorship" and "fascism" works against the opposition.

Because the extent of election fraud remained unclear and open to speculation, it would make sense to resort to the results of three national IISEPS polls conducted before and after the elections (Table 7.8). The results of the first postelection poll (March 27 to April 6, 2006), first made public on April 20 at a meeting in the British Embassy in Minsk, were not to the liking of either the government or the opposition. The results, obtained through face-to-face interviews of 1,496 randomly selected Belarusian adults, showed that 64.9 percent of those polled voted for Lukashenka, 21.4 percent voted for Milinkevich, and 5.0 percent voted for Kozulin (table 7.8). Because these results were called into question by many in the opposition, another national poll was conducted from April 16–29, 2006. For this second postelection survey, a different random sample of the same size was probed by a different group of face-to-face interviewers. The second postelection poll yielded results similar to the first. They also agree with the above-mentioned preelection polling by IISEPS (table 7.8) and the Russian firm VTSIOM, as well as with various other preelection forecasts. Yet, some opposition-minded analysts continued to doubt the validity of those surveys, arguing that in a country run by a dictator, no survey is reliable as people are afraid to betray their views.[63]

HOW RELIABLE ARE PUBLIC OPINION POLLS?

Because the poll-faulting argument is advanced from time to time, it makes sense to analyze its logic and function in light of known facts about Belarus, as well as about the national surveys conducted there.

The logic of the argument rests on the presumption that because "we all know" that Belarus is a dictatorship, by implication ordinary people should be afraid to openly express their opinions. Here, the emphasis is on "we all know." Like any preconceived notion, this one is hard to dispute. As was mentioned earlier in this book, most well-informed Belarus watchers not sympathetic or beholden to Lukashenka effectively call the dictatorial nature of the Belarusian regime into question, but even this fact does not come across as a strong counterargument. After all, "we all know."

Functionally, the argument in question purports to trivialize or downright eliminate a rich source of data about contemporary Belarus by declaring these data unfit. In my view, the thesis in question is advanced either by (1) those whose knowledge of Belarus comes from media, not personal exposure, or (2) those who may know Belarus well enough but refuse to acknowledge any mass opinions recorded by national surveys in Belarus that contradict their own views. For example, if "building a democracy" is possible through some kind of social engineering (e.g., as was supposed to be done in Iraq), then any inquiry into public opinion, particularly one showing that people are beset by "wrong" ideas, is not welcome.

In the end, the poll-faulting argument does not withstand scrutiny. Although Lukashenka's popularity ratings are high, they are not sky-high: from 30 percent to 40 percent of respondents probed in various surveys do not support him, and about 20 percent reveal that they voted for Milinkevich and Kozulin. Such people are too numerous to be labeled a bunch of heroes who managed to overcome paralyzing fear. With this many heroes, one may suggest that Belarus could have already become a country very different from what it is today. This, however, has not happened, which may only mean that not much heroism is required to acknowledge (in a face-to-face interview) that one actually dislikes Lukashenka.

In Belarus, the sociologist Andrei Vardomatskiy studied the influence of fear on responses to face-to-face interviews. Based on his 1999 research, he claimed that fearful respondents tend to refrain from definitive answers and therefore become a statistic in the "don't know" category. However, a person who does not support the president would rarely claim to support him out of fear.[64] In 2001, the same expert claimed that fear could artificially boost numbers of support for Lukashenka by 6 to 9 percent.[65] But in 2006, in his interview by Russia's *Kommersant*, Vardomatskiy related that because now Belarusians are content with the material quality of life, they are more willing than ever to overcome their fear, which is therefore not likely to affect election results.[66]

Perhaps the most important argument in favor of the IISEPS and other independent national surveys in Belarus is that the attitude toward Lukashenka revealed by those surveys correlates with other opinions not rigidly connected with political loyalty. Thus, Lukashenka supporters dislike entrepreneurs and the West, prefer state-owned enterprises, and value low, but steady, earnings over high, but unsteady, earnings. If the basic reason behind their ostensible support of Lukashenka were fear, then in response to all the other questions that are definitely not frightening, the "fake" Lukashenka fans would likely be expressing their true opinions: pro-European, liberal, and pro-market. The fact that Lukashenka supporters do not identify with those opinions means that they vote for Lukashenka because he actually personifies their values, such as attachment to economic security, dependency on the state, risk aversion, and distrust of private business.

The theory that people under authoritarian regimes hide their opinions also contradicts the experience of orange revolutions. Thus, in Ukraine, mass dissatisfaction with the institutions of power had been recorded by sociological surveys (including Gallup polls) well before the 2004 elections. According to a national survey conducted in Serbia in September 2000, Vojislav Koštunica enjoyed the support of 24 percent of adults as compared with the 18 percent that supported Slobodan Milošević.[67] In both cases, sociologists accurately predicted change at the helm of power. Although dissatisfaction with the government in Belarus is widespread, the number gap between the Lukashenka supporters and the supporters of, say, Milinkevich is simply too large. Consequently, it does not make sense to fault the surveys just because their results are not to one's liking.

A SOCIOLOGICAL PROFILE OF THE VOTERS

Surveys show that Lukashenka was favored more by women than men (the corresponding ratio of supporters being 63.8 to 51.5 percent[68]), whereas among the supporters of Milinkevich, men outnumbered women 21.1 to 17.7 percent.[69] Across the age groups, Lukashenka enjoyed minimal support among those from twenty to twenty-nine years of age and maximal support among the elderly. It is significant, however, that whereas those between the ages of twenty and twenty-nine voted in larger numbers for Milinkevich and Kozulin (combined) than for Lukashenka, the eighteen- and nineteen-year-olds threw their support behind the current president. Among these youngest voters, Lukashenka supporters were 2.5 times more numerous than supporters of both opposition candidates. This is in line with the observations of Vladimir Matskevich. A fierce critic of Lukashenka, Matskevich observes that "Belarusian youths now beginning to support the regime are proud that respect and [favorable] attitude were not just bestowed upon Belarus (as Bill Clinton did upon Stanislau Shushkevich) but have been earned or won in a fight. This is what makes this regime genuinely Belarusian in many people's eyes: the kind of leadership that nationalists dreamed about during their heyday in the early 1990s."[70]

As for the five social groups of Belarusians—private-sector employees, public-sector employees, students, retirees, and housewives and the unemployed —Lukashenka's edge is not only among the employees of the private sector; in fact, his advantage is at its highest among the retirees.

Across the regions, Lukashenka's edge is at its highest in Gomel, Mogilev, and Minsk oblasts and at its lowest in the city of Minsk and in Grodno Oblast. Note that among all the above-mentioned oblasts, only that of Minsk does not include the oblast capital, which in this case is the national capital as well. Also note that the same spatial pattern of Lukashenka support was characteristic for the elections of 2001. Lukashenka's voting percentages stand in inverse proportion to the settlement size, from the least support (41.6 percent) in the national capital to the most (72.4 percent) in rural villages.[71]

Because Russian is the language of the majority in Belarus, Russian speakers predictably prevail among those who cast votes for each candidate. However, there is a higher percentage of self-described Belarusian-language speakers among those who voted for Lukashenka (3.7 percent) than among those who voted for Kozulin (1.3 percent) or Milinkevich (3.2 percent). Lukashenka also holds a numerical advantage among those speaking Russian and Belarusian intermittently and a particularly strong advantage among *trasianka* speakers. Because *trasianka* is relatively more widespread among small-town and village dwellers and among people of older age, these results are not unexpected. That said, it is important to underscore that Belarusian speakers did not turn out in larger numbers for the opposition, a situation strikingly at odds with the image of the opposition as promoters of linguistic Belarusification of Belarus.

Finally, when asked to reveal their attitude toward the joint stand by the United States, EU, and Council of Europe, according to which the 2006 presidential elections in Belarus did not match the Organization for Security and Cooperation in Europe standards of fairness, 58 percent of those probed considered the above stance unfair, whereas 27.5 percent deemed it fair, and 14.2 percent were stumped for an answer.[72]

POSTELECTION BLUES

When it became clear how few Belarusians support the opposition and how many genuinely believe that life is improving under the current regime, the opposition plunged into a postelection depression. "A feeling of hopelessness begins to sink into the most tenaciously optimistic mind-set,"[73] observes Vital Silitski. Silitski, together with Andrei Dynko, Valer Bulgakau, and Igar Babkou, is part of the new wave of Belarusian-speaking nativist ideologues[74] who have replaced the old guard led by Zianon Pazniak. No less dedicated to battle against Russia's cultural colonialism, they are more tolerant, intellectual, scholarly, and versed in foreign languages. Apparently, they are also able to accept defeat without resorting to wild-eyed exaggerations and conspiracy theories (Pazniak's signature reactions). "The events on Kalinowski Square," writes Silitski, "reflected the mobilization potential of an illusion" as no action of the opposition could bring about political change in Belarus at this point. "The society objectively recognized the Lukashenka victory in 2006."[75] Whereas Valyantsyn Akudovich once talked about the "archipelago Belarus," a notion reflecting the multiple locations of the Belarusian-speaking promoters of the national idea, Silitski claims that, by now, this structure has been permeated by horizontal ties and has thus been "localized" by the regime. So, now it looks more like a ghetto.

Already some opposition-minded analysts are debating whether "ghetto" is an apt metaphor.[76] In any case, a consensus is emerging across this debate that the regime has consolidated and broadened its social base, whereas the current opposition does not stand a chance.[77] In an interview with the BS RL, Yury Drakakhrust, a talk show host, asked Silitski how is it that, according to Silitski's article in the *Arche*, no effort by the opposition would have led to a different electoral result, the regime has achieved equilibrium with society, the democratic community has become a ghetto, the society has recognized Lukashenka's victory, and there is no crisis of power in Belarus; yet, from all of these, a conclusion is drawn that one has to keep on doing what was being done before? Don't you see, insisted the talk show host, that your analysis actually shores up the viewpoint taken by Abramova, who calls upon the opposition to cut back on acrimony and try to reach some degree of mutual understanding with the Lukashenka team? No, replied Silitski. "I am in fundamental disagreement with you on that issue."[78]

I would remain forever mystified by the "fundamental" nature of Silitski's disagreement with his interviewer had I not read an English-language article by the same author released just months prior to the above-quoted Belarusian-language publication. As a Reagan-Fascell Fellow of the National Endowment for Democracy, Silitski wrote a piece about Lukashenka's tactics of preempting democracy, including the removal "from the political arena even those opposition leaders that are still weak"[79] and a "combination of pressure, slander and sophisticated propaganda"[80] used to accomplish this goal. In this English-language piece, the Belarusian people, if present at all, are victims of the regime, not by any means its social base, much less willing collaborators. The political correctness of this picture fits the official American pronouncements on Belarus, but I am afraid it does a disservice to whoever in the West is willing to grasp Belarusian realities as they are, without slotting them into a Western ideological template.

In the meantime, as shown above, Lukashenka's support is growing among Belarusian youths, a demographic with which the regime has not been particularly successful in the past. A well-known Belarusian journalist has already called the growing ranks of Lukashenka's young admirers "Generation L."[81]

QUO VADIS MILINKEVICH? QUO VADIS KOZULIN?

At this writing, Alexander Kozulin is still in jail. In late October 2006, Kozulin undertook a fifty-three-day hunger strike. It was terminated on December 11, 2006, after the American United Nations envoy raised the issue of political prisoners in Belarus at the Security Council's closed-door meeting only to be rebuffed by the Russian envoy, who said that this issue had not been on the agenda and would never have made it to the agenda of the Security Council's meeting. Ironically, most of Kozulin's international ties are with Moscow, not the West, which is what made Kozulin a more dangerous rival than Milinkevich in Lukashenka's eyes.

Up until the Russia-Belarus trade war of the winter of 2006–2007, it seemed that Kozulin was destined to spend his entire five-and-a-half-year jail term behind bars. Following that war, Western leaders began to seek direct contacts with Lukashenka, who is still officially non grata anywhere in the West. If this creeping change of heart on the part of Western leaders is to continue, it will require some face-saving gestures. Setting preliminary conditions for Lukashenka in exchange for unlimited contact with Europe may be one such gesture. The release of political prisoners is among such conditions, and Rene Van der Linden informed the leaders of the two chambers of the Belarusian parliament of this during his surprise January 2007 trip to Minsk. Shortly thereafter, on February 12, 2007, the chairman of the Supreme Court of the Republic of Belarus, Valentin Sukalo, released a statement indicating that should Kozulin apply for requalification and shortening of his prison term, the request would be considered.[82] It remains to be seen if anything happens to Kozulin as a result of the emerging political gambit.

Milinkevich's situation is not easy either. Shortly after the elections, the opposition party leaders floated the idea of convening the Congress of the

United Democratic Forces, the very same body that had made Milinkevich a presidential candidate. This time, however, the goal of the congress would be different: to deprive Milinkevich of legitimacy as the opposition leader so that the fate of Vladimir Goncharik, the 2001 presidential hopeful, would befall Milinkevich as well.

The most active role in discrediting Milinkevich was played by Anatoly Lebedko, chairman of the United Civic Party. At the previous (2004) congress, Lebedko was nominated alongside Milinkevich as a prospective presidential candidate on behalf of the united opposition, but Milinkevich won by a slim margin. There is, however, one important difference between Milinkevich and his 2001 predecessor Goncharik. The latter never visited a Western country as a presidential candidate. In contrast, Milinkevich visited many, and he was introduced to Western leaders who began to perceive him as the leader of the "democratic community" in Belarus. Until recently, Milinkevich and his wife were viewed as the key figures in distributing Western funds earmarked for Belarusian democracy. Milinkevich is particularly close to Poland, whose officialdom is eager to supervise the entire Western strategy of geopolitical reorientation of its eastern neighbors, Ukraine and Belarus. Although short-lived, the success of the orange revolution in Ukraine, in which Polish advisors and statesmen played an important role, evidently inspired Polish foreign policy makers. Some commentators believe that his Polish advisors were responsible for a controversial open letter that Milinkevich addressed to President Lukashenka in February 2007. "It is imperative to expeditiously overcome the schism in Belarusian society," wrote Milinkevich in that letter, "because only a consolidated nation can withstand challenges"[83] resulting from the trade war with Russia. "You underscore that one of the main goals of your policy is the retention of our statehood,"[84] Milinkevich also wrote, effectively legitimizing Lukashenka's role as the national leader. The ostensible goal of the letter was to suggest that the officialdom join the opposition in its upcoming celebration of the anniversary of the Belarusian People's Republic (BPR). The anniversary falls on March 25. On that day in 1918, the BPR had been proclaimed under German occupation. A quasistate that lasted for six months, the BPR has been viewed by many in the Belarusian opposition as the beginning of true Belarusian statehood, which was then brutally interrupted by the Red Army.

One of the reasons why some observers construe Milinkevich's offer to Lukashenka as a "Polish idea" is that it resembles the famous Polish Round Table Talks of 1989 whereby both the communist ruler of Poland, General Wojciech Jaruzelski, and the Solidarity's leader, Lech Wałęsa, found a way to come together as Polish patriots.[85]

Be that as it may, Milinkevich is now involved in delicate, but Byzantine, maneuvering. His letter to Lukashenka split the opposition, with seemingly equal numbers supporting and opposing the idea of such a letter. Milinkevich realizes that the credit of Western trust in him may expire unless he stays afloat politically at home. His success, however, looks exceedingly unlikely unless he is able to lead a certain political party. The problem is that Milinkevich is steadily associated with the BNF. However beset by an internal feud of its own, BNF is not going to coopt Milinkevich into its leadership. In light of this situation, Milinkevich began to create his own movement, *Za Svabodu* (For Liberty). It is, however, hard for Milinkevich to accomplish this task without making inroads into the BNF's turf. Recruitment efforts among the BNF members can only alienate its leaders from Milinkevich.

Needless to say, the continuing bickering does not benefit the Belarusian opposition, whose standing in the eyes of the Belarusian public risks plunging even lower than it already is. The very word combination "united democratic forces" sounds more like a parody, and it is hard to say which of the two adjectives—"united" or "democratic"—is more off the mark.

NOTES

1. Vital Silitski, "Pamiatats, shto dyktatyry ruinuyutsa," *Arche* 7 (2006), at http://arche.bymedia.net/2006-7/silicki706.htm.

2. Alexei Pikulik, 'Schaslivchiki i louzery: Balans sil," online conference, *Nashe Mneniye*, July 12–21, at www.nmnby.org.

3. IISEPS's national survey of May 2005, at www.iiseps.org.

4. Vladimir Berezin, "Dlya kogo veshchayet Radio Svaboda?" *Nashe Mneniye*, May 14, 2005, at www.nmnby.org.

5. IISEPS's national survey of April 2006, at www.iiseps.org.

6. IISEPS's national survey of April 2006.

7. IISEPS's national survey of March 26–April 6, 2006, at www.iiseps.org.

8. IISEPS's national survey of October 23–November 3, 2003.

9. IISEPS's national survey of October 2006, at www.iiseps.org.

10. IISEPS's national survey of March 2006, at www.iiseps.org.

11. IISEPS's national survey of December 2005, at www.iiseps.org.

12. Paval Sevyarynets, "Maloye sitna," January 9, 2005, at www.mfront.net/sev_dziasiatka.html.

13. IISEPS's national survey of October 2006, at www.iiseps.org.

14. IISEPS's national survey of March 2005, at www.iiseps.org.

15. IISEPS's national survey of March 2005.

16. IISEPS's national survey of May 2005, at www.iiseps.org.

17. IISEPS's national survey of March–April 2006, at www.iiseps.org.

18. IISEPS's national survey of March–April 2006.

19. IISEPS's national survey of December 2005, at www.iiseps.org.

20. "Tsi byla moladz galounai silai u gramadska-palitychnykh pratsesakh 2006 godu?" *Expertiza Svabody*, a talk show of the Belarusian Service of Radio Liberty, December 7, 2006, at www.svaboda.org.

21. Full results of this survey are available at www.kiis.com.ua/index.php?id=4&sp=1&num=24.

22. IISEPS's national survey of April 2006, at www.iiseps.org.

23. IISEPS's national survey of April 2006.

24. "Gde konchayetsia Yevropa?" Interpretation of the results of the April 2006 IISEPS's national survey, at www.iiseps.org.

25. Julia Korosteleva and Stephen White, "'Feeling European': The View from Belarus, Russia and Ukraine," *Contemporary Politics* 12, no. 2 (June 2006): 193–205.

26. IISEPS's national survey of April 2006, at www.iiseps.org.

27. IISEPS's national survey of June 2006, at www.iiseps.org.

28. Yury Drakokhrust, "Gde konchayetsia Belorussiya?" *Neprikosnovennyi Zapas* 47 (2006): 108–19.

29. "Pobediteli ne poluchayut nichego," *Belorussky Rynok*, November 24, 2001, at www.br.minsk.by/archive2001-46/sk14944.stm.

30. "Belarus' Bitter Election," *The Economist*, September 10, 2001, at www.economist.com.

31. "Pobediteli ne poluchayut nichego," *Belorussky Rynok*, November 24, 2001.

32. "Pobediteli ne poluchayut nichego," *Belorussky Rynok*.

33. Dmitry Vereshchagin and Sergei Lozhkin, "Rabota nad oshibkami," *Belorusskaya Delovaya Gazeta*, November 13, 2001, at http://bdg.press.net.by/2001/11/2001.

34. Vereshchagin and Lozhkin, "Rabota nad oshibkami." In one paragraph of the article, the authors claim that the share of undecided was 20 percent at the very least, whereas according to another paragraph, it could not be more than 15 percent.

35. Vereshchagin and Lozhkin, "Rabota nad oshibkami."

36. This was cited on February 17, 2007, by Alexander Feduta, a former press secretary of Alexander Lukashenka, at http://feduta.livejournal.com.

37. "Legko li byt yedinym," interview with Vladimir Goncharik, *Nashe Mneniye*, February 27, 2007, at www.nmnby.org.

38. Yanina Bolonskaya, "Nezakazannye tsifry," *Belorusskaya Delovaya Gazeta* 1483, November 26, 2004.

39. Pavliuk Bykovsky, "Reiting Lukashenko i yego konkurentov," at http://ru.belaruselections.info/current/2006/sociology/0022756.

40. Gallup: "Za Lukashenku gatovuya galasavats 53%, za Milinkevicha 21%" Belarusian Service of Radio Liberty, December 28, 2005, at www.svaboda.org.

41. Victor Boichenia, "Yedinyi: Politicheskii portret," *Belorusskaya Delovaya Gazeta,* March 7, 2006.

42. "Chamu Alyaxandar Milinkevich vystupau na telebachani pa-raseisku?" Belarusian Service of Radio Liberty, February 24, 2006, at www.svaboda.org.

43. "Alyaksandr Milinkevich: 'Belaruskaya mova verniotsia va uladu, universitety, shkoly,'" Belarusian Service of Radio Liberty, October 5, 2005, at www.svaboda.org.

44. Interview with Yury Khodyko, *Nashe Mneniye*, August 17, 2007, at www.nmnby .org.

45. Pavel Yakubovich, "Rozhdionnyi padat' letat ne mozhet," *Belarus Segodnia*, February 23, 2006, at www.sb.by.

46. Svetlana Alexievich is a Belarusian author with the highest name recognition outside Belarus due to her *Voices from Chernobyl: Chronicle of the Future* (London: Aurum Press Ltd., 1999) (a translation from the Russian). The book was later reprinted in the United States under the title *Voices from Chernobyl: The Oral History of a Nuclear Disaster* (Champaign, IL: Dalkey Archive Press, 2005). In 2006, Alexievich received a National Book Critics Circle Award for that book.

47. "Tsi zyavilas' u Belarusi alternatyva Alyaksandru Lukashenku?" *Prasky Accent*, a talk show of the Belarusian Service of Radio Liberty, January 29, 2006, at www.svaboda.org.

48. Pavel Starodub, "Liudi i kukly," *Belarus Segodnia*, March 23, 2006, at www.sb .by.

49. Sergei Nikolyuk, "Dogovor 2006," *Nashe Mneniye*, April 18, 2006, at www .nmnby.org.

50. Yury Drakokhrust, "Gde konchayetsia Belorussiya?", 108–19.

51. Andrei Piontkovsky, "Lukashenko stal istinnym otsom belorusskoi nezavisimosti," AFN, July 6, 2006, at www.afn.by.

52. Pavel Kirillov, "Oppozitsia mozhet poluchit vtoroi tur s pomoshchyu storonnikov Lukashenko," *Belorusskiye Novosti*, March 7, 2006, at www.naviny.by.

53. Kirillov, "Oppozitsia mozhet poluchit vtoroi."

54. Svetlana Martovskaya, "Pochemu Belarus' golosuyet za Lukashenko," *Telegraf*, September 14, 2005, at www.inosmi.ru/translation/222228.html.

55. Pavel Starodub, "Liudi i kukly", *Belarus Segodnia*, March 23, 2006.

56. Anatoly Levkovich, "Kogda eks-kandidat v tyurme eto problema vsego obshchestva," *Belorusskiye Novosti*, September 22, 2006, at www.naviny.by.

57. Alena Struve, "Yakiye paraleli pamizh belaruskai i ukrainskai situatsiyai?" Belarusian Service of Radio Liberty, at www.svaboda.org; March 21, 2006.

58. "Tsi magli padzei 19–25 sakavika skonchitsa inaksh?"*Prasky Accent*, a talk show of the Belarusian Service of Radio Liberty, April 2, 2006, at www.svaboda .org.

59. "Yakoye palitychnaye znacheniye meli tydniovyya pratesty apazytsii?" *Prasky Accent*, a talk show of the Belarusian Service of Radio Liberty, April 26, 2006, at www.svaboda.org.

60. Because this admission is more than believable, the falsifications appear to be counterproductive and irrational. My untested hypothesis is that, much like similar falsifications of the referendum, these took place in the precincts whose not-very-reflective bosses perceived themselves as revolutionaries fighting on street barricades

they had erected to repel their sworn enemies, generously funded by Western sponsors. Such were indeed the spirit, perception, and overall atmosphere within the Lukashenka camp. A collateral hypothesis would be that the Lukashenka electoral machine set out to make the impression of victory so overwhelming that the opposition would be shown unworthy of Western grants.

61. "Yakoye palitychnaye znacheniye meli tydniovyya pratesty apazytsii?" *Prasky Accent*, April 26, 2006.

62. "Yakoye palitychnaye znacheniye meli tydniovyya pratesty apazytsii?"

63. Yanov Polessky, "Razocharovat'sia v bolshinstve," *Nashe Mneniye*, April 27, 2006, at www.nmnby.org/print/0604/27-d_prn.html.

64. Andrei Vardomatskiy, "Belarus i mir: Sotsiologicheskoye issledovaniye," *Analiticheskiy Byulleten' Belorusskikh Fabrik Mysli*, No. 2 (1999): 20–23.

65. "Po dannym sotsiologov laboratorii Novak, negativnyy reiting Lukashenko rastiot," interview with Andrey Vardomatskiy, *Russia Online*, May 8, 2001, at www.rol.ru/news/misc/newssng/01/05/08_026.htm (accessed May 2001).

66. Valery Panyushkin, "Belorusskoy oppozitsii ne khvatayet narodnogo gniewa," *Kommersant*, March 18, 2006, at www.kommersant.ru/doc.html?DocID=658651&IssueID=30045.

67. Center for Political Studies and Public Opinion Research, Institute of Social Sciences, Belgrade, Serbia, at www.cpijm.org.yu.

68. IISEPS's national survey of March–April 2006, at www.iiseps.org.

69. IISEPS's national survey of March–April 2006.

70. Vladimir Matskevich, "Zhdat serioznykh postupkov ot takoy oppozitsii ne prikhoditsia," *Belorusskiye Novosti*, September 21, 2006, at www.naviny.by.

71. IISEPS's national survey of March–April 2006, at www.iiseps.org.

72. IISEPS's national survey of March–April 2006.

73. Silitski, "Pamiatats."

74. The group is tight-knit and possessed by its members' determination to lead in Belarusian nation-building. In his Belarusian Service of Radio Liberty interview on May 31, 2006, Bulgakau placed Silitski in an honorable thirteenth position in his list of the twenty most prominent Belarusians of the twentieth century. Not only does that list not include Lukashenka, it does not include Zianon Pazniak either.

75. Silitski, "Pamiatats."

76. Vladimir Matskevich, "Zhdat serioznykh postupkov ot takoy oppozitsii ne prikhoditsia," *Belorusskiye Novosti*, September 21, 2006.

77. Matskevich, "Zhdat serioznykh."

78. "Pamiatats, shto dyktatyry ruinuyutsa," *Prasky Accent*, a talk Show of the Belarusian Service of Radio Liberty, August 18, 2006, at www.svaboda.org.

79. Vital Silitski, "Preempting Democracy: The Case of Belarus," *Journal of Democracy* 16, no. 4 (2005): 83–97, at http://muse.jhu.edu/journals/journal_of_democracy/v016/16.4silitski.html.

80. Silitski, "Preempting Democracy."

81. Victor Martinovich, "Generation L," *BelGazeta*, September 5, 2005, at www.belgazeta.by/20050905.35./010080140.

82. Sergei Pulsha, "Kozulin mozhet vyiti na svobodu dosrochno," *Belorusskie Novosti*, February 22, 2007, at http://naviny.by/rubrics/politic/2007/02/12/ic_articles_112_149684.

83. Alexander Milinkevich, "Otkrytoye pis'mo Alexandru Lukashenko," *Charter 97*, February 7, 2007, at www.charter97.org/rus/news/2007/02/07/pismo.

84. Milinkevich, "Otkrytoye pis'mo Alexandru Lukashenko."

85. Pavel Sheremet, "Liderov ne vybirayut, imi stanoviatsia," *Belorussky Partizan*, February 19, 2007, at www.belaruspartisan.org/bp-forte.

Conclusion

It is vital that we develop a critical perspective on the seductive simple-mindedness of geopolitics.

—Geraóid Ó. Tuathail[1]

Belarus is the least studied and least understood European state to emerge from the breakup of the Soviet Union. But how indeed should "the country's problems be understood when so much is apparently paradoxical? A popular [autocrat] versus a squabbling opposition; consensual colonialism versus elitist nationalism."[2] Whether or not I have unraveled those paradoxes is up to the reader to decide. What is already clear, though, is that the picture I have painted is a tough sell to policy makers and even to part of the scholarly community. This may be because in my palette, ominous colors have been used sparingly, if at all. I have not assigned blame according to the preconceived notions and dominant expectations. Thus, I have not portrayed Lukashenka as a bloodthirsty tyrant or described Russia as a grizzly bear at Europe's doorstep, an image recently favored by *The Economist*. Contrary to the imputed logic, Russia seems to have lost Belarus, despite the fact that a few years ago it could have incorporated that country without causing mass protests by its citizenry. This picture is particularly at odds with that of the U.S. foreign policy makers. The major document of American policy with regard to Belarus is the Belarus Democracy Act. Adopted in 2004 and reauthorized in 2006, it denies entry into the United States of senior leaders of the government of Belarus and their immediate families, prohibits loans and investment by U.S. banks, and blocks U.S. assets of the members of Belarusian leadership.[3] To be sure, entry to the United States cannot be securely denied because of the location of the United Nations headquarters, so not only did Alexander Lukashenka participate in and speak at the United Nations General Assembly's meetings (the last time in September 2005), but also some of his ministers and members of his presidential administration took part in United Nations conferences held in New York as recently as March and April 2007. American banks have never been particularly active in Belarus, and no American assets of the members of Belarus's leadership have ever been located. Under these conditions, the act is largely a gesture of staunch disapproval of Belarus's ruling regime.

Short of questioning someone's authority to resort to such gestures, one would at least expect that, however symbolic, the punishment should fit the crime or that wrongdoers all across the world should be condemned in proportion to the reprehensibility of their acts. But while there is little doubt that on their home turf Belarusian authorities deviate from the accepted Western standards of decent behavior, the analysis contained in this book supports a fellow researcher's view that "the use of violence by the authoritarian Belarusian regime has been insignificant against the backdrop of authoritarian dictatorships elsewhere in the world, and even in the postcommunist era,"[4] and that "President Lukashenka consistently and vigorously pursued the policies that struck positive resonance with the society."[5] Apparently, no fewer than one hundred members of the United Nations would deserve identical democracy acts to condemn their respective domestic policies.[6] Yet, no similar documents were adopted for Turkmenistan or Azerbaijan, two sorely undemocratic countries rich in oil and gas and persistently courted by the West. In 2006, the president of Azerbaijan was graced by a White House reception. Likewise, in 2006, the leader of semidemocratic (at best) and oil-rich Kazakhstan met with both Vice President Dick Cheney and President George W. Bush. During his 2005 visit to the Republic of Georgia, Bush called it a "beacon of liberty." This beacon is barely flickering, and desperate attempts are underway to rekindle it.

Attending conferences and participating in discussions on Belarus, I invariably come across one peculiar line of reasoning in support of the American approach to Belarus. Belarusian authorities, the line goes, accuse us of a double standard. Why is it, they say, that you sanction us, instead of Azerbaijan or any of the Central Asian *stans*, which are even less democratic than we are? We do so, the standard response goes, because you are in Europe, while they are not. Being in Europe, you've got to be one of us. The last time I heard this reasoning was in September 2007 from Lubomir Rehak, Slovakia's charge d'affaires in Minsk, but I have heard it many times before. I find this pronouncement mischievous not only because of its self-serving nature but also because the eastern border of cultural Europe has never been set once and for all. It seems like Europe is expandable, and its configuration solely depends on one's geopolitical agenda. As was shown in chapter 3 of this book, a notable cultural frontier runs across Belarus, leaving just one of its regions—at best—on the side of the Western world. To the west of that frontier, the locus of responsibility and action is, for the most part, a person or individual; to the east, it is a collectivity or the people. Writing about Russian political culture, a political scientist with close ties to the Kremlin acknowledged that "the personification of political institutions and the great role of leaders . . . *make up for a deficiency in mutual trust*. That is why Russians lean not to institutions but to strong personalities" (emphasis added)[7] Apparently, Belarusians do the same, and the resulting conflict of values (between most Belarusians and the West) may or may not be politicized. Those choosing to politicize that conflict have their own goals, which they are of course free to present as care for the good of the Belarusian (or whatever) people.

Although scholars normally embrace a view of reality more multicolored and sensitive to nuances than that of politicians, at least part of Western scholarship on Belarus toes the line of the American foreign policy establishment, and some researchers even go ahead of the curve. Publications devoted to post-Soviet Belarus contain recurrent observations that can be summarized as follows:

> The Belarusian language is rarely used in everyday interpersonal communication, schooling, or in the news media; Russian dominates all these areas. The Belarusian ruling regime is autocratic; it represses independent media; Belarusian opposition is marginalized and muzzled, and the 2001 and 2006 presidential elections were rigged. Soviet and Russian-born symbols (the national flag and emblem, the name of the currency unit, and the celebration of a national independence holiday on the day of the liberation of Minsk from the Nazis by the Soviet Army) prevail over genuinely Belarusian symbols. Economic reform is in an embryonic stage; and the role of Russia in external economic and political ties is overpowering.

I do not doubt accuracy of these observations, but the "certitudes" that usually accompany them are a totally different matter. For example, it is not clear a priori which language is the native language of today's Belarusians and which symbols are genuinely Belarusian. Likewise, it should give any impartial observer pause to see that the Russian political regime under Vladimir Putin has drifted in the direction of autocracy and has significantly increased its approval at home (where "democracy" is perceived by many Russians as an impish term justifying the West's meddling in Russia's internal affairs and is "derisively called *dermocratiya,* or shit-ocracy"[8]). Consequently, if the wish for a strong hand is indeed paramount in neighboring Belarus, one cannot rule out the fact that the Belarusian regime fits dominant political culture. As noted in this book, 63 percent of Belarusians believe that maintaining order (as they see it) is their president's principal achievement.[9]

It is, however, "certitudes" of dubious nature—one may also call them tacit assumptions—that seem to unduly politicize almost every piece of news coming from the Republic of Belarus. Here are some of those assumptions reconstructed by way of reverse reasoning:

> Membership or belonging in a certain ethnic group is preset and derives from one's genealogy or ancestral roots; ethnic groups are spatially discrete and/or match the respective ethnographic areas; therefore, embracing extraterritorial (or "somebody else's") national symbols is an anomaly. Because Belarus is a sovereign country separate from Russia, to speak Belarusian would be more natural (and also more dignified and patriotic) than Russian. Consequently, it is negative, disapproving, and harmful that the "native" language is marginalized in Belarus, while a "foreign" one is promoted. Democratization is inseparable from the restoration of both national identity and language; dictatorship is a tool of Russian hegemony. Reunification with Russia is harmful for Belarus. And the Belarusian economy is destined to collapse because it takes guidance from central planning, the failed economic system of the former USSR.

When Belarusian realities are viewed through the prism of these assumptions, predictable conclusions emerge. Such conclusions may not necessarily be worded as follows, yet they appear to be accepted by implication: President Lukashenka of Belarus is a political degenerate who should be ostracized and snubbed. The democratic and nationalist opposition is worthy of support. The Soviet and pro-Russian indoctrination of the Belarusian populace has to be undone. And Belarus's economic growth is a hoax.

This book has sought to provide an alternative, depoliticized view of Belarus. Indeed, the research it contains has proven each of the above assumptions wrong. One exception concerns the would-be consequences of Belarus's unification with Russia, an issue I did not research. I nevertheless concur with the view that in the long run such consequences may be harmful, although not for the reasons routinely given. There is little doubt that Russians and Belarusians are as close to each other as any two peoples could be, and numerous statements to this effect by the national leaders of Russia and Belarus are in sync with popular perception. Likewise, the plausible but ever-less-likely Russia-Belarus unification cannot be faulted based on Russia's inherently undemocratic ways because the grassroots political cultures in Russia and Belarus are identical, and neither one attaches a high premium to Western-style democracy. Throughout history, however, it is the sheer magnitude of Russia's space that has inhibited Russia's economic and, consequently, sociopolitical development.[10] Any compact country like Belarus is bound to have fewer godforsaken places than even the European (let alone Asian) section of Russia has per commensurate unit of its territory. Already at this writing, Belarus is visibly better groomed than Russia, the shiny new look of the Russian capital notwithstanding.

That said, however, all the remaining tacit assumptions from the above list do not stand up to close analysis, and this book has, hopefully, made this clear. Thus, becoming a nation does not correlate with becoming a democracy.[11] In the specific case of Belarus, prior to 2002, making political decisions on the basis of popular preferences could easily have cost that country its statehood. Ironically, only the well-lubricated propaganda machine of a supposedly undemocratic leader has now made the sacrifice of Belarusian statehood less likely. By the same token, no truly democratic vote in today's Belarus would help make Belarusian the language of the majority. By all appearances, Russian is the mother tongue of most Belarusians because it is from their mothers that they learned to speak it. And yet, Russian-speaking Belarusians are every bit as patriotic as their Belarusian-speaking compatriots, if not more so. The grassroots demand for Belarusian may increase if Belarusian statehood is retained, but the sole agency with which realistic hopes for this retention now rest is Lukashenka's government. Realistically, nobody in the opposition can rise up to this task. The next Belarusian leader will, most probably, be promoted from among current Lukashenka loyalists.

The major problem Belarus faces is nation building. To this day, a single Belarusian identity has not crystallized. None of Belarus's present-day borders is a cultural or linguistic frontier, and the eastern and southern borders of Belarus are devoid of any cultural frontier characteristics at all. At the same time, as noted above, a cultural divide runs across Belarus, making it a cleft country. To some extent, this helps explain the constant tug of war over Belarus's "true" leanings and national symbols. Because, however, at least three-quarters of Belarus, by both land area and population, lies on the eastern side of the cultural divide, and the same language is used on both sides of Belarus's eastern border, ties between Russians and Belarusians are natural and do not derive from the alleged ploys of Russian imperialists. Even during the worst crisis in Russia-Belarus relationships, that is, during the winter 2006–2007 trade war, more Belarusians opted for unification with Russia than for joining the European Union (48.5 to 33.65 percent)[12]—when given only these options to select from.

Economic growth in Belarus is as real as it can be, and so are improvements in living conditions, particularly from 2004 to 2006. While major uncertainties lie ahead because of a significant increase in energy prices,

Belarus may well be able to adjust to them. While doing so, the country is not likely to rely on central planning to the extent the Soviet Union did. However, as a much smaller and better-managed economy than that of the Soviet Union at large, the economy of post-Soviet Belarus is not inimical to a certain dose of manual steering by the government, which is bent on safeguarding social equity.

What Belarusians definitely reject loud and clear is a call for blanket privatization. The application of this and other neoliberal remedies in the similar cultural environments of Russia and Ukraine has not earned the approval of Belarusians, who remain resentful of social stratification and favor a strong safety net. Upon coming to power, Lukashenka interiorized and acted upon these popular sentiments. Above all, he responded to the public call to restore economic ties with Russia. By doing so, while opposing the incorporation of Belarus into Russia, and by presiding over ten years of robust economic growth, Lukashenka has turned into a successful politician. Under his tutelage, Belarus has become an independent political player, a rare example of a country "ruled neither from Moscow, nor from Washington, nor from Brussels."[13] A self-made politician, Lukashenka has succeeded despite overwhelming odds, including having the world's most influential political players—the leaders of the United States, the European Union, and now also Russia—set against him.

Obviously, Lukashenka is an autocrat, but it is equally obvious that being an autocrat is in line with local political culture and that "coercion is not the sole foundation of Lukashenka's rule in Belarus."[14] If that's the case, Lukashenka's time may not have run out yet. As one rising star of the opposition-minded Belarusian community recently mentioned, it would be good if the National Endowment for Democracy only issued its reports every thirty years; this would be good because the average life span of an authoritarian regime is seventeen years no matter what we do. Indeed, while Lukashenka's government abides by its social contract with the majority of Belarusians by delivering on its promises to them, the Belarusian opposition is beset by internal feuds and is neither nationalist nor democratic as long as only a few Belarusians share its not always clearly identified goals and aspirations. This qualification pertains to much of the organized opposition, engaged as it is in client-patron relations with its foreign sponsors; it does not pertain by any means to anyone who may be opposed to, or critical of, the Lukashenka regime. There are plenty of reasons to be critical of an authoritarian regime. Some people have a hard time realizing, however, that there are even more reasons to resent (and fear!) a situation whereby the libertarian intentions of the rulers surpass the civic capacity of the ruled, or rulers' offer of democracy exceeds the ability and willingness of the ruled to digest it. According to a politically correct view, "It is 'cultural condescension' . . . to say that some na-tions are 'not ready' for democracy. The question, however, is not whether that idea is condescending but whether it is true."[15] By ostracizing and sanc-tioning the authoritarian government whose legitimacy in the eyes of most Belarusians is beyond doubt, and by communicating *only* with the externally sponsored and self-proclaimed democrats, the West has sowed seeds of doubt over the purity of its intentions, politicized a bona fide cultural divide, and made it easy for Lukashenka to portray all of the opposition as an antinational force.

One of the reasons modern Belarus baffles Western observers like no other post-Soviet state is that many of these observers take nation building for granted and are fixated on spreading democracy as a magical cure-all. Little attempt is made to understand Belarus on its own terms, that is, in the context of its location, history, emerging identity, and cultural leanings. Attaching po-litical labels to a situation whose roots transcend politics constitutes a critical weakness of Western approaches to Belarus.

While some Belarus analysts are diligent and act in good faith, the object of analysis is unusually elusive. No nation or *ethnie* is exempt from external influences, and hardly any is immune to them. But what is truly unusual about Belarus is the degree to which external factors have so far affected every fiber of its national fabric, every facet of Belarus's ethnonational setting: the econ-omy, politics, and, indeed, language and identity. After seven decades as a re-public of the Soviet Union and following sixteen years of full-fledged state-hood, Belarus has not yet found its bearings. It is therefore impossible to understand Belarus without immersing oneself deeply in the history and cur-rent affairs of Belarus's neighbors. In theory, national awakening is linked to modernization, but this term subsumes industrialization, advancement of the capital city and other urban centers, acquisition of statehood, and more, all of which came to Belarus from without or were conditioned by stimuli originat-ing in a larger entity of which Belarus was long a part. In contrast to what happened in Iran under the shah, these external influences were not deemed hostile and were therefore organically absorbed. It's no wonder that the ma-jority of Belarusians did not perceive that larger entity as the epitome of alien colonialism but as their own homeland.

Anthony Smith has acknowledged how "tempting [it is] to conclude that 'ethnicity' is in the eye of the beholder, that it is all 'situational,' a matter of time and context."[16] This is because "even ethnic communities, so easily rec-ognizable from a distance, seem to dissolve before our eyes the closer we come and the more we attempt to pin them down."[17] More of an allegory in-tended to underline the relativity of one's perspective on ethnicity than a statement of the obvious, this pronouncement could be taken literally when it comes to Belarusians. They are, in fact, not easily recognizable from a distance and never speak in one voice, so coming closer and sorting out forces instrumental in their collective evolution only renders their image fuzzier and harder to categorize.

Because of a bitter conflict over two sets of national symbols and the narratives glorifying them, the political scene of Belarus became bipolar. Throughout the 1990s, one's public persona was best discernible if one was either fervently pro-Russian and anti-Western or vice versa. One of the accomplishments of Lukashenka's administration has been that it came up with a certain middle ground and has been promoting it slowly but surely. Of course, the so-called national ideology of the Republic of Belarus is not exactly halfway between the two poles, but neither are most Belarusians whose cultural leaning toward Russia is pronounced. However, even as it endorses and embraces cultural closeness to Russia, Lukashenka's strand of nationalism is distinctly Belarusian. It is Belarusian in that most Belarusians have found it problematic to see themselves as a community apart from Russia, and so has their leader. For many Belarusians, things Russian no longer belong in "we" but cannot yet be assigned to "they." Yet, the country and its leader have made important steps in the direction of psychological (albeit not yet economic) independence from Russia. Significantly, they have done this in unison, without any attempt on the part of the leader to push it along, get ahead of his fellow countrymen, or preach historical myths that do not strike a chord with Belarusians.

Given that the split on the crucial issue of what it means to be a Belarusian has not yet been overcome, the West would be well served to promote national consolidation, not preclude it by sponsoring one minority strand (or occasionally two) of Belarusian nationalism. Only broad national consolidation, not forceful democracy promotion, will untether Belarus from Russia. The umbilical cord connecting Belarus to Russia will be cut as soon as most (not just some) Belarusians embrace their distinctiveness and refuse to trade their sovereignty for promises of a better life. It is highly unlikely that the Belarus Democracy Act helps to bring this outcome any closer. The exact opposite seems to be true.

Having said this, one last set of questions remains to be addressed: Why is it that the Western, particularly American, policies with regard to Lukashenka's Belarus have been so inefficient, or worse, counterproductive? Why is it that by professing staunch disapproval of Lukashenka's policies, the West has actually strengthened him? Why is it that the West ignores the genuine concerns of Belarusians and preaches democracy instead with the perseverance of a broken gramophone record? To be sure, the U.S. policy vis-à-vis Belarus has produced a genuine achievement—the one-liner about Europe's last dictatorship. A quality sound bite, it has added zing to public pronouncements about Belarus, it has turned up in the titles of papers by Western Belarus watchers,[18] and no primer in public speaking should pass it up. Yet, as one Belarusian journalist observes, "by now they have probably heard about Europe's last dictatorship as far away as Zanzibar, but is there anybody who has gained anything from that?"[19]

Earlier, I noted that certain idiosyncrasies make understanding Belarus difficult. Difficult, however, does not mean impossible, provided there is willingness to understand. This willingness has been largely absent, and no serious debate over policy toward Belarus has ever taken place. Even such critics of Bush's anti-intellectualism who see it as his leadership style (rather than the defining feature of his worldview) claim that it "has supplanted the more intricate, policy-oriented debate that should serve as the hallmark of deliberation in an extended democratic republic."[20] Internationally, the results of this deficiency have been disastrous. Simply, in some world regions the foreign policy failures and ensuing disasters have been more spectacular than in others. But there seems to be one recurrent theme to failures and disasters of varying proportions. As the world knows, weapons of mass destruction (WMD) were presented as the reason for the Iraq war. When those were not found, the justification became spreading democracy. Spreading democracy, of course, turned out to be even harder than finding the nonexistent WMD. However, the world has learned from a former boss of the U.S. Central Intelligence Agency that a commitment to invade Iraq was voiced by one of the chief architects of that invasion as early as September 12, 2001.[21] At that time, no ties with the perpetrators of September 11 could have been documented, no unassailable evidence on WMD had been collected, and although Saddam Hussein was a brutal dictator, Saudi Arabia and Syria were no more democratic than Iraq. William Kristol, who in 2002 wrote that a war with Iraq "could have terrifically good effects throughout the Middle East,"[22] noted in his January 2007 column that as a result of the last-straw American troop surge, "individuals and nations might decide that it is once again wiser to be a friend of the U.S. than an enemy."[23] This seems to be a frank confession. Looking at the map of the Middle East, one sees that besides possessing huge quantities of oil, Iraq is geographically central to that world region. Creating a friendly regime at the core of the Middle East was most probably the intention of the architects of the Iraq war, with a subsequent diffusion of "friendliness" outward from that core envisioned by those architects. Any knowledge about the Iraqi people, including their religious makeup, mutual tensions, and who or what actually kept them in check was not deemed worthy of consideration.

"To understand the appeal of geopolitics to certain intellectuals, institutions and would-be strategists," writes Gerard Toal, "one has to appreciate its mythic qualities. Geopolitics is mythic because it promises uncanny clarity and insight in a complex world. It actively closes down an openness to the geographical diversity of the world and represses questioning and difference. The plurality of the world is reduced to certain 'transcendent truths' about strategy. Geopolitics is a narrow instrumental form of reason that is also a form of faith, a belief that there is a secret substratum and/or a permanent set of conflicts and interests that account for the course of world politics."[24]

In the United States, where 63 percent of college-age people (18–24) cannot identify Iraq on the world map,[25] congressmen profess no knowledge of Shiite-Sunni differences,[26] and the words "freedom" and "democracy" (though profoundly meaningful in the context of American history) have a certain ritualistic ring to them, it was possible to sell the geopolitical rationale for the war as a fight for democracy and freedom.

Let us now get back to Belarus. "One may suspect," I wrote in 2003, "that the current Belarus regime frustrated certain *geopolitical* expectations related to that country. Yet it remains unclear whether such expectations were warranted in the first place."[27] Dimitri Simes, president of the Washington-based Nixon Center, echoed the same suspicion in a March 2006 interview given to the Russian daily *Nezavisimaya Gazeta.* "With all the imperfections of the Belarusian political system," observed Simes, "it is obvious that the disapproval of Minsk is founded not only on its domestic policy but also on the fact that Lukashenka makes no attempt to cooperate with the West and with the USA and, at least formally speaking, is more given to building a union with Russia."[28] "I think Lukashenka is anathemized because he refuses to play ball according to the dictates of U.S. foreign policy," an anonymous reviewer of my National Science Foundation proposal pointed out in 2006.

Whereas in the case of Iraq, the first offered justification of the geopolitical strategy was WMD, with spreading democracy being the second-best excuse, Belarus got rid of its last nuclear weapon in 1996, and so in the case of Belarus, democracy has become the first line of attack. But the rationale of the strategy toward Belarus seems to be just as geopolitical at its core as that toward Iraq. "The idiocy of moving NATO to Russia's doorstep"[29] drew from the profound delirium over winning the cold war. A traditional East European nationalism of the nativist strand, with more than a touch of anti-Russian sentiment, came in handy. This sentiment worked so well and in so many places that the same approach was rubber-stamped for Belarus. For a long time, however, Belarus showed signs of being different: what worked elsewhere did not work in Belarus, which became the stumbling block in the overarching task of reorienting the western neighbors of Russia. At the turn of the century, it became obvious that the foreign policy makers' expectations with regard to Belarus had been misguided all along. Adopted in 2004, the Belarus Democracy Act was thus a product of the establishment's lasting frustration over a stubborn little-known country unwilling to grasp where the true reward comes from. In the end, it seems that a foreign policy that continues to be fixated on the old-fashioned idea of the geographical centers of power and their polarities, a foreign policy that is in fact "insensitive to the particularity and diversity of the world's states,"[30] is flawed, which explains, if only in part, the monumental failure in Iraq and a less spectacular failure in Belarus.

In his eleventh thesis on Feurbach, Marx famously stated that "the philosophers have only interpreted the world in various ways; the point is to change it."[31] As we have seen disastrous attempts to change big chunks of the world without bothering to achieve any good understanding of them, the word "only" in Marx's thesis acquires a poignant irony. Certainly Belarus is no Iraq, but in any case, social scientists would do best to "only interpret." There is no reason to jump over one's head. Let us leave this to politicians.

NOTES

1. Geraóid Ó.Tuathail (Gerard Toal), "Understanding Critical Geopolitics," *Journal of Strategic Studies* 22, nos. 2–3 (1999): 107.

2. Eurozine—Articles, May 22, 2007, at www.eurozine.com/articles/2007-05-22-eurozinerev-en.html (accessed September 30, 2007).

3. H. R. 5948, [109th] Belarus Democracy Reauthorization Act of 2006, *GovTrack.us*, at www.govtrack.us/congress/billtext.xpd?bill=h109-5948&page-command.

4. Natalia Leshchenko, "The National Foundation of the 'Last European Dictatorship'" (paper presented at the Twelfth World Convention of the Association for the Study of Nationalities, Columbia University, New York, April 14, 2007, quoted with the author's permission).

5. Leshchenko, "The National Foundation."

6. While the rankings of the world's countries by some Washington-based agencies (e.g., Freedom House) can justify singling Belarus out, this could not be otherwise because these agencies are part and parcel of the same establishment that first makes political choices, then seeks to justify them.

7. Viacheslav Nikonov, "Gordoye soznaniye mogushchestva," *Izvestia*, 26 July 2007, www.izvestia.ru/comment/article3106530/?print.

8. David Remnick, "The Tsar's Opponent," *The New Yorker*, October 1, 2007, 67.

9. IISEPS's national survey of January 2007, at www.iiseps.org.

10. Some information to this effect is contained in Grigory Ioffe, Tatyana Nefedova, and Ilya Zaslavsky, *The End of Peasantry?* (Pittsburgh, PA: University of Pittsburgh Press, 2006), ch. 3.

11. Those willing to learn more about this lack of correlation may want to familiarize themselves with Ira Strauss's paper "Empire as Metaphor," presented at the Twelfth World Convention of the Association for the Study of Nationalities, Columbia University, New York, April 12, 2007.

12. IISEPS's national survey of January 2007, at www.iiseps.org.

13. These are the words of Belarus's foreign minister Sergei Martynov, quoted in Leshchenko, "The National Foundation."

14. Leshchenko, "The National Foundation."

15. George F. Will, "The New Math: 28 + 35 = 43," *Newsweek*, January 31, 2005, 60.

16. Anthony D. Smith, *The Ethnic Origins of Nations*, 12th ed. (London: Blackwell, 1999), 2.

17. Smith, *The Ethnic Origins of Nations*.

18. See, for example, David Marples, "Europe's Last Dictatorship: The Roots and Perspectives of Authoritarianism in 'White Russia,'" *Europe-Asia Studies* 57, no. 6 (2005), and Leshchenko, "The National Foundation."

19. Alexei Zolotnitsky, "Den Voli: Vlast i oppozitsia v starych okopakh," *Belorusskie Novosti*, March 25, 2007, at www.naviny.by.

20. Coleen J. Shogan, "Anti-intellectualism in Modern Presidency: A Republican Populism," *Perspectives on Politics* 5, no. 2 (2007): 301.

21. Scott Pelley's interview with George Tenet on *60 Minutes*, a CBS show, April 29, 2007, at www.cbsnews.com/stories/2007/04/25/60minutes/main2728375.shtml.

22. David Corn, "Kristol Clear at *Time*," *The Nation*, January 3, 2007, at www.outlawjournalism.com/news/?p=1434.

23. William Kristol, "There Is a Way Forward in Iraq," *Time*, January 4, 2007, at www.time.com/time/magazine/article/0,9171,1574144-2,00.html.

24. Tuathail, "Understanding Critical Geopolitics," 113.

25. "Study: Geography Greek to Young Americans," *CNN*, May 4, 2006, at www.cnn.com/2006/EDUCATION/05/02/geog.test.

26. Jeff Stein, "Can You Tell a Sunni from a Shiite?" *International Herald Tribune*, October 17, 2006, at www.iht.com/articles/2006/10/17/opinion/edstein.php.

27. Grigory Ioffe, "Understanding Belarus: Questions of Language," *Europe-Asia Studies* 55, no. 7 (2003): 1011.

28. Andrei Terekhov, "Oranzhevoi revolutsii v Minske ne budet," *Nezavisimaya Gazeta*, March 15, 2006. Here is a relevant quote from *The Economist*: "Two rigged elections, with political arrests before the vote and protests battered afterwards; behind them, two moustachioed, post-Soviet rulers. The balder one, Alyaksandr Lukashenka, was reviled by the U.S. before and after last month's pointless presidential poll in Belarus. The other—Ilham Aliev of Azerbaijan, whose allies swept the board in an absurd parliamentary vote last year—this week fulfills his long-standing ambition to meet George Bush in America." "Use a Long Spoon," *The Economist*, April 27, 2006.

29. Patrick Buchanan, "To Die for Tallinn," HumanEvents.com, April 5, 2007, at www.humanevents.com/article.php?id=20560.

30. Tuathail, "Understanding Critical Geopolitics," 107.

31. Karl Marx, *Theses on Feurbach*, Marx/Engels Internet Archive, at www.marxists.org/archive/marx/works/1845/theses/theses.htm (accessed September 30, 2007).

Bibliography

Akudovich, Valyantsyn. "Bez nas." *Nasha Niva*, April 28, 2003, at www.litara.net (accessed September 29, 2007).

———. "Vaina kulturau ili piramida Kheopsu za muram Mirskaga zamku." *Nashe Mneniye*, August 22, 2005, at http://www.nmnby.org/pub/220805/akudovich.html (accessed September 29, 2007).

Anderson, Benedict. *Imagined Communities.* London: Verso, 1991.

Babkou, Igar. "Genealyogiya belaruskai idei." *Arche* 3 (2005): 136–65.

Balmaceda, Margarita M., James Clem, and Lisbeth Tarlow, eds. *Independent Belarus: Domestic Determinants, Regional Dynamics, and Implications for the West.* Cambridge, MA: Harvard University Press, 2002.

Belarus: Window of Opportunity to Enhance Competitiveness and Sustain Economic Growth. Washington, DC: The World Bank, 2005.

Berdiaev, Nikolai. *The Origin of Russian Communism.* London: The Centenary Press, 1937.

Białokozowicz, Bazyli. *Miedzy wschodem a zachodem.* Bialystok: Bialowieża, 1998.

Bobkov, Igor. "Etika pogranich'ya: Transkul'turnost kak belorusskii opyt." *Perekriostki* 3–4 (2005): 127–36.

Bulakhov, Mikhail. *Evfimii Fiodorovich Karski, 1861–1931.* Minsk: BGU, 1981.

Bulgakau, Valerka. "Vybary prezydenta kreolau." *Arche* 4 (2001), at Arche.home.by/2001-4/bulha401.htm (accessed August 30, 2006).

Chua, Amy. *World on Fire: How Exporting Free Market Democracy Breeds Ethnic Hatred and Global Instability.* New York: Anchor Books, 2004.

Dean, Martin. *Collaboration in the Holocaust: Crimes of the Local Police in Belarus and Ukraine, 1941–1944.* New York: St. Martin's Press, 2000.

Drakakhrust, Yury. "Belorusskii natsionalism govorit po-russki." *Belorusskaya Delovaya Gazeta*, January 19, 1998.

———. "Gde konchayetsia Belorussiya?" *Neprikosnovennyi Zapas* 47 (2006): 108–19.

———. "Vayennaya khitrasts." *Arche* 5 (2004): 54.

———. "Velikoye kniazhestvo belorusskoye." *Belorusskiye Novosti*, August 15, 2003, at www.naviny.bu/ru/print/?id=18242.

———. "Zhaneuskaya kanventsiya dlya vainy kul'turau." *Arche* 3 (2004), at Arche .home.by/2004-3/drakachrust304.htm (accessed September 30, 2007).

Eberhardt, Piotr. "The Concept of Boundary between Latin and Byzantine Civilization in Europe." *Przegląd Geograficzny* 76, no. 2 (2004): 169–88.

Feduta, Alexander. *Lukashenko: Politicheskaya biografiya*. Moscow: Referendum, 2005.

Gapova, Elena. "On Nation, Gender, and Class Formation in Belarus . . . and Elsewhere in the Post-Soviet World." *Nationalities Papers* 30, no. 4 (2002): 639–662.

———. "The Nation in Between, or Why Intellectuals Do Things with Words." In *Over the Wall/After the Fall: Post-Communist Cultures through the East-West Gaze*, edited by Sibelan Forrester, Magdalena Zaborowska, and Elena Gapova. Bloomington: Indiana University Press, 2004.

Gellner, Ernest. *Nations and Nationalism*. Ithaca: Cornell University Press, 1983.

Golubovich, V. I., ed. *Ekonomicheskaya istoriya Belarusi*. 3rd ed. Minsk: UP Ecoperspectiva, 2004.

Goujon, Alexandra. "Language, Nationalism, and Populism in Belarus." *Nationalities Papers* 27, no. 4 (1999): 661–77.

Guthier, Steven L. "The Belorussians: National Identification and Assimilation, 1897–1970." *Soviet Studies* 29, no. 1 (1977): 37–61, and no. 2 (1977): 270–83.

H. R. 5948, [109th] Belarus Democracy Reauthorization Act of 2006, at www .govtrack.us/congress/billtext.xpd?bill=h109-5948&page-command (accessed September 30, 2007).

Harvey, David. *A Brief History of Neoliberalism*. New York: Oxford University Press, 2005.

Hroch, Miroslav. *Social Preconditions of National Revival in Europe: A Comparative Analysis of Patriotic Groups among the Smaller European Nations*. 2nd ed. New York: Columbia University Press, 2000.

Huntington, Samuel P. *The Clash of Civilizations*. New York: Simon and Schuster, 1996.

IMF Country Report No. 05/217, June 2005. *Republic of Belarus: Selected Issues*. IMF: Washington, DC, 2005.

Ioffe, Grigory. "Culture Wars, Soul-searching, and Belarusian Identity." *East European Politics and Societies* 21, no. 2 (2007): 348–81.

———. "The Phenomenon of Belarus: A Book Review Essay." *Eurasian Geography and Economics* 5 (2006): 622–34.

———. "Understanding Belarus: Belarusian Identity." *Europe-Asia Studies* 55, no. 8 (2003): 1241–71.

———. "Understanding Belarus: Economy and Political Landscape." *Europe-Asia Studies* 56, no. 1 (2004): 85–118.

———. "Understanding Belarus: Questions of Language." *Europe-Asia Studies* 55, no. 7 (2003): 1009–47.

———. "Unfinished Nation-building in Belarus and the 2006 Presidential Election." *Eurasian Geography and Economics* 48, no. 1 (2007): 37–58.

Ioffe, Grigory, Tatyana Nefedova, and Ilya Zaslavsky. *The End of Peasantry?* Pittsburgh, PA: University of Pittsburgh Press, 2006.

Kaplan, Robert. "Was Democracy Just a Moment?" *The Atlantic Online*, December 1997, at www.theatlantic.com/issues/97dec/democ.htm (accessed May 5, 2007).

Kipel, Vitaut. *Belarusans in the United States*. Lanham, MD: University Press of America, 1999.

Koriakov, Yury. *Yazykovaya situatsiya v Belorussii i tipologiya yazykovykh situatsii*. PhD diss., Moscow State University, 2003.

Korosteleva, Elena A., Colin W. Lawson, and Rosalind Marsh, eds. *Contemporary Belarus: Between Democracy and Dictatorship*. London and New York: Routledge/ Curzon, 2003.

Korosteleva, Julia, and Stephen White. "'Feeling European': The View from Belarus, Russia and Ukraine." *Contemporary Politics* 12, no. 2 (June 2006): 199–205.

Kupala, Janka. *Tuteishiya*. Munich: Vy-va Batskaushchyny, 1953.

Legvold, Robert, and Celleste Wallander, eds. *Swords and Sustenance: The Economics of Security in Belarus and Ukraine*. Cambridge, MA: MIT Press, 2004.

Lewis, Ann, ed. *The EU and Belarus: Between Moscow and Brussels*. London: Federal Trust for Education and Research, 2002.

Lindner, Rainer. "Besieged Past: National and Court Historians in Lukashenka's Belarus." *Nationalities Papers* 27, no. 4 (1999): 631–48.

Loftus, John. *The Belarus Secret*. New York: Alfred A. Knopf, 1982.

Marples, David R. *Belarus: A Denationalized Nation*. Amsterdam: Harwood, 1999.

———. *Belarus from Soviet Rule to Nuclear Catastrophe*. New York: St. Martin's Press, 1996.

———. "Color Revolutions: The Belarus Case." *Communist and Post-Communist Studies* 39, no. 3 (2006): 351–64.

———. "Elections and Nation-Building in Belarus: A Comment on Ioffe." *Eurasian Geography and Economics* 48, no. 1 (2007): 59–67.

———. "Europe's Last Dictatorship: The Roots and Perspectives of Authoritarianism in 'White Russia.'" *Europe-Asia Studies* 57, no. 6 (2005): 895–908.

Matikevich, Vladimir. *Nashestviye*. Moscow, 2004.

Matsuzato, Kamitaka. "A Populist Island in an Ocean of Clan Politics: The Lukashenka Regime as an Exception among CIS Countries." *Europe-Asia Studies* 56, no. 2 (2004): 235–61.

Mečkovskaya, Nina B. *Belorussky yazyk: Sotsiolinguisticheskie ocherki*. Munchen: Verlag Otto Sagner, 2003.

Mikulich, Tatyana M. *Mova i etnichnaya samasviadomasts*. Minsk: Navuka i Technika, 1996.

Natsional'nyi sostav naseleniya Respubliki Belarus i rasprostranionnost' yazykov. Minsk: Ministerstvo Statistiki i Analiza, 2001.

Nosevich, Viacheslav. "Belorusy: Stanovleniye etnosa is 'natsionalnaya ideya.'" In *Belorussiya i Rossiya: Obshchestva i gosudarstva*, 11–30. Moscow: Prava Cheloveka, 1998.

Orlov (Arlou), Vladimir, and Gennadz Saganovich. *Desiat' vekov belorusskoi istorii*. Vilnius: Nasha Buduchynia, 2001.

Pankin, Alexei. "Demos i kratos v Belorussii i v Rossii." *Izvestia*, November 3, 2004, at www.izvestia.ru/comment/629774_print (accessed November 4, 2004).

Putnam, Robert. *Making Democracy Work: Civic Traditions in Modern Italy*. Princeton, NJ: Princeton University Press, 1993.

Rahr, Alexander. "Lukaschenka: Die Opposition ist in Weißrussland keineswegs verboten." *Die Welt*, January 25, 2007, at www.welt.de/data/2007/01/25/1188208.html (accessed February 8, 2007).

"Report on Belarus, the Last Dictatorship in Europe, Including Arms Sales and Leadership Assets." White House Press Release, Office of the Press Secretary, Washington, DC, March 16, 2006.

Rubinov, Anatoly. "Yeschio raz ob ideologii." *Belarus Segodnia*, July 28, 2006.

Ryabchuk, Mykola. *Vid malorossii do ukrayiny*. Kyiv: Kritika, 2000.

Rykiel, Zbigniew. *Podstawy geografii politycznej*. Warsaw: Polskie Wydawnictwo Economiczne, 2006.

Sadowski, Andrzej. *Pogranicze polsko-bialoruskie: Tozsamosc mieskancow*. Bialystok: Trans Humana, 1995.

Sheremet, Pavel, and Svetlana Kalinkina. *Sluchainyi prezident*. St. Petersburg: Limbus Press, 2004.

Shevtsov, Yury. *Obyedinionnaya natsiya: Fenomen Belarusi*. Moscow: Yevropa, 2005.

Shushkevich, Stanislau. *Neo-communism v Belarusi*. Smolensk: Skif, 2002.

Silitski, Vital. "Pamiatats, shto dyktatyry ruinuyutsa." *Arche* 7 (2006), at http://arche.bymedia.net/2006-7/silicki706.htm.

Smith, Anthony D. *The Ethnic Origins of Nations*. 12th ed. London: Blackwell, 1999.

Trubachev, Oleg. *V poiskakh yedinstva: Vzgliad filologa na problemu istokov Rusi*. Moscow: Nauka, 1997.

Tsvikevich, Alexander. *Belarus: Politicheskii ocherk*. Berlin: Izdaniye Diplomaticheskoi Missii BNR, 1919.

———. *Zapadno-russizm: Narysy s gistoryi gramadskai mysli na Belarusi u 19 i pachatku 20 V*. Mensk: Belaruskaya Dziarzavnaye Vydavetstva, 1929.

Tsykhun, Genadz. "Krealizavany produkt: Trasianka yak ab'yekt lingvistychnaga dasledavannia." *Arche* 6 (2000), at http://arche.home.by/6-2000/cychu600.html (accessed May 9, 2003).

Tuathail, Geraóid Ó. (Gerard Toal). "Understanding Critical Geopolitics." *Journal of Strategic Studies* 22, nos. 2/3 (1999): 106–24.

Turonek, Jerzy. *Bialorus pod okupacja niemiecka*. Warsaw: Ksiazka i Wiedza, 1993.

Urban, Michael E. *An Algebra of the Soviet Power: Elite Circulation in the Belorussian Republic, 1966–1986*. New York: Cambridge University Press, 1989.

Vakar, Nicholas. *Belorussia: The Making of a Nation*. Cambridge, MA: Harvard University Press, 1956.

Vishvevsky, A. G. *Serp i rubl*. Moscow: OGI, 1999.

White, Stephen, Elena Korosteleva, and John Lowenhardt, eds. *Post-Communist Belarus*. Lanham, MD: Rowman & Littlefield, 2005.

Woolhiser, Curt. "Constructing National Identities in the Polish-Belarusian Borderlands." *Ab Imperio* (Kazan, Russia) 3 (2003): 293–346.

———. "Language Ideology and Language Conflict in Post-Soviet Belarus." In *Language, Ethnicity and the State*, edited by Camille O'Reilly, vol. 2, 91–122. London and New York: Palgrave, 2001.

———. "Metalinguistic Discourse, Ideology, and 'Language Construction' in the BSSR, 1920–1939," the English original of an article published in French as "Discours sur la langue, idéologie et 'édification linguistique' dans la RSS de Biélorussie, 1920–1939." In *Le discours sur la langue en URSS à l'époque Stalinienne*, edited by Patrick Sériot, 299–337. Cahiers de l'ILSL no. 14. Lausanne: University of Lausanne, 2003.

Yarashevich, Viachaslau. *Political Economy of Modern Belarus in the Context of Post-Socialist Transformation Discourse.* PhD diss., University of Kingston, Kingston-upon-Thames, United Kingdom, 2006.

Yermalovich, Mikola I. *Pa sliadakh adnago mifa.* Minsk: Belaruskaya Navuka, 2002.

Zaprudnik, Jan. *Belarus at a Crossroads in History.* Boulder, CO: Westview Press, 1993.

Zarzycky, Tomasz. "Uses of Russia: The Role of Russia in the Modern Polish National Identity." *East European Politics and Societies* 18, no. 2 (2004): 1–33.

Zen'kovich, Nikolai. *Tainy ukhodiashchego veka.* Moscow: Olma Press, 2000.

Index

Abushenka, Uladzimer, 90
Adamkus, Valdas, 149
Adamovich, Ales, 22, 138
Adradzhennye (Belarusian Revival), 81,
    92, 95. *See also* national
    awakening/revival
agitprop: American foreign policy, 146;
    Western, 137, 148
agriculture, 105, 109, 125
Akudovich, Valyantsyn, xx, 1, 28,
    95–96, 100, 203–4, 222
Alexievich, Svetlana, 84, 87, 88, 212,
    227n46
All-Belarusian Convention, 171, 195,
    216
Arche (journal), 38, 69n4, 80–85, 88,
    95, 222
Arlou (Orlov), Uladzimer, 19, 25, 26,
    28, 41, 66–67, 81
Armia Krajowa, 60
Astrousky, Radaslau, 58, 91
Aven, Piotr, 139–40, 143

Babkou (Bobkov), Igar, 81, 90, 222
Baranovichi (Belarusian city), 11, 177
Belarus: cities in, xvii, 2, 15; eastern,
    2, 15, 16, 18, 60, 107–9, 138;
    economic model, xiv, 124, 125, 129;

economy, subsidization of, 93,
    120–21, 124–25, 128, 172; ethnicity
    in, 38, 45, 61, 138; as "Europe's last
    dictatorship," xii, xviii, 146, 238,
    239; KGB (Committee for State
    Security) of, 32, 173, 174, 193, 195;
    mentality in, 155, 185; national idea
    of, xvi, 46, 47, 68, 80, 98, 100,
    101n3; national symbols of, xix, 18,
    37, 61–64, 68, 82, 208, 233–35,
    238; post-Soviet, 2, 189n10, 233,
    236; statehood of, xiv, xix, 68, 79,
    85, 94, 97, 100, 160, 170, 185, 186,
    224, 235, 237; television in, 3, 11,
    195; western, 2, 5, 16, 17, 18, 31,
    41, 53, 57, 63, 109, 120, 126, 138,
    147, 167, 170, 179; writers in, 14,
    19, 20, 22, 44. *See also*
    Belarusianness; Belarusification;
    ethnic Belarusians; nationalism,
    Belarusian; Soviet Belarus
Belarus Democracy Act, xii, xviii, 111,
    129, 171, 231, 238, 241. *See also*
    democracy; National Endowment for
    Democracy
Belarusian (language):
    dialects/vernaculars of, 1, 5, 14,
    16–18, 43; as a language of

broadcasting, 3, 11, 85–89; as a language of instruction/schooling, 3, 9, 10, 17, 19, 22, 36n134, 44, 46, 52, 60, 209; as a language of publications, 1, 2, 11, 14–16, 19–21, 23, 31n6, 38, 45, 46, 51, 83, 151, 153, 222; as native language, 3, 15, 17, 235; as official language, xx, 2, 16, 23; reform of, 16, 17; as a Slavic language, 1, 30; speakers of, 5, 8, 11, 15–17, 26, 28, 30, 44, 49, 52, 53, 79, 81, 85, 94, 157, 200, 212, 221; spread of and use in everyday life, 4–5, 7–8, 15–16, 22, 24, 26–28, 233, 235; as a standard language (of literary norm), 1–3, 5–6, 15, 17, 19, 29–30, 233; theaters in, 4, 21, 78. *See also* Belarusian Service of Radio Liberty

Belarusianness, 47, 49, 57, 93, 98

Belarusian People's Republic (BPR), 57–58, 68, 224

Belarusian Popular Front (Belarusky Narodny Front, BNF), xvi, 24, 45, 64, 81, 92, 152, 179, 197, 209, 211, 212, 217

Belarusian Service of Radio Liberty, 59, 84, 112, 151, 152, 177, 188, 195

Belarusian State University, 16, 195, 212

Belarusification, 10, 13, 15–17, 19, 24–25, 27, 30, 34n83, 57, 65, 81, 85, 95, 152, 221

Belarus-Russia union, 79, 121, 123, 125, 147, 149, 156, 158, 165, 185, 194

Belarus Segodnia (daily), 11, 211, 212, 216

Belaz (super-heavy trucks), 116

Belorussian Soviet Socialist Republic (BSSR), xiii, xiv, 2, 18–20, 23, 41, 57, 85, 92. *See also* Soviet Belarus

Beltransgaz, 118, 119, 121, 122, 159, 160

Berdiaev, Nikolai, 136–37

Bialystok (city in Poland), 41, 46, 48–52, 74n109

BNF. *See* Belarusian Popular Front

Boguševič, Frantsyšek, 43, 47

borderland, 8, 38, 41, 47, 49, 53

Borodin, Pavel, 159

BPR (Belarusian People's Republic), 57–58, 68, 224

Breault, Yann, 37, 153

Brest (city in Belarus), xx, 68, 70n16, 74n109, 91, 92, 100, 109, 128, 156

Brussels, 12, 187, 236

BSSR. *See* Belorussian Soviet Socialist Republic

Budinas, Yevgenii, 138–39

Bukchin, Semion, 83–84

Bulgakau, Valer, 38, 69n4, 81, 82, 86, 90, 222, 228n74

Bush, George W., xii, 129, 148, 171–72, 188, 191n40, 232, 239

Bykau (Bykov), Vasil, 2, 21, 47

Byzantine civilization, 98, 99

Catholic Church, 39, 44, 47, 48, 50, 65, 70n15, 212. *See also kościół*

Catholics, 14, 15, 38, 44, 47, 48, 51, 53, 54, 67, 137, 211; and anti-imperial ethos, 90; background/roots of, 16, 39, 45, 53, 91; priests, 39, 48

census: 1897 Russian, 15, 51, 71n49; 1959 Soviet, 2; 1989 Soviet, 50; 1999 Belarusian, 3, 6, 29, 50, 52, 56, 82; Polish, 50

Central Intelligence Agency, 239

central planning, 234, 236

Central Rada, 58

chauvinism, 57

Cheney, Richard, 149, 232

Chernobyl, xv, 144, 147, 150, 177, 184, 195, 198

China, 116, 118, 200, 201

Chua, Amy, 140–41

Chubais, Anatoly, 140, 178, 182–83

CIS. *See* Commonwealth of Independent States

cleft country (versus torn country), 100, 235
cold war, xvi, 59, 92, 129, 136, 200, 240
collective farm, 31n21, 120, 176, 213
collectivism, 136, 138. *See also* communalism
Commonwealth of Independent States (CIS), 65, 108, 112–16, 139, 154
communal ethos, 91, 93, 136, 168
communalism, 99, 138, 144, 155, 161, 189. *See also* collectivism
communism, 136, 137, 144
Communist Party, xviii, 12, 16, 20, 22, 107, 146, 152, 176, 179, 209
constitution, 9, 24, 147, 171, 172, 175, 187, 209
Constitutional Act of the Russia-Belarus Union, 121, 123, 157, 158, 160
constitutional referendum, 147, 209. *See also* referendum
corruption, 57, 97, 111–12, 141–43, 145, 159, 170, 174, 182, 196, 198–99, 212
Creoles, 89–97. *See also* national projects
Cyrillic, 1, 2, 15, 27, 44
Czechs, 21, 30, 42, 43, 97, 201
Czeczot, Jan, 43

Danilovich, Alex, 158
Dashkevich, Valery, 127
democracy: attitude toward, 54, 83; becoming a, 235; building, 219; concern for, 149; deviation from, 232; emphasis on, 182, 198; as an impish term/swear word, 142, 233; lacking, 142, 164, 203; as an obscure goal, 139; pre-empting, 222; pro-, 83, 87; promotion of, 127, 238; prospects for, 100; spreading, xii, xix, 237, 239, 240; Western funds for, 224; Western-style, 188, 234. *See also* Belarus Democracy Act; National Endowment for Democracy
Deutsche Welle, 86–89, 211

dictatorship, xii, xvi, xviii, 67, 146–53, 171, 218, 219, 232, 234, 238, 239
double standard, 232
Drakakhrust (Drakokhrust), Yury, xx, xxii, 24, 67, 83–88, 97–98, 100, 102n24, 204, 205, 214, 222
Dunin-Marcinkiewicz, Vincent, 43
Dynko, Andrei, xii, 81, 82, 88–90, 186–87, 222
Dzierzynski, Felix, 11, 69n10

East Prussia (Kaliningrad Oblast), 61
Eberhardt, Piotr, 98, 99
EBRD (European Bank for Reconstruction and Development), 126
economic growth, xiv, xvi, 110–13, 115, 117, 126, 129, 171, 188, 189, 206, 214, 234–36
elections, xix, xx, 7, 8, 24, 100, 128, 139, 146–47, 158–60, 171, 175–76, 181, 185, 188, 193, 195, 197, 200, 203, 205–22, 223, 233, 242n28
elite: bias against, 154; business/economic, 128, 143, 161; colonial, 186; cultural, 18, 27, 68, 95; imperial, 38; intellectual, 18, 135; liberal arts, 27; local, 177; versus masses, 110, 142, 162n6, 214; members of the, 95; national, 16, 19, 20; nationalist, 19; ruling (political), xiii, xiv, 110, 121, 128, 129, 145, 154, 156–57, 159–60, 164n37, 167, 212; Russian, 143, 161; Russified, 187; social, 89
emigration, 58, 81
energy, 93, 113, 121, 129, 136, 149, 160, 172, 186, 189, 235
engineering, mechanical, 107, 108, 117
enterprises, xvii, 12, 105, 107–10, 113, 116, 119, 121, 125–26, 173, 197, 220
equality, 162
equity, 114, 138, 236
ethnic Belarusians, xix, 2–3, 11, 15–16, 19, 42, 45, 56, 107, 138. *See also* Belarus

ethnic group, 13, 21, 38, 41, 42, 49, 52, 54, 61, 80, 98, 234. *See also* ethnicity

ethnicity, 3, 24, 38, 41, 44, 45, 50, 61, 62, 80, 81, 138, 211, 237. *See also* ethnic group

European Bank for Reconstruction and Development (EBRD), 126

European Union, xiii, 50, 85, 117, 152, 161, 187, 200, 235, 236

exports, xx, 70n17, 94, 107–8, 113, 115–18, 122, 124, 174, 187

falsifications, xvi, xix, 217, 227n60

Federal Security Service (FSB; of Russia), 174, 190n25

Feduta, Alexander, xxii, 36n139, 84, 87, 93, 152, 174, 179–85

Filaret (Orthodox supreme leader of Belarus), 39, 70nn16–17, 152

foreign policy, xi, xiii, 146, 212, 224, 231, 233, 239–41

FSB. *See* Federal Security Service

Gaidar, Yegor, 121, 139–40

Gallup (institution), 209–10, 220

Gapova, Elena, 148, 176–78

Gazprom (Russian company), 118–22, 183

GDP. *See* gross domestic product

geopolitics, 40, 86, 149, 231, 239, 240; agenda and, 233; catastrophe and, 182; expectations and, 240; leaning/orientation and, 93, 160, 203, 205, 224; niche and, 47; rationale and, 240; school of thought, 121; strategy and, 240

German Democratic Republic (GDR), 128, 144

give-and-take scheme, 123

gmina (civil subdivision), 51–52

Gomel (city in Belarus), xx, 6, 16, 17, 25, 26, 74n109, 106, 107, 108, 150, 182, 221

Gorbachev, Mikhail, 5, 10, 61, 63, 126, 139, 179

Grazhdanka (script), 44, 46

Great Patriotic War, 61, 67, 97. *See also* World War II

Greek Catholics. *See* Uniate Church

Grodno (city in Belarus), xx, 3, 4, 7, 14, 24, 31n21, 41, 46, 52, 53, 98, 100, 105, 108, 109, 179, 209, 211, 221

gross domestic product (GDP), 110, 112–15, 117, 119–20, 124, 126–27

guerillas, 56, 61, 63. *See also* partisans

Guthier, Steven, 15, 16, 19

Hajnówka (city in Poland), 51–52

Hebrew (language), 45

Hill, Ronald, xix, 167

Hroch, Miroslav, xx, 10, 38, 42, 62, 98

Huntington, Samuel P., 81, 98–100

Hussein, Saddam, 142, 239

identity: Belarusian, xii–xvi, 12, 37–38, 40, 43, 47, 56, 61–62, 65, 68, 77, 80, 98, 100, 235; blurred/weak, 39, 42, 154; civilizational, 93, 121; collective/shared, 40, 41, 42, 49, 65; dimensions of, 98; emerging, 237; ethnic, xix, xx, 40, 42, 49; formational, 124, 125, 127; insight into, 54; manifestation/token of, 61, 80; national, xxii, 37, 78, 81, 138, 208, 214, 234; Polish, 73n90, 162n15; religion and, 38–39; seeking, 81; separate, 38, 43, 135, 205; split-identity disorder, 68

IISEPS. *See* Independent Institute of Socio-Economic and Political Studies

IMF (International Monetary Fund), xix, 112, 185

immigration card, 156

importers, 110, 117

imports, 115, 116, 118, 121, 132

income disparity, 142, 171. *See also* inequality

incorporation, 15, 72n72, 121, 125, 128, 138, 236

independence, 11, 30, 67, 79, 81, 85, 90,
94, 98, 110, 161, 184, 188, 196, 198,
199, 214, 233, 238
Independent Institute of Socio-
Economic and Political Studies
(IISEPS), 7, 8, 10, 32n43, 79, 83, 84,
114, 193, 196, 198–99, 201–3, 205–7,
210, 213–15, 218, 219
inequality, 112, 136, 202. *See also*
income disparity
integration, 24, 158, 159, 161, 186, 203.
See also reintegration
International Monetary Fund (IMF), xix,
112, 185
investments, 106, 113, 119–20, 125,
171, 231
Iraq, xii, xiii, 142, 219, 239, 240
"iron curtain," 200
Ivashkevich, Victar, 97, 217–18
Izvestia (newspaper), 11, 169

Japan, 120, 148, 154, 181
Jews, xvii, xxivn38, 16, 19, 34n70, 42,
44, 45, 59, 71n49, 77, 91, 103, 138,
174, 175, 202

Kaliningrad, 61
Kalinkina, Svetlana, 175–79, 190n28
Kalinowski, Konstanty (Kastus), 46,
191
Kalinowski Square, 216, 222
Kaplan, Robert, 142
Karbalevich, Valery, 64
Karski, Yevfimii, 1, 13, 15, 17, 46, 47,
72n59, 73n105
Kazaniecki, Pawel, 216
Kaznacheyev, Vadim, 88
Kebich, Viacheslav, 175, 177, 179
Kiev, 64, 152, 217
Kievan Rus, 155
Kolas, Jakub, 2
Komsomolskaya Pravda v Belarusi
(daily), 83
Konoplev, Vladimir, 184
Koriakov, Yury, 18, 19

Korosteleva, Elena, xiv
Korosteleva, Julia, 204
kosciól, 39, 51, 78. *See also* Catholic
Church
Koyalovich, Mikhail, 46
Kozulin, Alexander, 8, 147, 195,
212–13, 215–16, 218–21, 223
Kresy Wschodnie (Poland's eastern
periphery), 14, 53, 78
Kristol, William, 239
Kuchma, Leonid, 199
Kupala, Janka, 2, 54, 77, 78, 92, 212
Kupala Theater, 3, 4, 21, 77
Kyrgyzstan, 199, 201

land reclamation, 109
language reform, 16, 17, 27
Latin America, 116, 154, 187
Latin civilization, 99
Latin script (Lacinka), 1, 15, 27, 43, 44,
46, 47
Latypov, Ural, 174
Lebedko, Anatoly, 152, 224
Lenin, Vladimir, 11, 57
Leningrad, 107
Leninism, 57
Lindner, Rainer, 64, 66, 168
Lithuania: authorities of, 45; border of,
4, 8; consulate of, 150; culture of, 44;
Grand Duchy of, xiv, 1, 13, 21, 23,
42, 43, 54, 56, 57, 63, 67, 68, 81,
208, 210; language of, 21; modern
state of, xx, 4, 12, 30, 32n43, 41, 42,
44, 48, 50, 54, 79, 108, 111, 118, 149,
151, 186, 193, 201; peasants of, 54;
people of, 42, 43, 71n49, 202; state
of, 44
Litvin, Vladimir, 188
Lukashenka, Alexander:
accomplishments of, 11, 128, 143,
172, 173, 174, 187, 217, 238; ascent
to power of, 111, 147, 170–71, 206;
attitude to the Belarusian language,
32n35, 94; as autocrat, 29, 172, 219,
236; as Batska ("father"), 125, 168;

electorate against, 82, 83, 85, 97, 119, 171, 177, 197; extracting concessions from, 123, 160; hometown of, 5; humble origins of, 183, 188, 210; inauguration of, 177; as leader of national project, 89, 90, 94, 96, 100, 186, 238; personality and medical record of, 173, 174, 178, 180; policy and politics, 126, 145, 151, 158, 161, 169, 172, 181, 187, 212, 215, 222; political instinct of, 181, 183; popularity/standing/reputation of, 90, 129, 158, 168, 170, 171, 184, 188, 199, 206, 213–15, 219; as president, xii, xiii, 29, 79, 95, 121, 128, 144, 152, 157, 174, 175, 187, 189, 232, 235; pronouncements of, 25, 79, 146, 149, 155, 156, 157, 159, 171, 183, 195, 204, 212; reflecting popular aspirations, xiv, 97, 169, 178, 184, 187, 188, 193, 214, 220, 236; regime of, xix, 29, 83, 84, 85, 90, 96, 146, 147, 148, 153, 174, 193, 236; relationship with Putin, 79, 159, 214; relatives and personal life, 169, 175, 213; as skilled, charismatic speaker, 6, 25, 26, 39, 91–93, 167, 175, 176, 181–83, 210, 212; as Soviet man, 210; spelling name of, xx; style and mannerisms of, 97, 154, 159, 168, 169; support and vote for, electoral victories, 8, 24, 111, 138, 152, 160, 153, 167, 175, 179, 184, 187, 199, 206–8, 210, 213, 215, 217, 220, 221, 223, 227n60
Lukashuk, Alexander, 188

Maksymiuk, Jan, 167, 217
Maldis, Adam, 21–22, 27
Manayev, Oleg, 32n43, 177, 193–94
Marcus, Ustina, 9
market: economy, xvi, xix, 91, 100, 112, 125, 138, 139, 141; farmer's, 19; foreign, 113, 171; fundamentalism, 126; minority dominated by, 140–42,

161, 206; paragons, 127; prices, 122; provincial, 112; pure, 154; raw, 161; reform, 124, 138, 144; Russian, 92; transition, 126
Markov, Sergey, 41, 54
Marples, David, xv, xvi, xviii, xxii, 4, 9, 14, 17, 62, 147, 167, 189
marshes, 109
Marx, Karl, 35n88, 78, 80, 136, 241
Marxism, 135–37
Masherov, Piotr, 20
Masherova, Natalya, 185
Matikevich, Vladimir, 173
Matskevich, Vladimir, 220
Matsuzato, Kamitaka, 154–55
Mazurov, Kirill, 20
Mečkovskaya, Nina, 40, 45
mentality, 49, 54, 137, 139, 155, 185, 205
Mickiewicz, Adam, 22, 91, 100
migration, 5, 12, 16, 19, 115
Milinkevich, Alexander, 8, 82, 152, 10–13, 215–21, 223–25
Milošević, Slobodan, 220
Minsk, xi, xiv, xv, xvii, xx, 2–12, 14–20, 24–29, 37, 40, 60–61, 63, 67–68, 77–79, 81, 83, 86, 89, 98–99, 105–10, 116, 129, 135, 147–51, 155–57, 171, 174, 176, 179, 182, 185–87, 189n10, 193, 195, 207, 209, 214, 218, 221, 223, 232–33, 240
mixed economy, 125
Mogilev (city in Belarus), xx, 15, 25, 100, 105, 107, 108, 111, 175, 221
Moscow, xiii, xvii, xviii, 11, 20, 22, 23, 28, 40, 42, 48, 57, 61, 64, 67, 68, 87, 88, 106, 107, 116, 117, 137, 138, 139, 142, 150, 156, 158, 173, 185, 187, 190n22, 206, 209, 210, 214, 223, 236
Moskovsky Komsomolets (Russian daily), 169, 171
mother tongue, 8, 29, 235. *See also* native language
Motyl, Alexander, 23

Mozyr (city in Belarus), xvii, 60, 107, 108, 116
Muscovite Liberals, 82, 85, 88, 94, 96
Muscovites, 139, 140

Narkomauka (orthography), xx, 216, 217
Nasha Niva (newspaper), 17, 23, 43, 44, 46, 81, 82, 83, 88, 89, 95, 151, 186, 211
Nasha Slova (newspaper), 23
national awakening/revival, 9, 96, 237
National Endowment for Democracy, 87, 153, 222, 236
nationalism, Belarusian: Catholic roots of, 65; fragile nature of, 47; golden age of, 15; multifaceted nature of, 68, 79, 85; versus older nationalisms, 38, 40; pendulum effect within, 45–49; role of Vilna, 44–45; Russian-speaking, 83; Westernizing/anti-Russian strand of, 53, 58, 60, 73n103, 83, 84, 238. *See also* national movement, Belarusian; national projects
national movement, Belarusian, xix, 15, 16, 19, 47–49, 58, 62, 66, 72n72. *See also* nationalism, Belarusian
national projects, 79–82, 87, 89, 94, 96, 164n37, 205, 211
National Socialism, xvii
nation building, xiv, xvi, xix, xx, 77, 95, 172, 228n74, 235, 237
native language, 3, 4, 10, 13, 15–18, 25, 37, 45, 50, 157, 233, 234. *See also* mother tongue
nativist, 81–85, 87, 88, 90–92, 94–96, 186, 205, 222, 240
NATO. *See* North Atlantic Treaty Organization
natsdems (national democrats), 57, 58
natural gas, 79, 93, 94, 113, 117–19, 122, 124, 132n56, 170, 214
Nazi collaborators, Belarusian, xvii, 58–62, 74, 58–62, 74n129, 103n51

Nemtsov, Boris, 175
neoliberalism, xiv, 121, 126–28, 161–62, 236
Netherlands, 117, 118
New Russians, 142–43
Nikoliuk, Sergei, 138
NKVD (secret police organization), 18
non-Western world, xii, 141, 142
North Atlantic Treaty Organization (NATO), 171, 200, 201, 203, 208, 240
Nosevich, Viacheslav, 80
Novopolotsk (city in Belarus), 107, 108
NPZ (Russian abbreviation for oil refinery), 107, 108, 116. *See also* oil refinery
Nuti, Mario, xiv, 114

oil, xii, 94, 106, 108, 110, 113, 114, 116–19, 122–25, 128–29, 143–44, 149–50, 158, 161, 183, 186, 197, 232, 239. *See also* petrochemicals
oil refinery, 107, 108, 116, 123, 124. *See also* NPZ
Okara, Andrei, 64, 65, 168
oligarchs, 122–24, 126, 141–42, 151, 159, 161, 197
opposition: activities/think tanks/scholars, 26, 32n43, 86, 112, 118, 125, 147, 148, 150, 151, 187, 193, 215, 218, 222, 236; Belarusian-speaking, 94, 221; congress of the united, 209, 211, 224; as heirs of the Grand Duchy, 54; leaders of, 21, 82, 197, 208, 216, 222–24; Lukashenka regime's stance toward, xiii, 150, 206, 217, 237; marginalized, beset by feuds, 233, 236; media of, 25, 32n35, 63, 79, 80, 83, 89, 97, 152, 175, 180, 181; members of, 27, 41, 160, 167, 170, 175, 186, 191n42, 218, 221, 235; "mentally sound," 169; opinions/worldview of, 138, 184, 194, 208, 218; parties, 152, 209, 233; presidential candidates from, 82, 152,

206–10, 213, 220, 224; relative standing of, 9, 79, 149, 177, 196, 197, 217, 221, 222, 225; Russian, 158; to Russia or Poland, 43, 45, 94; website of, 151, 209; Western support of, 199, 210, 212, 227n60, 236

orange revolution, 129, 160, 197, 199, 202, 203, 216, 220, 224

Organization for Security and Cooperation in Europe (OSCE), 97, 149, 188, 221

Orthodoxy, 14, 15, 38, 39, 44–48, 50–51, 53–54, 57, 65, 68, 69n10, 78, 92, 98, 152, 168, 211

OSCE. *See* Organization for Security and Cooperation in Europe

Pankin, Andrei, 97

Parliamentary Assembly of Europe, 149, 210

partisans, xiv, xvi, 59, 60, 63, 74n129. *See also* guerillas

passports, 24, 26, 41, 45, 49, 52, 56, 73n90, 90, 150, 156, 182

pauperization, 198

Pawluczuk, Wlodzimierz, 65

Pazniak, Zianon, 61, 64–66, 81–83, 169, 179, 197, 222, 228n74

peasantry: Belarusian, 14, 53, 67; local, 53; Orthodox, 46; Russian, 136, 137

peasants: being born as, 97, 176, 181, 183, 210; communes, 137–39, 144, 155, 161; farming of, 109; Lithuanian, 54; lives of, 45, 169; masses, 38, 42, 44, 135, 136; values of, 65, 120, 136, 138, 162n6, 168, 188; vernacular of, 14, 16, 21

perestroika, 61, 63, 138, 175, 179

Pesniary (rock group), 63

petrochemicals, 107, 108, 109, 159

Platonov, Andrei, 136

Podlaskie (Voivodship of Poland), 50–52

Poland, xx, 9, 14, 15, 16, 18, 26, 39, 41, 44, 45, 46–49, 50–53, 57, 64, 70n15,

71n58, 73n89, 78, 79, 92, 108, 111, 116, 118, 125, 128, 129, 148, 150, 162n15, 224, 186, 187, 197, 200, 201, 205, 210, 224; border with Belarus, 52, 176; people of, xv, 13, 26, 38, 40, 42–50, 52–56, 58, 60, 69n12, 71n49, 73n89, 73n90, 77, 138, 162n15, 177, 200, 202, 212; and Polishness, 44, 46, 48, 70n28, 212; rebellions and uprisings, 14, 216; *See also* Rzeczpospolita

Polesie (southern Belarus), 42, 109

political activists, xviii

Polonism, 17, 46, 48

Polonization, 43, 48, 50, 51, 53, 67, 72n72

Polotsk (city in Belarus), 28, 67

populism, 154

potassium, 108, 116, 117, 144

poverty, 92, 112, 126

powiat (civil division), 51, 52

Pravda (Russian daily), 11, 17

prices: of Beltransgaz, 119, 122; of energy supplies, 160, 172, 189; hikes of, 124, 158, 196, 198; liberalization of, 126; of natural gas, 93, 94, 110, 118, 122, 132n56, 170, 186; of oil, 110, 114, 116, 117, 122, 124, 186

Primakov, Yevgeny, 181

Pripet River, 109

privatization, 92, 110, 111, 114, 125–27, 139, 143, 145–46, 158, 182–83, 189, 236

propaganda, 11, 15, 18, 143, 145, 150, 184, 195, 211, 214, 222, 235

Pushkin, Alexander, 92, 142, 145, 180

Putin, Vladimir, 79, 97, 121, 124, 156, 158, 159, 161, 162n10, 170, 178, 182, 187, 204, 214, 233

Putnam, Robert, 141

Puzinovsky, Mikhas, 8–10

referendum: in an authoritarian country, 64; falsification, 227n60; idea of, 25; of 1995, 2, 9, 24, 26, 64; of 1996,

147; of 2004, 171, 172, 209; possible, 85

Rehak, Lubomir, 232

reintegration, 156–60. *See also* integration

Riasanovsky, Nicholas, 142

Rice, Condoleezza, 217

Romanchuk, Yaroslaw, 112, 124, 125

Rubinov, Anatoly, 90, 92, 145

Russia: affinity between Belarus and, 161, 201; and anti-Russian sentiment, 53, 67, 81, 93, 94, 210, 240; budget of, 117, 120, 123; culture of, xix, 17, 46, 56, 73n103, 83, 95, 100, 233; dependency on, 113, 128, 200; detaching Belarus from, 66, 68, 92, 93, 155, 184, 188, 204, 205, 234, 238; differences from, 154, 155, 157; economic growth in, 110, 113, 115; empire of, 21, 42, 65, 68, 72n72; exports to, 116, 118; federation of, 106, 186; government of, 44, 117, 125; imperial tradition of, 161, 178; import from, 92, 110, 116–18; incorporation into, 7, 9, 94, 125, 128; influence of on Belarus, xv, 87, 92, 160; inherently undemocratic, 82, 234; as integral to Belarusians' mental map, 204–5; leaders of, 145, 146, 169, 208, 212; leaning toward, xvi, 53, 54, 64, 85, 93, 98, 203, 238; military of, 67, 92, 109; monarchs/tsars and, 40, 154; national core (center) of, 49, 80; nationalism and, 40, 91; and non-Russians, 3, 12, 23, 61, 149; oil and, 116, 117, 122–24, 186; oligarchs and, 123, 124, 141, 142, 159, 161; Orthodox Church of, 39, 45–48, 57, 78; and peasantry, 136, 168; political establishment of, 97, 157, 161, 181; privatization in, 139–44, 182; provinces/regions of, 41, 120, 137; relations with Poland, 40, 45, 47, 48, 57; and Russian as ethnonym and/or

nationality, 12, 13, 16, 20, 21, 37, 38, 40, 42, 47, 49, 54, 56, 60, 63, 65, 67, 77, 78, 82, 83, 89, 121, 140–42, 146, 155–57, 162n11, 201, 202, 204, 208, 233–35; scholars/analysts/experts of, 14, 40, 41, 54, 120, 121, 124, 125, 135; society of, 54, 140; style in, 114, 125, 161, 189; television in, 151, 185, 195, 208, 214; ties/relationships with, xv, xvi, xix, 66, 83, 90, 93, 109, 111, 113, 125, 127, 129, 161–62, 182, 185, 201–2, 206, 212, 233, 236; trade war with, 121–24, 128–29, 149, 156, 158, 203, 224–25; trade with, 116, 116, 120; transit from, 106, 108, 117, 128; tsarist, 9, 21; as unfinished old foe, xviii; unification with, 78, 85, 93, 102, 159, 161, 170, 234, 235, 240; urbanization of, 136–37; war against, 56, 67, 81, 91. *See also* Russianness; Russification

Russian (language), xvi, xix, xx, 1–29, 31n21, 34n70, 34n84, 37, 39, 47, 52, 53, 60, 63, 64, 66, 78, 82–90, 94, 95, 96, 151, 173, 175, 178, 188, 190n24, 193, 195, 210–12, 221, 233–35; literature in, xvii, 179; publications/media in, xx, 11, 20, 83, 102n24, 111, 114, 143, 151, 169, 171, 182, 183, 185, 190n22, 215, 240

Russianness, 43, 46, 48

Russicisms, 23, 46

Russification, xv, 5, 11–13, 18, 20, 21, 29, 30, 46, 53, 64

Rzeczpospolita (Poland), 9, 65, 67, 81, 92, 160, 211. *See also* Poland

Sadowski, Andrzej, 49, 50, 52, 53

safety net, 127, 189, 236

Security Council, 223

Sevyarynets, Paval, 197–98

Sheiman, Victor, 174, 178, 190n26

Sheremet, Pavel, 175, 177–79

Shevtsov, Yury, 61, 80, 93, 98, 153, 169, 172

Shimov, Yaroslav, 148, 153

Shkialionek, Mikola, 48

shock therapy, 126, 140

Shushkevich, Stanislau, xi, 9, 25, 39, 63, 110, 154, 181, 197, 220

Shybeko (Szybeka), Zakhar, 45, 60

Silitski, Vital, 87, 96, 153, 193, 222, 228n74

Simes, Dimitri, 240

Sinitsyn, Leonid, 185–86

Skulski, Leopold, 53

Slavophiles, 56

Smith, Anthony David, xix, 38, 40, 54, 62, 66, 237

Sokolov, Maxim, 169

Soviet Belarus, 1, 2, 15, 21, 24, 50, 61, 63, 64, 74n109, 97, 109. *See also* Belorussian Soviet Socialist Republic

Soviet Union/USSR, xii, xiv, xvi, xvii, xviii, 12, 13, 22, 30, 35n97, 58, 63–65, 68, 80, 91, 92, 97, 106, 107, 109, 110, 115, 135–39, 142, 157, 160, 176, 179, 181, 182, 204, 231, 234, 236, 237

spatiality, 34n74, 40, 52, 53, 54, 85, 172, 204, 205, 221

Spengler, Oswald, 136

Stalin, Joseph, xvii, 19, 59, 60, 63, 80, 136, 146, 148, 188

Stalinism, xvii, 58–61

stratification, 114, 126, 236

Sukhorenko, Stepan, 195

Suvorov, Alexander, 68

Tarashkevitsa (orthography), xx, 2, 6, 23, 27

Taraškievič, Branislau, 1, 2, 18, 46, 71n54

tariffs, 94, 117, 122–24, 177

TBM (Belarusian Language Society), 2, 3, 8, 10, 11, 23, 24, 28

television sets, 106, 108, 109, 113, 116

Tereshkovich, L. V., 48

terrorism, 79, 170, 195

TI (Transparency International), 111

torn country (versus cleft country), 100

tractors, xv, 63, 106, 107, 113, 116, 119, 124, 211

transition (economic, post-Communist), 110, 113, 125–27, 139, 144, 158, 161

Transparency International (TI), 111

trasianka (language), 2, 4, 5, 7, 8, 19, 90, 183, 188, 210, 221

travel abroad, 146, 150

travel sanctions, 187, 189n10

trucks, 11, 63, 106, 107, 108, 113, 116, 209

Trusau, Aleh, 2, 6, 28, 138

trust, xii, 143, 187, 225, 233

Tsvikevich, Alexander, 44, 46, 47, 73n97

Turonek, Jerzy (Yury), 58, 60–61

tuteishiya (locals), 41, 77, 78

Tuteishiya (play by Janka Kupala), 54, 70n28, 77, 78

Ukraine, xx, 6, 13, 19, 23, 39, 50, 61, 64, 65, 74n109, 85, 100, 101n5, 106–09, 111, 113–16, 118, 130n8, 132n56, 141, 150, 154–55, 160, 186, 197, 199, 201–4, 216, 220, 224, 236; people of, 25, 89, 90, 202–4

Ukrainian (language), 1, 4, 5, 12, 13, 17, 25, 65, 80, 89, 90, 108, 111, 155, 188, 189, 212

UN. *See* United Nations

Uniate Church, 14, 38–39, 45, 48, 67, 69n10

union state, 157–60

United Kingdom, 117, 118

United Nations (UN), 1, 114, 115, 144, 223, 232

United States, xvii, 64, 99, 118, 127, 137, 141, 159, 186–88, 189n10, 202, 221, 231, 236, 240

Urban, Michael, xiii–xiv

urban areas, 3, 15, 30, 38, 43, 137

urbanites, 3, 4, 7, 16, 18, 19, 26, 41, 42, 82, 84, 137

urbanization, 42, 43, 135–37, 154, 176
urban population, 16, 137
USSR. *See* Soviet Union

Vakar, Nicholas, xiii, 17, 18, 50, 58, 66, 13
Viachiorka, Vintsuk, 82, 152, 225
Vilna (Wilno, Vilnius), 8, 14, 15, 17, 18, 23, 43, 44, 45, 58, 66, 69, 71n49, 151
Vinnikova, Tamara, 172, 177, 190n16
Vishnevsky, Anatoly, 135–36
Vitebsk (city in Belarus), xx, 7, 16, 17, 45, 46, 69, 98, 100, 105–7, 197
Voslensky, Mikhail, 135

Wałęsa, Lech, 224
weaponry, 174, 177
weapons of mass destruction (WMD), xii, 239
Western Europe, 40, 108, 113, 137, 145, 155
Western grants, 151, 212, 227n60
westernizers, 56, 57, 60–63, 65, 68, 73n103, 137, 139
Western sponsors, 150, 206, 209, 218, 227
Western world, xi, xiii, 2, 54, 59, 61, 63, 65, 85, 92, 98, 99, 100, 103, 103n51, 106, 110, 116, 118, 120, 121, 123, 137, 141, 145, 148, 150, 153, 160, 162n11, 169, 171, 172, 174, 182, 187, 188, 198, 200, 206, 212, 217, 220, 223, 232, 233, 237, 238, 240

West-Rusism, 46, 48, 57, 60, 61, 68, 73n97
White, Stephen, xiv, 204
White House, 232
white-red-white flag, 57, 58, 64, 78, 101n3, 176, 208
White Russia, 40
WMD (weapons of mass destruction), xii, 239
Woolhiser, Curt, xxii, 16, 41, 46
World Bank, xiv, xix, 96, 112, 144, 185
World War II, 11, 60, 91, 106, 138. *See also* Great Patriotic War

xenophobia, 86, 211

Yakovlev, Alexander, 175
Yakubovich, Pavel, 90, 174, 212
Yamal-Europe pipeline, 118, 120, 124
Yanukovich, Victor, 203
Yeltsin, Boris, 63, 121, 139, 140, 157, 158, 159
Yermalovich, Mikola, 41, 66
Yiddish (language), 2, 15, 16, 34n70

Zaprudnik, Jan, xiv, xv, xvii, xviii, xxii, 43, 48, 49, 59, 66
Zayiko, Leonid, 84, 118, 120, 122, 123, 124, 126, 127, 138
Zen'kovich, Nikolai, 13, 15, 20, 21
Zimianin, Mikhail, 20
Zlotnikov, Leonid, 84, 117, 124
Zyuganov, Gennady, 146

About the Author

Grigory Ioffe is professor of human geography at Radford University in Virginia. He is coauthor, with Tatyana Nefedova and Ilya Zaslavsky, of *The End of Peasantry? The Disintegration of Rural Russia* (2006) and numerous other publications.

CPSIA information can be obtained at www.ICGtesting.com
Printed in the USA
BVOW01s0156310714

360927BV00004B/9/P